CAMBRIDGE STUDIES IN
MEDIEVAL LIFE AND THOUGHT

Edited by M. D. Knowles, Litt.D., F.B.A.
*Emeritus Regius Professor of Modern History in the
University of Cambridge*

NEW SERIES VOL. XIV

THE SCHOOL
OF PETER ABELARD

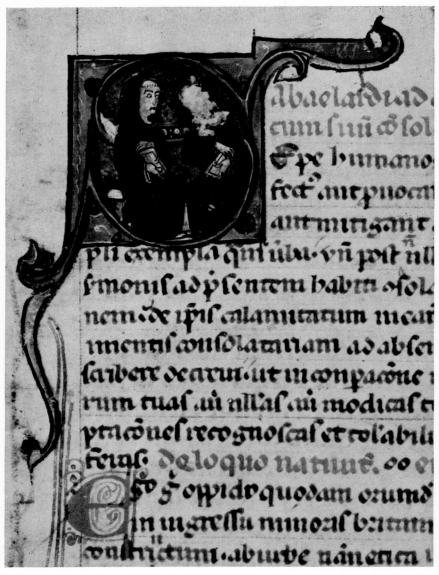

The opening of Abelard's *Historia Calamitatum* in the Paris MS., Bibl. nationale lat. 2923, f. 1r. Abelard and Héloïse appear in the initial but the face of Héloïse has been scratched out. The figures have no iconographical value since the manuscript was not copied before the mid-thirteenth century at the earliest. After *c.* 1337 it belonged to Petrarch who annotated it profusely. For references see J. Monfrin, *Abélard. Historia Calamitatum*, pp. 18–19. No other medieval representation of Abelard is known. The Oxford MS., Queen's College 284, contains a seventeenth-century drawing of Abelard but it does not appear to be of medieval inspiration.

THE SCHOOL
OF PETER ABELARD

THE INFLUENCE
OF ABELARD'S THOUGHT
IN THE EARLY
SCHOLASTIC PERIOD

BY

D. E. LUSCOMBE

Fellow of Churchill College, Cambridge

CAMBRIDGE
AT THE UNIVERSITY PRESS
1969

Published by the Syndics of the Cambridge University Press
Bentley House, P.O. Box 92, 200 Euston Road, London, N.W.1
American Branch: 32 East 57th Street, New York, N.Y. 10022

© Cambridge University Press 1969

Library of Congress Catalogue Card Number: 69-10431
Standard Book Number: 521 07337 5

Printed in Great Britain by
Alden & Mowbray Ltd
at the Alden Press, Oxford

IN MEMORY OF D. A. CALLUS, O.P.

CONTENTS

CONTENTS

PREFACE

This book represents an historian's attempt to discern the ways in which Abelard's thought reached and influenced his contemporaries and successors. The subject has attracted historical study for nearly a century if we take as a starting point the classic article by Heinrich Denifle entitled 'Die Sentenzen Abaelards und die Bearbeitungen seiner Theologia vor Mitte des 12. Jahrhunderts' which appeared in the *Archiv für Literatur- und Kirchengeschichte des Mittelalters* in 1885. Since that time much further knowledge of Abelard's school and of his disciples has accumulated and in addition a vast amount of scholarly energy has been devoted to the task of understanding and of bringing to life twelfth-century thought and learning in its many aspects and moods. With respect to Abelard's following it is perhaps a fitting time to draw together some threads and to offer an interpretation of its place in the evolution of the early scholastic movement.

The principal sources of this study are literary, biographical, palaeographical and doctrinal. The occasional surviving literary references to Abelard which were made in the twelfth century and later are numerous enough to convey the intensity and the scale of the disagreements which existed concerning his personality and achievement. The names of several of his disciples and hearers are also known and an examination is here attempted of their relationships to Abelard as well as of their reactions to his work and thought. However, information concerning twelfth-century personalities is seldom abundant and much can also be gained from studying the codicology of Abelard and his school. The surviving or known manuscripts of writings by Abelard and by his disciples offer further knowledge of Abelard's readership and following and therefore also of the general history of a formative period in medieval thought.

Abelard's public career was closed in 1140 by an ecclesiastical condemnation. As a condemned heretic whose errors had been vigorously denounced by, among others, Bernard of Clairvaux, Abelard's influence upon his age was limited and tainted. That he was survived by disciples is an established fact, but what was done by these disciples to develop or to qualify his teaching still requires examination. It seems that the condemnation of 1140 raised as many questions as it solved and that the conflicts between Abelard's critics and his defenders in the schools entailed serious disagreements not only over outlook and method but also over specific teachings which continued to be debated in the years that followed. The stimulus which Abelard gave to the study of particular ideas and themes outlived the condemnation of 1140 and some of the criticisms which were levelled against Abelard at this time were an insufficient guide to his contemporaries. Already within the school of Hugh of St Victor a more sophisticated and refined study of Abelard's thought was in progress, and it was this which provided the springboard for many future doctrinal developments. Throughout the 1130s, 40s and 50s the interaction of the rival traditions of the schools of Abelard and of Hugh is a striking feature of theological discussion. If the Sentences of Peter Lombard, which enjoyed such a prolonged influence throughout the medieval period, may be regarded as the climax of continuous activity by schoolmen during the first half of the twelfth century, then it is clear that Abelard, for all his exaggerations and errors, was a major and continuing stimulus to debate and thought.

I have tried in the following pages to illustrate primarily the development of theological thought in approximately the first half of the twelfth century by reference not only to Abelard's disciples but also to major teachers of the various schools of the period such as Gratian of Bologna, Hugh and Richard of St Victor, Peter Lombard and Robert of Melun. I have not tried to be exhaustive and much could be said about the relationship between Abelard and other writers; the Porretans in particular are little mentioned. So much is added yearly to knowledge of the literature and thought of this period that much of what appears below will soon be subject to modification and revision. At the present time the long needed critical edition of Abelard's theological writings, in the hands of Fr E. M. Buytaert, advances nearer to publication and the progress continues of the edition by Dom Jean Leclercq of the writings of Bernard of Clairvaux. To lack all the benefits that these editions can bring is, of course, a limitation. It is moreover necessary to add that Abelard's writings are not much less liable today than in the past to provoke varied responses from their readers; to attempt to discuss the responses which were formulated in the twelfth century is to expose oneself the more to the possibility of being unjust or merely tentative.

I have been greatly helped and encouraged by many, including Dr L. Minio-Paluello, the late Fr Daniel Callus, O.P., Professor C. R. Cheney, Dr R. W. Hunt, Dom J. Leclercq, Dr R. W. Lovatt, Professor D. M. MacKinnon, Miss B. Smalley, Professor R. W. Southern, Professor P. Zerbi and, not least, my wife. Librarians and custodians of manuscripts in many institutions in several countries have provided considerable assistance, notably in the Institut de Recherches et d'Histoire des Textes in Paris. I am most appreciative of the support given to me by the Provost and Fellows of King's College, Cambridge, and, more recently, by the late Master and the Fellows of Churchill College, Cambridge. Professor Dom David Knowles perceived the need for this study and has been its constant guide: *exemplum proposuit* (Abelard, *Theologia Christiana*, IV, PL. 178, 1279A).

D.L.

NOTE

Part of the material in chapter II first appeared, in a slightly different form, in 'Berengar, Defender of Peter Abelard', *Recherches de théologie ancienne et médiévale*, vol. XXIII, 1966, pp. 319–37.

The frontispiece appears by kind permission of the *Bibliothèque Nationale*, Paris.

LIST OF ABBREVIATIONS

AHDLMA   *Archives d'histoire doctrinale et littéraire du moyen âge*. Paris, 1926–

ASOC   Analecta sacri ordinis cisterciensis. Rome, 1945–

BGPTMA   Beiträge zur Geschichte der Philosophie und der Theologie des Mittelalters. Münster, 1891–

Bouquet, *Recueil*   M. Bouquet, *Recueil des historiens des Gaules et de la France*, 24 vols, 1738–1904.

Clm   Codex latinus monacensis (Bavarian State Library, Munich).

CSEL   Corpus scriptorum ecclesiasticorum latinorum. Editum consilio et impensis Academiae Litterarum Caesareae Vindobonensis. Vienna, 1866–

DDC   Dictionnaire de droit canonique, A. Villien, etc. Paris, 1924–

DHGE   Dictionnaire d'histoire et de géographie ecclésiastiques, A. Baudrillart, etc. Paris, 1912–

DTC   Dictionnaire de théologie catholique, A. Vacant, etc. Paris, 1915–

IRHT   Institut de recherches et d'histoire des textes. Paris.

MABK   P. Lehmann and P. Ruf, *Mittelalterliche Bibliothekskataloge Deutschlands und der Schweiz*, 3 vols in 6. Munich, 1918–39.

MGH.SS   Monumenta Germaniae Historica. Scriptorum series.

PL   J. P. Migne, Patrologia latina. Paris, 1844–

RFNS   *Rivista di filosofia neo-scolastica*. Milan, 1909–

RHE   *Revue d'histoire ecclésiastique*. Louvain, 1900–

RS   Rolls Series: Rerum Britannicarum Medii Aevi Scriptores. London, 1858–

RSPT   *Revue des sciences philosophiques et théologiques.*
          Paris, 1907–
RTAM   *Recherches de théologie ancienne et médiévale.*
          Louvain 1929–
S.C.   Summary Catalogue of Western MSS in the
          Bodleian Library at Oxford, F. Madan, etc.,
          7 vols in 9. London, 1895–1953.
ZKG   *Zeitschrift für Kirchengeschichte.* Gotha, 1877–

CHAPTER I

THE LITERARY EVIDENCE

Joseph de Ghellinck once observed that Abelard was perhaps the only medieval master whose contemporaries recorded his fame so universally and with such enthusiasm and horror.[1] From this rich crop of literary witnesses the ways in which Abelard impressed his contemporaries and their successors can be known. The most emphatic testimony to Abelard's fame was provided, however, by Abelard himself. In his fifties, *c.* 1133–6, Abelard wrote in the form of a letter to a friend his own *apologia*. In this traditionally entitled *History of My Troubles* Abelard made plain that he enjoyed to a remarkable degree the gift of attracting large numbers of followers; wherever he taught he gained crowds of admiring students.[2] Abelard also recorded

---

[1] *L'Essor de la littérature latine*, p. 44. André Duchesne first presented some of this evidence in *Petri Abaelardi . . . Opera* (reprinted in PL. 178, 91–6). For considerations of this material see especially R. L. Poole, *Illustrations of the History of Medieval Thought*, pp. 170–5, M. Grabmann, *Die Geschichte der Scholastischen Methode*, II, 170–2 and J. de Ghellinck, *Le Mouvement théologique du XIIe siècle*, pp. 151–4, 278–9. See also G. Paré *et al.*, *La Renaissance du XIIe siècle*, pp. 277–81.

[2] See the following passages in the *Historia Calamitatum*, throughout cited by lines from the edition of J. Monfrin (after disputing against William of Champeaux in Paris): 'Hinc tantum roboris et auctoritatis nostra suscepit disciplina, ut hii qui antea vehementius magistro illi nostro adherebant et maxime nostram infestabant doctrinam, ad nostras convolarent scolas', *ll.* 101–4. After lecturing on Ezechiel at Laon: 'Quo quidem audito, hii qui non interfuerant ceperunt ad secundam et terciam lectionem certatim concurrere', *ll.* 217–19. On returning from Laon to Paris Abelard lectured on theology and philosophy: 'Unde utriusque lectionis studio scole nostre vehementer multiplicate, quanta mihi de pecunia lucra, quantam gloriam compararent ex fama te quoque latere non potuit', *ll.* 248–51. Before facing his judges at Soissons in 1121: 'Ego autem singulis diebus, antequam sederet concilium, in publico omnibus secundum quod [Monfrin: quam] scripseram fidem catholicam disserebam, et cum magna ammiratione omnes qui audiebant tam verborum apertionem quam sensum nostrum commendabant', *ll.* 739–44. Dejected by his condemnation at Soissons Abelard set up an oratory in the diocese of Troyes: 'Quod cum cognovissent scolares, ceperunt undique concurrere, et relictis civitatibus et castellis solitudinem inhabitare, et pro amplis domibus

that his writings enjoyed a similar popularity.[1] In 1139 his opponent Bernard of Clairvaux complained that these writings had taken wing and had flown into many cities and castles and even into other lands.[2] Bernard tells us too of Abelard's boast that his works had been spread in Rome.[3]

[1] Of his glosses on Ezechiel begun at Laon in defiance of the most celebrated biblical commentator of the day Abelard wrote '. . . omnes pariter de transcribendis glosis quas prima die inceperam in ipso earum initio plurimum solliciti esse'. These glosses were finished in Paris: 'que quidem adeo legentibus acceptabiles fuerunt, ut me non minorem gratiam in sacra lectione adeptum jam crederent quam in philosophica viderant', *Hist. Calam.*, ed. Monfrin, *ll.* 219–21, 245–8. He wrote of his *Theologia* 'Summi boni': 'Quem quidem tractatum cum vidissent et legissent plurimi, cepit in commune omnibus plurimum placere, quod in eo pariter omnibus satisfieri super hoc questionibus videbatur.' His rivals alleged 'quod ad transcribendum jam pluribus eum ipse prestitissem', *ibid., ll.* 702–5, 851–2. In his *Dialogus* Abelard makes the Philosopher flatter both himself and 'opus illud mirabile theologiae, quod nec invidia ferre potuit, nec auferre praevaluit, sed gloriosius persequendo effecit', PL. 178, 1613D. He had begun his *Theologia* 'Scholarium' by referring to the pleasure which his writings on philosophy had aroused in their readers, *Prolog.*, PL. 178, 979A.

[2] 'Volant libri . . . Urbibus et castellis ingeruntur. Transierunt de gente in gentem et de regno ad populum alterum', *Epist.* 189 (PL. 182, 355A). Cf. William of St Thierry writing to Bernard in 1139: 'libri eius transeunt maria, transiliunt Alpes', *Epist.* 326 (PL. 182, 531B). Also Geoffrey of Auxerre: 'cum blasphemiis plena gravissimis volitare undique scripta coepissent, profanas novitates vocum et sensuum viri eruditi atque fideles ad Dei Hominem retulerunt', *S. Bernardi Vita Prima*, III, v (PL. 185, 310D–311A).

[3] 'Legite, si placet, librum Petri Abaelardi, quem dicit Theologiae: ad manum est enim; cum, sicut gloriatur, a pluribus lectitetur in curia', *Epist.* 188 (PL. 182, 353B). 'Sed in his omnibus gloriatur quod cardinalibus et clericis curiae scientiae fontes aperuerit, quod manibus et sinibus Romanorum libros et sententias suas incluserit', *Epist.* 338 (PL. 182, 543D). Cf. William of St Thierry, *Epist.* 326, *loc. cit.*, and the chronicler Richard of Poitiers, writing between 1142 and 1153: 'scripsit autem Petrus Baalardus opuscula quaedam, quae pluribus habentur in locis' (MGH.SS. XXVI, 81 and again in *Chronicon anonymi*, ed. M. Bouquet, *Recueil des historiens*, XII, 120); also William Godell, an English monk of St Martial of Limoges, writing *c.* 1173: 'scripsit et docuit plurima', *Chronicon* (ed. Bouquet, *Recueil*, XIII, 675). Alberic of Tre Fontane in the next century believed that Abelard's heresies drove his writings underground: 'Libri tamen eiusdem magistri diu in abscondito servati sunt ab eius

---

parva tabernacula sibi construere. . . . Quanto autem illuc major scolarium erat confluentia et quanto duriorem in doctrina nostra vitam sustinebant, tanto amplius mihi emuli estimabant gloriosum et sibi ignominiosum', *ll.* 1044–7, 1094–7.

Abelard's friends lauded his fame with enthusiasm. Héloïse wrote that such celebrity had never been enjoyed by any king or philosopher. Whole districts and towns would be excited at his coming.[1] Fulk, prior of the Benedictine house of St Eugène at Deuil in the valley of Montmorency, wrote in a letter of consolation after Abelard's mutilation and before 1118 that his school counted among its members Romans, Englishmen, Germans, Swedes and natives from every part of France. The dangers of travel meant nothing to them for they believed that Abelard could teach them everything.[2] During his trial at Soissons in 1121 the strength of the support for Abelard moved the bishop of Chartres, Geoffrey of Lèves, to warn the assembly of the risks involved in judging him a heretic.[3] Abelard was condemned but later his fortunes as a teacher revived. The chronicle of the abbey of Morigny in the diocese of Sens remarked of Abelard in the year 1131 that his students came from all parts of the Latin world.[4] In 1136 Walter of Mortagne wrote

[1] 'Quis etenim regum aut philosophorum tuam exequare famam poterat? Que te regio aut civitas seu villa videre non estuabat? Quis te, rogo, in publicum procedentem conspicere non festinabat ac discedentem collo erecto, oculis directis non insectabatur?' *Epist.* 2 (PL. 178, 185CD).

[2] *Epist. ad Abaelardum* (PL. 178, 371D–372B). On the text of this letter see D. Van den Eynde, 'Détails biographiques sur Pierre Abélard', pp. 219–20.

[3] Geoffrey's speech is known through Abelard's reconstruction in *Hist. Calam.*, ll. 791–802: 'Nostis, Domini omnes qui adestis, hominis hujus doctrinam, qualiscunque sit, ejusque ingenium in quibuscunque studuerit multos assentatores et sequaces habuisse, et magistrorum tam suorum quam nostrorum famam maxime compressisse, et quasi ejus vineam a mari usque ad mare palmites suos extendisse. Si hunc prejuditio, quod non arbitror, gravaveritis, etiamsi recte, multos vos offensuros sciatis et non deesse plurimos qui eum defendere velint, presertim cum in presenti scripto nulla videamus que aliquid obtineant aperte calumpnie; et quia juxta illud Jheronimi: "Semper in propatulo fortitudo emulos habet".'

[4] 'Petrus Abailardus, monachus et abbas, et ipse vir religiosus excellentissimus rector scholarum, ad quas pene de tota latinitate viri litterati confluebant', *Chronicon Mauriniacensis*, ed. L. Mirot, p. 54. Mirot believed that this anonymous

discipulis', *Chronicon* (MGH.SS. XXIII, 836). He may have drawn upon the information of Helinand of Froidmont (diocese of Beauvais) who wrote *c.* 1210: 'Libri tamen eius adhuc a multis curiose servantur, quibus aquae furtivae dulciores sunt, et panis absconditus suavior. Ego ipse in eis multa reprehensibilia inveni', *Chronicon* (PL. 212, 1035A).

B

4 THE SCHOOL OF PETER ABELARD

of the widespread tributes being paid to Abelard by his disciples.[1]
In a report made to the pope after the council of Sens in 1140,
the archbishop of Sens and his colleagues depicted Abelard as a
danger not only within the schools. He had spread throughout
Gaul, even among the uneducated, a habit of disputing the
nature of the Trinity.[2] Abelard was said by Bernard of Clairvaux
to have boasted of a following in the Roman Curia.[3] Bernard
belittled Abelard's theology but he never minimized its influence.
Hugh Métel, the loquacious canon of St Leo at Toul, described
the spread of Abelard's errors in terms of a plague which had struck
France. Hugh's fanciful polemic is merely an imitation of the
masterly appeals of Bernard, but he serves to impress upon us
the latter's greater realism.[4] After the second condemnation
Peter the Venerable, abbot of Cluny, was moved by Abelard's
plight to harbour him and to bring him to make his peace with
Bernard of Clairvaux. Peter marvelled at the contrast between
Abelard's present humility and his former universal fame.[5] As
after the judgment of Soissons, however, Abelard's following, if
temporarily silenced, was not considered to have been extin-

[1] Walter of Mortagne, *Epist. ad Abaelardum*, ed. H. Ostlender, p. 34.
[2] '... cum per totam fere Galliam in civitatibus, vicis et castellis, a scholari-
bus, non solum intra scholas, sed etiam triviatim; nec a litteratis aut provectis
tantum, sed a pueris et simplicibus, aut certe stultis, de sancta Trinitate, quae
Deus, est, disputaretur', printed among the letters of Bernard of Clairvaux,
no. 337 (PL. 182, 540C). William of St Thierry had written previously to
Bernard: 'novae eius sententiae de fide ... per provincias et regna ... cele-
briter praedicantur, et libere defenduntur', *Epist.* 326 (PL. 182, 531BC).
[3] See above, p. 2, n. 3.
[4] 'Percussa est Francia Aegypti plagis durissimis, percussa est loquacibus
ranis nec deest sciniphes ... Medendum est itaque his plagis, inflammandum
est cauterium ad cauteriatas conscientias medendas et velociter; velociter,
inquam, ne morbus invalescat', Hugh Métel, *Epist.* 4, ed. C. L. Hugo, *Sacrae
Antiquitatis Monumenta*, II, 332. On this one may consult de Fortia d'Urban,
Histoire et ouvrages de Hugues Métel, pp. 29–51, and the *Histoire littéraire de la
France*, XII, 493–511, here 497–8.
[5] 'Hoc magister Petrus fine dies suos consummavit, et qui singulari scientiae
magisterio, toti pene orbi terrarum notus, et ubique famosus erat', Peter the
Venerable, *Lib.* IV, *epist.* 21 (PL. 189, 352B.)

part of the chronicle where Abelard's presence at Morigny is recorded, was
composed by a monk of Morigny and probably in 1132 (*ibid.*, pp. viii, x).

guished. Nearly two decades later the Bavarian reformer Gerhoh of Reichersberg, to whom earlier Abelard's disciples had been as the locusts foreseen in the Apocalypse, claimed that the schools of Germany and France were still infested by his followers.[1] The writer of the *Metamorphosis Goliae episcopi*, in mentioning the scholastic celebrities of the day, added that very many followed Abelard.[2] In milder tone in 1159 John of Salisbury wrote that as a logician Abelard still had many disciples.[3]

Abelard was a free-lance teacher. Although his name has been traditionally believed to have been the spur behind the rise to fortune of the schools of Paris, he also taught for much of his career in a variety of places outside Paris. The convent of the Paraclete was his only abiding foundation. On account of his sojourn on the banks of the Ardusson near Troyes, Petrarch was able in his *De Vita Solitaria* to cite Abelard as a recent example of a philosopher who had chosen the life of solitude, although Petrarch had to add that even in hiding Abelard was pursued by his followers.[4] A circle of followers, however fluctuating and nomadic it may have been, usually represented for Abelard more than a distracting, if lucrative, retinue of young students. Abelard's own enquiries and speculations were largely conducted in the context of his activity as a teacher of students and as the head of

---

[1] 'Fumant scholae plures in Francia et aliis terris permaxime a duabus caudis ticionum fumigantium videlicet Petri Abaiolardi et episcopi Gilliberti', Gerhoh of Reichersberg, *Liber de novitatibus*, c. 20 (ed. E. Sackur, *Libelli selecti*, p. 301). Earlier in the same work (c. 4, *ed. cit.*, p. 292) Gerhoh quoted from an otherwise unknown letter which he sent to Pope Innocent II (1130–43): 'Nam de fumo putei abyssi, ut Iohannes in Apocalypsi previdit (9, 1 *et seq.*), nunc exierunt locustae, videlicet plures discipuli Petri Abaiolardi.'

[2]   'Celebrem theologum vidimus Lumbardum
        cum Yvone Helyam Petrum et Bernardum,
        quorum opobalsamum spirat os et nardum,
        et professi plurimi sunt Abaielardum',
Metamorphosis Goliae episcopi, ed. R. B. C. Huygens, p. 771. The poem was dated *c.* 1150 by H. Brinkman, 'Die Metamorphosis Goliae', pp. 32–4.

[3] 'Multos reliquit, et adhuc quidem aliquos habet professionis huius sectatores et testes. Amici mei sunt . . . ', John of Salisbury, *Metalogicon*, II, 17 (ed. C. C. J. Webb, p. 120).

[4] Petrarch, *De Vita Solitaria*, Book 2, tract. VII, ch. 1 (trans. J. Zeitlin, p. 270).

a band of scholars. He directly and enthusiastically addressed his *Theologia 'Scholarium'* and his *Logica 'Nostrorum petitioni sociorum'* to his followers and he revised some of his works in order partly to meet the criticisms of his opponents outside his school.[1] In the *Historia Calamitatum*, where Abelard described his disputes with other masters, he made it plain that he was a leader of men. The close union which existed between Abelard and his disciples is strikingly confirmed in some of the writings of the latter which so resemble Abelard's own that they have in the past been attributed to Abelard himself.[2]

Bernard of Clairvaux did not fail to take account of the vitality of this bond between Abelard and his disciples. We misinterpret the extraordinarily tense struggle between the abbot of Clairvaux and the Peripatetic from Le Pallet if we concentrate too much upon the clash between two strong personalities. Historians of this controversy have rightly paid much attention to Bernard's criticisms of the opinions of Abelard. Bernard's composition of a list of heretical propositions allegedly taken from Abelard's writings, his attitude to the application of reason in the study of the truths of faith, the tension between monastic and scholastic theology—these aspects of the quarrel have attracted much scrutiny. But Bernard did not only charge Abelard with propounding academic heresies. He was moved to such a degree of activity because of the extent of Abelard's influence upon other minds.[3] Bernard's strategy in 1140 comprised not only attempts to rouse the bishops of France and the Cardinals of Rome to take action against Abelard but also manœuvres to detach many followers from their support of Abelard.[4] Professor Klibansky

[1] Abelard's methods of revising his treatises were revealed by J. Cottiaux, 'La Conception de la théologie chez Abélard', H. Ostlender, 'Die Theologia Scholarium des Peter Abaelard' and B. Geyer, *Untersuchungen*, pp. 611–12.

[2] Such are the *Sententie* of Hermann and the *Glossae super librum Porphirii secundum vocales.*

[3] See above, p. 2, nn. 2 and 3, p. 4, n. 2.

[4] Cf. the report sent to Pope Innocent II by the archbishop of Sens and others after Abelard's trial: 'Plures etiam scholares adhortatus est ut et libros venenis plenos repudiarent et rejicerent et a doctrina quae fidem laedebat catholicam caverent et abstinerent' printed among the letters of Bernard of Clairvaux, no. 337 (PL. 182, 541B).

has recently republished a most important letter from Abelard to his *socii* in which he bitterly protests that Bernard had violently attacked him, not in his presence but before his own students and friends at Sens and at Paris.[1] It was as a result of visiting Paris and preaching there that Bernard converted into the Cistercian order Geoffrey of Auxerre who had at some previous time been a disciple of Abelard.[2] When Bernard bombarded the Curia in Rome with his requests for the condemnation, he in particular sounded the convictions of Master Guy of Castello, Cardinal priest of St Mark, who was said to be a friend of Abelard.[3] At the trial at Sens Abelard's supporters were present.[4] The presiding bishops reported to the pope that Abelard had been busy collecting his disciples from all quarters and that he had, as it were, put on the Whips for the occasion to make sure of their allegiance and common viewpoint.[5] When Pope Innocent II issued the letter of condemnation, it was directed against both Abelard and his followers and supporters.[6] There was to be no more direct collaboration between Abelard and the circle of his followers.

The fact that Abelard spent much of his career at the head of a group of scholars and students who attached themselves to him for personal reasons and not by reason of the fame of any institu-

[1] 'Sciatis autem ... quanta ille Datianus meus in me veneni sui probra vomuerit: primo quod Senonis in praesentia domini archiepiscopi et multorum amicorum meorum, quod deinde Parisius de profundo nequitiae suae coram vobis vel aliis eructuaverit', in Klibansky, 'Peter Abailard and Bernard of Clairvaux', p. 7. The letter was previously edited by J. Leclercq in his *Etudes sur S. Bernard*, pp. 104–5. See also J. G. Sikes, *Peter Abailard*, pp. 228–9.

[2] Geoffrey d'Auxerre, *S. Bernardi Vita Prima*, IV, 2, n. 10 (PL. 185, 327); *Vita Tertia, Fragmenta*, n. 49, ed. R. Lechat, 'Les Fragmenta de Vita et Miraculis S. Bernardi par Geoffroy d'Auxerre', pp. 115–16.

[3] Bernard of Clairvaux, *Epist.* 192 (PL. 182, 358–9).

[4] 'Adfuit magister Petrus cum fautoribus suis', Bernard of Clairvaux, *Epist.* 337 (PL. 182, 542A).

[5] 'Magister Petrus interim suos nihilominus coepit undequaque convocare discipulos, et obsecrare ut ad futuram inter se dominumque abbatem Claraevallensem disputationem una cum illo suam sententiam simul et scientiam defensuri venirent', *ibid.* (PL. 182, 541C).

[6] '... universos quoque erroris sui sectatores et defensores, a fidelium consortio sequestrandos et excommunicationis vinculo innodandos esse censemus', Innocent II, *Epist.* 447 (PL. 179, 517A).

tion which contained Abelard had, therefore, special consequences for Abelard and for his critics. There was in addition to this comment upon the force that Abelard and his entourage represented much further comment of a very varied character upon the leading features of Abelard's mind, of his personality and of his teaching. It is important to appreciate the variety and the content of this criticism before studying the fortunes of Abelard's known followers and the subsequent interest in, and development of, Abelard's teachings. One thing is very clear: Abelard's talents stimulated and received widespread respect and admiration of which the expression mainly confirms the reasons for self-congratulation contained in the *Historia Calamitatum*. The sharpness of Abelard's intellect, his *ingenium*, was repeatedly recorded.[1] Geoffrey of Auxerre remembered Abelard as a distinguished master.[2] An anonymous biographer writing before 1165 celebrated in Abelard an unbelievable subtlety, unheard of memory and superhuman ability, and he claimed that when Abelard had first lectured on theology and logic in Paris he swiftly and easily surpassed all the masters of France.[3] Goswin, prior of St Médard and later abbot of Anchin, who as a student in Paris had once sought to interrupt one of Abelard's lectures, facing him as David before Goliath but without the same success, acknowledged when Abelard was held in St Médard after the condemnation of 1121 his many victories and numerous pupils, his deep learning and lofty eloquence.[4] Over a century later a legend commemora-

---

[1] Cf. Otto of Freising, *Gesta Friderici*, I, 48 (ed. G. Waitz, p. 69); Fulk of Deuil wrote that Abelard's disciples were 'scientiae subtilitate permoti', *Epist. ad Abaelardum* (PL. 178, 372); Robert of Auxerre, *Chron*. (MGH.SS. XXVI, 235); William Godell, *Chron*., ed. Bouquet, *Recueil*, XIII, 675.

[2] 'Magister insignis et celeberrimus in opinione scientiae', Geoffrey of Auxerre, *S. Bernardi Vita Prima*, III, v (PL. 185, 310D). Cf. Alberic of Tre Fontane: 'magister Petrus Abaelardus in scientia celeberrimus', *Chron*. (MGH. SS. XXIII, 836); Helinand of Froidmont, *Chron*. (PL. 212, 1034D); William of Nangis, monk of St Denis, *Chron*., ed. H. Géraud, I, 32, n. 2.

[3] Ed. R. L. Poole, *Illustrations of the History of Medieval Thought*, pp. 314–15. Cf. Geoffrey, bishop of Chartres, as reported in Abelard's *Hist. Calam.*, *ll.* 794–5: '... magistrorum tam suorum quam nostrorum famam maxime compressisse'.

[4] Goswin 'proponebat ei, pro mulcendis eius auribus et animo deflectendo, profunditatem scientiae, torrentem eloquentiae ad quicquid vellet abun-

ted Abelard as the master who had taught in many places in spite of great opposition and whose students faithfully followed him wherever he went.[1] In an anecdote, contained in a sermon of the thirteenth century by Odo of Cherington, Abelard's opulence is represented. He is depicted as sumptuously attired, riding upon a fine horse amid an escort of mounted servants and fêted like a prince.[2] In the phrase of Peter the Venerable he exercised *singulare scientiae magisterium*.[3]

As a philosopher Abelard received high praise from chroniclers[4] and from John of Salisbury who considered him to be the leading logician of his time.[5] Richard of Poitiers coupled his name with that of Hugh of St Victor as a *lumen latinorum*, a very famous doctor and philosopher.[6] The epitaphs which Abelard's death occasioned are especially interesting. The tributes are flowery and exaggerated but it is as a philosopher skilled in the arts of dialectic that Abelard was celebrated. With his death philosophy too sinks into the grave.[7] He had been the master of the problem

[1] Cf. James of Vitry, *Exempla*, ed. J. Greven, no. 58, p. 36.
[2] *Cit.* B. Hauréau, 'Mémoire sur quelques maîtres du XIIe siècle', p. 234.
[3] See above, p. 4, n. 5.
[4] Cf. *Chronicon Britannicum*, ed. Bouquet, *Recueil*, XII, 558: 'Petrus Abalardus, mirae abstinentiae Monachus, tantaeque subtilitatis Philosophus, cui nostra parem, nec prima secundum saecula viderunt.' Also Robert of Auxerre, *Chron.* (MGH.SS. XXVI, 235): 'ingenio subtilissimus mirabilisque phylosophus'.
[5] 'Peripateticus Palatinus, qui logicae opinionem praeripuit omnibus co-aetaneis suis, adeo ut solus Aristotelis crederetur usus colloquio se omnes opposuerunt errori', John of Salisbury, *Metalogicon*, I, 5 (ed. Webb, p. 17).
[6] *Chron.* (MGH.SS. XXVI, 81); cf. *Chronicon anonymi*, ed. Bouquet, *Recueil*, XII, 120. Héloïse hailed Abelard as a philosopher, *Epist.* 2 (PL. 178, 185CD). Henry of Brussels wrote in the late twelfth century of Abelard: 'dialecticae peritia, imo omnium liberalium artium insignis', *De Scriptoribus Illustribus*, c. 16 (ed. A. Miraeus, *Bibliotheca ecclesiastica*, p. 164). Alexander Neckham commemorated him as a logician in company with Gilbert Porreta, Alberic (of Paris), Thierry and one Gualo, *Laudes divine sapientie*, cited by A. Vernet, 'Une épitaphe inédite de Thierry de Chartres', p. 166.
[7]   'Occubuit Petrus, succumbit eo moriente
          Omnis philosophus, perit omnis philosophia,
          Scinditur in partes jam vestis philosophiae',

dantem, numerositatem victoriarum quas conflictu literario conquisisset...',
Vita Gosvini, I, 18, ed. Bouquet, *Recueil*, XIV, 445.

of universals.[1] The much cited epitaph inscribed on Abelard's tomb proclaims that he alone had access to all knowledge.[2] He was for Peter the Venerable an Aristotle, the equal or the leader of all logicians.[3] There were some writers who would not pay unequivocal tribute to Abelard as a philosopher. The student Goswin had been warned in Paris by Jocelyn, the logician and later bishop of Soissons, that Abelard was a quibbling scoffer rather than a disputant, a jester rather than a teacher.[4] Otto of

[1]   'Errores generum correxit, ita specierum;
          Hic genus et species in sola voce locavit,
          Et genus et species sermones esse notavit',
anon. epitaph. no. 3 (PL. 178, 104C). This summary is accurate.

[2]   'Est satis in tumulo, Petrus hic jacet Abaelardus,
          Cui soli patuit scibile quidquid erat',
PL. 178, 103D. This inscription was frequently reproduced. Cf. an epitaph in cod. Zurich, Stadtbibl. C. 58, ed. J. Werner, *Beiträge zur Kunde der lateinischen Literatur des Mittelalters*, p. 24, no. 50, and the collection of epitaphs in cod. Soissons, Bibl. municipale, 24, f. 1, cited by C. C. J. Webb in his ed. of the *Policraticus* of John of Salisbury, I, xiii. Also the following chroniclers: Clarius, monk of St Pierre-le-Vif at Sens (ed. Bouquet, *Recueil*, XII, 184); *Chronicon Senonense Gaufridi de Collone*, cited by V. Cousin, *Opera P. Abaelardi*, I, 46; William of Nangis, *Chronicon*, ed. Géraud, I, 33; William Godell, *Chronicon*, ed. Bouquet, *Recueil*, XIII, 675; Robert of Auxerre, *Chronicon*, MGH.SS. XXVI, 235. In the twelfth-century grammatical commentary *Promisimus* cited by R. W. Hunt, 'Studies on Priscian in the Twelfth Century', II, p. 41, the inscription is said to have been composed 'a quodam clerico suo'.

[3] PL. 178, 103C; cf. anon. epitaph. no. 3 (PL. 178, 104C). Similar tributes were paid to other leading twelfth century masters. Clarembald of Arras described Thierry 'utpote totius Europae philosophorum praecipuus', *Epistola*, ed. N. Haring in 'The Creation and Creator of the World' according to Thierry of Chartres and Clarenbaldus of Arras', p. 183; and cf. A. Vernet, 'Une épitaphe inédite', p. 664.

[4] ' "Magistrum Petrum ... disputatorem non esse, sed cavillatorem; et plus vices agere joculatoris quam doctoris, et quod instar Herculis clavam non leviter abjiceret apprehensam, videlicet quod pertinax esset in errore; et quod si secundum se non esset, nunquam acquiesceret veritati" ', *Vita Gosvini*, ed. Bouquet, *Recueil*, XIV, 442–3.

---

anon. epitaph. no. 3 (PL. 178, 103D). Cf. also an epitaph uncertainly attributed to Ralph Tortaire:
          'Muta fit omnis, eo defuncto, philosofia,
          Logica conticuit, musica fit vidua',
Carmina, ed. M. B. Ogle and D. M. Schullian, p. 447. Ralph's authorship was rejected by E. de Certain in *Bibliothèque de l'Ecole des Chartes*, 4ème série, I (1895), p. 497. He is also credited with admiring verses published by C. Cuissard, 'Documents inédits sur Abélard', pp. 33 *et seq*.

Freising also charged Abelard with levity[1] and Walter Map declared that the logic of the prince of nominalists was a source of confusions to many.[2] In general, however, Abelard as a philosopher had won esteem and the writers of epitaphs on his death passed over in silence his stormy career, his condemnations as a heretic and his misfortunes as a teacher of theology.

Abelard's acknowledged reputation as a theologian was much less good. The judgment of Geoffrey of Auxerre that Abelard was a treacherous teacher of theology—*de fide perfide dogmatizans*[3] —was repeated by several later writers.[4] Clarembald of Arras attributed to Abelard a spirit of boastfulness and of impiety.[5] The attacks made upon Abelard's theology by Bernard of Clairvaux, Walter of Mortagne, William of St Thierry and Gerhoh of Reichersberg were successful both in procuring Abelard's condemnation and in generally impressing upon chroniclers and other writers the justice of this condemnation.[6] Abelard's defeat was an incontrovertible fact to all except William Godell, the English monk of St Martial at Limoges, who in 1173, impressed by the manner in which Abelard spent his last days on

---

[1] 'Plurimum in inventionum subtilitate non solum ad phylosophiam necessarium, sed et pro commovendis ad iocos hominum animis utilium valens', Otto of Freising, *Gesta Friderici*, I, 48, ed. Waitz, p. 69.

[2] '. . . magistri Petri, principis Nominalium, qui plus peccavit in dialetica quam in divina pagina; nam in hac cum corde suo disseruit, in illa contra cor laboravit, et multos in eosdem labores induxit', Walter Map, *De Nugis Curialium*, written between 1181 and 1193, ed. M. R. James, p. 38.

[3] Geoffrey of Auxerre, *S. Bernardi Vita Prima*, III, v (PL. 185, 310D–12A).

[4] Cf. Helinand of Froidmont, *Chron.* (PL. 212, 1034D) and thence Alberic of Tre Fontane, *Chron.* (MGH.SS. XXXIII, 836) and Vincent of Beauvais, *Bibliotheca Mundi*, t. IV, *Speculum historiale*, lib. XXVII, c. XVII, 1102. Also Gerard of Auvergne, cited in *Gallia Christiana*, XIV, 961A.

[5] 'Cum spiritu iactantiae et impietatis plenus, divinitati ignominiam inferre, sibi gloriam conatus est parare', Clarembald of Arras, Commentary on Boethius' *De trinitate*, ed. Jansen, p. 48*. According to some writers, e.g. Grabmann in *Geschichte*, II, 172, Hugh of Orleans (*Primas*) directed some verses against Abelard, but see F. J. E. Raby, *A History of Secular Latin Poetry*, 2nd ed., II, 179.

[6] Cf. the mid twelfth-century *Historiae Tornacenses* (MGH.SS. XIV, 328); Henry of Brussels in the later twelfth-century *De Scriptoribus Illustribus*, c. 16 and *Appendix*, c. 3, ed. A. Miraeus, pp. 164, 174 (the work is here ascribed to Henry of Ghent); the thirteenth-century *Chronicon Burchardi et Cuonradi Urspergensium* which celebrates St Bernard: 'contra Petrum Baiolardum haereticum firma disputatione contendit' (MGH.SS. XXIII, 342).

earth and no doubt very misinformed as to the facts of history, described the council of Sens as the occasion of Abelard's victory.[1] Otto of Freising, who could be critical of Bernard, nonetheless was a little severe about Abelard's teaching in his account of the condemnations of Soissons and of Sens,[2] and a continuator of his history wrote of Abelard's Arianism and of Bernard's magnificent triumph in securing the condemnation.[3] The Cistercian Helinand of Froidmont, writing in the early thirteenth century, tells us that he has himself seen much that is reprehensible in Abelard's writings.[4] Other chroniclers note the scandal caused by the 'profane novelty' of Abelard's teachings and they disapprove of his appeal from the jurisdiction of the council of Sens to that of the pope.[5] Dislike of Abelard's doctrines was very widely expressed and this no doubt contributed to the sometimes peculiar image of him which was transmitted to posterity. In the late thirteenth century Gerard of Auvergne, although he uses the judgment of Geoffrey of Auxerre, turns Abelard into a necromancer and a companion of the devil.[6] In the early fifteenth century an English writer wrote off Abelard as a senile fool[7]

[1] 'Qua de causa coacto Concilio affuit, et multa quae ei objiciebantur constantissime removit, et plurima sua non esse quae illius esse et ab eo dicta affirmabantur, luculenter approbavit. Verum omnem haeresim postremo abnegavit et catholicae Ecclesiae se filium fore confessus est et affirmavit, et in pace fraterna post hoc vitam finivit', William Godell, *Chron.*, ed. Bouquet, *Recueil*, XIII, 675.

[2] Otto of Freising, *Gesta Friderici*, I, 48–51 (ed. Waitz, pp. 69–74). Cf. R. Folz, 'Otton de Freising, témoin de quelques controverses intellectuelles de son temps', pp. 77–8.

[3] Otto of St Blaise, writing before 1210, *Ottonis Frisingensis Continuatio Sanblasiana* (MGH.SS. xx, 205).

[4] See above, p. 2, n. 3.

[5] Cf. *Sigeberti Continuatio Praemonstratensis*, written between 1146 and 1155 (MGH.SS.VI, 452), and thence Robert of Auxerre, in *c.* 1203, *Chron.* (MGH.SS. XXVI, 235); *Chronicon Turonense*, ed. Bouquet, *Recueil*, XII, 472, and in *c.* 1300 William of Nangis, *Chron.*, ed. Géraud, I, 32.

[6] 'Fuit enim nigromanticus et daemoni familiaris', cited in *Gallia Christiana*, XIV, 961A. In Breton folklore Héloïse became a sorceress; see *Barzas-Breis. Chants populaires de la Bretagne*, ed. M.Th.de la Villemarqué (Paris 1839), pp. 93 *et seq.*

[7] 'Ille delirus senex et haereticus'; 'haereticus tam famosus', Pseudo-Thomas Netter, *Confessio Magistri Johannis Tyssyngton de Ordine Minorum* in the *Fasciculi Zizaniorum Magistri Johannis Wyclif cum Tritico*, ed. W. Waddington Shirley,

and at the turn of the fifteenth and sixteenth centuries the recogniz-
ably modern interpretation of, and in this instance regret for,
Abelard's achievement as the introduction of secular philosophy
into the study of sacred theology is formulated by John Eck's
predecessor in the chair of theology at Ingolstadt.[1]

The rift between admirers of Abelard's work and those critical
or cautious of its theological worth was firmly established in
Abelard's lifetime and continued to be very clearly marked in the
rest of the twelfth century as well as in subsequent centuries.
Scarcely any of these commentators would utter a word explicitly
in favour of Abelard as a theologian. In the epitaphs there are
signs that admirers had been impressed and comforted by their
master's retirement in his last days from the turbulence of the
schools to the quiet of Cluny. This conversion softened the blow
of the condemnation; without it the continuation of expressions
of admiration might well have been less assured. Before 1165
Wolfger of Prüfening inserted Abelard's name into his list of the
'modern doctors'.[2] In the later middle ages the title of doctor
was again bestowed upon Abelard in company with saints
Anselm of Canterbury, Thomas Aquinas and Bonaventure.[3]

[1] 'Item a tempore Petri Abelardi philosophia secularis sacram theologiam
sua curiositate foedare coepit, qui anno 1140 vixit et condemnatus fuit cum
suis pravis doctrinis, agente sancto Bernhardo in Senonensi consilio.' The writer
is Georg Zingel (1428–1508) and the remark occurs in his *Lectura super epistola
ad Hebraeos* (written after 1497) found in cod. Munich, Univ. Bib., MS. 2°.
41 f. 571rb *in fine* and cited by P. Lehmann and O. Glauning, *Mittelalterliche
Handschriftenbruchstücke der Universitätsbibliothek und des Georgianum zu München*,
p. 92.
[2] G. Becker, *Catalogi Bibliothecarum Antiqui*, p. 209.
[3] See J. Leclercq, 'Une liste de docteurs dans un manuscrit de Tolède', pp.
23–4.

(RS 1858), pp. 134, 157, 165. The compiler has in view a corrupt version of
Abelard's eucharistic teaching.

CHAPTER II

ABELARD'S FOLLOWERS

The names of some twenty-one disciples and sometime pupils
under Abelard are known. In addition some fourteen anonymous
writers composed works of theology or of logic under Abelard's
inspiration. Pope Innocent II in 1140 forbad the followers of
Abelard to hold or to defend the mistakes of their master and
ordered Abelard's writings to be destroyed. The literary evidence
surveyed in the last chapter would lead by itself to the conclusion
that there was no future in attempting to develop Abelard's
theology. Yet there survive today, in addition to copies of
Abelard's own writings, eleven theological compositions produced
by his followers. The writings of the school are highly important
in the history of early scholastic theology and logic but most of
them are of obscure or anonymous authorship. All the logical
works which in the present state of knowledge can be assigned
to Abelard's school are anonymous.[1] Of the theological works,
the most central one is not merely anonymous; its existence is
only posited by the strong hypothesis of Dr H. Ostlender who
considered that the *Liber Sententiarum* wrongly attributed to
Abelard by Bernard of Clairvaux was the work of an anonymous
member of the school and acted as the main source for several
of the other sentence collections of the school.[2]

Some theological writings of the school do bear their authors'
names but the fact is not always a revealing one. One abbot
Bernard composed some Sentences *c.* 1140 but he seemingly
cannot be identified with any other known twelfth-century
abbot of that name.[3] Master Hermann who is presumed to have
written after 1139 the most widely conserved sentence work of
Abelard's school is otherwise wholly unknown.[4] Nothing

[1] See below, pp. 66, 70–4, 77, 82, 86–7, 89.
[2] Ostlender, 'Die Sentenzenbücher der Schule Abaelards', pp. 224–50.
Bernard's charge (see *Epist.* 188 and 190 in PL. 182, 353B and 1062C) was
repudiated by Abelard in his *Confessio fidei 'universis'* (PL. 178, 107–8).
[3] See below, pp. 234–6.　　　　　　　　[4] See below, pp. 158–64.

enables us to identify Master Hermann with any other contemporary bearer of this name, such as Hermann of Carinthia, the student of Arabic learning who had moved to Spain before 1138[1] or Hermann the Praemonstratensian abbot of Kappensberg or Scheida, an acquaintance of Rupert of Deutz and author of a work describing his conversion from Judaism.[2] St Bernard appealed to one Hermann, bishop of Constance (1139–66) and part author of Bernard's own life, to act against Arnold of Brescia, Abelard's partner in heresy.[3] After 1180 Cardinal Laborans dedicated to another Hermann a treatise against the Abelardians entitled *Secte Sabellianorum*.[4] But Abelard's disciple is known to us only through an apparent self-reference in a book of Abelardian sentences.[5] Likewise the *Ysagoge in theologiam*, a major work of the school, may be by one Odo who is distinct from other writers of that name and of those days but who is not at present otherwise identifiable.[6]

There are, however, two important sentence collections of the school by well-known authors. These are the Sentences of Roland Bandinelli who later became Pope Alexander III and the Sentences of Master Omnebene, later bishop of Verona. Roland Bandinelli completed his work in 1150.[7] He was born of an aristocratic Sienese family in the earliest years of the century.[8]

---

[1] Cf. C. H. Haskins, *Studies in the History of Mediaeval Science*, p. 55.

[2] Hermann of Kappensberg, *Opusculum de sua conversione*, PL. 170, 805–36; written *c.* 1137.

[3] Bernard of Clairvaux, *Epist.* 195 (PL. 182, 1281).

[4] Ed. Landgraf, *Laborantis Cardinalis Opuscula*, pp. 61–2.

[5] 'Diverso vero tempore prolata idem significant, ut si quis diceret heri: Hermannus leget cras, qui idem dicat: Hermannus legit hodie et cras idem dicat: Hermannus legit heri, idem significat, scilicet quod ego hodie legerim. Idem namque est me heri fuisse hodie lecturum et me hodie legere et cras me hodie legisse', PL. 178, 1728D. On this see Ostlender, 'Die Sentenzenbücher', pp. 210–13.

[6] See my article 'The Authorship of the *Ysagoge in theologiam*' which is to appear in the *AHDLMA*.

[7] Discovered by Heinrich Denifle, 'Die Sentenzen Abaelards', pp. 434–61 and ed. A. M. Gietl in 1891. On the date of composition see D. Van den Eynde, 'Nouvelles précisions chronologiques', pp. 100–10.

[8] On Roland's life see E. Portalié, 'Alexandre III', cols. 711–17; on his teaching career see also M. Pacaut, *Alexandre III*, pp. 52–77, and *idem*, 'Roland Bandinelli', cols. 702 *et seq.*

The place of his education is not known and nothing enables us to assume that he actually studied in northern France under Abelard. At the time of the publication of Gratian's *Decretum* he held a chair of theology at Bologna.[1] It is reasonable to suppose that during the 1140s Roland was an active promoter and critic of aspects of Abelard's theology. At the same time he was digesting the *Decretum* and writing his *Stroma* on canon law.[2] Robert of Torigny gives high praise to Roland as a teacher.[3] By 1149–50, however, Roland had left Bologna to become a canon at the cathedral of Pisa where perhaps he taught in the episcopal school. He was then on the threshold of very great fame. His *Stroma* was published by 1148 and his *Sententie* within another two years. In 1150 he was a cardinal, in 1153 he became chancellor of the Roman church and from 1159 to 1181 he was pope. His attachment to the teachings of Abelard did not impede the acquisition of the highest honours and paradoxically it was he who in 1174 raised Bernard of Clairvaux to the altars of the church.[4] Ironically too he condemned as pope in 1177 the doctrine of Christological nihilism which as a master and under Abelard's stimulus he had himself expounded in the schools of Bologna.[5]

Roland's contribution to the discussion of Abelard's thought in the schools of Bologna must have been weighty. But his attachment to Abelard's personal teachings appears very restrained

[1] The authority for this is the canonist Huguccio: 'Alexandro tertio Bononiae residente in cathedra magistrali in divina pagina', *Summa*, c. 31, C. 2, q. 6, *cit.* J. F. von Schulte, *Geschichte der Quellen und Literatur des Canonischen Rechts*, I, 115, n. 3; cf. F. Ehrle, *I più antichi statuti della facoltà teologica dell'università di Bologna*, p. lxviii, and Pacaut, *Alexandre III*, p. 59.

[2] Roland Bandinelli, *Stroma*, ed. F. Thaner. See also S. Kuttner, *Repertorium der Kanonistik*, I, 55, 127–9, 245.

[3] 'Fuit enim in divina pagina praeceptor maximus et in decretis et canonibus et in Romanis legibus praecipuus', *Chron.*, ed. Delisle, II, 108.

[4] For discussions of the negotiations preceding the canonization and of Alexander's delay in agreeing to the requests of the Cistercian order, see J. Leclercq, 'Recherches sur les Sermons sur les Cantiques. La Recension de Clairvaux' in *Recueil d'Etudes*, I, 267–8 and A. H. Bredero, *Etudes sur la 'Vita Prima' de S. Bernard*, pp. 40–1. On Bredero's thesis cf. the review by M. D. Knowles in the *English Historical Review*, LXXVII (1962), pp. 748–9.

[5] See J. de Ghellinck, *Le Mouvement théologique du XIIe siècle*, pp. 251–8.

when he is compared with his colleague Omnebene, who similarly was not prevented from pursuing a distinguished career.[1] He is plausibly identified with Omnebene the canonist master to whom Pope Eugenius III wrote during his pontificate (1145–53)[2] and who in about 1156 abbreviated the *Decretum* of Gratian.[3] In 1157 he became bishop of Verona and as such is said to have proved a faithful ally of Alexander III.[4] He died in 1185.

All these writers—Roland, Omnebene, Bernard, Hermann and 'Odo'—as well as the anonymous authors whose careers are not known to us are members of Abelard's school of theology. Each one produced a theological work or a scriptural commentary in which the opinions of Abelard were prominent. Some of these authors may never have been in Abelard's company in the schools and may only have encountered his ideas through his writings or even through those of other disciples. Héloïse, however, shared his company and enjoyed his teaching without belonging to the schools of the clerks. She had been his pupil in letters[5] but she also knew his theological work well. The oratory of the Paraclete was handed over by Abelard to her and to some of her sisters expelled from Argenteuil. The new community received from Abelard a Rule[6] and an exhortation to study the three biblical languages, Hebrew, Greek and Latin.[7] Abelard requested Héloïse and her sisters to imitate in the love and

[1] Omnebene's Sentences were discovered by Denifle, '*Die Sentenzen Abaelards*', pp. 461–9; see also A. M. Gietl, *Die Sentenzen Rolands*, pp. l–lvi and Grabmann, *Geschichte*, II, 227–8. The work is sadly still inedited, but many extracts are given in the footnotes of Gietl's work.

[2] *Epist.* 543 (PL. 180, 1564B), addressed to *magistrum Omnibonum*.

[3] I have not been able to see J. F. von Schulte, *Dissertatio de Decreto ab Omnibono abbreviato* (Bonn, 1892). Articles by G. Le Bras on two manuscripts of the *Abbreviatio Decreti* are found in the *Revue des sciences religieuses*, VII (1927), pp. 649–52, and VIII (1928), pp. 270–1; and see S. Kuttner, *Repertorium*, I, 259. The available details of Omnebene's life are collected by R. Chabanne, 'Omnibonus', cols. 1111–12; L. Saltet, *Les Réordinations au moyen âge*, p. 308 and J. F. von Schulte, *Geschichte*, I, 119–21.

[4] Cf. Saltet, *Les Réordinations au moyen âge*, p. 307.

[5] *Hist. Calam.*, ll. 280 et seq.

[6] The Rule has been critically edited by T. P. McLaughlin; cf. also PL. 178, 255–314. On the chronology of Abelard's writings to Héloïse see D. Van den Eynde, 'Chronologie des écrits d'Abélard à Héloïse'.

[7] *Epist. IX, de studio litterarum*, PL. 178, 325–336.

study of holy letters Paula and Eustochium whose requests to Jerome had resulted in many compositions.[1] To Héloïse Abelard owed the stimulus for much of his writing. The *Hymns and Sequences* were designed for the Paraclete and prefaced by a spiritual direction to the community;[2] so were a *Psalterium*[3] and a collection of *Sermons*.[4] The commentary on the *Hexaemeron* was written for Héloïse and her *Problemata* led Abelard to expound some forty-two Scriptural passages and difficulties. In addition to the series of personal letters Héloïse was the recipient of a *Confession of Faith* in which Abelard expressed his deepest wishes and convictions. 'The passionate drama of Héloïse and Abelard', as Monsieur Gilson once observed, 'was more fertile in ideas than one might suppose.'[5] Moreover, Héloïse herself shared in Abelard's ideas. Like Abelard's other disciples, who used and copied the arguments and authorities originally manipulated by their master, some of the statements of Héloïse are also to be found in Abelard's works. The arguments and the examples taken from Jerome and Seneca and others which Abelard in his *Historia Calamitatum*[6] puts into Héloïse's mouth as she attempts to dissuade the philosopher from marriage, are found as well in Abelard's *Theologia Christiana*.[7] They may not be any the less her own thoughts for being phrased by Abelard. Héloïse also adhered closely to Abelard's conviction that our intentions, not our deeds, count before God. She uses Abelard's own terminology sparingly, but the phrases she borrows are the key ones and of a kind which easily lodge in the memory.[8]

---

[1] *Epist. VIII, in fine* (PL. 178, 314B; McLaughlin, 'Abelard's Rule', p. 292).
[2] Ed. G. M. Dreves, *Petri Abaelardi . . . Hymnarius Paraclitensis* and again in Analecta Hymnica Medii Aevi, XLVIII, 141–223; cf. also PL. 178, 1771–1816.
[3] *Epist.* III (PL. 178, 187C); J. T. Muckle, 'The Personal Letters between Abelard and Héloïse', p. 73. Cf. *ibid.*, pp. 58–9.
[4] On the composition of Abelard's collection of sermons see D. Van den Eynde, 'Le Receuil des Sermons de Pierre Abélard'.
[5] Gilson, *The Mystical Theology of St Bernard*, p. 13.
[6] *Ll.* 425–558.
[7] *Lib.* II (PL. 178, 1195 *et seq.*). Cf. P. Delhaye, 'Le dossier antimatrimonial de l'Adversus Jovinianum et son influence sur quelques écrits latins du XIIe siècle'.
[8] 'Non enim rei effectus, sed efficientis affectus in crimine est. Nec quae

The literature inspired by the friendship of Abelard and Héloïse is aside from the main stream of the development of early scholastic theology; its influence was mainly felt in the Paraclete and in its dependencies. Yet to the Paraclete *la très sage Héloïs* brought and indeed applied some of the ideas which were principally to stimulate the professionals of the schools. She proposed that Abelard should write a Rule for women in accordance with his own fundamental principles and she applied Abelard's opinion that human works are morally indifferent and do nothing to secure either merit or blame, not only to their marriage (to which, she maintained, she had not consented and therefore she was innocent of the crime[1]) but also to the question of monastic observances. She questioned the value of the prohibition of meat in religious communities; in itself the taking of meat is neither good nor bad; its renunciation is an external practice common both to truly pious souls and to hypocrites. Only interior actions count for the Christian; the rest is Judiasm. Christianity has substituted the law of faith for the law of works.[2] Héloïse, like Abelard, minimized the differences between monks and layfolk by applying Abelard's ethical theory to the criticism of monastic 'Judaism' and of superstition concerning works.

Abelard's supporters and friends included people who were his disciples in the schools as well as others who were not. He received assistance in the course of his life from men who without being his students intervened on his behalf and some thereby supported his teaching. For example, Abelard was befriended in 1121–2 after his flight from the abbey of St Médard by Theobald, the

---

[1] *Epist.* IV (PL. 178, 195D–6A; Muckle, 'The Personal Letters', p. 80).
[2] *Epist.* VI (PL. 178, 220B *et seq.*; Muckle, 'The Letter of Héloïse on the Religious Life', pp. 248 *et seq.* For further criticisms by a disciple of Abelard of 'Judaism' in Christian moral thought, see below, p. 152.

---

fiunt quam quo animo fiunt aequitas pensat', *Epist.* II (PL. 178, 186A; Muckle, 'The Personal Letters', p. 72); cf. Abelard, *Ethica*, c. 3 (PL. 178, 644A). 'Nulla quidquid meriti apud Deum obtinent quae reprobis aeque ut electis communia sunt', *Epist.* IV (PL. 178, 198B; Muckle, p. 82); cf. *Ethica*, c. 7 (650B). Also, *Epist.* VI (PL. 178, 213–26, *passim*; Muckle, 'The Letter of Héloïse on the Religious Life', pp. 241–53. Some parallels are discussed by Muckle in 'The Personal Letters', p. 55.

c

count of Blois and of Champagne, and by the anonymous prior of St Ayoul at Provins in the diocese of Sens.[1] The permission required for Abelard to live the monastic life in a place of his own choosing was sought by the bishop of Meaux and then by Stephen de Garlande, the royal seneschal.[2] Of all Abelard's friends except Héloïse the one who perhaps most shaped his destiny was Peter the Venerable, who ensured that Abelard did not pass into the memory of posterity as an outcast but as a repentant heretic and unfortunate man of genius.

Other supporters were more involved with their master's opinions and teachings and their fortunes were of the most varied. The examples of Roland and Omnebene are not the only ones which suggest that adherence to Master Peter was not necessarily an obstacle to a successful career. When Bernard of Clairvaux was writing his series of letters to Pope Innocent and to members of the Roman Curia in a bid to secure Abelard's condemnation, he wrote a special letter to Master Guy of Castello, Cardinal priest of St Mark. Bernard stated here that be believed that Guy was a friend of Abelard yet he trusted that he was no friend of Abelard's errors.[3] He urged Guy to press for Abelard's condemnation and to beware of his errors. Guy had been a member of the Roman Curia at least since 1123 and in 1127 he had become Cardinal deacon of S. Maria in Via Lata.[4] At some time Guy had acquired the title *magister* and he enjoyed a reputation for learning.[5] Abelard and he had both attended a

---

[1] *Hist. Calam.*, ll. 987–1016. Abelard and Theobald figure together in a story told by Peter Cantor in *Verbum Abbreviatum*, c. 46 (PL. 205, 146B).

[2] *Hist. Calam.*, ll. 1017–1037.

[3] 'Injuriam facio vobis, si aliquem a vobis ita diligi credam, ut cum eo pariter eius errores diligatis . . . ', Bernard of Clairvaux, *Epist.* 192 (PL. 182, 358–9, here 358B). Cf. Alberic of Tre Fontane: 'De isto Guidone in epistolis beati Bernardi memoratur, quod fuerit magistri Petri Abaelardi discipulus, sed non est magistrum in errore secutus', *Chron.* (MGH.SS. XXIII, 837).

[4] On Guy's life see R. Mols, 'Célestin II' and A. Wilmart, 'Les livres légués par Célestin II à Città di Castello'. It is worth recalling that Fulk of Deuil in his letter to Abelard says that Romans were present among Abelard's audience before 1118 (PL. 178, 371C), but we do not know whether Guy attended a school in France.

[5] Cf. *Chronicon Mauriniacensis*, ed. L. Mirot, pp. 79–80: 'Celestinus, qui alio nomine magister Guido de Castellis nominatus est. Hic vero prelacione

consecration ceremony at the abbey of Morigny in the arch-diocese of Sens in the year 1131[1] and Guy was again in France for several months on a mission in 1139–40.[2] It is likely therefore that Guy had formed his friendship with Abelard in the course of one of his visits to France and, in view of Bernard's action, that they had met together in 1139–40. But this does not appear to have compromised Guy's reputation in Rome for in 1143 he was elected pope as Celestine II. Moreover, in the previous year Gerhoh of Reichersberg appears to have had no suspicions about Guy's orthodoxy for he wrote a tract against the teachings of Gilbert of Poitiers, whom Gerhoh elsewhere[3] links with Abelard as a propagator of heretical teachings, and he dedicated his work, the *Libellus de ordine donorum sancti spiritus*, to master Guy.[4] Guy is the only associate of Abelard, except for Héloïse, who is known to have possessed copies of Abelard's writings. Dom André Wilmart discovered in a manuscript of the thirteenth century a list of the books owned by him and bequeathed on his death in 1144 to the church of Città di Castello where he had

---

[1] Both Mols and Wilmart omit to mention this occasion, but see *Chronicon Mauriniacensis*, ed. Mirot, p. 53: 'Affuerunt ... diaconi cardinales ... Guido de titulo Sancte Marie in Via lata ... '; and for Abelard's presence see Mirot, p. 54 (cited above, p. 3, n. 4).

[2] Mols, 'Célestin II', col. 59.

[3] 'Fumant scolae plures in Francia et aliis terris per maxime a duabus caudis ticionum fumigentium videlicet Petri Abaiolardi et episcopi Gilliberti', Gerhoh of Reichersberg, *Liber de novitatibus*, c. 20, ed. E. Sackur, *Libelli selecti*, p. 301.

[4] Ed. D. & O. Van den Eynde and A. Rijsmersdael, *Gerhohi praepositi Reicherspergensis opera inedita*, I, 63–165. On the identification of Cardinal Guido mentioned in the opening of Gerhoh's work with Guy of Castello and on the date of composition (1142) see P. Classen, *Gerhoch von Reichersberg*, pp. 340 and 412 respectively. Later Guy, as pope, sent a letter of encouragement to Gerhoh (PL. 195, 1105D–1106B).

---

illa dignissimus erat, quoniam ei tria, que inter homines pene habentur pre-cipua, simul confluxerant, celebremque magistrum reddiderant: nobilitas scilicet generis, mentis industria in omni statu equalis, litterarum quoque, quarum doctrine intentissimus fuit, sciencia multiformis.' This part of the chronicle, book III, was written by a monk of Morigny after 1149 but before 1151 (Mirot, pp. xii, xiii). Bernard of Clairvaux also gives Guy the title of *magister* in the letter cited.

been a canon.[1] Here we find recorded Abelard's *Theologia* and *Sic et Non*.

A less discreet association with Abelard was pursued by Hyacinth Boboni who vigorously defended Abelard against Bernard but who became a cardinal soon after Abelard's death and many years later (in 1191) pope as Celestine III.[2] Hyacinth had been born in the early years of the century into a noble Italian family. He entered the papal court when young and his signature is found on papal documents from 1121 onwards. He became a subdeacon in 1126. Before and after the council of Sens in 1140 Bernard had occasion in his letters to Rome to deplore the malignant opposition of Hyacinth.[3] It is a likely inference from a remark of John of Salisbury in his *Historia Pontificalis* that Hyacinth was in France during the crisis.[4] The roles then played by Cardinal Guy and by Hyacinth help to explain why Bernard so energetically pressed his case in Rome; it may also help to explain why Abelard preferred to appeal from the bishops at Sens to the court of Rome.[5]

In spite of his embroilment in these disputes Hyacinth was elevated to the purple only four years later in 1144 and perhaps

[1] A. Wilmart, 'Les livres légués'.

[2] For details of Hyacinth's life see R. Mols, 'Célestin III'; also A. Hofmeister, 'Studien über Otto von Freising', I, pp. 142–3.

[3] 'Quanquam non iam parvulae nec pauculae, sed certe grandiusculae et multae sint, nec nisi in manu forti vel a vobis exterminabuntur. Jacinctus multa mala ostendit nobis; nec enim quae voluit, fecit, vel potuit. Sed visus est mihi patienter ferendus de me, qui nec personae vestrae, nec curiae in curia illa pepercit', Bernard of Clairvaux, *Epist.* 189 to Pope Innocent (PL. 182, 356D–7A); cf. *Epist.* 338 to the chancellor, Cardinal Haimeric (PL. 182, 543D),

[4] John is writing principally of Arnold of Brescia who 'adhesit Petro Abaielardo partesque eius cum domino Iacincto, qui nunc cardinalis est, adversus abbatem Clarevallensem studiosius fovit. Postquam vero magister Petrus Cluniacum profectus est, Parisius manens . . .', *Hist. Pont.*, ed. M. Chibnall, p. 63.

[5] The conjectures of Vacandard, while not altogether unreasonable, are not actually warranted by the evidence. Vacandard, in his *Vie de S. Bernard*, II, 141, 148, stated that Hyacinth was one of Abelard's 'imprudent advisers', was partly responsible for destroying the previously good relationship between Bernard and Abelard and brought from Rome the assurance that Abelard's *Theologia* was in the hands of the Cardinals. Vacandard further thought that Hyacinth may have challenged the authority of the council of Sens and that by giving 'flattering assurances' he partly caused Abelard to appeal to the pope.

by Celestine II who was pope in the first three months of that year and whose papal name Hyacinth was one day himself to assume. In the middle of the century Hyacinth seems to have possessed a reputation for orthodoxy. In the winter of 1163–4 Gerhoh of Reichersberg requested Hyacinth to employ his great prestige and authority in resisting heretical masters of the schools who denied the omnipotence of Christ.[1] Hyacinth, like Cardinal Guy in 1142, does not seem to have been suspect to Gerhoh as a result of his past association with Abelard but to what extent he had ever shown sympathy with the teachings of Abelard and to what extent he had simply been motivated by hostility towards the proceedings instituted by Bernard of Clairvaux, it is not possible to determine.[2]

At another extreme from the careers of Popes Celestine II, Alexander III and Celestine III there were disciples whose attachment to Abelard involved them in tragedy and misfortune. One such student is known to us through a short reference made by Gerhoh of Reichersberg in a letter to the cardinals in Rome written in the winter of 1163–4.[3] Gerhoh, now nearing his seventieth year, recalls his earlier struggles against the betrayers of the orthodox doctrine of the person of Christ.[4] He mentions

[1] '... doctrina pestifera in scholis discolis adeo crebrescit, ut jam plures magistrorum, et discipulorum et indisciplinatorum garriant adversus fidem catholicam'; '... qui vos in Ecclesia Romana gratia Dei plurimum valetis, cavete, ne sitis ingratus gratiae Dei, sed per ipsum resistite hostibus ejus', *Epist.* XIX (PL. 193, 573C, 574A). For Hyacinth's reply see *Epist.* XXII (PL. 193, 586). On the date of Gerhoh's letter see P. Classen, *Gerhoch von Reichersberg*, p. 392.

[2] In the *Dialogus Ratii et Everardi*, the author, Everard, now a Cistercian monk, declares: 'me fuisse clericum in Francia domini Hyacinthi, nunc Papae', ed. N. M. Haring, p. 248. Everard was also the author of a *Summula decretalium quaestionum* and, as the *Dialogus* shows, a firm disciple of Gilbert of Poitiers; see Haring, 'The Cistercian Everard of Ypres'. Haring mentions here (p. 143) that Cardinal Hyacinth was in France in 1162–5—at the time, that is, when Gerhoh was requesting action against heretical masters. It is just possible, on the other hand, that Everard was in the entourage of Hyacinth in 1140 when the latter was already called 'dominus'. In any case it is worth noting the association of a supporter of Gilbert with one of Abelard's sympathizers.

[3] *Epist.* XXI (PL. 193, 575–85). On the date of this letter see Classen, *Gerhoch von Reichersberg*, pp. 392–3.

[4] 'Cogor in senectute mea reminisci ex parte laborum juventutis meae', *Epist.* XXI (PL. 193, 575D).

first Master Liutolfus, the same Lotulph, in fact, who had accused Abelard of heresy at the synod of Soissons in 1121[1] and who, says Gerhoh, flourished under Pope Honorius II (1124–30).[2] Then he writes: 'Again on another occasion while I was in Rome, a certain canon of the Lateran called Adam, who had recently emerged from the schools of Master Peter Abelard, attempted to demonstrate that Christ was partly God and partly man.'[3] Gerhoh implies that he personally intervened against Adam who later apostatized and retired to Apulia as a direct result, it would seem, of his thinking.[4] Gerhoh next cites a third instance ('tertia vice') which occurred during the schism of Anaclete (1130–7).[5]

It would thus seem that the possibly direct acquaintance of Gerhoh with Adam occurred while Gerhoh was in Rome in 1126 or at least before the beginning of the schism of Anaclete

---

[1] Cf. Abelard, *Hist. Calam.*, *ll.* 710 *et seq.*; also Classen, *Gerhoch von Reichersberg*, p. 90, and D. Van den Eynde, 'Du nouveau sur deux maîtres lombards contemporains du Maître des Sentences', pp. 7–8.

[2] *Epist.* XXI (576C). M. Chossat, *La Somme des Sentences*, pp. 67–8 and Van den Eynde, 'Du nouveau sur deux maîtres lombards', view Lotulph as a disciple of Abelard. Gerhoh accused him of adoptianism ('dum astruere conaretur Christum, secundum quod homo est, hominis quidem filium esse naturalem, sed Dei Patris filium adoptivum', *Epist.* XXI (576C)). Van den Eynde explains Gerhoh's failure to record Lotulph's association with what he considered to be Abelard's teaching on the ground that he knew Lotulph to be an adversary of Abelard. But does Gerhoh credit Abelard with the same thesis? In 1147 he wrote to Bernard of Clairvaux: 'Mirati sumus valde, pater sancte, in catalogo heresium Petri Abaiolardi hoc te pretermisisse, quod ille dictis ac scriptis asseruit, hominem de virgine natum non proprie sed figurative dici deum . . . ', ed. G. Hüffer, 'Handschriftliche Studien zum Leben des hl. Bernhard von Clairvaux', p. 270, and dated by Van den Eynde, *L'oeuvre littéraire de Géroch*, p. 61. Earlier in 1141 he wrote to Pope Innocent II (PL. 193, 584C–5C) that many disciples of Abelard affirmed that the man born of the Virgin is only called God in figurative speech; on this letter and Gerhoh's lost tract, *De glorificatione filii hominis*, cf. Van den Eynde, *op. cit.*, pp. 49–65. But Gerhoh does not associate discussion of the adoptive sonship of Christ with Abelard's school.

[3] *Epist.* XXI (576D).

[4] 'Sancta Romana Ecclesia mihi astitit meamque fidem fideliter approbavit in tantum, ut cum postea praedictus Adam factus apostata ivisset in Apuliam, diceret mihi unus cardinalium, recte illum pro sua perfidia relictum a Christo', *ibid.* (577A).

[5] *Ibid.* (577B).

in 1130.[1] Adam, having recently come from France, had probably been one of the band of enthusiastic followers who had accompanied Abelard into comparative isolation near Quincey between 1122 and 1125.[2] The error cannot be found in any of Abelard's writings, although even the earliest version of the *Sic et Non*, perhaps prepared between 1122 and 1126,[3] contains texts grouped under the question whether Christ was partly God and partly man.[4] Moreover, since some of the sentence collections of the school assert that Christ is partly God and partly man, Abelard may well have considered the proposition favourably[5] and Adam would appear to show that Abelard did so while teaching at Quincey. There were other reasons too for which men criticized Abelard's activities and his teachings at Quincey.[6]

[1] Cf. Classen, *Gerhoch von Reichersberg*, p. 36, n. 13. Chossat, unconvincingly in my view, stated (*La Somme des Sentences*, pp. 67–8) that Gerhoh disputed with Adam *c.* 1133.

[2] After *c.* 1125 Abelard, as abbot of St Gildas of Ruys, retired from teaching until the early 1130s.

[3] Statements about the composition of the *Sic et Non* have to be received with caution until all the known manuscripts have been critically examined. But for this dating cf. J. Cottiaux, 'La Conception de la théologie', p. 268. Sikes, *Peter Abailard*, p. 267, suggests the years 1122–3, but the reasons he gives are not of the most persuasive. An even earlier date for the beginning of this work is conceivable; A. M. Stickler, *Historia Iuris Canonici Latini*, I, 193, considers it to have been elaborated 'variis in recensionibus continuis ab a. 1115/17'.

[4] This question, which is the sixty-sixth in the printed version of PL. 178, 1434–6, is found in all the manuscripts of the *Sic et Non* except cod. Douai 357 where the text is short owing to the loss of leaves. The presence of the same question in a number of manuscripts does not preclude differences in the selection and arrangement of the relevant *auctoritates*.

[5] Hermann, *Sententie*, c. 24 (PL. 178, 1733BC); *Sententie Florianenses*, ed. H. Ostlender, p. 17 and *Sententie Parisienses I*, ed. A. M. Landgraf, pp. 31–2.

[6] In the *Hist. Calam.*, *ll.* 1201–12, Abelard complained of criticisms levelled against him at Quincey by two 'novi apostoli': 'quorum alter regularium canonicorum vitam, alter monachorum se resuscitasse gloriabatur. Hii predicando per mundum discurrentes et me impudenter quantum poterant corrodentes, non modice tam ecclesiasticis quibusdam quam secularibus potestatibus contemptibilem ad tempus effecerunt, et de mea tam fide quam vita adeo sinistra disseminaverunt . . .' The critics are usually identified as Norbert of Xanten and Bernard of Clairvaux. A. Borst's suggestion ('Abälard und Bernhard', pp. 502–3) that the two were Norbert and his successor as abbot of Prémontré, Hugh of Fosses, does not quite satisfy the distinction which Abelard here makes between canons and monks: 'alter regularium canonicorum

The case of Adam illustrates how quickly Abelard's teaching could be carried far and wide, even to Rome and more than a decade before William of St Thierry and Bernard of Clairvaux became anxious about the support for Abelard that existed in the centre of Latin Christendom. Gerhoh's action leads one to wonder how many other students of Abelard returned to their own lands to preach and to teach the new learning in the 1120s. To men such as Gerhoh, Adam's apostasy and, as it would seem, exile were a striking testimony to the danger presented by Abelard to the enquiring mind.

Pope Innocent's condemnation in 1140 bore not only against Abelard and his followers but also against Arnold of Brescia.[1] Arnold, a man of great austerity and uncommon appeal, was born in the late eleventh century and after many vicissitudes of fortune was hanged in Rome in 1155. A political agitator and vehement critic of ecclesiastical abuses, in the nineteenth century he came to share with Abelard a reputation as an anti-clerical freethinker.[2] Arnold was the most luckless supporter of Abelard. But why should the Italian reformer have been mentioned by name in Innocent's condemnation of Abelard? The cause would seem to lie in the letters of Bernard of Clairvaux who, when writing to Rome to secure the papal verdict before and after the council of Sens, depicted Arnold as the shield bearer of Goliath or Abelard. The Italian and the Frenchman were as two

[1] 'Mandamus quatenus Petrum Abaelardum et Arnaldum de Brixia, perversi dogmatis fabricatores, et Catholicae fidei impugnatores, in religiosis locis, ubi vobis melius visum fuerit, separatim faciatis includi', Innocent II, *Epist.* 447 (PL. 179, 517BC).
[2] On Arnold's life there is an abundant literature; see especially E. Vacandard, 'Arnaud de Brescia', F. Vernet, 'Arnaud de Brescia' and G. W. Greenaway, *Arnold of Brescia*.

---

vitam, alter monachorum se resuscitasse gloriabatur'. The *De baptismo* of Bernard of Clairvaux (PL. 182, 1031–46), which answers questions put by Hugh of St Victor and which is directed against rumours or reports of Abelard's teaching in circulation, is now most commonly dated *c.* 1125. Cf. Sikes, *Peter Abailard*, pp. 214–15; A. Borst, 'Abalard und Bernhard', p. 500; L. Ott, *Untersuchungen*, pp. 495 *et seq.*, 499 *et seq.*, 527 *et seq.*, 539 *et seq.*; D. Van den Eynde, *Essai sur . . . Hugues de S. Victor*, pp. 132–7. On the disorders of the school cf. below, pp. 54–5.

hissing bees which had united against the Lord.[1] The Roman Curia was meant to gain the impression that Abelard was in league with the unruly Arnold who had lately been expelled from Italy. Bernard may thus have intended to make it more difficult for the Curia to avoid condemning an ally of Arnold but in any case, as may be suggested from the references to the alliance between Arnold and Abelard contained in the accounts of Otto of Freising and of John of Salisbury, the fact was itself sufficiently prominent to occasion a mention in the letters of Bernard. Otto of Freising, who was once a student in Paris, tells us that Arnold had been a pupil of Abelard.[2] E. Vacandard, in a remarkable study of Arnold which cleared away so many legends and misinterpretations, accepted Otto's word and deduced that Arnold would thus have been a student in Paris *c.* 1115 and would then have formed an intimate relationship with the philosopher.[3] Other scholars, writing more recently, have heavily criticized Otto's statement; and A. R. Motte in particular, noting the silence of John of Salisbury and of Bernard of Clairvaux on the nature of this relationship, distrusted as well the general reliability of Otto's account of the crisis of 1140.[4] John of Salisbury wrote in his *Historia Pontificalis* that Arnold allied with Hyacinth and Abelard against Bernard and that after the council of Sens Arnold remained on the Mont Sainte-Geneviève where Abelard

---

[1] 'Procedit Golias procero corpore, nobili illi suo bellico apparatu circummunitus antecedente quoque ipsum eius armigero Arnaldo de Brixia. Squama squamae coniungitur, et nec spiraculum incedit per eas. Siquidem sibilavit apis quae erat in Francia, api de Italia: et venerunt in unum adversus Dominum', Bernard of Clairvaux, *Epist.* 189 (PL. 182, 355BC). Cf. *Epist.* 330 (535C).

[2] 'Arnaldus iste . . . Petrum Abailardum olim preceptorem habuerat', Otto of Freising, *Gesta Friderici*, II, xxviii (ed. Waitz, p. 133). Cf. *Sigeberti Auctarium Affligemense*: 'Arnaldus hereticus et scismaticus de Brixia, discipulus magistri Petri Abailart', MGH.SS. VI, 403; *Annales Sancti Taurini Ebroicensis*: '1178 [*sic*]. Hoc tempore surrexit quidam magister Arnaudus nomine, magistri Petri Abelardi discipulus, qui multa contra Romanam ecclesiam predicabat', MGH.SS. XXVI, 509.

[3] Vacandard, 'Arnaud de Brescia', pp. 55–7.

[4] Motte, 'Une fausse accusation contre Abélard et Arnaud de Brescia', pp. 39–42. Cf. Sikes, *Peter Abailard*, p. 26 and A. Frugoni, *Arnaldo da Brescia nelle fonti del secolo XII*, p. 56. Greenaway, however, inclines to accept Otto's statement (*Arnold of Brescia*, pp. 28–30).

had previously lodged and there propounded his reformist anti-authoritarian views to the few down-and-outs who alone were attracted to his lectures.[1]

John of Salisbury does not elucidate Arnold's motives in supporting Abelard but contents himself with the observation that he had made common cause with Abelard against the abbot of Clairvaux. Nevertheless the spectacle of the extreme moral reformer from Italy in league with the Parisian master in a dispute concerning scholastic heresy is an intriguing one and if the existence of a master-pupil relationship is at best dubitable, the motives of this relationship are as unclear as those of Abelard's relationships with Hyacinth and with Guy. Some writers have posited a vague spiritual kinship between the herald of emancipated reason and the prophet of a new church order,[2] and more recently the two have been seen as bourgeois with Arnold, the 'shield bearer', acting as the executor of Abelard's anti-feudal and anti-ecclesiastical theories.[3] It is true that Abelard manifested a reformer's spirit[4] but the condemnation of abuses alone would not suffice to bring an Abelard and an Arnold together. Moreover, Abelard did also hold some radical opinions on the nature of ecclesiastical authority. In the *Ethica* he denied that every bishop possessed the power of binding and loosing the sins of men and

---

[1] 'Ob quam causam a domino Innocentio papa depositus et extrusus ab Italia, descendit in Franciam et adhesit Petro Abaielardo, partesque eius cum domino Iacincto, qui nunc cardinalis est, adversus abbatem Clarevallensem studiosius fovit. Postquam vero magister Petrus Cluniacum profectus est, Parisius manens in monte sancte Genovefe divinas litteras scolaribus exponebat apud sanctum Hylarium, ubi iam dictus Petrus fuerat hospitatus. Sed auditores non habuit nisi pauperes et qui ostiatim elemosinas publice mendicabant, unde cum magistro vitam transigerent . . . Episcopis non parcebat ob avariciam et turpem questum, et plerumque propter maculam vite, et quia ecclesiam Dei in sanguinibus edificare nituntur', *Hist. Pont.*, ed. Chibnall, pp. 63–4.

[2] Cf. Vacandard, 'Arnaud de Brescia', pp. 57–8.

[3] See the remarks made in a spoken discussion by E. Werner and reported in *La Vita Comune del Clero nei Secoli XI e XII*, I, 345–6 and 348. And for criticism of Werner see P. Classen, *ibid.*, pp. 346–7, 348.

[4] Cf. *Hist. Calam.*, ll. 1255 *et seq.*, 1534 *et seq.* In sermon XXXIII (PL. 178, 588B–589A) Abelard castigated monkish litigiousness over tithes and monks who lived outside their abbey. In his *Epistola ad quemdam canonicum* (PL. 178, 343–52) Abelard defended the superiority of the monastic over the clerical state.

he preferred to hold as his own belief that this power only existed in those bishops who had qualities of discretion and of holiness and who by their merits were worthy successors of the apostles.[1] Similar beliefs are associated with Arnold who is presumed to have preached that the unworthiness of a priest rendered invalid his administration of the sacraments.[2] But we have little precise knowledge of the teachings of Arnold. We do not know of any opinion held by him that need have been inspired by Abelard or any contemporary suggestion that Arnold derived his teachings from Abelard. Common harassment by ecclesiastical authority and by Bernard of Clairvaux is perhaps more likely to have proved in some unknown way a factor bringing together two men who otherwise had only a vague affinity with each other.

Arnold, like Adam, incurred censure as a direct result of his association with Abelard and he was sentenced to confinement in a religious place. A third victim and sufferer of misfortune was Berengar, Abelard's bizarre apologist, who complained to the bishop of Mende about the ill treatment he was receiving from supporters of Bernard of Clairvaux.[3] The cause of this hostility was his writing of an *Apologeticus* which is in fact the only surviving work of protest written on Abelard's behalf by one of his supporters between the council of Sens and the violent outburst of Robert of Melun in his *Sentences*, which appeared in the 1150s.

The *Apologeticus*[4] of Berengar of Poitiers[5] has been chiefly

---

[1] *Ethica*, c. 26 (PL. 178, 673–8); and also the continuation of this chapter printed from the Oxford manuscript (Balliol College 296, ff. 78v–79v) by C. Ottaviano in the *Rivista di Cultura*, XII (1931), here pp. 442–3. Cf. L. Hödl, *Die Geschichte der scholastischen Literatur und der Theologie der Schlüsselgewalt*, I, 79–86; P. Anciaux, *La Théologie du sacrement de pénitence*, pp. 286–8.

[2] Cf. Vernet, 'Arnaud de Brescia', cols. 1973–4.

[3] Berengar, *Epist. ad episcopum Mimatensem*, PL. 178, 1871AB.

[4] First edited by A. Duchesne, *Petri Abaelardi ... Opera* (Paris, 1616), pp. 302–20 and thence reprinted in PL. 178, 1854–70 and in V. Cousin, *Opera Petri Abaelardi*, II, 771–86. The title of Berengar's tract, *Apologeticus*, is known from a reference in the letter which Berengar wrote later to the bishop of Mende (PL. 178, 1872B); in manuscripts of the work, however, it is called *Apologia*. Five manuscript copies are known. Of these the earliest was not copied until after the

remembered on account of its fantastic and fanciful reconstruction of Abelard's trial at Sens. In Berengar's account the judges
are said to be drunk, the proceedings an orgy and Bernard of
Clairvaux a heretic himself and author of impudent verses.

---

mid thirteenth century, viz. cod. Paris, Bibl. nat. lat. 2923, ff. 43–5; see *Catalogue
général des manuscrits latins de la Bibliothèque nationale*, III, 282–4; J. Monfrin,
ed., *Abélard. Historia Calamitatum*, pp. 18–19. The manuscript was later (after *c.*
1337) in Petrarch's collection; see P. de Nolhac, *Pétrarque et l'humanisme*, II, 217–
24 and J. Leclercq, 'L'amitié dans les lettres au moyen âge. Autour d'un manuscrit de la bibliothèque de Pétrarque', p. 391. The manuscript was also known to
V. Cousin, *op. cit.*, II, 771, but much of the text of the *Apologeticus* is missing
from it (cols. 1862–70 of the Migne impression). There are three fourteenth-
century copies: cod. Bruges, Bibl. municipale 398, ff. 17r–20v, which contains
only extracts from the work; see A. de Poorter, *Catalogue des manuscrits de la
Bibliothèque de la Ville de Bruges*, n. 398; cod. Oxford, Bodleian, Add. C. 271,
ff. 76r–81v; see F. Madan, *A Summary Catalogue of Western Manuscripts in the
Bodleian Library at Oxford*, v, n. 29565 and J. Monfrin, ed., *Hist. Calam.*, pp.
23–5; cod. Paris, Bibl. nat. lat. 1896, ff. 185v–189v; see P. Lauer, *Bibliothèque
nationale: catalogue général des manuscrits latins*, II, 228–9. Cod. Orleans, Bibl.
municipale 78, f. 63 *et seq.* is of the fifteenth century; see C. Cuissard, *Catalogue
général des manuscrits des bibliothèques en France, Départements XII, Orléans*,
p. 39. The Oxford and the two Parisian manuscripts contain, besides the
Apologeticus, Berengar's letters to the bishop of Mende and to the Carthusians,
whereas the Orleans manuscript has only the letter to the bishop of Mende
and the Bruges manuscript presents only extracts from this letter. The letter to
the Carthusians is also found in another Oxford MS., Bodleian, Add. A. 44, f. 53;
see F. Madan, *op. cit.*, v, n. 30151 and R. Klibansky, 'L'Epitre de Bérenger
de Poitiers contre les Chartreux', pp. 314–16. A lost manuscript of St Victor
in Paris, GGG 17, in the sixteenth-century catalogue of Claude de Grandrue,
is known to have contained the *Apologia*, see Monfrin, ed., *Hist. Calam.*, pp.
42–3. A. Duchesne used for his edition of Berengar's writings one manuscript
found 'in the library of the most Christian King' (*Petri Abaelardi . . . Opera*,
p. 302) and cod. Paris 1896 had entered the royal collection by the mid
seventeenth century at the very latest. A note printed by Duchesne on
Berengar's letter to the bishop of Mende (see PL. 178, 1873, n. 9) is in fact taken
from cod. Paris 1896 *in margine*, but there are variants between the texts of
Duchesne (= Migne) and of this manuscript.

[5] The only evidence for associating Berengar with Poitiers is the rubric
title of his *Apologeticus* in cod. Paris Bibl. nat. lat. 2923, f. 43 (late thirteenth
century or fourteenth century: 'Apologia Berengarii Pictavensis pro magistro
Petro Abaelardo') and in cod. Bruges 398, f. 17v. There is no evidence at
all for assuming, with A. Duchesne, *Petri Abaelardi . . . Opera*, p. 302, that
Berengar was a *scholasticus*, nor for thinking with J. G. Sikes, *Peter Abailard*,
pp. 233, 239, that Berengar was a monk. On the contrary, a phrase in his
letter to the bishop of Mende suggests that he was not: 'quid ergo peccavi si
. . . saecularis religiosum redargui?' (PL. 178, 1872B).

This tract has not been the subject of much modern discussion; Berengar later recanted it and historians have usually dismissed it as worthless diatribe.[1] Yet however insulting Berengar was, he merits a patient historical consideration, for he surely incorporates into his polemic something of the immediate popular reaction to Abelard's prosecution and condemnation.[2] He had been young at the time of the trial[3] and he is, as Professor Klibansky observed,[4] a representative of the younger generation which had been so captivated by Abelard. His intention had been to justify Abelard's condemned teachings in a second part of his *Apologeticus*, but no such continuation ever appeared, because, as he later claimed, he had 'grown wiser'.[5] His attachment to Abelard—*praeceptor meus*[6]—had earned him the disfavour of those who respected the abbot of Clairvaux to whom, as to a chief prosecutor, Berengar had directly addressed his *Apologeticus*. From the heat of his resentment, it would appear

---

[1] E. Vacandard, 'Bérenger de Poitiers', cols. 720–2; also *idem, Vie de S. Bernard*, II, 170–4, is impatient with Berengar. The late Dom O. Lottin, 'Pierre Bérenger', col. 379, wrote that the historian has nothing to learn from the fantastic description of the meeting *inter pocula*, but G. W. Greenaway, *Arnold of Brescia*, pp. 73–5, admits the truth of Berengar's claim that the verdict against Abelard was determined before the council meeting, and J. G. Sikes, *op. cit.*, p. 233, also accepts that a preliminary meeting occurred even though the details of Berengar's account are libellous. For other considerations of Berengar see *Histoire littéraire de la France*, XII, 254–60 (reproduced in PL. 178, 1854–6); E. Gilson, *The Mystical Theology of St Bernard*, Appendix III, 167–9 and R. Klibansky, 'L'Epitre de Bérenger de Poitiers'.

[2] Cf. E. Gilson, *op. cit.*, p. 167: 'Berengar's pamphlet . . . is rich in historical sidelights on the state of mind that prevailed in Abelard's entourage.' It is now more than twenty years since R. Klibansky, 'L'Epître de Bérenger de Poitiers', p. 314 called for a deeper study of the human and literary aspects of Berengar's writings.

[3] 'Eram ea tempestate adolescens, nondumque impuberes malas nubes lanuginis adumbrabat', Berengar, *Epist. ad episcopum Mimatensem* (1872A).

[4] 'L'Epitre de Bérenger de Poitiers', p. 314.

[5] 'Quae autem dixerit, et quae non dixerit, et quam Catholica mente ea quae dixerit senserit, secundus arrepti operis tractatus Christiana disputatione ardenter et impigre declarabit', *Apolog.* (1862D); also, *ibid.* (1870D) and in the letter to the bishop of Mende: ' "Sed cur, inquiunt, expleto primo volumine, secundum, ut spoponderas, non texis?" Quia processu temporis meum sapere crevit' (1873A).

[6] *Epist. ad episc. Mimatensem* (1872A).

that Berengar had written this work not long after the papal condemnation of July 1140.[1]

The *Apologeticus* opens with a rude and mocking tribute to Bernard's fame and sanctity and to his skill in composing farcical songs and polished verses.[2] But Bernard has also used Berengar's master as a target for his arrow.[3] He has declared him a heretic before an assembly of bishops and has plucked him from the womb of mother church.[4] In Berengar's account the council of Sens is made to seem even more farcical than the synod of Soissons had appeared in Abelard's *Historia Calamitatum*. At an after-dinner gathering of prelates one of the company is depicted as loudly declaiming passages from a book by Peter (*liber Petri*) while the others engaged in a drinking bout.[5] The bishops gnashed their teeth against Peter on hearing a theological point of unusual subtlety and wagging their heads like the Jews they said: 'Look at him who destroys the temple of God.'[6] Then they became drowsy and the reading ceased.[7] The lector put the question to the deaf ears of the bishops: 'Damnatis?' The priests of Bacchus could scarcely respond '–namus'—'we swim'.[8] Thus the trial of Master Peter was to be as unjust as that of Our Lord and Berengar accordingly relates it in the terms used by St John the Evangelist in his account of the passion of Christ:[9] 'The chief priests and the pharisees gathered a council and said: What do we, for this man doth many miracles? If we let him alone so, all will believe in him. But one of them, named Bernard the abbot, being the high priest of that council, prophesied, saying: It is expedient for us that one man should be exterminated by the people and that the whole nation perish not. From that day therefore they devised to have him condemned.' Meanwhile Peter prayed: 'O Lord, deliver my soul from wicked lips and a deceitful tongue.'[10] On the next day the council met, like the

---

[1] Berengar does not refer to Abelard's death in 1142 and could well have written before then.

[2] 1857A. E. Vacandard argued that, at least as a monk, Bernard never composed licentious poems, 'Les poèmes latins attribués à S. Bernard', pp. 223–4.   [3] 1858A.   [4] 1858B.   [5] 1858C–9A.

[6] 1859B. Cf. *Matt.* 27, 40.   [7] 1859C.   [8] 1859D.

[9] 1860AB. Cf. *Joh.* 11, 47–53.   [10] 1860C. Cf. *Ps.* 119, 2.

council of vanity of Ps. 25, 4 and after one bishop of famous memory[1] had spoken stupidly, Abelard appealed to Rome. To Berengar this appeal to Rome appears as a justifiable attempt to seek asylum,[2] but unlike St Paul, who had been allowed to appeal to Rome by the governor Festus, Abelard's right to do the same was, according to Berengar, flatly denied by Bernard.[3] So the mouth of reason, the trumpet of faith, the abode of the Trinity was condemned straightway by the Roman see, in his absence and with his case unheard.[4]

Berengar's satire is built upon a basis of truth and strong feeling. He had probably been one of Abelard's *fautores*[5] who had attended the trial at Sens and he was surely accurate in distinguishing two meetings at the first of which the bishops determined their attitude towards Abelard.[6] He attributes the mental fuzziness of Abelard's judges to the effects of strong drink, but he perhaps also reflects a feeling shared by some of Abelard's supporters that the judges were incompetent.[7] Berengar presents Bernard

[1] The identification of the bishop referred to by Berengar is not a matter of importance, and if the words 'quidam memoriae celebris episcopus' be taken to mean a bishop who died before the writing of the *Apologeticus*, there is no obvious candidate from among those prelates known to have been present at Abelard's trial. Henry of Sens, who died 10 January 1142, was an archbishop and Geoffrey of Châlons-sur-Marne died on 27 or 28 May 1142 which was a month after Abelard's own death (21 April 1142) which we might expect Berengar to have mentioned if he had known of it. But can we be certain that Abelard died in 1142?

[2] 1861A.   [3] 1861AB.

[4] 'Damnatur, proh dolor! absens, inauditus et inconvictus' (1861B).

[5] This is the expression used by the bishops in their letter to Pope Innocent (printed among Bernard's, no. 337 (PL. 182, 542A)) and we know from both them and Abelard that Abelard had collected his supporters together for the meeting at Sens. Cf. *ibid.* (541C) and Abelard's letter to his *socii*, ed. J. Leclercq, *Etudes sur S. Bernard*, App. V, pp. 104–5 and R. Klibansky, 'Peter Abailard and Bernard of Clairvaux', pp. 6–7.

[6] The bishops in their letter to Pope Innocent II admit this: 'pridie ante factam ad vos appellationem damnavimus', *Epist.* 337 (PL. 182, 542C).

[7] Abelard throughout thought unfavourably of his accusers and of their accusations; see his *Confessio fidei ad Heloisam* ('opinione potius traducuntur ad judicium quam experientiae magistratu', PL. 178, 375C), his *Confessio fidei* 'universis' (PL. 178, 105–8) and his *Apologia*: 'ex tuis potius figmentis quam ex dictis meis arguere laboras', ed. P. Ruf and M. Grabmann, 'Ein neuaufgefundenes Bruchstück der Apologia Abaelards', p. 12.

as the persecutor-in-chief and Abelard as a Christ-like victim and he accuses Bernard throughout of manœuvring unfairly to prevent Abelard from gaining a fair hearing. It appears in fact to be true that the papal condemnation was merely an acceptance of the report of the judges at Sens[1] and that it was issued before Abelard had made any representations in Rome. Moreover, the impression which Berengar attempts to convey of the unfairness of the trial was shared by others. When in his *Historia Pontificalis* John of Salisbury came to describe the trial in 1148 of Gilbert of Poitiers, he mentioned a meeting preceding Gilbert's trial at which Bernard of Clairvaux produced *capitula* answering the teachings of Gilbert and submitted them for the approval of leading churchmen who were present. John tells us that those cardinals who were at Rheims were angry on hearing of this meeting 'saying that the abbot had attacked master Peter in exactly the same way, but he (Peter) had not had access to the apostolic see, which was accustomed to confound schemes of this kind and snatch the weak from the clutches of the strong'.[2] John does nothing himself to deny the cardinals' explanation but, as John's editor, Mrs M. Chibnall, has observed,[3] he does explicitly consider other more exaggerated suspicions of Bernard's methods to be false. Both Berengar and the cardinals at Rheims in 1148 seem therefore to have felt strongly that at the council of Sens Abelard had been deprived of the opportunity to defend himself by virtue of the unfair manœuvrings of the abbot of Clairvaux.

Berengar now abandons the Bacchanalian scene and pauses in his satire. He becomes more serious and attempts to assess the justice of the condemnation. The points that he makes are less telling. He asks why both sides had not been equally able to

---

[1] Cf. Innocent II, *Epist.* 447: 'Dolemus autem quoniam, sicut litterarum vestrarum inspectione et missis a fraternitate vestra nobis errorum capitulis cognovimus ... Nos itaque ... communicato fratrum nostrorum episcoporum cardinalium consilio, destinata nobis a vestra discretione capitula, et universa ipsius Petri dogmata ... damnavimus' (PL. 179, 515C–517B, here 516C–517A).

[2] *Hist. Pont.*, c. 8 (ed. M. Chibnall, pp. 19–20).

[3] *Ibid.*, p. 20, n. 1.

present their case.[1] The whole trial, he claims, had been rigged by Bernard and even later in his letter to the bishop of Mende, where he withdraws his criticisms of Bernard, he still implies that the refusal to hear Abelard was unfair.[2] We seem to hear an echo of lively debates between the two parties when Berengar states that Bernard's supporters justified the prosecution on the ground that the abbot of Clairvaux had sincerely wished to lead Abelard to correct his errors.[3] But Berengar reproaches Bernard for having acted against Abelard out of vengeance, tyrannically and with rancour, rather than out of a desire to correct him.[4] That is Berengar's case, but it is flatly opposed by the reference of the bishops gathered at Sens to earlier private meetings between Bernard and Abelard at which the abbot 'had in friendliness and familiarity admonished him to correct his books'[5] and also by their clear and emphatic statement that at the council session Abelard had been given a chance to speak in his own defence, but that he refused this chance, appealed to the pope and together with his entourage left the meeting. The bishops' view of the proceedings was that Abelard had stopped his own trial and although they perhaps should have proceeded to a condemnation there and then, they decided to follow him in referring the case to Rome.[6]

[1] 'Cujus unquam, Jesu bone, culpa tam caecos habuit judices, ut non utrinque causae latera ventilarent, ut non in quam potissimum partem jus vergeret elimarent', *Apolog.* (1861BC).

[2] 'Damnaverat, inquam, Abaelardum, et vocem ejus sine audientia strangulaverat', Berengar, *Epist. ad episc. Mimatensem* (1872A).

[3] 'Sed corrigere, inquiunt fautores abbatis, Petrum volebat. Si Petrum, bone vir, ad integrum fidei statum disponebas revocare, cur ei coram populo aeternae blasphemiae characterem impingebas? Rursusque, si Petro amorem populi tollebas, quomodo corrigere disponebas?' *Apolog.* (1861C).

[4] *Ibid.* (1861D).

[5] Among the letters of Bernard, no. 337 (PL. 182, 541AB). Cf. Geoffrey of Auxerre, *S. Bernardi Vita Prima, lib.* III, c. 5 (PL. 185, 311A).

[6] 'Dominus abbas cum librum Theologiae magistri Petri proferret in medium, et quae adnotaverat absurda, imo haeretica plane capitula de libro eodem proponeret, ut ea magister Petrus vel a se scripta negaret; vel, si sua fateretur, aut probaret, aut corrigeret; visus diffidere magister Petrus Abaelardus et subterfugere, respondere noluit: sed quamvis libera sibi daretur audientia, tutumque locum et aequos haberet judices, ad vestram tamen, sanctissime Pater, appellans praesentiam, cum suis a conventu discessit. Nos autem, licet appellatio ista

D

Berengar makes no reference to Abelard's refusal to speak in his own defence; in his view, the assembly was packed with stupid judges and Abelard rightly sought refuge at Rome. Abelard, says Berengar, had a right to find refuge at St Peter's chair because he professed the faith of St Peter. Berengar produces an otherwise inextant letter from Abelard to Héloïse in which Abelard confessed the correctness of his faith: the use of logic has been the cause of the opposition to his teaching, for Abelard's enemies have asserted that his dialectical subtlety has taken precedence over his faith. In a celebrated phrase, Abelard affirmed that he had no wish to be a philosopher in order to repudiate Paul nor to be an Aristotle at the price of being separated from Christ.[1] This letter is proof for Berengar that Abelard was not impugning the faith of St Peter and it is a complete reply to the argument that Bernard used in his letter to Pope Innocent that Abelard, having impugned the faith of Peter, should not find refuge at Peter's chair.[2] But, unless our text of Bernard's letter has undergone an alteration of which we have no knowledge, this was not quite what Bernard wrote; Bernard in fact asked the pope to judge whether one who impugns the faith of Peter should

---

[1] *Confessio fidei ad Heloisam* (PL. 178, 375C). D. Van den Eynde, 'Chronologie des écrits d'Abélard à Héloïse', pp. 344–7 demonstrates that this *Confessio* was written in 1139 before Abelard's trial.

[2] 'Testatur etiam rancorem animi ejus epistola ad Innocentium papam directa, in qua sic stomachatur: "Non debet, inquit, refugium invenire apud sedem Petri, qui fidem impugnat Petri",' *Apolog.* (1861D).

---

minus canonica videretur, Sedi tamen apostolicae deferentes, in personam hominis nullam voluimus proferre sententiam', among the letters of Bernard, no. 337 (PL. 182, 542AB). Cf. Geoffrey of Auxerre, *S. Bernardi Vita Prima, lib.* III, c. 5 (PL. 185, 311C). Why Abelard appealed over the heads of his judges has never been quite clear. Berengar implies that his motive was to seek refuge from biased judges. Otto of Freising, *Gesta Friderici,* I, 48 (ed. Waitz, p. 70) states that Abelard was afraid that the excited populace would rise against him. 'De iusticia veritus' say *Sigeberti Continuatio Praemonstratensis* (MGH.SS, VI, 452) and Robert of Auxerre, *Chronicon (ibid.,* XXVI, 235). Geoffrey of Auxerre writes: 'nec volens resipiscere, nec valens resistere sapientiae et spiritui qui loquebatur, ut tempus redimeret, Sedem apostolicam appellavit' and he repeats a story that Abelard lost his head, *S. Bernardi Vita Prima, lib.* III, c. 5 (PL. 185, 311C).

find refuge in Rome.[1] Bernard meanwhile bombarded members of the Curia with his own appeals;[2] Abelard, so far as we know, did not attempt to rival Bernard's campaign to influence the Curia and after starting out for Rome, turned aside to enter Cluny. Thus, when the pope acted, or so Berengar claims, he had been completely hoodwinked by Bernard's rhetoric.[3]

Berengar tells us that Bernard produced at Sens a short list of errors which he has seen but which does not represent Abelard's teachings at all; it contains only the headings of an execrable fabrication.[4] But, after quoting in a rough manner five of the propositions,[5] he heavily qualifies this judgment in asserting that Abelard did teach some of the extracted opinions, but

[1] 'Verum tu, o successor Petri, judicabis, an debeat habere refugium ⟨apud⟩ sedem Petri, qui Petri fidem impugnat', Bernard of Clairvaux, *Epist.* 189 (PL 182, 356B). The bishops too told Pope Innocent that further action would be his responsibility, since they had proceeded as far as they could. They had no doubt but that the pope should act against Abelard but they acquiesced in Abelard's appeal: 'Processimus in hoc negotio quousque ausi sumus: tuum est de caetero, beatissime Pater, providere ne in diebus tuis aliqua haereticae pravitatis macula decor Ecclesiae maculetur', among the letters of Bernard, no. 191 (*ex persona domini archiepiscopi Remensis*, PL. 182, 358AB). Geoffrey of Auxerre was cynical about Abelard's appeal, but does not deny Abelard's right to seek refuge in Rome: 'Quando vero Petrus ille refugium inveniret in Sede Petri, tam longe dissidens a fide Petri?' *S. Bernardi Vita Prima*, lib. III, c. v (PL. 185, 311D).

[2] *Epist.* 192, 193, 331–6, 338 (PL. 182, 358–9, 536–40, 542–4).

[3] 'Deberet ergo refugium apud sedem Petri invenire, si non illecebrae tui eloquii clausissent viscera misericordiae Romanae Ecclesiae', *Apolog.* (1862B).

[4] *Ibid.* (1862C). Putting words into Bernard's mouth Berengar wrote: ' "foedum illud sacrilegumque dogma manuali quodam indiculo complosi, ne scilicet breviter volentibus attingere summam rei, onerosum esset ire per spatiosos saltus voluminum Abaelardi" ', *ibid.* On the list of errors see below, chap. IV, *passim*.

[5] 'Quod scilicet Pater sit omnipotentia, Filius quaedam potentia, Spiritus sanctus nulla potentia; quod Spiritus sanctus, licet sit ejusdem substantiae cum Filio, non tamen est de eadem substantia; quod homo sine nova gratia possit operari; quod Deus non possit plus facere quam facit, nec melius facere quam facit, nec aliter facere quam facit; quod anima Christi non descendit ad inferos', *ibid.* (1862D). These propositions correspond to capitula 1, 2, 5, 6, 18 in the numbered list of J. Rivière, 'Les "capitula" d'Abélard condamnés au concile de Sens', pp. 16–17. But Leclercq (*Etudes sur S. Bernard*, p. 102) has shown that only some of the *capitula* were condemned by the bishops at Sens. These were marked with an asterisk in the manuscripts and Leclercq finds that they were nos. 1, 2, 4 and 13 of Rivière's list. Thus Berengar's selection does

always in a Catholic spirit.[1] The weakness of Berengar's position with respect to the condemned errors is even more apparent later in his letter to the bishop of Mende. Here he says that, having grown wiser, he is now in agreement with the abbot of Clairvaux: he had no wish to defend statements which give a bad impression but of which the meaning is sound.[2] The ebullience which sustained the attack on Bernard's behaviour throughout the first part of the *Apologeticus* vanishes at the point where Berengar is faced with the real issue at stake, for in the matter of the errors Berengar could do no better than sit on a fence.

Berengar admits that Abelard has occasionally erred, but in order still to maintain that the condemnation of these errors was unjust, Berengar has to resume his biting criticism of the impudence and imprudence of Bernard's actions. Now, however, as Berengar embarks on the third and last phase of his polemic, his satire comprises less comic fancy. What follows is the satire of exposure, the returning of the charges made by an opponent with the retort that he is no better than his victim. Berengar's purpose is now to urge that Bernard himself is not free from error: 'Peter had erred: so be it. You, though, how have you erred? You have erred, whether knowingly or not. If you erred knowingly, you are a proven enemy of the Church; if you erred unknowingly, how are you, who know not how to discern error, a defender of the Church?'[3] Berengar alleges that Bernard has taught that souls have their origin in heaven and that he is ignorant of the canons of good taste in literature. With these two errors, Berengar's charge sheet does not seem very full and to boost his accusations he is not opposed to making more fun at Bernard's expense. He caricatures Bernard as a naive monk who is constantly stating the obvious. Berengar quotes some of Bernard's sayings: 'I am my mother's son', 'my head is bigger

---

[1] *Apolog.* (1862D). Berengar here also promises to reveal in a continuation of the *Apolog.* which Abelard had said and which he had not said, and with what a Catholic mind he felt what he had said.

[2] 1873AB.   [3] 1863A.

---

not seem to correspond to the selection made by the bishops from the list put before them.

than my fist', 'midday occurs in daytime' and so on.[1] Berengar
is right in thinking that there is a streak of simplicity and obvious-
ness in Bernard's writings, but the greater naivety of isolating
statements outside their contexts can scarcely provoke a cheap
laugh. However, Berengar also pokes fun at Bernard's contem-
plative writing: to one thick camel, with an inflated Roman
neck, who had enquired of Bernard what is to be loved, the abbot
answered 'God'. 'Our philosopher', wrote Berengar, enjoined
that neither virtue nor pleasure but God should be the object of
our love; this is an answer worthy of a learned man but known
also to any mean woman and extreme idiot. It is thus that little
old ladies philosophize at their weaving. But our archimandrite,
having given a rustic reply, which no one would dispute, to a
Roman who as a member of the Curia had learned to love gold
and not God, rises suddenly to a higher level and exclaims that
the measure (*modus*) of loving God is to love Him without measure (*sine modo*)—an unintelligible impossibility. Christ never
hid his meanings in unclear speech, but Bernard's writings are
full of these ludicrous sayings. Bernard, who should be turning
swords into ploughshares, is turning ploughshares into swords
when he picks out faults in Abelard's teaching.[2] In all this Berengar
is lampooning Bernard's De diligendo deo,[3] written at the request
of Cardinal Haimeric, chancellor of the Roman church, a work
of which Mabillon, sensitive to Berengar's diatribe, wrote:
'nullum tamen fere aut Bernardo dignius, aut religioni utilius
ab eo scriptum existimo'.[4] Berengar was partly mimicking
Bernard's own assaults upon Abelard's writings and teachings:

[1] 1867C.

[2] 1867B–8D. What Berengar here criticized was upheld by Abelard's disciples,
Hermann, Sent., c. 32 ('in dilectione Dei nullus modus', PL. 178, 1748C) and
Roland, Sent. ('Deus . . . sine mensura omnifariam est diligendus', ed. Gietl,
p. 319).

[3] S. Bernardi Opera, Vol. III. Tractatus et Opuscula, ed. J. Leclercq and H. M.
Rochais, pp. 119–54, especially here Prologus and c. 1, pp. 119–20 (or in PL.
182, 973–4). According to Leclercq and Rochais, pp. 111–12, the De diligendo
deo was composed c. 1126–41 and perhaps after 1136.

[4] Admonitio (PL. 182, 971–2). For a modern appreciation of the content of
the De diligendo deo see E. Gilson, The Mystical Theology of St Bernard, passim
(on Berengar, see p. 169).

the ironic references to 'philosophus noster' return Bernard's ironic appellation of Abelard as 'theologus noster'[1] and both protagonists find naiveties in the works of their victims. When Berengar attributes to Bernard the sentence 'Quaeris quid sit diligendum. Cui breviter respondeo: Deus', either he is fabricating or he possessed a text of the De diligendo deo which we do not know;[2] and if he is fabricating, then Berengar, to his discredit, is acting against Bernard in the manner which, Abelard complained, had been employed by Bernard.[3] Berengar's ranting only demonstrates the width of the gulf separating him from Bernard. To Berengar, filled with enthusiasm for Abelardian dialectic, the statement 'modus est sine modo diligere'[4] meant nothing at all.

To return to Bernard's 'errors', however, Berengar accuses Bernard of writing at length, for nearly two whole quires, on the subject of the death of his brother in the course of his commentary on the Song of Songs, that is, in a context which required the commentator to treat of nuptial joy, not of sadness, and not to turn canticles into an elegy and songs into lamentations.[5]

---

[1] Cf. Bernard, *Epist.* 190 (PL. 182, 1055C, 1059C), 332 (538A), 338 (543A). W. W. Williams in *Select Treatises of S. Bernard of Clairvaux*, p. 5, suggested—unconvincingly, I think—that two allusions in the De diligendo deo were directed against ideas of Abelard.

[2] *Apolog.* (1867B). According to Bernard, Haimeric asked 'quare et quo modo diligendus sit Deus' (and not 'quid sit diligendum'), *De diligendo deo*, c. 1 (Leclercq and Rochais, p. 119; PL. 182, 974A).

[3] Cf. *Confessio fidei 'universis'*: 'Quod autem capitula contra me scripta tali fine amicus noster concluserit, ut diceret: "Haec autem capitula partim in libro Theologiae magistri Petri, partim in libro Sententiarum ejusdem, partim in libro cujus titulus est: *Scito te ipsum*, reperta sunt", non sine admiratione maxima suscepi, cum nunquam liber aliquis qui Sententiarum dicatur, a me scriptus reperiatur. Sed sicut caetera contra me capitula, ita et hoc quoque per malitiam vel ignorantiam prolatum est' (PL. 178, 107). Cf., above, p. 33, n. 7. On this *Liber Sententiarum*, now lost, which was not written by Abelard but by one of his disciples, see H. Ostlender, 'Die Sentenzenbücher der Schule Abaelards', pp. 224–50.

[4] Mabillon observed (see Bernard of Clairvaux, *Opera*, PL. 182, 973, *in nota*) that this 'dictum aureum' came from Severus Milevitanus, correspondent of St Augustine, *Epist.* 109 (PL. 33, 418–9, here 419).

[5] *Apolog.* (1863D–6B). Cf. Bernard, *Super Cantica Sermo* 26, ed. J. Leclercq, I, 171–81 (or PL. 183, 904D–12).

Berengar arraigns Bernard for violating the dictates of Horace's *Ars poetica*.[1] Berengar was neither the first nor the last to uphold canons of classical taste, whereas Bernard's sermons on the Canticle, which embraced subjects scarcely suggested by the words of the Canticle itself, were inspired by a genuine spontaneity.[2] However, this charge was not Berengar's only grief against St Bernard's teaching and it perhaps was not even his real complaint. He implies later in his letter to the bishop of Mende that parts of the *Apologeticus* may have to be read with a sense of humour.[3] His intent was satirical and his main object here was surely to return some of Bernard's criticisms of Abelard. Berengar argues that Bernard had no right to level his charges against Abelard because he himself was capable of departing from the traditions of his fathers and of desiring to be novel. By commenting on the Song of Songs at all, Bernard was displaying presumption. Since Origen, Ambrose, Reticius[4] and Bede have already fully expounded it, Berengar can only assume that Bernard's motive had been a desire for novelty. But even in this desire Bernard has failed for Berengar finds, as he handles Bernard's exposition, nothing that had not been said before.[5] He quotes two passages which he says he finds (unless he is mistaken—'ni fallor') in Bernard's work but which Berengar claims are both lifted from a work which Ambrose composed on the death of his brother Satyr. However, neither of Berengar's quotations

---

[1] *Apolog.* (1864C–5A). Cf. Horace, *De Arte Poetica*, *ll.* 1–5, 9–13, 8–9, 15–16, 273–4,

[2] Cf. E. Gilson, *The Mystical Theology of St Bernard*, pp. 168–9. Also J. Leclercq, *Etudes sur S. Bernard*, p. 122: 'saint Bernard n'est pas guidé par les lois de la composition scolaire; c'est un génie, c'est un poète, c'est un prophète: il ne se soumet qu'à son inspiration, et il fait un chef d'oeuvre'. For some contemporary tributes to Bernard's commentary, cf. Leclercq, *op. cit.*, p. 123. Another disciple of Abelard, who in his way admired Abelard as much as did Berengar, could appreciate the subtlety and value of Bernard's exposition 'quam procul dubio per os eius dictavit Spiritus sanctus', John of Salisbury, *Historia pontificalis*, c. 11 (ed. M. Chibnall, p. 25).

[3] '... si quid in personam hominis Dei (*sc.* Bernardi) dixi, joco legatur, non serio' (1873B).

[4] Berengar's information concerning the little known Retius (or Reticius) of Autun (*Apolog.* 1863CD, 1864B) is valuable; cf. G. Morin in *Revue bénédictine*, XIII (1896), pp. 340 *et seq.*   [5] *Apolog.* (1863B–D).

can be found in Bernard's Sermons as we know them and only one of the two has been found in the work by Ambrose.[1] That Bernard, lamenting the death of his brother, Gerard, might have wanted to turn to Ambrose's expression of a similar grief is not reprehensible. But Berengar is irrepressible; having suggested that Bernard's illicit desire for novelty resulted in no novelty whatsoever, but in a slavish repetition of patristic achievements, Berengar now insists that in his lament Bernard did pass beyond the limits set by the Fathers: 'Tu vero terminos transgrediens, quos posuerunt patres tui, Cantica in elegos, carmina in threnos sorte miserabili convertisti.'[2] Clearly this is a *tu quoque*: Berengar is flinging back to Bernard the very words he used about Abelard in epistle 193: 'Transgreditur terminos quos posuerunt patres nostri: de fide, de sacramentis, de sancta Trinitate disputans.'[3] Berengar thus 'finds' in Bernard's own writings parallels to the contempts and insults which Abelard was accused of offering to the Fathers[4] as well as a readiness to show himself independent of the early doctors of the church.[5]

Bernard's second 'error' consists in a heretical misinterpretation, made in the course of the same commentary, of St Paul's statement that our true home is in heaven ('Nostra autem conversatio in caelis est', Philipp. 3, 20); according to Berengar, Bernard explains this as meaning that our souls originate in heaven. In his commentary Bernard does indeed compare the 'heavenly origin' of the soul of the Spouse with the earthly origin of the body. Her soul displays the marks of coming from heaven in its love for angelic and not for earthly pleasures. Here, in this region of dissimilitude, the soul keeps its original resemblance with heaven by leading an angelic life in a beast's body:

---

[1] Cf. Mabillon's note printed in Bernard, *In Cantica Sermo* 26 (PL. 183, 903D) and Ambrose, *De excessu fratris sui Satyri, lib.* I, 8, ed. Faller (CSEL, LXXIII), p. 213, *ll.* 2–4. Cf. P. Courcelle, *Les Confessions de S. Augustin dans la tradition littéraire*, pp. 301–4.   [2] *Apolog.* (1864O).   [3] PL. 182, 359.

[4] Bernard, *Epist.* 188: 'patrum probra atque contemptus', 'insultatur patribus' (PL. 182, 353).

[5] *Apolog.* (1864C). Cf. Bernard, *Tractatus de erroribus Abaelardi*, c. 5: 'Sed qui venerunt post apostolos, doctores non recipis, homo qui super omnes docentes te intellixisti' (PL. 182, 1063D).

this marvel, says Bernard, proves the 'heavenly origin' of the soul. In an imitative sense, a holy soul is heaven; the sun, moon and stars of heaven correspond to intellect, faith and virtues in the soul.[1] Bernard's contrast between the earth, the land of exile, the terrestrial condition, and heaven, man's true homeland, the spiritual condition, the angelic life, amounts to an affirmation that in this world the soul is a stranger, but in heaven, where it bears resemblances with the world of spirits, it is indigenous and in its own country.[2] Berengar interprets these references to the heavenly origin of the soul in a literal sense. He believes that Bernard has here adopted the error of Plato, of Pythagoras and of Origen's *Peri archon* as well as of the philosophers who followed them—an error which had been opposed by the Fathers. Bernard, in preferring an error of the philosophers, thus flies in the face of patristic teaching.[3] In one sense Berengar was right: Bernard was a Platonizer and he was in some respects a follower of the philosophers; his world was strongly tinged with platonism and he naturally used platonic language and platonic expressions.[4] But the text which Berengar interprets so literally does not amount to a denial by Bernard of the doctrine that souls are created by God and we should not take it too seriously. Berengar is principally intent upon returning Bernard's accusation that Abelard had preferred the teachings of the philosophers to those of the Fathers.[5] He delights to quote the Fathers against Bernard.[6]

---

[1] Bernard, *Super Cantica Sermo*, ed. J. Leclercq, I, 185–8 (or PL. 183, 915C–18B and Mabillon's note below 915C). Sermons 26 and 27 were not written before the summer of 1138 (Bernard, *Opera*, ed. Leclercq, I, xv–xvi); Berengar's *Apolog.* constitutes a *terminus ante quem*.

[2] Cf. J. M. Déchanet, 'Aux sources de la pensée philosophique de s. Bernard' in *S. Bernard Théologien. Actes du Congrès de Dijon* (ASOC, IX (1953)), p. 70. Also G. Dumeige, 'Dissemblance', cols. 1330–46, especially 1338–42 and J. Châtillon, 'Les Régions de la dissemblance', pp. 237–50.

[3] *Apolog.* (1866C–7B).

[4] Cf. Déchanet, 'Aux sources de la pensée philosophique' in *S. Bernard Théologien*, p. 73; M. D. Chenu, 'Platon à Cîteaux'.

[5] 'Tu itaque a doctrinae salutaris tramite devius, in philosophorum scopulos ruis', *Apolog.* (1867A). Cf. Bernard, *Epist.* 189: 'In sugillationem doctorum Ecclesiae, magnis effert laudibus philosophos; adinventiones illorum et suas novitates catholicorum Patrum doctrinae et fidei praefert.' (PL. 182, 355C).

[6] Berengar's source on the previous history of Bernard's error may have

If Bernard had alighted upon this silliness in Abelard's writings, Berengar triumphantly exclaims, he would undoubtedly have placed it on his monstrous list of *capitula*.[1]

Thus Berengar, having maintained that Bernard has misinterpreted Abelard, replies to Bernard by revealing his own errors, or at least by making misinterpretations in mock imitation of Bernard's own alleged misinterpretations. Both Bernard and Abelard have made mistakes, Abelard in his teachings and Bernard in his own teachings as well as in his misunderstanding of Abelard's teachings. So Berengar pleads the fallibility of all men and argues from this to the unwisdom of condemning Abelard. St Jerome and St Hilary themselves made mistakes but they were not assigned into the fellowship of heretics. Claudian of Lyons tells us that Hilary taught that Christ did not feel suffering during his passion and that no incorporeal thing is created, but Claudian maintained that Hilary had not thereby lost his merit as a confessor. The church pardoned Hilary, whereas, says Berengar, if Peter had said these things, Bernard's severity would have sanctioned stoning him to death.[2] Similarly if Peter had inveighed against marriage as cruelly as did St Jerome in his *De nuptiis*, where commenting on 1 *Cor.* 7, 1 ('it is good for a man not to touch a woman') Jerome says that it is consequently bad to touch a woman, for nothing except evil is the contradiction of good, Bernard would immediately have armed cohorts of married people to effect his destruction. As Berengar rightly says, Jerome's severities caused great upset in his day.[3] St James

---

[1] *Apolog.* (1867B).

[2] *Apolog.* (1869AB). Cf. *De statu animae*, II, 9 in *Claudiani Mamerti Opera*, rec. A. Engelbrecht (CSEL, XI, 134–5. Claudian says Hilary redeemed his fault by virtue of confession ('Hilarius opinionis huiusce vitium virtute confessionis abolevit'). Berengar makes Claudian say—or else found him saying—that Hilary erred without losing his merit as a confessor—which, of course, suits Berengar's argument better.

[3] *Apolog.* (1869B–70A). Cf. *Adversus Jovinianum*, lib. I, 7 (PL. 23, 218 *et seq.*).

---

been St Jerome, *Epist. 126 ad Marcellinum et Anapsychiam* (PL. 22, 1085–7, here 1085). His quotation from Augustine (*Apolog.* 1867A) cannot be found in the *De genesi contra Manichaeos*, lib. 2, c. 8 (PL. 34, 201–2) nor in the *De genesi ad litteram*, lib. 7, ed. I. Zycha (CSEL, XXVIII. Sectio III, Pars 2.), pp. 200 *et seq.*, but the content is not dissimilar.

reminds us that 'all of us often go wrong; the man who never says a wrong thing is a perfect character' (*Jac.* 3, 2). So, when Peter erred, Bernard should have displayed mercy rather than anger.[1] Berengar, therefore, places on a similar level the errors of Abelard, Jerome and Hilary and wonders why of these Abelard alone should have incurred such misfortune. For Berengar the errors of Abelard are purely mistakes made by a fallible human being. But he passes in silence over the failure of earlier peaceful efforts to persuade Abelard to correct his errors.[2] Moreover, since Abelard did change his ways after Rome had spoken, it could be argued that Berengar had underestimated the need for stern medicine.

At no point in his *Apologeticus* does Berengar impress us that he would, had he ever written his promised continuation, have been able to expound and defend Abelard's theological ideas with skill. His involvement in this crisis was too personal and too temperamental and too contrived. He saw the controversy between Bernard and Abelard as similar to the great patristic controversies of Augustine and Jerome and Origen, but he himself, as Mabillon observed, 'flocci fuit ac nullius auctoritatis'.[3] He did not acquit his master of the charges laid against him, and he went too far in his denunciation of Bernard of Clairvaux: 'putida mendacia evomuit, tamque indigna calumniarum monstra'.[4] The concentration of all his antipathy upon the abbot of Clairvaux reveals Berengar's limitations as the defender of Abelard, for Bernard's engagement in this strife came as the culmination of a whole movement of agitation against Abelard which had been fostered by Hugh of St Victor, the author of the *Summa Sententiarum*, Walter of Mortagne and William of St Thierry. No doubt at the very end of the 1130s, Bernard by entering into the fight had come to seem responsible for the train of events which led to Abelard's condemnation,

---

[1] *Apolog.* (1870B). [2] Cf. above p. 35 and n. 5.
[3] See Mabillon's *Praefatio generalis* in Bernard of Clairvaux, *Opera* (PL. 182, 43). Cf. the verdict of Petrarch on the *Apologeticus*: 'non magni quidem corporis, sed ingentis acrimoniae', *Invectiva contra Gallum* in Librorum F. Petrarche impressorum annotatio (Venetiis 1501, unpaginated).
[4] Mabillon, note on Bernard, *In Cantica Sermo* 26 (PL. 183, 903D).

but he had his reasons and there was a background to those reasons which Berengar does not discuss. Berengar views the whole crisis as the result of the hostility which Bernard felt towards Abelard. What provoked Berengar more than anything else was Bernard's attack upon Abelard his hero, and his denigration of the latter's character and achievement. Although Berengar certainly allowed his passions to outrun his judgment, he was right to criticize some of the manœuvres of Bernard. But his invective was limited and circumscribed by his inability to question the validity, as opposed to the fairness, of the ecclesiastical sentence of excommunication. Neither the pope nor the Church become targets for Berengar.[1]

Berengar's weakness as a defender of Abelard's cause is also seen clearly in the manner in which he employs his own not inconsiderable learning. The use which Berengar makes of pagan classical literature testifies to a grounding in the arts of the trivium. He flings the doctrines of Horace's *Ars poetica* against Bernard's own compositions. As a satirist he peppers his tract with lines from Lucilius, Persius and Martial and he embroiders the drinking scene with snatches of Gallus and of the *Odes* of Horace. Equally appositely Berengar introduces phrases from the Old Testament and he skilfully likens his subjects and their situations to comparable ones found in the New Testament. Berengar's pen is sharp and practised, yet his employment of non-Scriptural Christian writings is unscrupulous and uneven. He knows the *Confession of Faith* which Abelard wrote for Héloïse and he knows the accusations brought against Abelard, but he gives no indication that he is acquainted with other writings by Abelard. The most recent letters and sermons of Bernard were available to Berengar, but he misquotes the *De diligendo deo* and makes the apparently false claim that Bernard had plagiarized the *De excessu Satyri* of Ambrose and had composed worldly songs. Berengar seems to use, but without acknowledging his indebtedness, a letter by St Jerome in which the origin of souls is discussed.

---

[1] Cf. J. de Ghellinck, *L'Essor de la littérature latine au XIIe siècle*, p. 448: 'Le XIIe siècle pouvait se permettre des libertés de langage, qui attaquaient vivement les personnes, sans ébranler les institutions, qu'on respectait.'

He knows and cites from the *De nuptiis* of Jerome, the *Retracta-tiones* of Augustine and the *De statu animae* of Claudian, but he perverts the sense of the last of these. Berengar also knows of commentaries on the Canticle by Origen, Ambrose, Bede and Reticius, although he cites from the last of these alone. Berengar's erudition is quite ample, but on the whole he is more concerned to apply it satirically and unfairly rather than seriously.

Berengar's *Apologeticus* has perhaps only an incidental value for historians who are concerned with the trial at Sens and with the feelings and issues aroused by the debates of that time. But it does deserve to be treated as a historical document and not to be brushed aside as simply the invective of a passionate follower of Abelard. Berengar provides a valuable additional testimony concerning the sequence of events at Abelard's trial; he illumi-nates one state of mind that existed among Abelard's *fautores* and in addition he preserves for us Abelard's moving confession of faith made to Héloïse—perhaps Abelard's last communication to Héloïse. An unreliable witness can also be a useful one and Berengar is both. Invective and parody of Berengar's kind were common enough in the late eleventh and the twelfth centuries, and crude and coarse as much of it seems to us,[1] the *Apologeticus* is also in parts a *disputatio* and a satire from which ingenuity and sense are not wholly absent. Rudeness, violence, dishonesty and sheer wrongness mar the *Apologeticus* but are not its only attri-butes, for the *Apologeticus* is above all 'an expression of the pain felt by the disciples of Abelard at the persecution directed against a master whom they dearly loved'.[2] Berengar, though always ready for a fight, was obviously tormented by the spectacle of his hero being overthrown with great force and nothing in the *Apologeticus* can make us think that this anguish was insincere. The *Apologeticus* is Berengar's attempt to come to terms with this anguish.

Writing before 1150 to William III, bishop of Mende (1109–50),

---

[1] One might compare with Berengar's work the *Invectio in Gillibertum abbatem Cadomi* by Serlo of Bayeux, ed. T. Wright, pp. 251–4. Other examples are discussed by P. Lehmann, *Die Parodie im Mittelalter*, pp. 25 *et seq.*
[2] Gilson, *The Mystical Theology of St Bernard*, p. 167.

Berengar claimed that the first and only completed part of his *Apologeticus* had spread far and wide throughout Italy and France and could not now be withdrawn from circulation, although he would withdraw it if he could.[1] Berengar begs the protection of the bishop of Mende against the enmity of those who have resented his attack upon Bernard.[2] He argues, as in the *Apologeticus*, that Bernard is not infallible,[3] and he defends the right of philosophers of unequal distinction to dispute with one another.[4] If he has treated Bernard unfairly he is willing to be corrected,[5]

---

[1] '... viva exemplaria, quae jam per totam Franciam et Italiam concurrerunt' (PL. 178, 1873B). No twelfth-century copy of the *Apolog.* survives, but if the provenances of the surviving manuscripts are at all indicative of the location of their earlier exemplars, they seem to support Berengar's claim. Cod. Paris, Bibl. nat. lat. 2923 was perhaps produced in south France after the mid thirteenth century and passed into Petrarch's hands after *c.* 1337. Cod. Bruges, Bibl. municipale 398, a volume containing much Parisian material, perhaps originated in Paris in the fourteenth century. Cod. Oxford, Bodleian, Add. C. 271 is perhaps of Italian (fourteenth-century) origin, but was in Cambrai in 1471. The fifteenth-century cod. Orleans, Bibl. municipale 78 comes from Fleury on the Loire. The origin of the fourteenth-century cod. Paris, Bibl. nat. lat. 1896, which was in the royal collection at least by the seventeenth century, is unknown.

[2] 'Sis igitur Ulysses meae causae, ut Circe, quamvis filia Solis, jus meum magico murmure non audeat immutare, ut sidus meae conscientiae non possit invidia denigrare. Minus certe dolerem si fauces lupi biberent meum sanguinem, quam si ovium dentibus in frusta minuerer. Corrige igitur, pastor bone, tuas oves, ne contra me balent, quia non sum lupus insidians, sed canis protegens ovem. Fretus tandem vestro favore sermoni vela levabo, et inter oblatrantium linguarum Scyllas firmae rationis remigio navigabo. Imponit plurima dira meae personae religiosa manus, et sacro criminum diademate caput innocentis honorat' (1871AB). There is no evidence to suggest that Berengar fled to the Cévennes or that he was wandering there nor to say that the *Apologeticus* itself had been written there, although many historians have made all these assumptions, e.g. O. Lottin, 'Pierre Bérengar', col. 379, who says that Berengar was forced to expatriate himself, and J. G. Sikes, *Peter Abailard*, p. 239, who says that Berengar was 'forced to leave his native Poitiers for the district of the Cévennes'.

[3] 'Nondum sol est, nondum fixus est in firmamento; satis est, si luna est ... Ego ita sentio de abbate quod sit lucerna ardens et lucens; sed tamen in testa est' (1871D–2A). Berengar pronounced a similarly solemn judgment upon the Carthusians: 'Non est Carthusia coelum, non est Carthusia paradisus. Adhuc est Carthusia inter flumina Babylonis', *Epist. contra Carthusienses* (PL. 178, 1876BC).

[4] *Epist. ad episc. Mimatensem* (1872C–3A).

[5] 1872B.

but his criticisms of Bernard were not meant to be read seriously.[1] Berengar, however, descends to the lowest depth of absurdity when he pleads for pardon although innocent, but adds that if he is required to confess that he is guilty, he will do so.[2] In the last resort, Berengar would only equivocate in Abelard's defence; in his self-appointed role as Abelard's apologist he was a failure. Time itself was a better defender of Abelard; Berengar's failure did not prove the bankruptcy of Abelard's thought. But his uniqueness as an outspoken defender of Abelard at this time, if it is not a mere example of the fortuitousness of historical survivals, may well be significant of the completeness of Abelard's defeat in 1140.

It would seem most improbable that Berengar's tract could be read as a convincing demonstration of the ignorance of Abelard's accusers, yet in the mid fourteenth century it was so read by the Parisian Thomist master, Jean de Hesdin, who found in Berengar evidence that Abelard had been a teacher of 'doctrina sana' and was much to be admired in the anti-intellectualist atmosphere of the post-Ockhamist period.[3] In the twelfth century, however, when memories of the council of Sens would have been more vivid, one may well doubt whether Berengar would ever have gained such credence.

Arnold and Berengar sustained Abelard's cause to the point of infamy. Other friends and disciples repudiated it forthrightly. William of St Thierry, who precipitated the controversies of 1139–40 after reading the *Theologia* and being shocked by its daring and new modes of enquiry, wrote that he had once loved

---

[1] 'Damnabo, inquam, tali conditione, ut, si quid in personam hominis Dei dixi, joco legatur, non serio' (1873B). But cf. also: 'legant eruditi viri Apologeticum quem edidi, et si dominum abbatem juste non argui, licenter me redarguant' (1872B).

[2] 'Veniam rogo innocens; et si magis placet, veniam postulo reus' (1874D).

[3] See B. Smalley, 'Jean de Hesdin O. Hosp. S. Ioh.', pp. 292–4, It was in the fourteenth century that three out of the five surviving exemplars of the *Apologeticus* were copied and then too that Petrarch became interested in Berengar (see above p. 30 n.). Jean Gerson, confusing Berengar of Poitiers with Berengar of Tours, told how Berengar of Poitiers confessed on his death bed to having espoused errors on the doctrine of the eucharist, *Tractatus contra Romantium de Rosa* in *Joannis Gersonii . . . Opera omnia . . . opera & studio L. Ellies du Pin*, III, 301.

Abelard.[1] When and how he had encountered Abelard is, how-ever, an open question.[2] Another abbot who wrote a *Disputatio* against Abelard while confessing that he had once been bound to Abelard in the closest familiarity[3] is now confidently identified as Thomas of Morigny.[4] Thomas wrote at the bidding of Hugh, archbishop of Rouen,[5] and although he declares that he had once also written a treatise on universals for Master Thierry[6] and although he had perhaps once been in the schools, he was no recent convert to the monastic life but a monk of some forty, and an abbot of some thirty, years' standing. From 1140 to 1144, suspended from his functions by the archbishop of Sens, he lived in Paris at St Martin-des-Champs where he probably wrote his tract before Abelard's death in 1142. The chief target of his attacks was the recently condemned *capitula* and he drew upon his own knowledge of Abelard's *Theologia* and *Apologia*.[7]

A third abbot, Geoffrey of Auxerre, stated in his *Sermon* on the Resurrection that he had once been a disciple of Abelard. He had, however, been converted away from the schools of Paris and into the Cistercian order by the sermon *de Conversione* which Bernard of Clairvaux preached there in 1139 or 1140.[8] Thereafter Geoffrey attached himself wholeheartedly to Bernard as his secretary and travelling companion from 1140 to 1145 and subsequently as his biographer and as editor of his corres-

[1] 'Dilexi et ego eum et diligere vellem, Deus testis est', *Epist.* 326 (PL. 182, 532D).

[2] J. Déchanet, 'L'amitié d'Abélard et de Guillaume', considered that William was with Abelard at Laon in 1112–13. For caution concerning this thesis see M. M. Davy, *Un traité de la vie solitaire*, p. 17 and J. R. Williams, 'The Cathedral School of Rheims', p. 95.

[3] 'Cui strictissima familiaritate coniunctus fui', *Disputatio* (PL. 180, 283B).

[4] M. B. Carra de Vaux Saint Cyr, 'Disputatio catholicorum patrum'. For long this *Disputatio* (PL. 180, 283–328) was attributed to William of St Thierry, but see A. Wilmart, 'La série et la date des ouvrages de Guillaume', pp. 161–2; also E. Vacandard, *Vie de S. Bernard*, II, 164.

[5] PL.180, 310C, 321C.

[6] 'Tractatus de rebus universalibus ad Magistrum Theodoricum', PL. 180, 321A. Cf. Wilmart, 'La série et la date', p. 161.

[7] On Thomas see again below, pp. 109–10.

[8] See Geoffrey's own statement in the *Fragmenta de vita et miraculis S. Bernardi*, ed. R. Lechat, no. 49, pp. 115–16. The sermon is ed. J. Leclercq, *S. Bernardi Opera*, IV, *Sermones* I, 69–116; on its date, *ibid.*, p. 61.

pondence. From 1162 to 1165 he was himself abbot of Clairvaux.[1] In 1148 he took part in Bernard's campaign to have Gilbert of Poitiers convicted of heresy and in the combined account of the trials of Abelard and of Gilbert which Geoffrey gives in his *Life of Bernard*, he has harsh comments to make about Abelard's teaching.[2] In his *Sermon* on the Resurrection he firmly indicates the inadequacy and the one sidedness of Abelard's account of the Redemption as an example of virtue and as a stimulus to love. He blesses God for giving in Bernard a better master to refute the ignorance and to confound the insolence of Abelard.[3] It has been suggested by one student of Geoffrey's *Vita* that in its second recension, which was probably prepared between 1163 and 1165 in a renewed attempt to obtain Bernard's canonization from Pope Alexander III, Geoffrey moderated his attitude towards Abelard by omitting two words referring to him as a heretic.[4] The omission is perhaps not explicable with certainty nor does it greatly modify the sense of the passage.

Other disciples and pupils and hearers of Abelard became in their turn important figures in the French scholastic scene and by their perpetuation of his teaching and of his memory they form a major link between Abelard and other schools of France. The most able sympathizer with Abelard at the end of his career

---

[1] Geoffrey's career has been outlined by J. Leclercq, 'Les Ecrits de Geoffroi d'Auxerre' in *Recueil d'Etudes*, I, 27–46.

[2] *S. Bernardi Vita Prima*, III, v (PL. 185, 310D, 312A).

[3] 'Ceterum ego mihi aliquando magistrum fuisse recordor qui cum pedibus et intestinis nil amplius de agno paschali, aut ipse vorans, aut discipulis exhibens, et se pariter et suos omnes non modica eius parte fraudabat. Siquidem pretium redemptionis evacuans, nil aliud nobis in sacrificio passionis dominicae commendabat nisi virtutis exemplum et incentivum amoris ... Et quidem magna haec et vera, sed non sola. Benedictus Deus qui mihi simul et vobis magistrum dedit postea meliorem (sc. Bernardum), per quem prioris redarguit ignorantiam, insolentiam confutavit', *Sermo VIII, de Resurrectione Domini* (PL. 180, 331–2). Helinand of Froidmont glosses this text of Geoffrey in his *Chronicle*, PL. 212, 1035. Cf. J. Leclercq, *Etudes sur S. Bernard*, pp. 152–3.

[4] A. H. Bredero, *Etudes sur la 'Vita Prima' de Saint Bernard*, pp. 19–22. The passage referred to is the following: 'Et ipsum (sc. Abaelardum) ergo auctorem eadem sententia cum erroribus suis apostolicus presul involvens hereticumque denuntians, scripta incendio, scriptorem silentio condempnavit.' In the second recension the words 'hereticumque denuntians' are omitted and they do not appear in PL. 185, 311D–312A.

E

was Robert of Melun who had begun to teach in the *schola artium* on Mont Sainte-Geneviève in about 1137 and who ended his career as bishop of Hereford from 1163 to 1167. In his own theological teaching he could be very critical of Abelard yet he had the greatest esteem for his work and he was most critical of Bernard's prosecution of Abelard.[1] One anonymous master, on the other hand, who was taught by John of Tours and Peter Lombard and who had heard Abelard teaching, was little influenced by the latter. On the single occasion on which he apparently alludes to his own hearing of Abelard's teaching he registers a disagreement in a question concerning the divine power.[2] John of Salisbury was silent concerning Abelard's theology,[3] but he describes in the *Metalogicon*, written in 1159, how he had come to France as a young student in 1136 and had learned the elementary principles of dialectic from Abelard on Mont Sainte-Geneviève, 'drinking in . . . every word that fell from his lips'.[4] John discusses the various masters of the time but accords the chief place among them to Abelard.[5] He referred to Abelard's logical teaching on several occasions in his *Metalogicon*.[6]

Besides the theologians and the logicians Abelard's followers also included grammarians, poets and administrators. Master Hilary, poet, dramatist and grammarian, was attached to Abelard's school at the Paraclete. There he composed a short

[1] See below chap. XII.

[2] 'Magister P(etrus) Abaelardus dicebat, quod Deus non potest facere nisi quod facit . . . Sic audivi illum docentem . . . Nos autem non alligavimus divinam potentiam hoc modo', ed. J. P. Pitra, *Questiones Magistri Odonis Suessionis*, p. 113. For Abelard's teaching see below, pp. 127–8. I. Brady, 'Peter Manducator', p. 465, finds that the author of the group of questions 288–334 ed. by Pitra is not Odo of Ourscamp, but a contemporary; I am not clear whether Brady means to suggest that this master is Peter Manducator.

[3] However, see above, p. 34, where it is suggested that John may have been critical of Bernard's conduct towards Abelard in 1140.

[4] 'Cum primo adolescens admodum studiorum causa migrassem in Gallias, anno altero postquam illustris rex Anglorum Henricus, Leo iustitie, rebus excessit humanis, contuli me ad Peripateticum Palatinum qui tunc in monte sancte Genovefe clarus doctor et admirabilis omnibus presidebat. Ibi ad pedes eius prima artis huius rudimenta accepi et pro modulo ingenioli mei quicquid excidebat ab ore eius tota mentis aviditate excipiebam', *Metalog.*, II, x (ed. Webb, p. 78).   [5] *Ibid.*, I, v (ed. Webb, p. 17).

[6] *Ibid.*, III, i, iv, vi (ed. Webb, pp. 120, 123, 136, 144).

poem in elegiac form on the disorders of Abelard's students.[1]
His relationship with Abelard is otherwise unknown although
something of the rest of his career is known from evidence which
in parts is ambiguous.[2] Although some of Hilary's poetic subjects
are English it would be unsafe to conclude that Hilary himself
was English.[3] He is first found in 1116 and 1121 as a canon of
Ronceray, a convent of nuns at Angers.[4] Around 1125, on the
break up of the school of the Paraclete, Hilary is found in Abelard's circle and expressing in a lament over the failure of the
school his admiration for Abelard's teaching. He was probably
then in his middle age.[5] Either before 1116 or after c. 1125
Hilary spent eight years in the service of the bishop of Orleans
at Sainte-Croix without succeeding to procure a post that he
desired.[6] There is a presumption that Hilary went to Orleans
from the Paraclete because while he was at Orleans Master
Vasletus asked Hilary to replace him as *scholasticus* at Angers
under Ulger who was bishop from 1125 to 1148/9.[7] At another

[1] Printed in PL. 178, 1855–6 and in J. J. Champollion-Figeac, *Hilarii Versus
et Ludi*, pp. 14–16; also in F. J. E. Raby, *The Oxford Book of Medieval Latin
Verse*, pp. 243–5. I have not been able to see L. B. Fuller, *Hilarii versus et ludi*
which, according to a review by K. Young in *Speculum*, v (1930), pp. 112–14,
does not supersede the edition of Champollion-Figeac.

[2] See *Histoire littéraire de la France*, XII (1763), 251–4 (and reprinted in PL.
178, 1851–4); T. Wright, *Biographia Britannica Literaria. Anglo-Norman Period*,
pp. 91–4; Champollion-Figeac, *Hilarii Versus*, introduction; A. Luchaire,
*Etudes sur quelques manuscrits de Rome et de Paris: Recueils épistolaires de Saint
Victor*, pp. 70–3; E. Lesne, *Les Ecoles de la fin du VIIIe siècle à la fin du XIIe*,
pp. 129, 131–3, 181–4, and P. Marchegay, 'Charte en vers de l'an 1121 composée par Hilaire, disciple d'Abailard et chanoine du Ronceray d'Angers',
pp. 245–52. On Hilary's writings see especially K. Young, *The Drama of
the Medieval Church*, II, 211–18, 276–86.

[3] So Champollion-Figeac, *Hilarii Versus*, pp. vii–viii and Young, *The
Drama of the Medieval Church*, II, 211. But others state that Hilary was English
by origin, e.g. J. Mabillon (cited in PL. 178, 1851), Wright, *Biographia Britannica*
pp. 91–4, Lesne, *Les Ecoles*, p. 273, Raby, *The Oxford Book*, p. 243.

[4] Marchegay, 'Charte en vers', pp. 245–52.

[5] Hilary's *gravitas* and the length of the journey prevented him from following Abelard's students from the Paraclete to Quincey, *Elegia*, PL. 178, 1856A;
but over twenty years later he was alive and corresponding with Bernard,
bishop of Nantes, 1148–69 (Luchaire, *Etudes*, p. 72).

[6] See the letters of Hilary and of Hugh of Orleans in Luchaire, *Etudes*, pp.
70–1.

[7] See the letter of Vasletus in Luchaire, *Etudes*, p. 71; also *ibid.*, the letter of

time too he was asked to return to Orleans to refresh the study of letters in that place.[1] Hilary therefore does not seem to have been stimulated by Abelard to teach either logic or theology. The suggestion[2] that Hilary died as a canon of St Victor is not a firm one; it rests only on the facts that the necrology of St Victor contains an undated reference to the death of one Hilary and that the manuscript which contains the letters of Hilary (and those of others besides Hilary) was formerly at St Victor.

Abelard describes the experiment of the Paraclete in his *Historia Calamitatum*.[3] There he invokes the support of St Jerome and of Plato to justify the advantages to the philosopher of living in solitude and in rustic simplicity. However, Abelard was not left alone for long and he boasts that the Paraclete became a flourishing school. It lasted at most for four years and in about 1125 Abelard departed for Brittany to become abbot of St Gildas of Ruys. Abelard attributes the disintegration of his foundation to a campaign of detraction which had been waged by ecclesiastical authority. He withholds the details of the school's decline but the setback was severe enough for Abelard to claim that he had contemplated flight outside Christendom altogether in order to find peace among the enemies of Christ. Hilary in his *Elegia* gives a more explicit and not incompatible explanation of the closure of the Paraclete. According to this a clerk who was Abelard's servant infected his master with false rumours of the bad behaviour of the students whereupon the students had to disperse. If we combine the two sources it is reasonable to conclude that the disorders of Abelard's pupils were a factor in the anxiety felt on the part of ecclesiastical authority and in the dissolution of the school. The picture which Abelard gives in the

[1] See the letters of Hugh and of Hilary in Luchaire, *Etudes*, pp. 70–1.
[2] Luchaire, *Etudes*, p. 70.
[3] Ed. Monfrin, *ll.* 1038–1227.

Herbert to Hilary: 'Attende quoque, quia Magister Ulgerius bonos clericos magnipendit, & si vmquam eos retinere potest, amplis ipsos honoribus extollit ... Vasletum Magistrum Scolarum ... tibi in exemplum afferas.' Lesne, *Les Ecoles*, p. 182, unaware of Marchegay's article, assumed that Hilary came to the Paraclete after spending eight years at Orleans.

Historia Calamitatum of a large band of young and adventurous students thirsting for instruction but also feeding themselves, building their own lodgings and caring too for Abelard, is surely idealized. Flights to the wilderness were not uncommon in the eleventh and twelfth centuries but the experience of monastic communities suggests that such experiments did not endure without the most careful organization. To this perhaps Abelard did not sufficiently turn his attention and after reading Hilary it is no surprise to learn from Abelard that ecclesiastical authority was perturbed.

Another master in the arts, whom Gerald of Wales describes as a leading disciple of Abelard and an excellent rhetorician, was Master Meinerius, who died after 1175. Gerald recalls in his *Speculum Ecclesiae* an occasion when Meinerius apparently lamented, in the course of a lecture to a large audience in Paris, the coming triumph of laws over letters.[1] Gerald was writing between 1190 and 1215/6 but he himself had first gone to Paris as a young student *c.* 1165 and had taught there, although not continuously, until 1180. Meinerius' lecture therefore belongs probably to the later 1160s or 1170s. Earlier in the *Metamorphosis Goliae*, which was written anonymously *c.* 1150 by an Englishman, Meinerius was praised for his lofty speech and profound discourse.[2] He may reasonably be identified with the Mananerius who, together with a master Alberic and a master Garnerus, is associated with Abelard's school in a story found in an anony-

---

[1] The only surviving manuscript of the *Speculum Ecclesiae* (British Museum, Cotton Tib. B xiii) suffered damage in the fire of 1731 and the additions within brackets are the work of Gerald's editor who used a transcript made before the fire: 'Tempus enim de quo Sibyllae vaticinium olim mentionem fecit, quod magistrum Meinerium, principalem Petri Abalardi discipulum et rhetorem incomparabiliter eximium, in auditorio suo Parisius coram multitudine scholarium recitantem audivimus et plangentem, damnisque futuris ⟨valde compatientem, jam advenit. Erat autem vaticinium tale⟩: "Venient dies ⟨et vae illis⟩ in quibus leges ⟨obliter⟩abunt scientiam literarum'," *Proemium*, ed. J. S. Brewer, *Giraldi Cambrensis Opera*, IV (RS), 7.
[2]   'Adest et Manerius quem nullis secundo,
         alto loquens spiritu et ore profundo,
         quo quidem subtilior nullus est in mundo',
ed. R. B. C. Huygens, *ll.* 206–8. On the date see H. Brinkmann, 'Die Metamorphosis Goliae', pp. 32–4.

mous grammatical commentary composed in the late twelfth century in the school of Ralph of Beauvais.[1]

The chronicler Helinand of Froidmont says of his own master, the Englishman Ralph of Beauvais and the leading grammarian of the 1160s and 1170s, that he had been a pupil of Abelard.[2] He must have come to France by 1140 at the latest but the date and place of Ralph's attachment to Abelard's school are not clear. Peter of Blois mischievously remarked of him that on his centenary he had not advanced beyond the elementary stage of teaching grammar,[3] but Helinand here praises both his theological and secular learning. We cannot say whether he learned theology or the arts or both from Abelard.

In the above-mentioned story concerning Abelard's school and found in a grammatical work from the school of Ralph, a Master Vasletus is also mentioned.[4] Vasletus succeeded Ulger as *scholasticus* of Angers when the latter became bishop in 1125 and he describes himself as the *socius inaequalis* of Master Hilary who was also a former member of Abelard's school.[5] He was already an established logician whom Abelard cited in the early 1120s referring to him as *Magister*.[6] Although successful at Angers he once asked Hilary after 1125 to relieve him of his duties as *magister scholarum* and thus to give him the opportunity to fulfil his great wish, now that he had the means, to visit other schools.[7] E. Lesne believed that Vasletus did not in fact leave Angers for his name is found as *magister scholarum*, *archidiaconus* and *archischolaster* in various documents from the reign of bishop Ulger

[1] Cf. R. W. Hunt, 'Studies on Priscian, II. The School of Ralph of Beauvais' (1950), pp. 16, 40–1.

[2] 'Huius etiam Petri Abaelardi discipulus fuit magister meus, qui me docuit a puero, Radulfus, natione Anglicus, cognomento grammaticus, ecclesie Belvacensis, vir tam in divinis quam in saecularibus litteris eruditus', *Chron.* (PL. 212, 1035D). Cf. Gerald of Wales: 'in literatura nostris diebus praecipuus', *Gemma Ecclesiastica*, D. II, c. XXXVII, ed. Brewer, *Giraldi Cambrensis Opera*, II, 348. On Ralph and his work see Hunt, 'Studies on Priscian', II, and *idem*, 'The Introductions to the "Artes" in the Twelfth Century', p. 100.

[3] *Epist.* VI (PL. 207, 16–19, here 18A).

[4] Hunt, 'Studies on Priscian', II, 16, 40.   [5] Lesne, *Les Ecoles*, p. 129.

[6] *Logica 'Nostrorum petitioni sociorum'*, ed. B. Geyer (BGPTMA, XXI, 4), p. 544. On the date of this work see Geyer, *Untersuchungen*, pp. 597–603.

[7] Lesne, *Les Ecoles*, p. 130.

(1125–1148/9).[1] It is not possible to say exactly where or when Vasletus came into contact with Abelard.

There remains a figure who gave incidental support to Abelard. In the *Historia Calamitatum* Abelard relates how at his trial at Soissons in 1121 a master of the Schools, *Terricus quidam*, spoke out against the ineptitude of his accusers.[2] According to Abelard, as his *Theologia* was put in the flames, one of his accusers, anxious to make clear that the book was truly heretical, proclaimed that in it Abelard had attributed the divine omnipotence to God the Father alone. The papal legate, Cono of Praeneste, interjected that not even a child should believe this for common faith professed that all the persons of the Trinity were omnipotent. Thierry then mockingly (*irridendo*) quoted a sentence from the Pseudo-Athanasian Creed where omnipotence is attributed uniquely to the Father. For this contempt of the judges he was harshly called to order by his bishop (*episcopus suus*) on whom Thierry then turned in anger.[3] *Terricus* may well be the philosopher who became the chancellor of Chartres from 1142.[4] Abelard's reference is the first recorded mention of him for he does not appear again until the following decade when he was a master in Paris.[5] One cannot be certain who his bishop was in 1121. Geoffrey of Lèves, bishop of Chartres, is, apart from the legate, Cono of Praeneste, the only bishop whom Abelard mentions by name in his account of the synod, but there were other bishops present and, according to Abelard, Geoffrey had himself spoken against the condemnation and had declared that

---

[1] *Ibid.* [2] Ed. Monfrin, *ll.* 877–890, *et in notis.*
[3] Abelard attributes the following protest to Thierry: ' "Sic fatui, filii Israel non judicantes, neque quod verum est cognoscentes, condempnastis filium Israel. Revertimini ad judicium, et de ipso judice judicate, qui talem judicem quasi ad instructionem fidei et correctionem erroris instituistis; qui cum judicare deberet, ore se proprio condemnavit, divina hodie misericordia innocentem patenter, sicut olim Susannam a falsis accusatoribus, liberante" ', ed. Monfrin, *ll.* 883–90. Thierry is adapting the words spoken by Daniel against the judges of Susanna; cf. Dan. 13, 48–9.
[4] See A. Vernet, 'Une épitaphe inédite de Thierry de Chartres', p. 661. On Thierry's work and thought see now the survey by E. Jeauneau, 'Note sur l'école de Chartres', pp. 821–39, 853–5.
[5] A. Vernet, 'Une épitaphe inédite', p. 661.

there was no open calumny in Abelard's work.[1] This should make us cautious of assuming that it was Geoffrey who reproved Thierry or that Thierry was then associated with the schools of Chartres. In an incomplete, anonymous and perilously unreliable biography of Abelard written before 1165 and placed before the St Emmeram copy of Abelard's *Scito te ipsum*, a *magister Tirricus* is cited as the giver of secret lessons in mathematics to Peter who, although already successful as a master in Paris, had never studied the *quadrivium*.[2] He found this course difficult and *magister Tirricus* jokingly conferred on him a new name, *Baiolardus*, the product of a simile drawn with a dog which when full would only lick fat (*lardum baiare*). Abelard, however, renounced the name since it indicated a weakness in him and he substituted the more flattering form, *Habelardus*, which was to signify that he was on top of the arts after all.[3] The anecdote probably shows *Tirricus* and Master Peter playing with the possibilities of meaning and of orthography of an already existing cognomen, *Abelardus*.[4]

[1] Ed. Monfrin, *ll.* 791–802 (cited above, p. 3, n. 3). E. Vacandard, *Vie de S. Bernard*, II, 144, described Geoffrey, without justification, as a former pupil of Abelard.

[2] Clm. 14,160, f. 1, printed by B. Pez, *Thesaurus anecdotorum novissimus* III, I, xxii and reprinted with comments by R. L. Poole, *Illustrations of the History of Medieval Thought*, pp. 314–15. Pez (and therefore Poole) missed a last sentence which exists in the manuscript but which does not complete the biography: '... ad adipem. Nam processu tempris se usque adeo de lardo quadruvii potenter intromisit ut nos opera illius de geometricis et arithmeticis subtilitatibus usque hodie plura videamus'.

[3] In the *Dialectica*, however (ed. L. M. De Rijk, p. 59), Abelard disclaims all arithmetical ability: '... etsi multas ab arithmeticis solutiones audierim, nullam tamen a me proferendam iudico, quem eius artis ignarum omnino recognosco'.

[4] A. Vernet, however ('Une épitaphe inédite', p. 661), believes that the detached tone in which Abelard speaks of Thierry in the *Hist. Calam.* ('Terricus quidam, scolaris magister') tells against his having been a pupil of the latter. But Abelard may only have had a few private tutorials from Thierry ('clam magistro Tirrico in quasdam mathematicas lectiones aures dabat'); Poole was probably right in seeing no reason for doubting the truth of the bare fact that Thierry taught Abelard. We may record here that there is no real reason for claiming Master John Planeta as a pupil of Abelard. He appears in one of Walter Map's stories; as a letter of Bernard of Clairvaux on the errors of Abelard was being read before Archbishop Thomas Becket and two Cistercian abbots, he recounted an incident highly damaging to Bernard's reputation for

These long pages represent an attempt to list accurately and to discuss the evidence concerning Abelard's known followers, friends, hearers and above all disciples. The known names no doubt represent only a fraction of the total of those associated with Abelard in the schools. Joseph de Ghellinck wrote with an engaging definiteness: 'La liste est longue de ceux qui ont écouté ses leçons: il n'y manque, peut-on dire, qu'un petit nombre des noms illustres de l'époque: papes, cardinaux, archevêques et evêques forment un groupe imposant parmi ses anciens élèves et les disciples de sa pensée, voire même parmi ses amis et ses admirateurs.'[1] As a group Abelard's known followers form a most interesting and varied company. Abelard taught indeed some of the most illustrious personages of the twelfth century, among them popes, bishops and abbots. He also influenced some whose names became infamous. In this his school was as ambivalent as his own reputation. The opposite extremes of fortune encountered by Abelard's followers are far apart from each other and the troubles of 1140 as well as of previous years must have caused a very widespread disturbance in the French scholastic scene and elsewhere. It is particularly noticeable that Abelard's followers include a number of the successful masters of France in the great age of revival. These masters were not only theologians but rhetoricians, grammarians and logicians. Abelard did not only rouse the schools to controversy nor was his impact upon the schools merely a passing shock, for he himself trained a series of masters and was survived by many scholars who were interested in his teaching and who could be found after his death in Paris, Rome and Bologna, at Beauvais, Orleans, Angers and elsewhere.

[1] *Le Mouvement théologique*, p. 154.

---

miracles. Map's editors thereupon add that he was probably a pupil of Abelard, see *De Nugis Curialium*, ed. M. R. James, p. 38; also MGH.SS. xxvii, 64. Map, who wrote between 1181 and 1192/3, was, of course, a hostile critic of the white monks. John Planeta was a clerk in the service of Becket as archbishop (1162–70), see Becket in *Materials for the History of Thomas Becket*, ed. Robertson and Sheppard, iii, 59, 131.

CHAPTER III

THE DIFFUSION OF
ABELARDIAN WRITINGS

The literary evidence concerning Abelard's following is rich in human information and interest. It outlines features of personal conflict and loyalty. We know of some of the men who came into contact with Abelard as a teacher and also of some of those who were his disciples. But more can be learnt concerning Abelard's influence and appeal in his own generation and afterwards from evidence of a less personal and less explicit kind. The evidence provided by statements and by anecdotes and by the discussion of theological and logical doctrines can be combined with, and supplemented by, bibliographical and palaeographical evidence. The surviving manuscript books containing works by Abelard and by his students and disciples have a history and reveal much about the activities of the anonymous students of Abelard's thought. They were produced, exported, copied and read at great labour and for particular reasons. In their character, in the markings which they bear, in the frequency with which they are encountered in libraries, in the relationship of the copies to each other, can be found indications of the kinds of interests which were aroused by Abelard's teachings and of the uses to which they were put. This is as true of copies of Abelard's own works as of those of his disciples. The study of the diffusion of these manuscripts is complex but it is also the study of the geography of twelfth-century thought and learning; it assists our appreciation of the widespread interest in Abelard's writings and by implication in those of other masters. Our main concern is with manuscripts produced before 1500 and containing the major doctrinal works of Abelard and of his disciples. The poems, the personal correspondence with Héloïse, the smaller occasional letters and pieces are less instructive in this respect than the logical writings, the biblical commentaries, the *Theologia* and *Sic et Non* in their many versions, the *Ethica* and the *Dialogus*. Manuscripts produced after the twelfth century are less relevant, but are none the less valuable because they presuppose earlier exemplars and because they witness to the history of the copying of particular works.

Several of Abelard's writings are wholly lost. The glosses on Ezechiel which Abelard delivered at Laon and then finished at Paris were transcribed and circulated but do not now survive.[1] The letter in which Abelard attacked Roscelin of Compiègne is only known through Roscelin's reply[2] and from a reference in a letter which Abelard wrote to the bishop of Paris. His *Grammatica* is lost,[3] as is the *Exhortatio* which he delivered to the monks of St Denis.[4] Héloïse received from him a *Psalterium* which consisted perhaps of a series of collects to follow the recitation of the Psalms.[5] It is even possible that Abelard wrote both an *Anthropologia* (the counterpart in his teaching about man of the *Theologia* which concerns God and the Trinity)[6] and a *Rhetorica*.[7] He may also have written glosses on the *De syllogismo categorico* and *De syllogismo hypothetico* in his *Introductiones parvulorum*,[8] a commentary on the *De syllogismo hypothetico* in his *Logica 'Ingredientibus'*[9] and further commentaries in the *Logica 'Nostrorum'*. Even of Abelard's surviving works the varying versions and revisions are not fully available. Analysts of Abelard's texts have posited the existence of two versions preceding the

[1] *Hist. Calam.*, *ll.* 196–248.

[2] Ed. J. Reiners, *Der Nominalismus*, pp. 63–80; an earlier edition is in PL. 178, 357–72, and see Abelard, *Epist. ad G. episcopum Parisiensem*, (PL. 178, 355–358). Also D. Van den Eynde, 'Les Ecrits perdus', p. 469 and H. Ostlender, *Abaelards Theologia 'Summi boni'*, pp. xviii–xx.

[3] References from the *Theologia Christiana* and *Theologia 'Scholarium'* are analysed by Van den Eynde, 'Les Ecrits perdus', pp. 473–6. See also M. Dal Pra, *Pietro Abelardo. Scritti filosofici*, p. xxxiii, n. 20.

[4] Van den Eynde, 'Les Ecrits perdus', pp. 469–73.

[5] *Ibid.*, pp. 476–80.

[6] Cf. Abelard, *Expositio in 'ad Romanos'* (PL. 178, 901A); also Buytaert, 'Critical Observations', p. 402, n. 4.

[7] References in Abelard's *Super Topica Glossae*, ed. Dal Pra, p. 263, *l.* 25, p. 267, *l.* 16; also *ibid.*, pp. xxxii–xxxiii.

[8] *Pietro Abelardo. Scritti filosofici*, ed. Dal Pra, pp. xxv and xxvi.

[9] References, as to a work yet to be written, are in the *Logica 'Ingredientibus'* ed. Geyer, p. 291, *l.* 25 and p. 389, *l.* 7 and in the *Super Topica Glossae*, ed. Dal Pra, p. 325, *l.* 10. Further evidence in M. Grabmann, 'Kommentare', p. 200.

surviving version of the *Dialectica*[1] as well as of other versions of his *Logica*.[2] Fr Buytaert believes that the earliest version of the *Sic et Non* is lost.[3] Moreover, among the extant versions completeness is all too infrequently found. Losses have occurred too among the writings of Abelard's followers. The authors of the *Sententie Hermanni*[4] and of the *Sententie Parisienses I*[5] may have composed commentaries on St Paul's Epistle to the Romans, while a *Liber Sententiarum*, containing opinions which appeared to be derived from Abelard's teaching, crossed the path of Bernard of Clairvaux in the period before the council of Sens.[6]

The surviving copies of Abelardian works are, however, numerous enough to permit a consideration of the extent and the manner of their diffusion and appeal. Of Abelard's own major works the *Theologia* is found in eighteen manuscripts, the *Sic et Non* in ten, the *Ethica* in five, the *Dialogus* in three, the commentary on the *Hexaemeron* in four and that on Romans in three. A single manuscript contains a fragment of the *Apologia* and there are single copies of Abelard's logical works.[7] In addition there are single copies of the several theological and logical works belonging to Abelard's school with the exception of the Sentences of Omnebene, of which three copies are known, and of those of Hermann which survive in seven manuscripts. In three of these manuscripts the *Sententie* of Hermann are attributed to Abelard;[8] the rest lack an attribution. It is possible that the relatively higher number of copies of this work is due to an awareness that it contained opinions ascribed to Abelard.

An assumption that the controversies surrounding Abelard's

[1] N. d'Olwer, 'Sur la date de la Dialectica', pp. 375–90 and L. M. De Rijk, *Petrus Abaelardus. Dialectica*, pp. xxii–xxiii.
[2] Geyer, *Untersuchungen*, pp. 611–12.
[3] 'The Greek Fathers in Abelard's *Sic et Non*', p. 414.
[4] Cf. Ostlender, 'Die Sentenzenbücher', pp. 214–15.
[5] *Sent. Paris.*, ed. Landgraf, p. 29; also Ostlender in *Bulletin Thomiste*, VIII (1931), p. 229.   [6] See above, p. 14.
[7] The commentary on the *De interpretatione* in the *Logica 'Ingredientibus'* is an exception; two copies are known, see below, p. 89.
[8] Clm. 14,160, f. 2r (*Sentencie magistri Petri Abelardi*); Princeton, Garret 169, f. 83r (*Sentencie petri baiolardi*) and Pavia, Aldini 49, f. 73r (*Sententie magistri petri abaialardi de fide et caritate et sacramento*).

doctrines impeded the diffusion of his writings would be difficult to demonstrate and justify. The *Theologia* 'Summi boni' was publicly condemned and burnt at Soissons in 1121[1] and books containing further condemned teachings were said by Geoffrey of Auxerre to have been publicly burnt in St Peter's, Rome, after the condemnation by Pope Innocent II.[2] The *Theologia* 'Scholarium' was found by Walter of Mortagne to contain deviations from the traditions of orthodox writers and to be propagating opinions rather than the truth.[3] Bernard of Clairvaux, stimulated by William of St Thierry, branded the *Theologia*—or *Stultilogia*—and the *Scito teipsum* as sacrilegious and erroneous. Yet for all this stigmatization Abelard always presented his writings in a successful light. He introduced the *Theologia* 'Scholarium' and *Logica* 'Nostrorum petitioni sociorum' as works requested by his students and associates and he claimed in the *Historia Calamitatum*[4] that the *Theologia* 'Summi boni' was widely read. In the *Dialogus* Abelard allows his *Theologia* to be hailed as marvellous[5] and the personal correspondence with Héloïse contains another reference, due to Héloïse, to this glorious work.[6] It is true that in 1138 or 1139 William of St Thierry remarked that the *Ethica* and *Sic et Non* appeared to be shunning the light and circulating in a mysterious way[7] and that he had come to read the *Theologia* only by chance.[8] But Signy was in the Ardennes; moreover, William also complained that Abelard's writings were circulating too well.[9] An enforced general suppression of Abelard's writings after the second condemnation would have been virtually inconceivable, but in 1210 Helinand of Froidmont did report that although many kept copies of Abelard's writings, their continuing possession had come to be regarded as curious and the motives of their owners were suspect.[10] Writing before 1153 the chronicler

---

[1] *Hist. Calam.*, ll. 868–71.
[2] *S. Bernard vita prima*, III, v and *Epist. ad Albinum* (PL. 185, 311BC and 595BC).
[3] *Epist. ad Abaelardum*, ed. Ostlender, pp. 34–7.
[4] Ed. Monfrin, ll. 702–3.   [5] PL. 178, 1613D.
[6] *Epist.* 2 (PL. 178, 181C); ed. Muckle, 'The Personal letters between Abelard and Héloïse', p. 68.
[7] *Epist.* 326 (PL. 182, 532D–533A).   [8] *Ibid.* (531C).   [9] *Ibid.* (531B).
[10] *Chron.* (PL. 212, 1034D–35A).

Richard of Poitiers also stated that Abelard's writings were to be found in many places.[1] Some modern writers have even thought that the surviving copies bear the scars of earlier battles. Jean Mabillon thought that the *Theologia* was mutilated by posterity because of its unorthodoxies[2] and Dr de Rijk surmised that the reason for the loss of the earlier folios of the unique manuscript of Abelard's *Dialectica* was that the owners, the canons of St Victor in Paris, suppressed them, for they probably contained sharp attacks on the doctrines of William of Champeaux, the founder of their house.[3]

In fact Abelardian writings spread far and wide and did so quickly. To appreciate the evidence of surviving manuscripts and of library catalogues we shall divide the area of Europe into four zones consisting of France and the French-speaking part of Switzerland, the German-speaking lands, including for this purpose Denmark, Italy and England. Each of these zones has characteristics of its own which may have affected the circulation of these writings. Since it is difficult for a student to form firm judgments about particular manuscripts belonging to library collections with which he has not had long familiarity, my impressions are presented with timidity.

Scholastic forms of organization and scholastic activities in the twelfth century flourished most in northern France. In Germany, where the life of the schools was less developed, the libraries of religious houses contain a relatively good number of manuscripts containing the writings of Abelard's followers. These were perhaps brought home by clerics who had been in the French schools; these copies may also perhaps have served as substitutes for copies of the original writings of Abelard. The relative scarcity of manuscripts containing the works of Abelard's followers and now surviving in French libraries may be due to the greater availability of Abelard's own writings in and near these schools. Yet in France Abelard's own writings did not survive by belonging to scholastic libraries—the libraries, that is, of the schools run by cathedrals and other great churches. Abelardian

---

[1] *Chron.* (MGH.SS. xxvi, 81).   [2] PL. 182, 1047.
[3] *Petrus Abaelardus. Dialectica*, ed. de Rijk, p. 13.

manuscripts in France and elsewhere survived usually because they found their way into the libraries of religious houses. No institution, the convent of the Paraclete apart, was inseparably associated with Abelard's name and work. The Mont Sainte-Geneviève was an important theatre for Abelard, but the improvised oratory of the Paraclete near Quincey, with its huts of mud and wattle, appears to have been, while Abelard taught there, an encampment. At St Denis, at St Médard and at St Gildas Abelard's relationships with the monastic community were far from being harmonious. Only the Paraclete under Héloïse appears to have been a major repository for copies of Abelard's writings and was still such a repository in early modern times when D'Amboise and Duchesne and Camuzat read, used and printed writings by Abelard. But those manuscripts are now lost.[1]

The house of St Victor in Paris, founded by William of Champeaux and rising to fame with Hugh, was in Abelard's day and afterwards a prominent centre of study and thought. The numerous surviving manuscripts from its library contain several works by Abelard including some of his smaller pieces.[2] The house probably had in the thirteenth century a modestly prepared twelfth- or early thirteenth-century copy of Abelard's *Theologia 'Scholarium'*, now in the Arsenal Library in Paris,

[1] The manuscripts seen at the Paraclete by F. d'Amboise and A. Duchesne in preparation for the first printed edition of Abelard's works in 1616 have been discussed by J. Monfrin in an excellent introduction to his edition of the *Hist. Calam.*, pp. 41–6. Monfrin believes that the copy containing the correspondence between Abelard and Héloïse and the *Regula Sanctimonialium* with the *Institutiones* which was seen by d'Amboise is now lost together with the copy of the *Sermo ad virgines Paraclitenses*. However, the Troyes MS., Bibl. municipale 802 (Monfrin, pp. 9–18), has texts according to the tradition of the Paraclete.
[2] Cod. Paris, Bibl. nat. lat. 14,511 (late twelfth or early thirteenth century) contains commentaries by Abelard on the Lord's Prayer, Apostles Creed and Pseudo-Athanasian Creed as well as the *Problemata Heloissae* and the *Sermo ad virgines Paraclitenses*; it appears in the early sixteenth-century catalogue of the library made by Claude de Grandrue as bbb. 19 (A. Franklin, *Les anciennes bibliothèques de Paris*, I, 176). Cod. Paris, Arsenal 1030, ff. 24v–26r (15th century) contains Abelard's letter on St Denis (de Grandrue: eee. 5; cf. Franklin, *loc. cit.*). Two other manuscripts mentioned by de Grandrue have not been traced: p. 13 containing the *Confessio fidei* (but p. 13 is now Paris, Bibl. nat. lat. 14,669 which lacks this work) and bbb. 17 containing his letters (cf. Franklin, *op. cit.*, I, 175, 176).

MS. 265, ff. 65r–92v.[1] An incomplete copy of glosses on Aristotle's *De Interpretatione* (Paris, Bibl. nat. lat. 15,015, ff. 180r–199r), composed by a disciple of Abelard, also belonged to the library of St Victor in the thirteenth century.[2] Two further manuscripts, however, may not have belonged to St Victor until the later middle ages since the earliest *ex libris* inscriptions are of the fourteenth or fifteenth century. They are cod. Paris, Arsenal 1116, which contains on ff. 80r–84v a twelfth-century copy of an anonymous and incomplete abridgment of Abelard's Commentary on *Romans* in which passages from the *De Sacramentis* of Hugh of St Victor have been incorporated,[3] and cod. Paris, Bibl. nat. lat. 14,614 which has on ff. 117r–202r the unique extant text of Abelard's *Dialectica* in an incomplete twelfth-century copy.[4] It is hardly likely, in such a large collection, that these four manuscripts were the only representatives of Abelard's writings in the medieval library of St Victor; as we shall see in later chapters several Victorine writers of the mid twelfth century possessed an extensive knowledge of Abelard's theological teaching.

Other manuscripts are also associated with Parisian libraries.

[1] A thirteenth-century *ex libris* inscription of St Victor is found at the end of the text of the *Theologia* on f. 92v (or 94v if two fly-leaves are counted). For descriptions of the manuscript see H. Ostlender, 'Die Theologia Scholarium', p. 274 and H. Martin, *Catalogue*, I, 151–3. This manuscript is hh. 13 in the catalogue of de Grandrue (cf. Franklin, *Les anciennes bibliothèques*, I, 176).

[2] A thirteenth-century *ex libris* inscription is found on f. 199v. Cf. Geyer, *Untersuchungen*, p. 615, and V. Cousin (who edited fragments), *Fragments philosophiques*, II, 408–16.

[3] F. 1r bears the abbey's crest. An intriguing note by the copyist is in the upper margin of f. 80r: 'Fidem dedi ego et Gauterius ne darem hunc quaternionem, quamdiu dominicus erit in Francia'; the quire is now ff. 79–86. Descriptions of the manuscript are given by A. Landgraf in his edition, *Abaelardi Expositionis . . . Abbreviatio*, pp. 3–4 and by H. Martin, *Catalogue*, II, 286–9.

[4] F. 202v contains an *ex libris* inscription; the manuscript is MMMC in the catalogue of de Grandrue (cf. Franklin, *Les anciennes bibliothèques*, I, 176: mmm. 6). Full edition by L. M. De Rijk, *Petrus Abaelardus. Dialectica* (with description of the manuscript, pp. xii–xiii); partial ed. by V. Cousin, *Ouvrages inédits*, pp. 171–503. References to Abelard's logical teachings are made in another Victorine MS. (Paris, Bibl. nat. lat. 15,141, ff. 1–46; twelfth century) containing a *Summa Sophisticorum Elenchorum*; see L. Minio-Paluello, 'Jacobus Veneticus Grecus', p. 304.

The church of Notre Dame sold a manuscript of Abelard's Commentary on the *Hexaemeron* (Vatican, lat. 4214, ff. 1–30) to one of its canons, Annibale de Ceccano, at some time before he became archbishop of Naples in 1326,[1] and it owned, at least in the eighteenth century, another manuscript (Paris, Bibl. nat. lat. 17,251) containing two differing thirteenth-century copies of the same work.[2] The inventories of the library of the Louvre in the late thirteenth and early fourteenth centuries record two manuscripts, apparently now lost, one of which perhaps contained the *Theologia 'Scholarium'*.[3] Three sentence works by followers of Abelard are found in a miscellaneous volume formerly belonging to the priory of St Martin-des-Champs (Paris, Bibl. nat. lat. 18,108).[4] The three works, which are all

[1] Fly leaf: 'Iste liber est reverendi domini Annibaldi Dei gratia archiepiscopi neapolitani quem emit ab ecclesia parisciensi antequam esset archiepiscopus.' It appears in the catalogue of Vatican manuscripts made by the Maurist Dom Claude Etiennot (Stephanotius) and published by B. Montfaucon, *Bibliotheca Bibliothecarum*, I, 138D: P. 2 'Petri Abailardi Capitula Genesis. 117'. See also F. Stegmüller, *Repertorium Biblicum*, IV, n. 6376. On Annibale, who was Provisor of the Sorbonne from 1320 to 1326, see P. Glorieux, *Aux Origines de la Sorbonne*, I, 136–9.

[2] Identified by B. Hauréau in his *Notices et Extraits*, V (1892), p. 236; previously inedited sections of the commentary are printed here, pp. 237–44. See too L. Delisle, 'Inventaire des mss. latins de Notre Dame', no. 17,251. Ff. 33v–46r contain the prologue and an incomplete commentary; ff. 31r–33v contain a shorter fragment of the commentary which Fr Buytaert (in correspondence) suggests may be the work of a disciple.

In 1297 the chapter of Notre Dame received a legacy of books from Pierre de Joigny including *Sermones Petri Abalardi, qui incipiunt 'Ascendat puteus'* (L. Delisle, *Le Cabinet des manuscrits*, III, 4), but since no known sermon by Abelard bears this *incipit* the ascription to Abelard is uncertain.

[3] One MS. appears in the inventories of 1411 and 1413 with the description: 'Liber Hermetis, liber Vacce, Petrus Abaelardi et alia quaedam' (Delisle, *Le Cabinet des manuscrits*, III, 146). The other appears in inventories from 1373–80 onwards: 'Un très vieil cayer en latin, intitulé Incipit prefacio Petri Abaelardi et fut de maistre Jean de Marrigny, second fol inc. *Et sont in fide*' (Delisle, *op. cit.*, III, 147). Jean de Marigny might be the former chancellor of France and, from 1347 till his death in 1351, archbishop of Rouen. The work may be the *Theologia 'Scholarium'*; cf. the rubric of that work which appears in codd. Douai 357, f. 108r and London, British Museum, Royal 8. A. I, f. 3r: 'Petri Abaialardi in tractatum eius qui dicitur scolaris prefacio.'

[4] L. Delisle, 'Inventaire des manuscrits latins de Notre Dame', no. 18,108. There is a full description by A. Landgraf in his edition of the *Sententie Parisienses I, Ecrits théologiques*, pp. xv–xxv.

F

incomplete twelfth-century copies, are the *Sententie Parisienses I* (ff. 70r–75v), the *Sententie Hermanni* (ff. 76v–77v; chapters 12–18 of the Rheinwald-Migne edition) and the inedited *Sententie Parisienses II* (ff. 170r–177v). In 1140 St Martin-des-Champs housed Thomas of Morigny who wrote a *Disputatio* in criticism of Abelard's *Theologia* and *Apologia*.[1] However, the three sentence works belong to a volume which was bound in the eighteenth century and the origins and early peregrinations of its many parts are unclear.

Outside Paris a number of manuscripts can be related, with widely varying degrees of certainty, to some French monastic libraries. A Benedictine monk of the second half of the twelfth century, Rainerus Iuvenis, on leaving his abbey at Liessies to join the monks of nearby Hautmont in the diocese of Cambrai, offered as a token of his worth to the new community the copy he had made of Abelard's *Theologia* '*Summi boni*' (now cod. Berlin, Staatsbibliothek, theol. lat. oct. 95).[2] The history of cod. Tours, Bibl. municipale, 85 is less clear. The volume contains the *Sic et Non* on ff. 106r–118v and the *Theologia Christiana* and *Theologia* '*Scholarium*' on ff. 133r–158v and it belonged to the Benedictine abbey of Marmoutier near Tours when Dom Martène and Dom Durand made use of it for their edition in 1717 of the *Theologia Christiana*.[3] But the present codex is a composition of three manuscripts or parts of manuscripts and the second part which largely relates to Abelard has no indication of its provenance. The third part of the volume belonged to the priory of Ploermel, a dependent of Marmoutier, in 1254 and it

---

[1] Cf. above, p. 50.

[2] For a description of the manuscript see Ostlender, *Abaelards Theologia* '*Summi boni*', p. xii. Rainerus also copied on ff. 65r–93r the *De planctu naturae* of Alan of Lille; the date of this work is uncertain but it is unlikely to be before *c.* 1160; see M.-T. d'Alverny, *Alain de Lille*, p. 34. So this Rainerus should not be confused with an earlier Rainerus, also a scribe and abbot of Liessies who died in 1124, on whom see J. Peter, *L'Abbaye de Liessies*, p. 19 and M. Jacquin, *Etude sur l'abbaye de Liessies*, p. 335. On manuscripts of Liessies see J. Leclercq in *Scriptorium*, VI (1952), pp. 51–62.

[3] *Thesaurus novus anecdotorum*, V, 1139–1359 (reprinted in PL. 178, 1113–1330; also ed. V. Cousin, *Opera*, II, 357–566). On the defects of the impressions of Martène-Durand and of Migne see Buytaert, 'Critical Observations'.

is possible that Abelard's works soon found their way to Marmoutier or to one of its dependent houses.[1] Similar difficulties prevent one ascertaining the early history of a twelfth-century copy of Abelard's Commentary on *Romans* and of a thirteenth-century copy of the *Theologia 'Scholarium'* and the *Sic et Non*. The former (now cod. Angers, Bibl. municipale 68, ff. 1r–26r)[2] probably belonged in the eighteenth century to the Maurist abbey of Saints Sergius and Bacchus in Angers and[3] the latter, now cod. Douai, Bibl. municipale lat. 357, ff. 108r–155v, was found by Dom Martène in the abbey of Anchin near Douai.[4] But in neither case is it possible to be sure that these abbeys were the earliest repositories.

Four manuscripts are associated with the abbey of Mont St Michel. A thirteenth-century copy of the *Sic et Non*, cod. Avranches, Bibl. municipale 12, ff. 132r–207r, bears an *ex libris* inscription of the fourteenth or fifteenth century on f. 207r.[5]

[1] See the handwritten description by Mme J. Barbet available at the IRHT, Paris; also M. Collon, *Catalogue général*, XXXVII. *Tours*, I, 47. Collon (*ibid.*, pp. vi–vii) observes that book-marks of Marmoutier are in general not earlier than the seventeenth century. See also Ostlender, 'Die Theologia Scholarium', p. 269.

[2] See A. Molinier, *Catalogue général*, pp. 210–11 and W. Affeldt, 'Verzeichniss der Römerbriefkommentare', p. 395.

[3] 'P. Abaelardi 4 commentariorum libri in Epistolam ad Romanos', B. Montfaucon, *Bibliotheca Bibliothecarum Manuscriptorum*, II, p. 1219B.

[4] *Thesaurus novus anecdotorum*, V, 1148; cf. the remarks of Martène in the *Voyage littéraire de deux religieux bénédictins*, cited by C. Dehaisnes, *Catalogue général, Ancienne série*, VI, 772. For descriptions of the manuscript see an unsigned handwritten notice at the IRHT in Paris and Dehaisnes, *op. cit.*, pp. 190–1. Cf. also Ostlender, 'Die Theologia Scholarium', p. 270. The present volume has three parts; the second part, ff. 108–155, appears to share the same place of origin as the first part, ff. 1–107, since the rubrics and initials are in the same hand; moreover the name of a scribe, Sego, who wanted a drink, appears on f. 106v. J. W. Bradley, *A Dictionary of Miniaturists*, III, 222, states that Sego 'wrote many MSS some of which are in the Library at Douai', but he offers no references other than to Douai 96 (the present 357). Sego can hardly be Siger, the monk of Anchin who *c.* 1165 made the first collection of the writings of Bernard of Clairvaux (cf. J. Leclercq, *Etudes sur S. Bernard*, pp. 124–33).

[5] For descriptions see H. Omont, *Catalogue général ... Départements*, X, 11, and a handwritten notice by Mme J. Barbet in the IRHT, Paris. The manuscript may be the one seen by B. Montfaucon, *Bibliotheca Bibliothecarum*, II, 1361, no. 237, and it was used by V. Cousin in his edition of the *Sic et Non* (*Ouvrages inédits*, pp. 3 *et seq.*). G. Nortier, 'Les bibliothèques médiévales des

Abelard's commentary on the *Hexaemeron* was found by Dom Martène in the abbey in a manuscript of the twelfth or thirteenth century and now cod. Avranches 135, ff. 75r–90r.[1] When André Duchesne published Abelard's commentary on Romans for the first time in 1616, he did so from a manuscript then in the abbey but now apparently lost.[2] A twelfth-century copy of a *Tractatus de intellectibus* attributed by the scribe to Abelard but probably composed by a very close disciple is now Avranches 232, ff. 64r–68v.[3] The abbey of Mont St Michel through its abbot from 1154–86, the bibliophile and benefactor of the library, Robert of Torigny and through his relationship with Richard 'the Bishop', archdeacon of Coutances and bishop of Avranches from 1170 to 1182, became the repository of several important translations of Aristotle's writings made in particular by James of Venice *c.* 1130–40.[4] Dr L. Minio-Paluello has suggested that the copy of the *Metaphysica vetustissima* which is found in this volume on ff. 201r–225v, as well as other Aristotelian texts found in another manuscript from the abbey, now Avranches 221, ff. 2r–88v, were probably written in the circle of Robert and Richard.[5] The present cod. Avranches 232 has nine parts and the

[1] *Thesaurus novus anecdotorum*, v, 1361–1416. G. Nortier, 'Les bibliothèques médiévales' (1957), p. 145, n. 60, considers that this manuscript was copied and bound in the scriptorium of the abbey in the thirteenth century. For descriptions see H. Omont, *Catalogue général . . . Départements*, x, pp. 62–3 and the Abbé Desroches in *Mémoires de la Société des antiquaires de Normandie*, 2e sèrie, 1 (1837), p. 144, MS. 204.

[2] *Petri Abaelardi Opera*, pp. 491–725. Reissued in PL. 178, 783–978 and ed. V. Cousin, *Opera Petri Abaelardi*, II, 152–356.

[3] Ed. V. Cousin, *Opera Petri Abaelardi*, II, 733–53 (and earlier in *Fragments philosophiques*, II, 461–92). C. Prantl, *Geschichte der Logik*, II, 206 *et seq.*, and B. Geyer, *Untersuchungen*, pp. 612–15, determined that the *Tractatus* was the work of a disciple of Abelard. For descriptions of the MS. see H. Omont, *Catalogue général . . . Départements*, x, 110–12, L. Delisle, *Catalogue général . . . Départements*, IV (4° series), pp. 543–7, *Aristoteles Latinus. Pars Prior* (G. Lacombe and others), pp. 437–8, and Mme J. Barbet in a handwritten notice (1957) available at the IRHT, Paris.

[4] See L. Minio-Paluello, 'Iacobus Veneticus Grecus', pp. 292–4.

[5] *Ibid.*, pp. 293–4.

___

abbayes bénédictines de Normandie' (1957), p. 144, n. 59, considers that this manuscript was written at Mont St Michel.

survival on f. 199v of a fragment of an earlier binding impedes the assumption that the earlier folios had the same origin as the *Metaphysica vetustissima*.[1] But the volume is a deliberately formed collection of Aristotelian translations and of other philosophical works transcribed, as the hands suggest, in the course of the twelfth and early thirteenth centuries. Moreover, the *Tractatus de intellectibus* is sandwiched between anonymously made translations of the *De generatione et corruptione* (ff. 11r–63r) and of a part of the *Nicomachean Ethics* (ff. 73r–77r) which, according to Dr Minio-Paluello,[2] may well have belonged to the group of scholars associated with Robert and Richard. John of Salisbury was related to this circle. Richard 'the Bishop' had been his esteemed master and in *c.* 1167 John was still in touch with him and making enquiries with him concerning the translations of Aristotle's writings.[3] What John says in his *Metalogicon*[4] in praise of Abelard's ability to clarify logic and to teach the subject without becoming embroiled in its difficulties finds a close echo in one of a series of five *quaestiones* which follow the *Tractatus de intellectibus* on ff. 68v–71v.[5] Here an anonymous student acknowledges that Abelard and his adherents have clarified logic, in particular by opposing contemporary currents of idealist thought. If it is plausible to associate the *Tractatus* with a disciple of Abelard whose work appealed to a student or students in northern France who, like John of Salisbury, were in touch with other scholars in Coutances or Mont Saint

[1] An *ex libris* inscription of the 14th century is found on f. 255v and one of the 18th century on f. 1r. The codex was a unity when Montfaucon printed a catalogue of Mont St Michel in *Bibliotheca Bibliothecarum*, II, 1359, 1356.

[2] L. Minio-Paluello, *op. cit.*, p. 294.

[3] John of Salisbury, *Metalogicon*, I, xxiv; II, x (ed. Webb, pp. 57, 80); *Epist.* 211 (PL. 199, 234–5). Cf. Minio-Paluello, *op. cit.*, p. 292.

[4] 'Non enim occasio querenda est ingerende difficultatis, sed ubique facilitas generanda. Quem morem secutum recolo Peripateticum Palatinum . . . malens instruere et promovere suos in puerilibus quam in gravitate philosophorum esse obscurior', III, 1 (ed. Webb, p. 120).

[5] 'Alii autem qui quasdam formas essentias esse, quasdam minime perhibent, sicut Abaelardus et sui qui artem dialecticam non obfuscando sed diligentissime perscrutando dilucidant, nullas formas essentias esse approbant, nisi quasdam qualitates', f. 69r (ed. V. Cousin, *Opera Petri Abaelardi*, II, 755).

Michel, it follows that in that circle Abelard's reputation as a logician stood very high.

The abbey of Mont Saint Michel had, then, four Abelardian manuscripts, perhaps acquired at an early date. With manuscripts of Abelard coming from the abbey of Saint Benoit at Fleury on the Loire the origins are more difficult to detect. One of these manuscripts, Paris, Bibl. nat. lat. 13,368, contains on ff. 128r–231v a long series of logical commentaries copied in the twelfth century.[1] The first four belong to Abelard's *Introductiones parvulorum*.[2] Then follow the *De generibus et speciebus* (ff. 168ra–175va) and the *De propositionibus modalibus* (ff. 175va–177ra) by a pupil of Jocelyn of Bourges, bishop of Soissons from 1126 to 1152.[3] Ff. 177rb–231vb contain several commentaries and fragments of commentaries among which are anonymous glosses on Porphyry's *Isagoge* (ff. 215ra–223vb) which offer similarities with Abelard's own glosses on the same text at ff. 156r–162v of the codex.[4] The northern French character of these contents is also underlined in a fragment of a commentary on Porphyry which contains on ff. 178 and 179 references to various masters of the time such as Jocelyn, Roscelin and Ulger. Otherwise, however, the early history of the volume is unknown.

A second twelfth-century manuscript, which is also of high importance in the history of medieval logic, was at Fleury before entering the town library of Orleans (no. 266) but it does not contain any obvious indication of its origin and its identification with an entry in the catalogue of Fleury books made in 1552 is not entirely certain.[5] It contains some twenty-eight

---

[1] For partial descriptions see *Pietro Abelardo. Scritti filosofici*, ed. M. Dal Pra, pp. xiv–xvii; B. Geyer, *Untersuchungen*, pp. 593–4 and *Ouvrages inédits d'Abélard*, ed. V. Cousin, pp. xii–xvii. F. 9r bears an eighteenth-century inscription: 'Bibliotheca Floriacensis'. C. Oudin (cited in PL. 178, 66) noted this manuscript twice, once at Fleury and again when it was at St Germain-des-Prés.

[2] Ed. M. Dal Pra, pp. 1–203 and incompletely by V. Cousin, *Ouvrages inédits*, pp. 551–601.

[3] Cf. B. Geyer, *Untersuchungen*, pp. 594–5. The *De generibus* was ed. by V. Cousin, *Ouvrages inédits*, pp. 505–50 as a work by Abelard.

[4] Cf. Geyer, *Untersuchungen*, pp. 595–6.

[5] See C. Cuissard, *Catalogue général ... Départements*, XII, 128–9. Cuissard,

logical works, most of which are inedited, and as in the Paris collection the references to the masters of the day, for example to Roscelin, Jocelyn, Ulger and Abelard, underline its northern French origin.[1] The relationship of many works in the volume to contemporary currents of thought is at present unclear, but the collection does contain an analysis of a paralogism and some problems on 'totum' which may have been written by Abelard himself and which bear the title *Sententie secundum Magistrum Petrum*.[2] Also present is an anonymous treatise on predication entitled *Positio vocum sententie* (pp. 276a–278b) and copied in the same hand. The author is concerned to strengthen the distinction between the individual and the universal and this concern had been shared by Abelard who believed that the realists destroyed this distinction.[3] The work appears to depend, in many places verbatim, upon a lost gloss on Porphyry written by Abelard after his *Logica 'Ingredientibus'* and before his *Logica 'Nostrorum petitioni sociorum'*, and it may have been written between *c.* 1110 and 1124.[4] It is further likely that other works in this volume were produced by Abelard's circle. Mme Lebreton and Mme Pellegrin have suggested this in respect of a commentary on

---

[1] For analysis of the logical contents see L. Minio-Paluello, *Abaelardiana inedita*, pp. xli–xlvi. A handwritten description of the MS. by M. M. Lebreton and E. Pellegrin is available at the IRHT in Paris. Cf. also B. Geyer, *Unter-suchungen*, p. 595, and *Patristische und Scholastische Philosophie*, pp. 145–6, 209, 211–13.

[2] Identified and ed. by Minio-Paluello, *Abaelardiana inedita*, pp. xxxix–xlviii, 109–21. See also M. T. Beonio-Brocchieri Fumagalli, *La Logica di Abelardo*, pp. 80–7.

[3] Cf. *Logica 'Ingredientibus'*, ed. Geyer, p. 15: 'Restat autem nunc, ut eos oppugnemus qui singula individua in eo quod aliis conveniunt, universale appellant et eadem de pluribus praedicari concedunt, non ut plura essentialiter sint illa, sed quia plura cum eis conveniunt'; also *ibid.*, p. 37, *l.* 3 *et seq.*

[4] I have studied and edited this treatise in my unpublished Fellowship dissertation, pp. 295–323, in King's College Library, Cambridge.

---

p. vi, identified the manuscript with the 1552 catalogue entry: 'Boetii commentaria in topica ciceronis ac eiusdem de topicis differentiis, quod libros praecedunt II paginae quorum[!] prioris initium est "Condidisti".' The manscript contains two added folios of theological matter (pp. 1–4) but neither of these begins with the word 'Condidisti'. Apart from these folios, the description would suit both cod. 266 and cod. 267.

Boethius' *De differentiis topicis* (pp. 43a–78a) and of one on Aristotle's *De interpretatione* (pp. 5a–43a), which may be based on the *Logica 'Ingredientibus'*, as well as of glosses on Boethius' *De divisione* (pp. 122a–149a) which may be based on the *Introductiones parvulorum*.[1]

A third manuscript from Fleury may be mentioned here because of the similarities which exist between its contents and those of the Paris and Orleans volumes. Cod. Vatican Reginensis lat. 230, a late twelfth- or early thirteenth-century manuscript which may be identifiable with an entry in the Fleury catalogue of 1552,[2] contains an anonymous commentary on the *De differentiis topicis* of Boethius (ff. 72r–79v) which is seemingly the same as one in the Orleans manuscript (pp. 43a–78a). There are similarities between commentaries on the *Categories* and the *De interpretatione* found in the Vatican manuscript (ff. 41r–71r and 80r–87r) and in the Parisian manuscript (ff. 195v–210v and 225rb–231vb). Moreover, the *De generibus et speciebus* and *De propositionibus modalibus* by a pupil of Jocelyn are found in an identical arrangement in the Paris and the Orleans manuscripts.[3] Fleury therefore at some time but not necessarily in the twelfth century held these three interesting manuscripts which are related to each other in their contents. Of studies at Fleury in the twelfth century little is known[4] although one of the monks, Ralph Tortaire, did write some enthusiastic verses about Abelard,[5] and in addition the abbey was near to the schools of Orleans where the study of the arts flourished.[6] Whether or not these logical collections belonged in the twelfth century to Fleury, they were formed by scholars who followed closely the thought of the prominent logicians of northern France and they witness to the importance attached by contemporaries to the logical commentaries and exercises of Abelard and of his circle.

A number of other manuscripts survive which appear to have

---

[1] Cf. their handwritten notice mentioned above, p. 73, n. 1.
[2] See A. Wilmart, *Codices Reginenses Latini*, I, 545 *et seq.*
[3] See Minio-Paluello, *Abaelardiana inedita*, pp. xliii–xliv.
[4] Cf. E. Lesne, *Les Ecoles*, p. 195.
[5] See above, p. 10, n.   [6] Cf. Lesne, *op. cit.*, pp. 175–91.

been produced in France although their early histories are often far from clear. Two volumes among Queen Christina's manuscripts in the Vatican, *Reginenses lat.* 159 and 242, ff. 1r–74v— a *Theologia Christiana* copied in a French school hand of the second half of the twelfth century[1] and a late twelfth- or early thirteenth-century copy of the commentary on Romans[2]—came from the collection of Alexander Petau, but their earlier repositories are unknown.[3] Only one copy of the *Ethica* has been associated with France, Clm. 28,363, ff.103r–132v. The script is of the twelfth century and the volume lacks inscriptions of provenance, but appears to have been in Italy in the fourteenth or fifteenth century.[4] Three sermons by Abelard are found, without title or name of author, on ff. 151r–160v of a twelfth-century manuscript which once belonged to the Austin canons of Marbach in the diocese of Basle (Haut-Rhin) and now to the town library of Colmar, no. 128.[5] A *Theologia 'Scholarium'*, Paris, Bibl. nat. lat. 14,793, copied in a hand of the fourteenth or fifteenth century and lavishly illuminated and gilded, belonged in the early fifteenth century to a Norman humanist, Simon de Plumetot, whose library was transferred to the abbey of St Victor *c.* 1440.[6]

---

[1] Wilmart, *Codices Reginenses Latini*, I, 377–8. The text was identified by M. Grabmann, *Geschichte*, II, 175, n. 1, and a fragment not previously printed was published by C. Ottaviano, 'Un brano inedito'. E. Buytaert, 'An Earlier Redaction', p. 495, considers this text to represent a second recension.

[2] Wilmart, *Codices Reginenses Latini*, I, 578–9. Cf. Grabmann, *Geschichte*, II, 175, n. 1, and H. Denifle, *Die abendländischen Schriftausleger*, pp. 49–52.

[3] Neither volume is mentioned by K. A. De Meyier, *Paul en Alexandre Petau*.

[4] P. Ruf and M. Grabmann, 'Ein neuaufgefundenes Bruchstück', especially pp. 5–9. The *Ethica* is followed on ff. 132v–135v by a fragment of Abelard's *Apologia*.

[5] Identified by D. Van den Eynde, 'Le Recueil des Sermons', p. 19. The inscription of provenance appears on f. 1 and was kindly communicated to me by M. P. Schmitt. The catalogue of the manuscripts of Colmar is at present being published.

[6] I owe this information concerning de Plumetot to the kindness of M. G. Ouy. The manuscript was numbered ggg 18 on the fly-leaf by the sixteenth-century librarian of St Victor, Claude de Grandrue (bbb. 18 according to A. Franklin, *Les anciennes bibliothèques*, I, 175). It is the basis of the editions of Duchesne (pp. 973–1136), Migne (PL. 178, 979–1114) and Cousin (*Opera*, II, 2–143); some notes which accompany the Duchesne-Migne editions are

De Plumetot may be added to the interesting but short list of later medieval humanists who concerned themselves with Abelard's writings and most usually with his letters. They include Roberto de' Bardi, chancellor of Paris university, who bought a manuscript of Abelard's letters (now Troyes 802) in 1346,[1] and his friend Petrarch who owned the collection in Paris, Bibl. nat. lat. 2923,[2] as well as Coluccio Salutati who in 1395/6 asked Jean de Montreuil for a manuscript of Abelard's letters.[3] In England a gift of books to Oxford University made in 1443 by Duke Humphrey of Gloucester included the letters of Abelard.[4]

A neat but incomplete copy, probably made in the thirteenth century, of Abelard's glosses on the *De differentiis topicis* of Boethius is found in cod. Paris, Bibl. nat. lat. 7493, ff. 168r–183v.[5] The glosses belong to the *Logica 'Ingredientibus'* and they are present without annotations in a volume of miscellaneous texts copied in various periods. The cipher of the ill-balanced Charles IX, king of France from 1560 to 1574, appears at the head of the volume, but no early indication of the volume's origin is to be found. The unique and early thirteenth-century copy of a part of the *Logica 'Nostrorum petitioni sociorum'* survives in the town library of Lunel in the département of Hérault as cod. 6, ff. 8r–41r.[6] The volume belonged to the collection of L. Médard

[1] Cf. J. Monfrin (ed.), *Abélard. Historia Calamitatum*, p. 13.
[2] Cf. *ibid.*, pp. 18–19 for further references.   [3] *Ibid.*, p. 50.
[4] Cf. *Epistolae Academicae Oxonienses*, ed. H. Anstey, I, 235. This manuscript appears now to be lost; it may be added to the list of Monfrin (ed.), *Hist. Calam.*, pp. 50–1.
[5] Ed. M. Dal Pra, pp. 205–330 and partially by V. Cousin, *Ouvrages inédits*, pp. 603–10. The manuscript is described by Dal Pra, *ed. cit.*, p. xxix, by Cousin, *ed. cit.*, pp. viii–x and in the *Catalogus Cod. MSS. Bibliothecae Regiae*, IV (1744), 366, no, 7493. C. Oudin (cited in PL. 178, 65) noted it as cod. Bibl. regia 5492.
[6] Ed. Geyer, *Abaelards Philosophische Schriften*, II. The manuscript is partially described *ibid.*, I, x–xi and inaccurately in *Catalogue général . . . Départements*, XXXI, 167.

none other than fifteenth-century marginalia in the manuscript itself. Ostlender 'Die Theologia Scholarium', p. 274, determined that the text was the fourth recension although Buytaert, 'Critical Observations', p. 390, n. 4, prefers to consider it as a slightly annotated version of the third recension.

which was bequeathed to the town in *c.* 1830 and its earlier provenance is unknown.[1] The text suffers from omissions and transpositions which suggest that it had been rehandled to an uncertain extent by a pupil, and the presence in the same volume on ff. 41r *et seq.* of glosses on the *De syllogismo categorico* of Boethius in which Abelard is cited by name[2] seems to suggest that these copies or their exemplars were produced by active followers of Abelard's teaching. A late thirteenth-century copy of the *Sentences* ascribed to Hermann is found now in the Bibliothèque Inguimbertine at Carpentras, cod. 110, ff. 55r–65v.[3] Mgr d'Inguimbert, who was bishop of Carpentras from 1735 to 1757 and formerly librarian to Cardinal Corsini (Pope Clement XII) formed his collection by purchases made in Italy and especially in Aix-en-Provence from the collection of Thomassin de Mazauges.[4] The earlier history of this particular volume is not known although in view of the remaining theological contents in the volume and perhaps also in view of the marks on the paper fly-leaves ('Gaii Hirdon' and 'E. Bowzond'), a French origin is likely.

France must, of course, be the graveyard of many other manuscripts and the survivals are no doubt not merely of the fittest nor wholly the result of a natural selection. It is nonetheless worth underlining the presence among French manuscripts of a number of logical texts which may justly reflect the important place held in some French centres by the study of logic in general and of Abelard's logical thought in particular. On the other hand, the small number of theological texts composed by disciples may suggest, although the suggestion must be made timidly, that these texts were less actively circulated both because

---

[1] Médard notes that the ornamental title page on f. 1v was written by one Cauvas-Masson.

[2] F. 69, cited by Geyer, *Abaelards Philosophische Schriften*, I, xi.

[3] Inaccurately described by M. Duhamel, *Catalogue général . . . Départements*, XXXIV, i, 57–8. The work was identified by Ostlender in *Bulletin Thomiste*, VIII (1931), p. 229; cf. *idem*, 'Die Sentenzenbücher', p. 210. The text contains a supplementary fragment on the priestly power to remit sin (f. 65v) which is printed for the first time below, App. I. Nevertheless the Sentences remain incomplete.

[4] I owe this information to M. C. Sibertin-Blanc, Conservateur at the Bibliothèque Inguimbertine.

original works by Abelard were more easily obtainable and because newer works by masters who out-lived Abelard attracted attention more swiftly than in the more distant parts of Europe.

The number of Abelardian manuscripts found in Germanic regions, including the Baltic lands, is relatively very high and some of these were certainly produced in the *scriptoria* of German religious houses or by German scribes and were not merely imported from France.[1] The Benedictine abbey of Einsiedeln in the diocese of Constance produced in the twelfth century a version of the *Sic et Non* as well as five sermons in a Christmas cycle which are explicitly attributed to Abelard (cod. Einsiedeln, Stiftsbibl. 300, pp. 1–74 and 74–94).[2] A very finely written twelfth-century copy of the Sentences of Hermann, St Gall, Stiftsbibl. 69, pp. 417–448, was produced in the St Gall *scriptorium* in the diocese of Constance.[3] In Skåne, Sveno Symonis, a twelfth-century Cistercian at Herisvad, a daughter house of Cîteaux founded by archbishop Eskil of Lund in 1144, copied Abelard's commentary on the *Hexaemeron* but attributed it to Peter, abbot of Cl(uny?). The manuscript is now in the Royal Library at Copenhagen, E don. var. 138.[4] A fifteenth-century copy of the third recension of the *Theologia 'Scholarium'* was made at Cusa,

---

[1] Early scholastic manuscripts in Bavaria and Austria have been the subject of an excellent study by P. Classen, 'Zur Geschichte der Frühscholastik in Österreich und Bayern'. I follow this in a number of respects and have attempted to complete Classen's information concerning Abelardian manuscripts.

[2] See G. Meier, *Catalogus*, I, 274–5, who compares the script with that in other Einsiedeln manuscripts; A. Brückner, *Scriptoria*, V, 182, who affirms on calligraphical grounds that the manuscript originated at Einsiedeln; also a typewritten notice by E. Pellegrin, D. de Saugy and H. Dupont available at the IRHT, Paris. The manuscript was also at Einsiedeln in the fourteenth century, see G. Meier, *Heinrich von Ligerz*, pp. 21, 60. On the texts see E. Buytaert, 'Sic et Non', pp. 415, 423, and D. Van den Eynde, 'Le Recueil des Sermons', pp. 18–19.

[3] See G. Scherrer, *Verzeichniss*, p. 30. The *Sentences* were identified by M. Grabmann, *Geschichte*, II, 223. The origin of the manuscript was determined by A. Brückner, *Scriptoria Medii Aevi Helvetica*, III. *St Gallen*, II, 47, who also found it mentioned in the catalogue of 1461.

[4] The scribe's signature appears on f. 1r and Abelard's text on ff. 19–25. For descriptions see A. Krarup, *Katalog*, II, 17–18, A. Landgraf, 'Zur Methode der Biblischen Textkritik', pp. 445–7, and F. Stegmüller, *Repertorium Biblicum*, IV, n. 6376, VI, n. 9473–94. The manuscript was given to the University Library,

now cod. Ehrenbreitstein (Koblenz), Archives of the Rheno-Westfalian Province of the Capuchins, no number, ff. 103r–161v.[1] The manuscript formerly belonged to the Hospital Library planned c. 1456 by Cardinal Nicholas of Cusa, who is responsible for marginal annotations in this manuscript. Recently Professor R. Klibansky has revealed how these notes formed the basis of discussions which occur in Nicholas' *De pace fidei*.[2] In 1469 Oswald Nott of Tittmoning, a prolific scribe of the monastery of Tegernsee in Bavaria, copied Abelard's *Scito te ipsum* (Clm. 18,597, ff. 1r–47v).[3] Tegernsee was then a centre of reform and its monks have left a great harvest of ascetical literature such as Nott himself was prone to copy.[4] The *Scito te ipsum* is not a work of this variety, yet it aroused some interest in the house. A small leaf inserted between ff. 5 and 6 contains a *Questio* on Abelard's thesis that actions do not add to human merit and another inserted leaf, f. 9rv, contains a discussion with references to the teaching of Alexander of Hales and of John of Asti and concerning the role of human actions in the commission of sins. Another fifteenth-century student who had clearly been reading the Tegernsee copy of the letters of Bernard of Clairvaux (Clm. 18,211, marginalia on ff. 47va, 56rb, 57rab) where he found criticisms of the *Scito te ipsum* has inscribed lengthy warnings in Nott's copy [5] to deter the incautious reader. In 1458 Henry of Waldkirch, a bachelor of arts from Vienna, copied the same work at Heidelberg (cod. Mainz, Stadtbibl. 76, ff.292v–320v).[6] This together with a

[1] Identified by J. Koch, see L. Meier in *Zentralblatt für Bibliothekswesen*, LX (1943), p. 152.
[2] *Nicolai de Cusa De Pace Fidei*, ed. R. Klibansky and H. Bascour, p. 70, n. 7, p. 78, n. 21.
[3] Nott signs and dates his copy on f. 47v; the manuscript is also entered in the Tegernsee catalogue of 1483, Clm. 1925, f. 84v. A description of the manuscript appears in the *Catalogus* (C. Halm *et alii*), II, iii, 187.
[4] On Nott see P. Lindner, *Familia S. Quirini*, pp. 74–5, and V. Redlich, *Tegernsee*, pp. 136, 140, 184, 193.
[5] On f. 1r and on the third unnumbered leaf before f. 1.
[6] On the copyist and provenance of this manuscript see H. Schreiber, *Die Bibliothek der ehemaligen Mainzer Kartause*, p. 62. This copy of the *Ethica* was

Copenhagen, by Count Christian Rantzau, perhaps in 1731 (information of Mr Tue Gad).

row of other Heidelberg manuscripts, some of them copied by Henry himself, came subsequently to the Mainz Charterhouse and it can be traced in the late fifteenth-century catalogue of the Charterhouse books, cod. Mainz, Stadtbibliothek 577, f. 210v.

In the case of several other manuscripts of which the origin cannot be so clearly indicated, indications of provenance are to be found and sometimes these are of an early date. The most beautifully written *Theologia 'Summi boni'* in the twelfth-century Lyell MS. 49, ff. 101r–128v in the Bodleian Library at Oxford,[1] as well as an exceptionally fine twelfth-century copy of the *Sententie Hermanni*, now in Princeton University Library, cod. R. Garrett 169, ff. 83r–151v,[2] belonged in 1376, when the first catalogue of Peter of Arbon was prepared,[3] to the abbey of Admont in the archdiocese of Salzburg and may have originated in the abbey's *scriptorium*. A mid twelfth-century copy of the *Theologia 'Summi boni'*, Erlangen, University Library lat. 182, ff. 27r–65v,[4] which was based upon an exemplar similar to that used by the scribe of the Admont copy, belonged to the abbey of Heilbronn in the diocese of Eichstätt and on the road from

---

[1] Summarily described by R. W. Hunt, 'The Lyell Bequest', p. 76, and fully by N. M. Haring, 'A Third MS. of Peter Abelard's Theologia Summi boni', p. 215.

[2] See S. de Ricci, *Census of Medieval and Renaissance MSS.* II, n. 2295 (then in Baltimore Library), A. M. Gietl, *Die Sentenzen Rolands*, pp. xxii–xxiii, and H. Ostlender in *Bulletin Thomiste*, VIII (1931), p. 229, and also 'Die Sentenzenbücher', pp. 210–12 (then Admont 729).

[3] *Mittelalterliche Bibliothekskataloge Österreichs*, III, 19 ('sentencie Petri Baiolardi') and 30 ('Item Boecius glosatus de sancta trinitate incipit "Investigatam"; in eodem conmentum super Boecium et magister Helias super Boecium').

[4] This manuscript was edited by R. Stölzle and again by H. Ostlender. For descriptions see Ostlender, *Abaelards Theologia 'Summi Boni'*, p. xi, Stölzle, *Abaelards . . . Tractatus*, pp. x et seq., xxxiii et seq., and H. Fischer, *Katalog*, I, 202 et seq. (superseding J. C. Irmischer, *Handschriften Katalog*, n. 229). See too M. Grabmann, *Geschichte*, I, 167–8, and on the relationship with the Admont manuscript, Haring, 'A Third MS. of Peter Abelard's Theologia Summi boni', p. 216.

---

signalled by M. Bernards, 'Zur Überlieferung mittelalterlicher theologischen Schriften', p. 332 and by A. Landgraf, *Introducción*, p. 106; previously by M. Manitius, *Geschichte*, III, 112.

Ansbach to Nuremberg at least by the late thirteenth century.[1] Heilbronn, a Cistercian house, had been founded in 1132 from Ebrach, a daughter of Morimond, and had received books in its earliest days from the nearby Black monks of Michelsberg who were well supplied with philosophical codices.[2] A poor twelfth-century fragment of the *Theologia 'Scholarium'*, Heiligenkreuz, Stiftsbibl. 153, ff. 83r–87v,[3] belonged at least by 1381 to the Cistercians of Heiligenkreuz (diocese of Passau) who had come to the Vienna Woods from Morimond in 1134 or 5.[4] The twelfth-century catalogue of books at Engelberg in the diocese of Constance mentions a lost volume which probably contained the *Sic et Non*[5] as well as another lost volume which probably contained the Sentences of Hermann.[6] This catalogue was compiled between 1147 and 1178 during the abbacy of Frowin who was himself a critic of Abelard's notions of free will and of original sin.[7] Prüfening in the diocese of Regensburg seems to have produced before 1165, the date of Wolfger's catalogue, a most elegant volume containing the *Scito te ipsum* and the Sentences of Hermann, Clm. 14,160, ff. 39v–67r and 1v–39r.[8] The Austin

---

[1] H. Fischer, *op. cit.*, p. 566, no. 92. The catalogue entry reads: 'Boaetius de trinitate in duobus', P. Ruf, *MABK*, III, 2. *Bistum Eichstätt*, p. 212.

[2] H. Fischer, *op. cit.*, pp. 547 *et seq.* and see Ruf, *MABK*, III, 3. *Bistum Bamberg*, pp. 348–65, where many Boethian manuscripts of Michelsberg are noted.

[3] First noticed by M. Grabmann, *Geschichte*, II, 175, n. 1; see also H. Ostlender, 'Die Theologia Scholarium', p. 267, and B. Gsell, *Xenia Bernardina*, II, 159. D. Van den Eynde, 'La "Theologia Scholarium" ', pp. 225–7, considers that the scribe actually copied this text from the Fritzlar manuscript mentioned below, p. 84.

[4] *Mittelalterliche Bibliothekskataloge Österreichs*, I (T. Gottlieb), p. 66, *l.* 19.

[5] 'Imago mundi, dialogus Tullii ad discipulum de moralitate factus, sermones, excerpta auctoritatum a Petro Baiulardo collecta sub eodem volumine', P. Lehmann, *MABK*, I, 32, *ll.* 31–3.

[6] 'Liber magistri Petri de fide et Caritate et de Sacramentis', Lehmann, *MABK*, I, 32, *l.* 9. Cf. the title given to the *Sententie* of Hermann in cod. Pavia, Aldini 49, f. 73r: 'Sententie magistri petri abaialardi de fide et caritate et sacramento.' The tripartite division of sentence works into sections dealing with faith, charity and sacrament is a conspicuously Abelardian feature.

[7] Cf. O. Bauer, 'Frowin von Engelberg', especially p. 300.

[8] See *Catalogus* (C. Halm *et alii*), II, ii, 137–8, and Wolfger's catalogue, ed. G. Becker, *Catalogi*, p. 214, n. 144: 'Sententiae Petri baiol. et liber eius qui

canons of Indersdorf in the diocese of Freising owned in the twelfth century a manual on confession entitled by its anonymous author *Enchiridion*, Clm. 7698, ff. 43r–73v. The work is homiletic and in it Abelard's theory of sin figures prominently amid exhortations to priests to practice confession.[1] Two compendia of dialectic, Wolfenbüttel, Herzog-August-Bibl. 3614 (56,20. Aug. 8vo), ff. 149v–155v and 156r–162r, which contain references to and quotations from Abelard, appear to have been copied in the twelfth century at St Michael's Abbey, Hildesheim,[2] and logical commentaries in the twelfth-century manuscript of St Gall 833, of which the origin is uncertain, are also known to have been influenced by Abelard's teaching.[3]

There are several later manuscripts containing works by Abelard and associated with the Germanic zone. Tegernsee in the diocese of Freising possibly possessed as early as the thirteenth century a copy made in the same century of the *Sic et Non*,

[1] See f. 1r: *Iste Liber est monasterii in undestorf* (twelfth century). The work was identified and discussed by H. Weisweiler, 'Eine neue Bearbeitung', pp. 369–71; cf. also H. Ostlender, 'Die Sentenzenbücher', p. 251.

[2] See M. Grabmann, 'Bearbeitungen', pp. 26–31, and O. von Heinemann, *Die Handschriften der Herzoglichen Bibliothek, 2e Abtheilung. Die Augusteischen Hss.*, v, 84–5.

[3] See Grabmann, 'Bearbeitungen', pp. 46–7, 54. Also G. Scherrer, *Verzeichniss*, p. 283; the manuscript appears to have been produced in a German environment.

---

dicitur scito teipsum et sent. m. Hugonis in uno volumine.' On the recto side of the fly-leaf at the front of the volume, the inscription 'Emmerammum' has been added over an erasure and, as A. Boeckler has also observed (*Die Regensburg-Prüfeninger Buchmalerei*, p. 120), the capitals in the volume are in the style of the Prüfening school of illumination. However, H. Weisweiler (*Das Schrifttum*, p. 27) has reported an opinion advanced by Dr L. Ott that the manuscript is not identical with that recorded in the Prüfening catalogue because Clm. 14,160 contains a further work copied by the same scribe ('Liber domini Hugonis de claustralibus', ff. 157v–206v) which would not have escaped the notice of a cataloguer. No doubt Prüfening could have produced two nearly similar volumes, the larger of which had already been sent to St Emmeram in Regensburg before Wolfger compiled his catalogue, but Ott's opinion rests on an argument from silence and on the assumption that Wolfger was not content with or capable of a partial summary of the contents of this manuscript.

now Clm. 18,926,[1] and it also owned the now lost Clm. 19,134, which contained a late twelfth- or early thirteenth-century version of the *Sentences* of Omnebene.[2] Klosterneuberg in the diocese of Passau, a house of which Otto of Freising was once provost, owned in the thirteenth century a copy made early in that century of the *Dialogus* as well as of the *Exortatio magistri ad discipulum de inquisitione summi boni* (Vienna, Nationalbibliothek lat. 819, ff. 1r–59v and 59v–61a).[3] Jodocus Chuon, a chaplain of the Grossmünster in Zurich in 1447, is the earliest known possessor of an early thirteenth-century copy of the *Sic et Non*, cod. Zurich, Kantons- und Universitätsbibliothek (Stiftsbibliothek) Car. C. 162, ff. 23r–38v.[4] The Dominicans of Soest near Arnsberg had at some date in the middle ages a late thirteenth-century manuscript containing Abelard's Sermon *de dedicatione* and his commentaries on the Lord's Prayer and the Apostolic and Pseudo-Athanasian Creeds; the codex, however, Münster

[1] See *Catalogus* (C. Halm *et alii*), II, ii, 221, and E. L. T. Henke and G. S. Lindenkohl, *Petri Abaelardi Sic et Non*, pp. vi–xii (reprinted in PL. 178, 1331–4). A thirteenth-century inscription appears inside the cover and the manuscript is recorded in the 1483 catalogue, Clm. 1925, f. 84v. I have been unable to identify the (apparently fifteenth-century) gift mentioned by V. Redlich, *Tegernsee*, p. 237 (cited from Clm. 1005, f. 50r): 'D. Conradus Nüssl pleb(anus) in Ismaning (*alia manu*) dedit librum Abalardi in pergameno.'
[2] This manuscript was destroyed at Louvain in the first world war. A. M. Gietl's full transcript survives in the Bavarian State Library, Clm. 19,134A, as well as a photographic copy given by J. de Ghellinck, Cod. Sim. 168. See also Gietl's edition of the Sentences of Roland, *Die Sentenzen Rolands*, pp. XXIII, L.
[3] The manuscript was used by F. H. Rheinwald for his edition of the *Dialogus* (reprinted in PL. 178, 1609–1682 and in Cousin, *Opera*, II, 643–718). For descriptions see M. Denis, *Codices*, I, ii, 1996 *et seq.* (cod. DXXI (666)); and *Tabulae Cod. MSS.* (W. von Hartel *et alii*), I, cvp. 819. The manuscript title (f. 1r) is identical with the entry in the Klosterneuberg catalogue: *Dialogus Petri Baiolardi* (*Mittelalterliche Bibliothekskataloge Österreichs*, I (T. Gottlieb), p. 99).
  P. Lehmann mistakenly thought that cod. Prague, University Library XXIII E 63, Lobkovic 444, ff. 7r–117v, contains the *Dialogus* and Abelard's Sermons, *Mitteilungen aus Handschriften*, III, 22, n. 30 (and hence too A. Landgraf, *Introducción*, p. 107). Lehmann was misled by an inaccurate twelfth- or thirteenth-century rubric on f. 7r ('Incipiunt sermones petri baiolardi') and by the *incipit* on the same folio ('Aspiciebam ego in visione noctis').
[4] C. Mohlberg, *Katalog*, I, i, 136; A. Brückner, *Scriptoria*, IV, 98; P. Lehmann, *MABK*, I, 461.

G

University, Bibliotheca Paulina 81 (312), was destroyed in the last war and more precise indications of its history are not possible.[1] Another lost manuscript, a *Theologia 'Scholarium'* of uncertain date, is mentioned in the late fifteenth-century catalogue of the Dominican house in Vienna which was founded in 1226.[2] A fifteenth-century copy of the *Theologia 'Scholarium'* survives today in the German State Library in Berlin. The version, formerly of the Magdeburg Domgymnasium 34, ff. 193r–261v, may have been transcribed in or near Magdeburg and is textually similar to the one found in the Hospital Library of Nicholas of Cusa.[3] Finally, two further copies, both of the twelfth or thirteenth century, exist of which the whereabouts in the middle ages are unknown. They are codd. Fritzlar, Pfarrbibliothek, no number, ff. 94v–101r (now in the Priesterseminar Library at Fulda),[4] and Zurich, Zentralbibliothek C. 61, ff. 53v–60v.[5]

Works by Abelard's disciples are also relatively well represented in Germanic areas and some of these have already been mentioned; eight remain. The regular canons of St Nicholas near Passau possessed in their library a disorderly hotchpotch of theological texts which had interested an unknown student of the twelfth century who may have been a canon at St Nicholas. On ff. 104r–142v of the present Clm. 16,085 he copied and annotated

---

[1] Identified by H. Weisweiler, *Maître Simon*, pp. xxxiv–xxxv; see also J. Staender, *Catalogus*, p. 18.

[2] 'Summa theologie magistri Petri, incipit Scholarium nostrorum peticioni', *Mittelalterliche Bibliothekskataloge Österreichs* (T. Gottlieb), 1, 343, *l.* 36.

[3] Identified by Dr J. Koch, see H. Ostlender, 'Die Theologia Scholarium', p. 270. H. Dittmar, *Die Handschriften und alten Drucke des Dom-Gymnasiums*, 1 (Magdeburg 1878) has not been available to me. Dr Hans Lülfing of the Deutsche Staatsbibliothek (in correspondence) describes the manuscript as middle German with 424 folios; a date, 1452, is found on f. 284v. On the textual similarity with the Cusa manuscript see Buytaert, 'Thomas of Morigny', p. 83.

[4] Identified by A. Landgraf in *Scholastik*, IX (1934), p. 227. Cf. *idem, Ecrits théologiques*, pp. xiii, 293, and H. Ostlender, 'Die Theologia Scholarium', p. 281, n. 89. Full description by H. Weisweiler in *Scholastik*, XXXI (1956), p. 475; Weisweiler, unlike Landgraf, dates the copy as twelfth century.

[5] H. Ostlender, 'Die Theologia Scholarium', p. 267; C. Mohlberg, *Katalog*, 1, i, 34; H. Weisweiler, *Das Schrifttum*, pp. 161 et seq., and D. Van den Eynde, 'La "Theologia Scholarium"', pp. 227–8.

the *Sentences* of Hermann.[1] St Peter's in Salzburg owned, according to its late twelfth-century catalogue, a now lost copy of the *Sententie Petri Bailardi* which are probably the *Sentences* compiled by Hermann.[2] Some extracts concerning the sacrament of the eucharist and taken from the same work were identically reproduced in two manuscripts, the first of the twelfth century, Cologne, Stadtarchiv W. 137, f. 5rv which belonged at an unknown date to the regular canons of Niederwerth near Vallendar[3] and the second, Trier, Stadtbibliothek 591, ff. 114v–115v,[4] a copy of the twelfth or early thirteenth century, which was probably at St Eucharius in Trier in 1243[5] and certainly at St Matthias in Trier in the mid fifteenth century.[6] The former manuscript also contained on f. 179v the now erased beginning of what appears to be a twelfth-century copy of the *Theologia*

---

[1] See H. Weisweiler, 'Un manuscrit inconnu', pp. 245–69. Since the manuscript contains the *De vitanda missa uxoratorum sacerdotum* attributed to Berwin, abbot of Reichersberg, and found only here and in a manuscript from Lamspringe (Wolfenbüttel 782; twelfth century), a German origin is likely.

[2] G. Becker, *Catalogi*, 237, n. 211. Cf. the titles given to this work in three other manuscripts: Princeton, Garrett 169, f. 83r ('Sentencie petri baiolardi'), Clm. 14,160, f. 2r ('Sentencie Magistri Petri Abelardi') and Pavia, Aldini 49, f. 73r ('Sententie magistri petri abaialardi...'). On the other hand St Omer 115 ('Sententiae Petri Abaelardi') contains Abelard's verses to Astralabe. Among extant Viennese manuscripts cod. Nationalbibliothek lat. 2486 of the late twelfth century and containing on ff. 45r–60v a commentary on the *Isagoge* of Porphyry with references to Abelard, probably comes from one of the Salzburg libraries. See *Tabulae codicum MSS.*, II, 82 ('Salisb. 388') and M. Grabmann, 'Ein Tractatus', pp. 63–4.

[3] Noticed by H. Weisweiler, 'Un manuscrit inconnu', p. 265. *Ex libris* inscriptions of Niederwerth ('Liber monasterii beate Marie in Insula prope Valender ordinis canonicorum regularium' and, in a later hand, 'Liber Societatis Jesu confluen(tie)') were found on f. 1 when Dr Kelleter compiled his handwritten description of the manuscript collection (1894–7), but are now missing. Dr Gerig of the Stadtarchiv considers that the inscription now present on f. 225r ('Liber monasterii beate Marie virginis in Insula sub confluentia ordinis Canonicorum Regularium', i.e. Beatusberg, diocese of Trier; cited also by Weisweiler, *Das Schrifttum*, p. 211) appears as the result of a binder's mistake made in 1897.

[4] H. Weisweiler, 'Eine neue Bearbeitung', pp. 366–8; the extract, entitled *De specie panis et vini*, is edited from the Trier manuscript, here p. 368 (= PL. 178, 1743B–1744A).

[5] M. Keuffer, *Beschreibendes Verzeichniss*, V, 45.

[6] J. Montebaur, *Studien*, pp. 71–2, no. 236.

'*Scholarium*'.[1] The regular canons of St Florian (diocese of Passau) were the possessors of the only surviving copy of a Sentence work written under Abelard's inspiration (Sankt Florian XI 264, ff. 147r–163v).[2] Benediktbeuern abbey in the diocese of Freising came into possession at an uncertain date of a work dependent upon Abelard and upon the *Summa Sententiarum* and entitled *Bernardi abbatis sententie*; the single copy, Clm. 4,600, ff. 68r–72v, is of the twelfth century.[3] The *Sentences* of Roland Bandinelli, which survive only in a late twelfth- or early thirteenth-century manuscript, Nuremberg, Stadtbibliothek, Cent. III 77, ff. 144r–178r, cannot be traced before the mid sixteenth century when they appear in the catalogue of the books of St Egidius in Nuremberg.[4] Finally two twelfth-century codices, belonging formerly to St Emmeram in Regensburg, contain many indications of Abelard's logical teaching. Clm. 14,779 contains a row of glosses which resemble the *Introductiones Parvulorum*[5]

---

[1] See my Ph.D. dissertation, *Peter Abelard's Following* (Cambridge University Library, 1964), pp. 114–21.

[2] Identified by H. Denifle, 'Die Sentenzen Abaelards', pp. 424–34 and edited by H. Ostlender. Cf. E. Bertola, 'Le "Sententiae Florianenses"', pp. 368–78, M. Grabmann, *Geschichte*, II, 224, and Ostlender, 'Die Sentenzenbücher', p. 218. On the manuscript see A. Czerny, *Die Handschriften*, p. 110, and B. Geyer, 'Neues und Altes', p. 618. Against the suggestion of A. Gietl (in his edition of Roland's Sentences, p. xxiii) that the author of the *Sententie* lived in Italy see Ostlender, *ed. cit.*, p. vi.

[3] The text is analysed by H. Weisweiler, 'Eine neue Bearbeitung', pp. 346–71; Weisweiler's transcriptions are sometimes faulty. See too *Catalogus cod. lat. Bibl. Regiae Monacensis*, ed. altera, I, i, 213. The manuscript does not appear to be listed in the thirteenth-century Benediktbeuern catalogue published by P. Ruf, *MABK*, III, i, 64–5, and it lacks medieval inscriptions of provenance.

[4] Described by A. Gietl, *Die Sentenzen Rolands*, pp. VI–VII, LXVIII–LXX. The Nuremberg Stadtbibliothek possesses photographs of *Kataloge von Klosterbibliotheken von Nürnberg 1554/1555*. These catalogues were compiled after the secularization of the religious houses in 1538 and in the *Catalogus Liborum Monasterii Egidiani*, p. 30, we read: 'M(embraneum). Sententie Berdlandi E. 21'. Cf. the rubric on f. 144r of the manuscript: *InCipiunt Sententie Rddlandi bononiensis magistri Auctoritatibus Rationibus fortes* and, in another hand, *berddlandi.sententie*.

[5] Neither G. Shepss, 'Zum lateinischen Aristoteles', nor S. Brandt, *Boethii operum pars I, Prolegomena*, pp. lxvi–lxvii, decided the exact literary relationship between the two sets of works. I have argued in my unpublished disserta-

and on ff. 67v–86v a commentary on Boethius' *De syllogismo hypothetico* which refers often to Abelard.[1] Clm. 14,458, ff. 45r–56r contains a *Dialectica* in which Abelard is much cited.[2]

The manuscripts of the Germanic zone are particularly interesting. They suggest strongly that several of the theological works of Abelard's followers were written by German students and that in addition Gerhoh of Reichersberg had some basis for his protests against the progress of Abelardian as well as of Porretan teachings in the middle of Europe. The good number of south German and of Austrian manuscripts shows that something was stirring in the religious houses of this part of the world and that scholasticism of the French type had penetrated into the cloisters of central Europe. It is particularly important to note the concentration of manuscripts in the circle of adjacent dioceses constituted by Salzburg, Passau, Freising, Regensburg, Eichstätt and Constance. Many of these manuscripts were produced locally and were not merely imported.

By contrast, Italian manuscripts with an Abelardian interest are rare and difficult to identify. The best attested of them appears to be lost: Bernard of Clairvaux hinted that a member or members of the Roman Curia possessed the *Theologia* when he wrote to them: 'Read, if you please, the book of Peter Abelard which he entitles *Theology*, since you have it at hand',[3] and among the books bequeathed by Cardinal Guy (Pope Celestine II) on his death in 1144 to the church of Città di Castello in Umbria where he seems to have been a canon, were copies of the *Sic et Non* and of the *Theologia cum libro 'retractationum'*.[4] Extracts, apparently from Hermann's Sentences or from a very similar collection and concerning the Redemption, are now found inserted among Augustinian fragments in a twelfth-century manuscript, Florence, Medicea Laurenziana, Aedilium 142, pp.

[1] M. Grabmann, 'Bearbeitungen', pp. 24–6.
[2] *Ibid.*, pp. 16–24.   [3] *Epist.* 188 (PL. 182, 353B).
[4] A. Wilmart, 'Les livres légués par Célestin II'.

tion (King's College Library, Cambridge), pp. 225–34, that the glosses on the *Isagoge* (ff. 31r–36v) are the work of a disciple and dependent upon the glosses of Abelard.

199b–203, which may have been copied in central or western Italy and which belonged to the cathedral library of Florence in the fifteenth century.[1] The origins of all the other Italian manuscripts are obscure. The Monte Cassino manuscript 174.0, which like the manuscript of Cardinal Guy contains the *Theologia Christiana* (pp. 133–276)[2] and the *Sic et Non* (pp. 277–451),[3] together with the *Retractationes* of Augustine (pp. 53–132), is apparently of the twelfth century[4] and has been said to have been locally produced.[5] Two manuscripts of the *Sentences* of Master Omnebene of Bologna are in Italy: cod. Monte Cassino 386 G, pp. 57–87, of the twelfth or early thirteenth century,[6] and cod. Naples, Biblioteca Nazionale VII. C. 43, ff. 1r–90v, of the twelfth century and belonging to St Severinus in Naples in the sixteenth century.[7] The very important cod. Milan, Ambrosiana M. 63 sup. which contains on ff. 1r–72r a large part of the *Logica 'Ingredientibus'* in a copy of the late twelfth or early thirteenth

---

[1] The extracts constitute the so-called *Homilia*, PL. 47, 1211–19, properly identified by J. Rivière, 'Quelques faits nouveaux'. See also A. M. Bandinius, *Bibliotheca Leopoldina Laurentiana*, I, especially 416, 418. I am grateful to the Director of the Bibl. Medicea Laurenziana for information concerning the history of this manuscript.

[2] Identified by L. Tosti, *Storia di Abaelardo*, pp. 283 *et seq.* after B. Montfaucon, *Bibliotheca Bibliothecarum*, I, 223 had attributed it to St Augustine. Tosti published previously inedited fragments, pp. 286–94; cf. *Bibliotheca Casinensis*, IV, 5 *et seq.* Further textual analysis by D. Van den Eynde, 'Les Rédactions' and by E. Buytaert, 'Critical Observations'.

[3] Fragments were published by Tosti, *op. cit.*, pp. 295–315 (with facsimile on p. 279); cf. *Bibliotheca Casinensis*, IV, *loc. cit.* Textual discussion by M. Deutsch, *Peter Abaelard*, p. 457, and by E. Buytaert, 'Sic et Non'.

[4] In favour of the twelfth century are the *Bibliotheca Casinensis*, IV, *loc. cit.*, Van den Eynde and Buytaert; M. Inguanez, *Catalogus*, I, i, 257–8, and H. Ostlender, *Abaelards Theologia 'Summi Boni'*, p. xxvii, thought it to be of the thirteenth century.

[5] So Buytaert, 'Sic et Non', p. 415, without giving reasons. Tosti, *op. cit.*, p. 285, thought it was brought to Monte Cassino from Provence by Bernard Ayglier, abbot of Lerins from 1256 and of Monte Cassino from 1263 to 1282; but he produced no evidence and on the previous page had suggested that the manuscript supported the complaints made by Bernard of Clairvaux that Abelard's writings were circulating south of the Alps.

[6] Identified by A. Landgraf in *Divus Thomas* (Freiburg), XI (1933), p. 159, n. 4. Cf. Inguanez, *Catalogus*, II, 248–9.

[7] Identified by M. Grabmann, *Geschichte*, II, 227.

century has been in the Ambrosian Library since its foundation in the early seventeenth century;[1] it was received by Cardinal Federigo Borromeo as a gift from Camillo Bossi of Modena in 1605, but its earlier history is not known.[2] The last part of the commentary on Aristotle's *De interpretatione* contained in this manuscript has been shown by Dr Minio-Paluello[3] to have issued from a circle in which were debated problems similar to those discussed by Abelard, and the same manuscript also contains on ff. 72v–81v a commentary on Porphyry's *Isagoge* composed by a disciple of Abelard.[4] Dr Minio-Paluello believes that the authentic and complete version of Abelard's commentary on the *De interpretatione* in the *corpus* of his *Logica 'Ingredientibus'* is found in a copy made by an Italian scribe of the late twelfth century in cod. Berlin, Deutsche Staatsbibliothek lat. fol. 624, ff. 97r–146r. This manuscript belonged to St Victor in Paris in the later middle ages.[5] Italy is known to have played a part in the cultivation of logical studies in the twelfth century. Italy provided translators such as James of Venice and Burgundio of Pisa.[6] John of Salisbury

---

[1] Ed. from this manuscript by B. Geyer; for descriptions see Geyer, *Abaelards Philosophische Schriften*, I, x, and L. Minio-Paluello, *Abaelardiana Inedita*, p. xvi. The manuscript was noted by B. Montfaucon, *Bibliotheca Bibliothecarum*, I, 521D and in the *Histoire littéraire de la France*, XII (1763), 130.

[2] According to the handwritten *Inventario Ceruti* (information of the Prefect, Mgr C. Castiglione): 'Hic codex fuit ad ill.mum card. Federicum a Camillo Bossio mutina dono missus anno 1605. Olgiatus scripsit.' Antonius Olgiatus was prefect of the Library till 1647. Bossius or Bossi is also known to have given in 1606 four Greek manuscripts of the fifteenth and sixteenth centuries; these manuscripts contain philosophical and especially Aristotelian writings, see A. Martini and D. Bassi, *Catalogus cod. graecorum*, nos. 200, 298, 688 and 1042. G. Mazzuchelli, *Gli Scrittori d'Italia*, II, ii, 1839, says that Bossi acquired manuscripts for Borromeo from Reggio and Modena. I have been unable to consult the letters to Borromeo from Bossi listed in *Card. Federico Borromeo. Indice delle lettere a lui dirette conservate all'Ambrosiana* (Fontes Ambrosiani, XXXIV. Milan 1960), p. 79.

[3] *Abaelardiana inedita*, pp. xvi–xxi.

[4] *Glossae super librum Porphyrii secundum vocales*, ed. C. Ottaviano; incomplete ed. by B. Geyer. See also Geyer, *Untersuchungen*, pp. 601–12.

[5] The commentary was discovered by M. Grabmann, 'Kommentare', pp. 203–5, and the latter part of it is ed. by Minio-Paluello, *op. cit.*, pp. 1–108. For descriptions of the manuscript see Grabmann, 'Kommentare', especially pp. 185–6, and Minio-Paluello, *op. cit.*, pp. xii–xvi.

[6] See Minio-Paluello, 'Jacobus Veneticus Grecus'.

tells in his *Metalogicon* how his own master within the years 1136 to 1148, Master Alberic, a zealous anti-nominalist who 'even in the bulrush would be sure to discover knots in need of untying', left Paris for Bologna. When he returned to Paris he 'untaught' what he had 'unlearned' in Bologna.[1] One possible implication of this remark is that Bologna was not a place where the serious logician, or at least an Alberic, should stay for too long. But it is interesting that in one of the other commentaries in the Berlin manuscript, a commentary on Porphyry's *Isagoge* (ff. 73vb–76rb), the opinions of a Master A. whom Grabmann[2] considered to be Master Alberic are often preferred to those of Abelard, and also that the scribe was, if not certainly resident in Italy, at any rate Italian.

Two other manuscripts, now in Italian libraries, are also of unknown origin. One of these, cod. Brescia, Biblioteca Queriniana A.V. 21, ff. 17r–64v, contains the *Sic et Non* in a copy of the twelfth century[3] and the other, which is likewise in a good script of the twelfth century, contains the *Sentences* of Hermann, cod. Pavia, University Library, Aldini 49, ff. 73r–88v.[4] The relatively small number of Abelardian manuscripts in Italy today does not necessarily reflect the way in which such manuscripts were diffused in the twelfth century. It is possible that the progress of enquiries into the identification of early scholastic texts is made with greater difficulty in Italy than elsewhere. Moreover, texts do not only immigrate; they also emigrate, as may be the case with the Berlin manuscript. Neither Roland nor Omnebene at Bologna could have lacked some texts from France; in addition, Bernard's complaint that Abelard's writings circulated in Rome seems, from the example of Cardinal Guy, to have been accurate.

The yield of English libraries is similar in terms of numbers of

---

[1] John of Salisbury, *Metalogicon*, II, 10 (ed. Webb, pp. 78–9).
[2] 'Kommentare', pp. 194–9. I have studied and edited this commentary in my Fellowship Dissertation (King's College Library, Cambridge), pp. 235–94.
[3] First signalled by P. Ruf and M. Grabmann, 'Ein neuaufgefundenes Bruchstück', p. 21, n. 2.
[4] See L. de Marchi, *Inventario*, I, 21–2; H. Ostlender in *Bulletin Thomiste*, VIII (1931), p. 229 and *idem*, 'Die Sentenzenbücher', pp. 210–12.

manuscripts to that of Italian libraries and in terms of their significance. In addition provenance is much more easily established. Cod. Durham, Cathedral Library A. IV. 15, ff. 57r–65v appears to be an original Durham copy of the first book of the *Theologia Christiana* made in the mid twelfth century.[1] Other Durham manuscripts suggest that there were good contacts between the cathedral and the schools of France in the twelfth century and an anonymous gloss on St John's Gospel, 1, 1–21, 18, which appears on ff. 17–56 of cod. A. IV. 15, is in other manuscripts ascribed to Anselm, perhaps Anselm of Laon.[2] Durham's prior, Lawrence (d. 1154), was cited with Abelard in a small French collection of theological extracts, cod. Rouen, Bibl. municipale 553.[3] The *Sic et Non* was copied in the twelfth century in England by three or four fine hands which show affinities with the scripts of the Canterbury school, cod. Cambridge, University Library Kk. iii. 24, ff. 67v–159r.[4] The unique copy of the *Ysagoge in theologiam*, cod. Trinity College, Cambridge, B. 14. 33, was written in England in the twelfth century and belonged c. 1200 to the abbey of Cerne in Dorset.[5] Moreover, a rearrangement of a large part of the *Ysagoge* is found in two manuscripts,

[1] First identified by E. Rathbone in her dissertation *The Influence of Bishops*. See R. A. B. Mynors, *Durham Cathedral MSS.*, n. 61, pp. 51–2, and T. Rud, *Catalogus*, pp. 66–7. Also E. Buytaert, 'An Earlier Redaction', and D. Van den Eynde, 'Les Ecrits perdus', pp. 473–4.
[2] Mynors, *Durham Cathedral MSS.*, loc. cit.
[3] F. 135va: *Laur(entius) dunellensis*; f. 134ra: *M(agister) P(etrus) Abaelardus*. H. Omont, *Catalogue général . . . Départements, I*, 131 and E. Jeauneau, 'Glâne chartraine', pp. 3, 7.
[4] Mr H. L. Pink of the University Library kindly identified the hands for me. M. R. James, in a handwritten description of the manuscript available in the University Library, also identified one of the hands (beginning on f. 87r) as reminiscent of Christ Church, Canterbury. The manuscript was noted by C. Oudin as cod. 168 (cf. PL. 178, 64); E. von Dobschütz, *Das Decretum Gelasianum*, p. 151, suggested (without foundation) that the manuscript came from France. See also *A Catalogue of the Manuscripts*, III, 631–3. A sixteenth-century transcript, apparently of the University Library copy of the *Sic et Non*, is found in the Library of Corpus Christi College, Cambridge, cod. 165. See E. Bernard, *Catalogi*, I, iii, n. 1658; C. Oudin (cit. PL. 178, 64); W. Cave, *Scriptores*, I, 653, and M. R. James, *A Descriptive Catalogue*, I, 374.
[5] Ed. Landgraf. On the complicated history of this manuscript see my forthcoming article in the *AHDLMA*.

both apparently English in origin.[1] One, cod. British Museum, Harley 3038, ff. 3r–7v, belonged in 1176 to the Cistercian abbey of Buildwas, near Shrewsbury,[2] and the other, British Museum, Royal 10. A. XII, ff. 117v–123r, was acquired for Rochester priory in 1202 or slightly later.[3] Buildwas was also the twelfth-century home of the only extant copy of a lengthy Pauline commentary written by a faithful disciple of Abelard, the *Commentarius Cantabrigiensis* which is found in the twelfth-century Cambridge manuscript, Trinity College, B. 1. 39.[4] A late twelfth- or early thirteenth-century copy of a part of the *Sic et Non* and of a part of the *Dialogus* belonged to the Austin priory of Merton in Surrey at least by the fourteenth century and is now in the British Museum, Royal 11. A. V, ff. 73r–98v and 99r–109v.[5] A thirteenth-century copy of the *Theologia* '*Scholarium*', now British Museum, Royal 8. A. I, ff. 3r–69r, belonged once, according to a deleted inscription on f. 1v, to a monastery or church whose name ended in -*ford*.[6] A most valuable fourteenth-century collection of the major theological works— the *Theologia* '*Scholarium*', *Dialogus*, *Commentary on Romans* and *Scito te ipsum*—which is now in Balliol College, Oxford, cod. 296, was produced in England and the copyists knew of two differing

---

[1] I am most grateful to Miss E. Rathbone for lending me her notes of this discovery.

[2] An *ex libris* inscription is found on f. 7v; see *A Catalogue of the Harleian Manuscripts* (R. Nares and others), II, 727.

[3] An *ex libris* inscription is found on f. 8r; see G. F. Warner and J. P. Gilson, *Catalogue*, I, 307–9.

[4] Ed. Landgraf. An *ex libris* inscription is found on f. 1r and the manuscript is described by Landgraf, *Commentarius Cantabrigiensis*, part I, vii–x, and by M. R. James, *The Western MSS. in the Library of Trinity College*, I, 50–2.

[5] See G. F. Warner and J. P. Gilson, *Catalogue*, I, 337; E. Bernard, *Catalogi*, II, n. 8206. In the twelfth century John of Salisbury had been connected with the priory, see R. L. Poole, 'The Early Lives of Robert Pulleyn and Nicholas Breakspear', p. 66. An opinion of Abelard on the fixity of the divine power is cited in a thirteenth-century manuscript given to Merton by David of London and also containing works by Stephen of Tournai and Alan of Lille; British Museum, Royal 9. E. XII, f. 255v, cited by A. Landgraf, 'Beiträge', p. 363; see also Warner and Gilson, *op. cit.*, I, 296–9.

[6] See Warner and Gilson, *op. cit.*, I, 207 and H. Ostlender, 'Die Theologia Scholarium', p. 270. The earliest reference to the manuscript is by E. Bernard, *Catalogi*, II, i, n. 8670.

exemplars of the 'Scholarium' and the Scito te ipsum. The manuscript may have belonged to William Gray, bishop of Ely, who died in 1478.[1]

The evidence of all these manuscripts contributes to an understanding of the nature of the appeal of Abelard's writings and of those of his followers to twelfth-century scholars. Manuscripts containing Abelard's logical writings are relatively few in number. Although, as John of Salisbury shows in his Metalogicon and Abelard in his Historia Calamitatum, logic was the subject of passionate disputes arousing widespread interest, documents presenting these debates are not abundant.[2] Of Abelard's logical writings some are lost and only one (the commentary on the De interpretatione in the Logica 'Ingredientibus') survives in more than a single copy. Yet in comparison with the works of contemporaries, those of Abelard survive extremely well for the logical writings of Roscelin, William of Champeaux, Master Alberic, Jocelyn of Soissons, Bernard of Chartres and Robert of Melun are entirely lacking while from Adam of the Petit Pont we have only two copies of the Ars disserendi.[3] The habit of publishing one's logical teaching may have been under-developed among the logicians and quite possibly manuscripts of logic have had a poorer chance of surviving through the centuries. Those of Abelard are for the most part exceptional in bearing clear, contemporary indications of their author. The evidence collected suggests that the logical teaching of Abelard and of other masters was discussed not only in Paris but also in several other centres, at Fleury on the Loire, in the circle of Robert of Torigny, in some of the religious houses of Germany and possibly too in Italy. Copying, however, appears to have ceased in the thirteenth century and it is then that a new period begins in the history of logic characterized by the work of such masters as Lambert of Auxerre, William of

---

[1] For a full and excellent description see R. A. B. Mynors, *A Catalogue*, pp. 314–17; cf. for some further details on seventeenth-century copies made from the Balliol manuscript my 'Towards a new edition of Peter Abelard's *Ethica*', pp. 123–6.

[2] To say this is not to ignore the series of discoveries made by the late M. Grabmann in several of his more recent articles.

[3] Ed. L. Minio-Paluello.

Shyreswood and Peter of Spain and by the absorption of further translations of Aristotle's logical writings.

The appeal of Abelard's theological writing was more varied and complex. Two of the three extant copies of the *Theologia* '*Summi boni*' —the two copies are related and perhaps by a common exemplar circulating somewhere in Germany[1]—are found in the midst of other Trinitarian works of Boethian inspiration. The influence of the tradition of commenting upon the *De trinitate* of Boethius is perhaps responsible for Abelard's work being described in these manuscripts as *libri de trinitate*, although the correct title was in fact *Theologia*.[2] The work must have appealed, by virtue of its discussions of the theses of the *pseudo-dialectici* of the day, to those working within the Boethian philosophical tradition which was soon to flower, in the years after the condemnation of this work in 1121, at Paris and Poitiers with Thierry and Gilbert. Both the *Theologia* '*Summi boni*' of Abelard and the Trinitarian work of Gilbert were the subject of heresy trials in 1121 and in 1148 respectively and it is significant that Master Thierry was out of sympathy with the judges of Abelard's book at Soissons.

The *Theologia Christiana* and *Theologia* '*Scholarium*' were fuller in content and in range of discussion than the '*Summi boni*', richer in the citation of prophetic, philosophical and patristic material and more elaborate in the analysis of many central questions about the divine trinity and unity. But these works are monographs written when a strong theological current favoured the systematization of all theological *quaestiones* in collections of *sententie*. The *Sentences* of the Lombard largely grow out of the Victorine *Summa Sententiarum* which themselves largely grow out of the sentence collections of the Laon school. Abelard, on the other hand, preferred, like Anselm of Canterbury, to write theological monographs: a *Theologia* on God, an *Ethica*, even perhaps an *Anthropologia*. Only in the *Sic et Non* did Abelard sketch out a comprehensive list containing at its fullest 158 questions which would have been an adequate schema for a *summa*

[1] See above, p. 80.
[2] Cf. Ostlender, *Abaelards Theologia 'Summi Boni'*, pp. xx–xxiii.

if Abelard had been intent on providing solutions as well as texts in the way that Peter Lombard was later to do. In the *Theologia* and *Ethica* as well as in the commentary on Romans, the author's personal slant or bias is much in evidence and the high points occur when Abelard is formulating a pronouncedly personal thesis: 'Sufficit mihi in omnibus que scribo opinionem meam magis exponere quam diffinicionem veritatis promittere.'[1] To judge by the standards of discretion and sobriety followed by Hugh of St Victor, Abelard's major works seem immodest or certainly unsuitable to become a general basis for teaching. When many of Abelard's followers presented his opinions in the sentence works, the brevity of discussion tended to make the controversial opinions appear all the more controversial.

The state in which Abelard's texts were circulated is another most important factor concerning their appeal and influence. The texts of many of Abelard's writings are found in the manuscripts in a fluid state of continual evolution and alteration. Many texts are moreover incompletely present. The *Theologia 'Summi boni'* survives in two forms; the *Theologia Christiana* in four; the *'Scholarium'* in five. All the ten manuscripts of the *Sic et Non* contain different features. Some works appear to have been rehandled by pupils; such are the Paris copy of the Commentary on the *Hexaemeron*, the commentary on the *De interpretatione* in the Milan copy of the *Logica 'Ingredientibus'*, and the Commentary on the *Isagoge* in the *Logica 'Nostrorum petitioni sociorum'*.[2] It would not be possible to produce for any of these works a text such as Dom Schmitt presented of St Anselm's *Cur Deus Homo* which corresponds letter for letter with the text carefully fixed by Anselm himself. Abelard so tinkered with his texts that some additions were only incorporated by the copyists with great difficulty and amounted to poorly inserted duplications of previous passages.[3] It would appear that Abelard did not care overmuch about editing his work for publication and that he sometimes made his writing available as it stood, warts and all, for transcription and for circulation among an unsettled, even

---

[1] *Ethica*, I (cod. Oxford, Balliol College, 296, f. 79v).
[2] See above, pp. 67, 89, 77.   [3] See Buytaert, 'Critical Observations'.

rootless, public. He told in his *Historia Calamitatum* how many came to transcribe his expositions of Ezechiel before they were finished.[1] In later days Abelard might possibly have spared himself some anguish if the versions of his teaching which were circulating and which provoked his critics could have been previously subject to stricter control by himself. The sheer chaos of the varieties of the versions of the *Sic et Non* constitutes an editorial nightmare and it is no wonder that a modern editor should describe such volatile texts as 'poor'.[2] But, as with the far more numerous and complicated versions of the *Concordia* of Gratian which too almost defies being constricted within the stable limits of a modern printed edition, the varieties in the texts are rich evidence for the historian of the progress of the composition as well as of the research and the thought and the activities of master and students. Abelard swelled the repertory of texts in the *Sic et Non* by additions and by the formulation of further questions while his Prologue remained virtually unchanged, and as his inventories grew, the copies that were made and were taken away by students were varied. The complexity of these textual traditions is a vivid witness to the atmosphere of some schools, to the pressure of the demand for texts, to the liberty with which they were shared and to the composition of the readers—a bystanding audience of visiting students who, if we may believe Abelard, pressed him to write up his teaching in the *Logica 'Nostrorum petitioni sociorum'* and *Theologia 'Scholarium'* and who occasionally converted his texts for their own use. To an Anselm of Canterbury such a scene might have appeared riotous.[3]

[1] '... omnes pariter de transcribendis glosis quas prima die inceperam in ipso earum initio plurimum solliciti esse ... Post paucos itaque dies, Parisius reversus ... glosas illas Hiezechielis quas Lauduni inceperam consummare studui' (ed. Monfrin, *ll.* 219–21, 241–5).

[2] Buyteart, 'Sic et Non'.

[3] Monastic literature came nonetheless to share many similarities of production. Dom Jean Leclercq has underlined how frequently in the twelfth century monastic writings were subjected to friendly or secretarial processing (*Recueil d'Etudes*, I, 3–5) and how in the 'mobile' texts of St Bernard's writings we can observe their genesis and growth (*Recueil d'Etudes*, II, 14).

About eighty manuscripts containing writings of Abelard survive today; Bernard of Clairvaux, on the other hand, is represented in some 1,500 manuscripts.[1] The two men wrote such different kinds of works and addressed themselves in the main to such different audiences that comparisons between their literary fortunes must become contrasts. When Abelard wrote for monks he wrote in criticism as at St Denis or as the preacher of sermons. His writings to Héloïse and to the Paraclete are quite numerous but the dependencies of the Paraclete cannot compare as a distributing agency with the great Cistercian networks. Abelard's pupils dispersed from his school, as we have seen, to go in all directions and about all manner of purposes, but no organized and continuing means for the diffusion of his work existed as it did for the classics written by such Cistercians as Bernard, William of St Thierry and Ailred of Rievaulx. It is the books of monasteries which have chiefly survived from the middle ages, and haphazard and perilous though the preservation of monastic collections has been in the course of the centuries, Abelardian manuscripts which have survived have usually had to cross a line which divided the schools from the monasteries—and scholasticism from monasticism. William of St Thierry read Abelard by chance[2] and he read William of Conches only because someone who had the *Summa philosophiae* entered the monastery of Signy as a novice.[3] The arrival of Abelard's writings upon monastic shelves may be less a sign of how these writings circulated than of how they ceased to circulate.

Comparisons between the ways in which different works have been preserved in manuscripts have only a limited usefulness since the survival of manuscripts through eight centuries is the result of many different kinds of chance. But it would seem that the writings inspired by the traditions of the school of Anselm of Laon and of William of Champeaux and to a still greater extent the scholastic and exegetical writings of the Victorines were much in demand in the libraries of monasteries. Some sixty

---

[1] J. Leclercq, *Etudes sur S. Bernard*, p. 17.
[2] *Epist.* 326 (PL. 182, 531C).
[3] *De erroribus Guillelmi de Conchis* (PL. 180, 333B).

manuscripts of theological discussions emanating from the school of Laon have been listed by the late Dom Lottin[1] and the biblical commentaries of the school exercised an almost universal appeal.[2] The Victorine *Summa Sententiarum*, which was apparently finished before 1140 when Abelard's career was drawing to its close, survives in some fifty-five manuscripts.[3] Even the luckless Gilbert of Poitiers who, like Abelard, suffered strong criticism from Bernard of Clairvaux and, even more than Abelard, open criticism from many masters, has fared better.[4] The suggestion that Abelard's writings enjoyed a more ephemeral popularity must arise from evidence such as this. H. Weisweiler concluded his thorough survey of manuscripts in German libraries relating to the school of Anselm of Laon and of William of Champeaux by contrasting the favour accorded by religious foundations to the 'patristic' theology of the schools of Laon and of St Victor with the silent opposition of monks and canons to the 'dialectical' theology of Abelard, Gilbert of Poitiers and even Anselm of Canterbury.[5] Moreover, Professor C. R. Cheney, surveying English Cistercian libraries of the twelfth century, has reflected on the 'feeble influence' of the new scholasticism upon the works represented in those libraries.[6] No particular religious order seems to have led such opposition in Abelard's case; his writings

---

[1] Lottin, 'Nouveaux fragments théologiques' (1947), pp. 170–3. On the appeal of Anselm of Laon see also *idem, Psychologie et morale*, v, 442 *et seq.*

[2] Manuscripts are listed by W. Affeldt, 'Verzeichniss', pp. 373–4.

[3] F. Stegmüller, *Repertorium commentariorum*, I, 390.

[4] Twenty-two good and complete twelfth and thirteenth-century copies survive of Gilbert's commentaries on the *Opuscula sacra* of Boethius (N. Haring, 'The Commentary of Gilbert, bishop of Poitiers, on Boethius' *Contra Eutychen et Nestorium*', p. 243) and eighteen of his commentary on Boethius' *De hebdomadibus* (Haring, 'The Commentary of Gilbert of Poitiers on Boethius' *De Hebdomadibus*', pp. 178–80).

[5] *Das Schrifttum*, pp. 244–7.

[6] 'Les Bibliothèques cisterciennes en Angleterre au XIIe siècle' in *Mélanges S. Bernard*, pp. 375–82. Cf. C. H. Talbot, 'Notes on the Library of Pontigny', p. 106, who describes the Pontigny scriptorium in the twelfth century as very busy in producing Patristic classics. In quoting these judgments I do not wish to oversimplify monastic attitudes to study nor to overlook their variety, but to underline their main bias; cf. M. A. Dimier, 'Les premiers Cisterciens étaient-ils ennemis des études?'

entered Cistercian houses, or were ignored by them,[1] just as they fared with the Black monks and with the regular canons.[2]

The manuscripts sometimes provide explicit information concerning the attitudes of the readers of Abelard's writings. Some copies contain warnings to the reader to remember that Abelard was a heretic who should be read cautiously in view of what Bernard of Clairvaux had thought about him.[3] Yet early manuscripts also contain signs of a serious and profitable interest taken in the doctrines of the works, as well as expressions of admiration for Abelard. The Lyell manuscript in Oxford which contains such a beautiful copy of the *Theologia 'Summi boni'* was attentively studied by a contemporary of the mid twelfth-century copyist who noted and attempted to enumerate Abelard's questions and solutions concerning the divine properties and concerning the polemics with Roscelin of Compiègne and Alberic of Rheims. The Heilbronn copy of the same work begins: '*Incipiunt capitula librorum de trinitate magistri Petri, clarissimi atque doctissimi viri, cognomento adbaiolardi.*'[4] The twelfth-century Zurich manuscript of the *Theologia 'Scholarium'*—*tractatus utilis de sancta trinitate*[5]— is accompanied by questions in one of which an opinion of Abelard on the power of the keys is quoted;[6] marginal annotations accompany the *Theologia* continuously. The Prüfening *Ethica* and *Sententie Hermanni* are prefaced by a curious piece of flattering

---

[1] Cf. Erlangen 182 (at Heilbronn in the late thirteenth century), Heiligenkreuz 153 (at Heiligenkreuz in 1381), Copenhagen, E don. var. 138 (at Herisvad in the twelfth century), Cambridge, Trinity College B. I. 39 and British Museum, Harley 3038 (at Buildwas in the twelfth century).

[2] Besides the manuscripts at St Victor cf. Clm. 7698 (at Indersdorf in the twelfth century), Vienna 819 (at Klosterneuberg in the thirteenth century), British Museum, Royal 11. A.V (at Merton in the fourteenth century), Colmar 128 (Marbach), Clm. 16,085 (St Nicholaus-vor-Passau) and the Sentences of St Florian.

[3] Cf. Clm. 18,597 (above, p. 79). In St Gall 69 (*Sententie* of Hermann) a reader has twice added the word *Cave* in the margin of f. 128r where Abelard's doctrine of the Incarnation is presented (PL. 178, 1757D). In Erlangen 182, f. 27r a fifteenth-century hand has written 'Cave ne haurias venenum quo hic ... quod beatus arguit Bernardus in quadam epistola ad Innocentium papam: lege prius eandem consulo tibi.'

[4] Erlangen 182, f. 27r.

[5] Zurich, Zentralbibl. C. 61, f. 53v.   [6] Cf. below, p. 177 and n.

H

biography of Abelard.[1] Nicholas of Cusa in the mid fifteenth century read the *Theologia 'Scholarium'* with an especial interest in Abelard's use of pagan philosophical writings;[2] in a similar way an anonymous thirteenth-century reader of the Arsenal copy of the same work has annotated the passages in which Abelard justifies the reading of pagan philosophy and the understanding of God's revelation to both gentiles and prophets.[3] Notes and jottings and discussions arising out of the contents, sometimes controversial, of the *Sententie Hermanni* are found in Clm. 16,085 and in Pavia, Aldini 49; in the anonymous *Enchiridion* on confession the author refers to *ille summus peripatethicus* who proves (*probat*) that the human will, distinct from human actions, is the instrument of man's salvation or damnation.[4]

The compilers of manuscript volumes, when they selected a text by Abelard for copying or for binding in a volume, were usually also engaged in selecting other works to form a collection of a certain kind. The dominance of patristic theological literature ensured that any twelfth-century work of theology was liable to accompany works of the Fathers. A striking example is the inclusion of passages containing Abelard's pronounced theses on the Redemption in a collection of Augustinian fragments in a Florentine manuscript.[5]

It is often difficult to know when a series of texts was collected and united in a codex and it is also often difficult to know whether Abelard's authorship was appreciated by medieval owners of some of his works of which the copies lack attributions. Nevertheless, several volumes containing works by Abelard are now collections of early scholastic writings by several authors. For example, although the school of Laon and that of Abelard pursued quite different paths, and although Abelard's revolt against the teaching of Anselm was followed by many years of resistance by Anselm's supporters—Alberic of Rheims and Lotulph of Novara brought him to trial in 1121 and Walter of Mortagne wrote against

---

[1] See above, pp. 8, 58.   [2] See above, p. 79.
[3] Paris, Arsenal 265, ff. 81v and 83r (cf. PL. 178, 1044B, *l.* 8–1046A, *l.* 6 and 1053D, *l.* 1–1055B, *l.* 7).
[4] Cf. below, p. 170.   [5] See above, pp. 87–8.

him in 1136—yet the works of the two rival traditions were both wanted by students. *Quaestiones* prepared by members of the Laon school are found with the *Theologia* 'Scholarium' in the Zurich and Fritzlar manuscripts, with the *Sic et Non* in the British Museum manuscript, with the *Sententie Hermanni* in several of its copies[1] and with the *Sententie Bernardi abbatis*. Writings by Walter of Mortagne accompany the *Ethica* in Clm. 28,363 and the *Theologia* 'Scholarium' and *Sic et Non* in Tours 85. The Parisian MS., Bibl. nat. lat. 18,108, which contains three sentence collections from Abelard's school, also contains works by the élite among twelfth-century theologians—by members of the Laon school, by Hugh of St Victor and his disciples, by Bernard of Clairvaux and Odo of Ourscamp—although the union of these works occurred at an unknown date.[2] Writings by Gilbert of Poitiers and his disciples also accompany those by Abelard. Gilbert's commentary on 1 *Corinthians* was bound with Abelard's on *Romans* at least by the fifteenth century in the Vatican MS. Reginensis 242, and a Porretan commentary on 1 *Corinthians*[3] also accompanies in the Paris MS. Arsenal 1116 a twelfth-century abbreviation of Abelard's Commentary on Romans. The Sentences of St Florian follow the Porretan *Sententie Divinitatis*. The *Librum hunc* by Thierry of Paris and Chartres accompanies the *Theologia* 'Summi boni', the condemnation of which Thierry appears to have regretted, in two manuscripts[4] while the *Philosophia* of William of Conches accompanies the *Sic et Non* in Zurich Car. C. 162.

Works by the Victorines are also found in the manuscripts of Abelard. A striking combination is of Abelardian works and of the *Summa Sententiarum* produced by a leading disciple of Hugh who also made use of Walter of Mortagne and who wrote sharp criticisms of Abelard's theses. In the Zurich MS., Zentralbibl.

---

[1] Princeton, Garrett 169; Clm. 16,085; Cologne, Hist. Archiv W. 137; Trier 591.

[2] Abelard is moreover cited in three collections of sentences of the school of Laon, British Museum, Royal 9. E. XII, f. 255v, and Royal 8. C. IX, f. 165; also Bamberg Patr. 128, f. 36; cf. Landgraf, 'Beiträge', pp. 362-4.

[3] *Commentarius Porretanus*, ed. Landgraf.

[4] Oxford, Bodley, Lyell 49 and Erlangen 182.

C. 61, the *Theologia 'Scholarium'* and the *Summa Sententiarum* are written in the same twelfth-century hand and they are also found together in Arsenal 265. In the Prüfening manuscript and in Clm. 28,363 the *Summa* accompanies the *Ethica*; in the Carpentras manuscript it accompanies the *Sententie Hermanni*. Works by Hugh accompany works by Abelard in the manuscripts of Tours, Münster, Copenhagen, Fritzlar, Mainz and Balliol College and they also accompany works of Abelard's school in the Cologne manuscript and in Clm. 4,600 and 19,134. It would seem that although Abelard's works do not survive in great numbers of manuscripts, they were nonetheless given an important place in volumes containing other leading works of the day and were not infrequently the object of kindly comment and serious attention. The combination of Abelard and Hugh in the manuscripts is especially interesting for the same combination of their names was also achieved by the chroniclers. Richard of Poitiers before 1153 wrote of the two masters as *duo Latinorum lumina* and Ralph of Coggeshall believed that Abelard, Hugh and Gilbert were the leading masters of their generation.[1]

[1] See above, p. 9; also Ralph of Coggeshall, *Chronicon Anglicanum*, ed. J. Stevenson, p. 11. R. L. Poole, *Illustrations*, p. 173, describes this as 'a favourite combination, the very incongruity of which makes no small part of its significance . . . The juxtaposition would be inexplicable but on the assumption to which we have already been led, namely, that piety was an essential ingredient in the popular idea of Abailard.' Poole's remark is stimulating but the following chapters may make it appear only partially truthful. The doctrines of Abelard and Hugh were found to be together stimulating.

CHAPTER IV

THE CONDEMNATION OF 1140

An appreciation of Abelard's influence upon men's minds and upon their writings in the twelfth century must rest, at least in part, upon an understanding of how his contemporaries and successors discussed the content of his teaching, both logical and theological. How Abelard's logical teaching was received and developed will not be considered here; such a study would have to take into account a number of hitherto inedited texts which still await scientific study. It is fortunately more possible to consider Abelard's influence in theology and it is especially desirable to consider what those writers who most closely depended upon Abelard attempted themselves to do. Ever since Heinrich Denifle first revealed in 1885 the existence of such dependent writings, more and more texts by disciples of Abelard have been discovered and edited. These works are far from being merely the abridged reportings or the mirrored reflections of Abelard's own extant writings and we shall enquire how they presented or developed Abelard's theses and how some of them were stimulated by the criticisms of his opponents. The ways in which other active masters, too independent or eclectic to be classified as followers, continued to debate Abelard's opinions also require a historical examination. The fundamental concern of the following pages is, then, the role of Abelard's teachings in the evolution of early scholasticism. But first it is essential to appreciate the climate of controversy into which Abelard's principal teachings entered and to understand the reasons for which Abelard was condemned, justly or unjustly, in 1140.[1] The teachings of Abelard's followers are barely comprehensible outside the context of Abelard's own difficulties.

Abelard was powerfully attacked as a heretic and, according to his opponents, not merely on account of peripheral exuberances or exaggerations; his critics found his main teachings and indeed

[1] On the date of the council of Sens see J. G. Sikes, *Peter Abailard*, pp. 229–31.

his whole theological style to be objectionable. At Soissons in 1121, when Abelard's *Theologia 'Summi boni'* was burnt in the presence of a synod, Abelard complained that the accusations were neither sufficiently specific nor based upon a thorough examination of his teaching.[1] He appears to have been accused of tritheism, of the denial of the proposition *Deus seipsum genuit* and of exclusively associating omnipotence with God the Father.[2] Otto of Freising reported that Abelard was thought to have overemphasized the differences between the divine persons.[3] Previously Roscelin of Compiègne, whom Abelard had criticized in the *Theologia 'Summi boni'*,[4] had sent the book to the bishop of Paris on suspicion of heresy.[5] In 1121 Abelard's principal opponents were Alberic of Rheims and Lotulph of Novara whom he described as the successors of their own masters, Anselm of Laon and William of Champeaux.[6] Otto of Freising explained that the cause of their disquiet was a feeling that Abelard had incautiously mixed logic with theology.[7]

The victory of Alberic and Lotulph foreshadowed Abelard's future difficulties although at the time it marked only a temporary

---

[1] *Hist. Calam.*, ed. Monfrin, *ll.* 737–8, 845–6, 868–70.

[2] *Ibid., ll.* 725, 757–81, 871–906.

[3] '. . . de sancta trinitate docens et scribens tres personas, quas sancta aecclesia non vacua nomina tantum, sed res distinctas suisque proprietatibus discretas hactenus et pie credidit et fideliter docuit, nimis adtenuans, non bonis usus exemplis, inter caetera dixit: 'Sicut eadem oratio est propositio, assumptio et conclusio, ita eadem essentia est pater et filius et spiritus sanctus', *Gesta Friderici*, ed. Waitz, p. 69. Ostlender, *Abaelards Theologia 'Summi Boni'*, p. xxii, considers that Otto may have had in mind a passage of the *'Summi boni'*, *ibid.*, p. 59, *ll.* 12 *et seq.* A good summary of the episode of 1121 is found in J. Hofmeier, *Die Trinitätslehre des Hugo von Sankt Viktor*, pp. 31–35.

[4] Ostlender, *Abaelards Theologia 'Summi Boni'*, pp. xviii–xx.

[5] Cf. Abelard, *Epist. ad G. episcopum*, PL. 178, 357A.

[6] *Hist. Calam.*, ed. Monfrin, *ll.* 708–13. Cf. Otto of Freising, *loc. cit.*: 'Suessionis provinciali contra eum synodo sub presentia Romanae sedis legati congregata, ab egregiis viris et nominatis magistris Alberico emense et Letaldo Novariense Sabellianus hereticus iudicatus . . . ' On Albeic, see J. R. Williams, 'The Cathedral School of Reims in the time of Marster Alberic' and on Lotulph see D. Van den Eynde, 'Du nouveau sur deux maîtres lombards contemporains du Maître des Sentences', pp. 7–8.

[7] 'Sententiam ergo vocum seu nominum in naturali tenens facultate non caute theologiae admiscuit', *loc. cit.*

setback in his teaching career.[1] The *Theologia 'Summi boni'* was revised to become the *Theologia Christiana* and the *Theologia 'Scholarium'*. Between 1121/2 and *c.* 1125 Abelard maintained a school at Quincey although he was opposed by two *novi apostoli*, who are usually thought to be Bernard of Clairvaux and St Norbert,[2] and although he was criticized by Gerhoh of Reichersberg.[3] Bernard's *De baptismo* is generally held to have been written *c.* 1125 to counter rumours of Abelard's teaching or of that of one of his disciples[4] and Bernard was soon to criticize as well the version of the Lord's Prayer which Abelard recommended to the nuns of the Paraclete.[5] In the 1130s Abelard reappeared in Paris after leaving the abbey of St Gildas; he was found in Paris in 1136 by John of Salisbury[6] who also informs us that at the time of the council of Sens Abelard was lodged in the parish of St Hilary on the Mont Sainte-Geneviève.[7] In these years as in the previous decade Abelard was the object of criticism, and tracts appeared which were exclusively devoted to disputing his doctrines. The first known of such critics in the 1130s is Walter of Mortagne, who had been at Laon and who had also been a student in the second decade of the century under Alberic of Rheims.[8] He is reported to have thought of Abelard as Abelard thought of Anselm of Laon: 'erat homo in lectione satis diffusus ... sed non adeo in quaestionum solutione'.[9] His letter to Abelard[10] some twenty years later in about 1136 or 1137[11] was a courteous and cautious enquiry softened by acknowledgements of Abelard's distinction, even of his modesty, and tempered by a *caveat* against the unreliable gossip of students who spread rumours

[1] Cf. above, p. 3.
[2] *Hist. Calam.*, ed. Monfrin, *ll.* 1200–12. Cf. above, p. 25, n. 6.
[3] Cf. above, p. 24.
[4] Cf. above, p. 26n.
[5] Abelard, *Epist. X ad Bernardum* (PL. 178, 335–340).
[6] *Metalogicon*, II, 10 (ed. Webb, p. 78).
[7] See above, p. 28, n. 1.
[8] The best analysis of Walter's career is by L. Ott, *Untersuchungen*, pp. 126–38.
[9] *Vita Hugonis abbatis Marchianensis*, ed. Martène, *Thesaurus novus anecdotorum*, III, 1712E–1713A. Cf. *Hist. Calam.*, ed. Monfrin, *ll.* 167–70.
[10] Ed. Ostlender. Cf. Ott, *Untersuchungen*, pp. 234–66.
[11] A precise date cannot be given but see Ott, *Untersuchungen*, pp. 240–1.

about Abelard's teaching.[1] Walter controlled what such students reported and also what he himself had heard from Abelard by reading the *Theologia 'Scholarium'* in its first version.[2] Nonetheless, even with such good evidence he preferred to present himself as a scholar who hoped to have the basis for his anxieties removed by explanations from Abelard given in friendly correspondence. In another work, the *Tractatus de trinitate*, Walter's civility towards Abelard disappeared.[3]

In 1138 or 1139 William of St Thierry, then a Cistercian monk at Signy, interrupted his second commentary on the Canticle considering that he was no longer able to give himself 'to a task of such pleasant leisure within while Abelard without was so cruelly laying waste the regions of the faith with unsheathed sword'.[4] He wrote a *Disputatio* against him[5] and sent it with a list of the thirteen offending teachings which he had controverted in the *Disputatio* to Bernard of Clairvaux and Geoffrey, bishop of Chartres.[6] William's list of *capitula* had a marked influence upon the final list sent after the council of Sens to Pope Innocent II. He had found his evidence in 'duo . . . libelli idem pene continentes nisi quod in altero plus, in altero minus aliquanto inveniretur';[7] one of these *libelli* was the *Theologia 'Scholarium'* in its third version and the other was a *Liber Sententiarum* by

[1] 'Solet autem frequenter contingere, quod discipuli discordent a sensu magistrorum, sive per imperitiam verba eorum male exponendo, sive ad ostensionem sui aliquas novitates inducendo, quas causa maioris auctoritatis magistris suis, licet ignorantibus, consueverunt ascribere', Walter of Mortagne, *Epist. ad Abaelardum*, ed. Ostlender, p. 34.

[2] Cf. Walter of Mortagne, *Epist. ad Abaelardum*, ed. Ostlender, pp. 35-6nn. and Ostlender, 'Die Theologia Scholarium', pp. 266-9.

[3] PL. 209, 575-90, here especially c. 13 (588-90). The date of this work is thought to be *c.* 1125, although the arguments given by L. Ott, 'Der Trinitäts-traktat Walters', p. 233 and by M. Chossat, *La Somme des Sentences*, p. 86, may be thought to be not of the most convincing. On the text of the *Tractatus*, see L. Ott, *Untersuchungen*, pp. 138-40.

[4] *Epistola ad Fratres de Monte Dei, Prologus*, ed. Wilmart, p. 239; also PL. 184, 305-6.

[5] PL. 180, 249-82.

[6] *Epist.* 326, 3 (PL. 182, 531-3). J.-M. Déchanet, *Guillaume*, p. 69, suggests that the letter and *Disputatio* were sent in March 1138, but R. Klibansky, 'Abailard and Bernard', p. 12, n. 1, argues in favour of Lent 1139.

[7] *Epist.* 326 (PL. 182, 531c).

someone other than Abelard.[1] He seems in chapter seven of the *Disputatio* to have known what some students of Abelard were saying about the Atonement,[2] but he had sought in vain Abelard's *Scito te ipsum* and *Sic et Non*.[3] William claimed to have urged against Abelard only what could be drawn from patristic founts. For this reason some ten years later he asked the Carthusians of Mont-Dieu to suppress his name from the headings of this and of his other writings.[4]

The consequences of William's initiative are well known and Bernard met Abelard who, according to Geoffrey of Auxerre, at first agreed to correct his works but quickly changed his mind.[5] At about this time Abelard issued a fifth version of his *Theologia* '*Scholarium*' in which he reacted to his critics.[6] The details of the continuing hostilities are often unclear but there can be no doubt that Bernard gained a tactical superiority. In his short letters to Rome and above all in his *Tractatus de erroribus Petri Abaelardi* Bernard secured support in Rome and eventually Abelard's condemnation by Pope Innocent. The *Tractatus* and the other letters owed much to William's *Disputatio* but Bernard seems to have handled the *Theologia* and the *Liber Sententiarum* as well as the *Scito te ipsum* and the *Expositio* of Romans.[7] Moreover an anonymous *Excerptor* compiled damaging quotations to

[1] 'Die Theologia Scholarium', pp. 272-3 and 'Die Sentenzenbücher', pp. 225-9.
[2] PL 180, 269C, 276C
[3] *Epist*. 326 (532D-3A).
[4] *Epist. ad Fratres de Monte Dei*, ed. Wilmart, p. 239.
[5] *S. Bernardi Vita prima*, III, 5 (PL. 185, 311A). The report to the pope after the council of Sens signed by the archbishop of Sens and the bishops of his province mentions two meetings (printed among the letters of Bernard of Clairvaux, no. 337 (PL. 182, 541 AB)).
[6] Ostlender, 'Die Theologia Scholarium', pp. 275-81
[7] See *Epist*. 188, 190 (PL. 182, 353B, 1062C) and the conclusion of the list of 19 *capitula* now printed by L. Grill, 'Die neunzehn "Capitula"', p. 237. Through the kindness of Dom A. Stacpoole I have been able to read the proofs of an article by Dom J. Leclercq, 'Les Formes successives de la lettre-traité de saint Bernard contre Abélard', which is to appear in the *Revue bénédictine*. Leclercq has found an earlier form of the *Tractatus* in cod. Charleville 67 (from Signy; twelfth century); he also underlines Bernard's indebtedness to William of St Thierry.

support fourteen *capitula haeresum* many of which are identical with the list of nineteen *capitula* which Bernard sent to Rome.[1] The *Excerptor* found his texts partly in the *Theologia 'Scholarium'* but mainly in a source or sources not known to be by Abelard but which is probably the anonymous *Liber Sententiarum*. Some of the excerpts are identical with those used by William and Bernard and the *explicit* of the collection—'Haec sunt Capitula Theologiae, imo Stultilogiae Petri Abaelardi'—is a pun which was also enjoyed by Bernard.[2]

The list of nineteen propositions which has entered into the handbooks as the official list of heresies condemned by Pope Innocent II was collected by Bernard and transmitted by him to Rome at the end of his *Tractatus*.[3] Bernard explains that he found these *capitula* partly in the *Theologia*, partly in the *Liber Sententiarum Magistri Petri* and partly in the *Scito te ipsum*, and, moreover, that 'we have replied' to those which are marked with a sign.[4] Dom Jean Leclercq, on the basis of an examination of the manuscripts, believes that the *capitula* originally so marked correspond to nos. 1, 2, 4 and 13 in the list established by J. Rivière from Abelard's *Apologia*, although in the *Tractatus*

---

[1] *Capitula Haeresum Petri Abaelardi* (PL. 182, 1049-54). I know of three manuscripts containing this work: Vatican lat. 663, f. 3 (on which the printed edition is based), London, British Museum, Royal 8. F. XV ff. 1r-2v and Paris, Bibl. de l'Arsenal 268 ff. 248r-9v.

[2] *Tractatus* or *Epist.* 190 (PL. 182, 1061B).

[3] J. Leclercq, *Etudes sur S. Bernard*, App. V, *Autour des capitula d'Abélard*, pp. 101-3. The list was printed by L. Grill, 'Die neunzehn "Capitula"', pp. 236-7 from cod. Heiligenkreuz 226, f. 93rv. Grill's choice of this single manuscript was regretted by J. Leclercq, 'Les Etudes bernardines', p. 134. In 'Les Formes successives', pp. 103-4 Leclercq has re-edited the list using thirty manuscripts; he warns that Bernard may not be the original compiler of the *capitula* which he collected.

[4] 'Sunt et alia in aliis scriptis non pauca nec minus mala capitula, ad quae nec temporis nec epistolae angustia respondere permittit . . . Collegi aliqua tamen, et transmisi. Ad capitula tantummodo ista respondemus quae signo tali * nota sunt . . . Haec capitula partim in libro theologiae, partim in libro sententiarum magistri Petri, partim in libro, cuius est titulus: scito te ipsum, reperta sunt', Grill, *loc. cit.* The manuscript reading *respondemus* makes little sense, even if the letter was sent to the pope before the council of Sens; Leclercq, *Etudes sur S. Bernard*, p. 102, states that most manuscripts have *respondimus*.

Bernard himself replied to nos. 1, 2, 3 and 14.[1] Nevertheless, whichever *capitula* came to the fore in discussion among Abelard's critics at the time of the council of Sens, the whole list was generally condemned by the Pope,[2] and Abelard felt constrained to answer the whole list in his *Apologia* and again in his *Confessio fidei 'universis'*.

Abelard was furious about Bernard's statement that he had extracted the *capitula* from the *Theologia*, *Scito te ipsum* and *Liber Sententiarum* and not only on the ground that he disclaimed the authorship of the *Liber Sententiarum*. He marvelled that Bernard should have been duped by this work. His fury was mixed with gratitude that the charges against him had never appeared in his own writings: 'The devil even if he does interpret Scripture badly at least gives the actual words of Scripture which he mis-interprets. But you are so far from both my words and my meaning and you labour over arguments taken from your inventions rather than from my sayings.'[3] In the *Confessio fidei 'universis'* he wrote: 'There is a well known proverb: Nothing is so well said that it cannot be twisted'[4] and he claimed that the charges had been framed in malice or in ignorance. Abelard's *Apologia* was answered by Thomas of Morigny who issued a *Disputatio* in which, however, there is no reference to Abelard as condemned[5] In addition to criticizing Abelard's teaching on

---

[1] Leclercq, *Etudes sur S. Bernard*, p. 102 and cf. J. Rivière, 'Les "Capitula" d'Abélard', pp. 16–17. Leclercq concludes that the marked *capitula* were probably answered in the council of Sens and that the *Tractatus* was probably sent after the council. Leclercq's new edition ('Les Formes successives', pp. 103–4) of the list is taken from Bernardine manuscripts; that of Rivière was constructed from Abelard's *Apologia*. The arrangement of the two lists is not identical. Bernard's *Tractatus* counters the first, second and thirteenth of the *capitula* as edited by Leclercq; only three manuscripts have signs placed against these *capitula*.

[2] '... destinata nobis a vestra discretione capitula', *Epist.* 194 (PL. 182, 361B).

[3] *Apologia*, ed. Ruf and Grabmann, p. 12.   [4] PL. 178, 105–6.

[5] PL. 180, 283–328 and cf. above, p. 50. On Thomas's criticisms of Abelard's presumptuous use of dialectic cf. R. Klibansky, 'The Rock of Parmenides', p. 184. Whether Abelard's *Apologia* was written before or after the council of Sens is uncertain, although Otto of Freising, *Gesta Friderici*, 1, 51 (ed. Waitz, p. 74), reported that it was written when Abelard went to Cluny.

the basis of the third[1] version of the *Theologia 'Scholarium'*, Thomas sought to show that his *Apologia* was an unconvincing attempt to demonstrate his orthodoxy.

Walter, William, Bernard and Thomas not only tried to find where the weaknesses in Abelard's errors lay but also complained about Abelard's method and general theological outlook with a unanimous voice. Walter found that Abelard's *Theologia* departed from the tradition of orthodox writing, taught *opinio* rather than *veritas* and laid claim to a perfect and full knowledge of the Trinity. William objected that Abelard was too free in subtracting from and adding to faith and prone to teaching without Scriptural authority and against the plain teaching of the Fathers. His *nobis videtur* was a cry of revolt and a proclamation of independence. Thomas's stance was similar and he found *multae . . . profanae et mortiferae novitates*; Abelard courted Plato, Virgil and Macrobius with excessive zeal and by imitating John the Scot Eriugena lapsed into heresy. With Bernard proclamations of Abelard's wrongness almost exceed explanations of his errors. Bernard loosed off many brilliant phrases which must have burned deep into the minds of both parties. The harm done to Abelard by the exposure of his preference for his own *aestimatio* could not be repaired overnight.

William, Bernard and Thomas were all monks and Bernard and William are very great representatives of a golden age of monastic theology. Much recent study has not only pronounced Bernard cleared of the charge of being an enemy of speculation or of dialectic or of the schools as such, but has also found, especially since the appearance of E. Gilson's famous study of his mystical thought, that Bernard had as a theologian a very considerable speculative and synthesizing

[1] H. Ostlender, 'Die Theologia Scholarium', p. 263, and E. Buytaert, 'Thomas of Morigny', who, however, does not observe Ostlender's previous assertion of the same conclusion. Buytaert also overlooks both the fact that W. Meyer, *op. cit.*, pp. 417–18, printed a fragment of the 'lost' opening of the *Disputatio* and the existence of the manuscript from which Meyer took his text, cod. Berlin, Philippicus 1690, f. 246 *et seq.* (seventeenth century). The manuscript is described by V. Rose, *Die Handschriften-Verzeichnisse der Königlichen Bibliothek zu Berlin*, XII, 1, 468–9.

ability.[1] William, too, has to be seen not simply as an informer against Abelard but as a powerful thinker who in his *Enigma fidei* attempted to meet Abelard on a speculative level.[2] The conflicts between Abelard and the two leading monastic theologians of the day should be seen not merely as disputes between the upholders respectively of faith and of reason but as the effects of the realization of structural differences between two traditions of theological analysis and reflection. The flourishing tradition to which Abelard's monastic critics adhered was a prolongation of patristic theology, meditative, conservative, rich in psychological and moral experience, able to detect acutely real weaknesses in the work of schoolmen and in addition to attract and to convert men from the schools to the life of the cloister by virtue of its own intellectual strength.[3] This monastic opposition to Abelard has recently been, to misappropriate a word which once tended to be used of Abelard himself, rehabilitated and it is now quite common to find writers who underline the positive doctrinal and methodological contributions which Bernard himself made to, and did not merely borrow from, scholastic thought.[4] The tensions which existed between the rival but also intercommunicating schools of the towns and the monastic cloisters were, as M. D. Chenu has suggested, abusively symbolized by the sharp clash between Bernard and Abelard.[5]

The overtly polemical critics of Abelard in his later years included Walter of Mortagne, who was not a monk. The critics of Abelard were not only secular as well as monastic but were

[1] See Gilson, *Mystical Theology of Saint Bernard*, E. Bertola, *San Bernardo*, W. Hiss, *Die Anthropologie Bernhards*.
[2] See Gilson, *Mystical Theology*, App. V, pp. 198–214, M.-M. Davy, *Un traité de la vie solitaire*, idem, *Théologie et mystique de Guillaume de S. Thierry*, I, J. M. Déchanet, *Guillaume de S. Thierry*, O. Brooke, 'The Speculative Development of the Trinitarian Theology of William'.
[3] See J. Leclercq, *L'Amour des lettres*, idem, 'S. Bernard et la théologie monastique du XIIe siècle' in *S. Bernard Théologien*, pp. 7–23. Also, J. M. Déchanet, 'Aux sources de la pensée philosophique de S. Bernard' in *S. Bernard Théologien*, pp. 56–77.
[4] E. Kleineidam, 'Wissen, Wissenschaft, Theologie bei Bernhard von Clairvaux' in *Bernhard von Clairvaux. Monch und Mystiker*, pp. 128–67.
[5] Chenu, 'Platon à Cîteaux', p. 99.

moreover not confined to those who issued broadsheets or agitated for a condemnation. As we shall see in later chapters, substantial criticisms of Abelard were also produced by other scholastics in the context of their regular teaching and writing. To identify the motives of the monastic opposition to an Abelard or to a Gilbert of Poitiers is perhaps to ascertain only the most readily perceptible sources of criticism. Moreover, monastic criticism, however soundly motivated, failed, as J. Cottiaux established,[1] to comprehend accurately some important aspects of Abelard's attitude to theology, its object, its form and its methods. In particular Bernard interpreted in an unfavourable sense Abelard's wish to formulate *aestimationes*: 'quasi cuique in ea sentire et loqui quae libeat liceat; aut pendeant sub incerto in vagis ac variis opinionibus nostrae Fidei sacramenta, et non magis certa veritate subsistant. Academicorum sint istae aestimationes, quorum est dubitare de omnibus, scire nihil.'[2] When Abelard used the term *aestimatio* in respect of faith in things unseen, he did not intend to minimize the certitude of faith but to define the nature of an act of knowledge which is not yet *experientia* and which does not attain to *cognitio*. His method involved no break in the links binding the teaching of the faith to its revealed sources. His search for the correct use of language in theological discourse was to some extent misunderstood as an attempt to alter the content of faith.

The analysis by historians of both the opportuneness and the shortcomings of the criticisms directed against Abelard in publicly polemical writings has been pursued further in respect of Abelard's methods than of the content of his teaching.[3] J. Cottiaux insisted vigorously that there was no disparity between Abelard's principles and their applications, yet he himself did relatively

[1] Cottiaux, 'La Conception de la théologie'. Cf. M. M. Davy, *Théologie et mystique de Guillaume de S. Thierry*, I, 52–65.
[2] *Tract. de erroribus*, c. 4 (PL. 182, 1061C). Cf. William of St Thierry, *Disputatio*, c. 1 (PL. 180, 249–50).
[3] Cf. for example a recent and excellent study by J. Jolivet, 'Sur quelques critiques de la théologie d'Abélard', p. 25: 'ici on s'occupe plutôt de sa méthode, et du sens de cette méthode, tels qu'ils peuvent être révélées sous le jour particulier des critiques'.

little to justify, at least in respect of non-Trinitarian teachings, the claim that the particular controverted teachings, which were the applications of his methods, were free from error.[1] More commonly a distinction is proposed between the orthodoxy of Abelard's methods and intentions and the unorthodoxy of some of their applications.[2] Abelard's methods are generally agreed to have proved an inestimable stimulus upon twelfth-century thinking. The powerful advocacy of reason, the development of the *quaestio* in biblical exegesis, the propagation of techniques for harmonizing concepts, propositions and the documents of the faith by a dialectical hermeneutic, have assured for Abelard an exceptional place of honour in the history of the twelfth-century revival.[3] But the methodological interpretation of Abelard's contribution to thought has developed further than the understanding of Abelard's doctrinal influence which has sometimes been overlooked or at best briefly noticed by even the most eminent historians of twelfth-century thought.[4] In the slow elaboration of scholastic doctrines Abelard has a place, but is it merely that of the nuisance-maker and heretic whose inherently fruitful methods were imprudently applied by their own author? Evidence of Abelard's nuisance value is provided by the list of *capitula* condemned by Pope Innocent, and Dom Jean Leclercq has claimed that by his interventions Bernard enabled others to avoid and to forget these errors of Abelard as well as those of Gilbert of Poitiers, thereby saving for the future the proper

[1] Cottiaux, *op. cit.*, pp. 810–21.

[2] E.g. J. de Ghellinck, *L'Essor de la littérature latine*, pp. 49–50: 'actuellement on est presque unanime à dire que les convictions personelles d'Abélard sont inattaquables . . . l'application de ses théories aux dogmes n'est pas toujours en harmonie avec ses déclarations de foi chrétienne'.

[3] For interesting refinements to this view see M. D. Chenu, 'Un Essai de méthode théologique'.

[4] Grabmann's *Geschichte* was expressly concerned with scholastic method, and therefore studied only Abelard's use of reason and his *Sic et Non* technique. E. Gilson in his *History of Christian Philosophy*, p. 163, is content to indicate the fecundity of the new spirit witnessed by Abelard's disciples and the intellectual 'standard' which Abelard, so to speak, imposed. De Ghellinck, *Le Mouvement théologique*, pp. 156–7, refers the reader to particular histories of particular doctrines discussed by Abelard.

application of dialectic.[1] Yet Dr C. H. Talbot has written that in his attacks upon Abelard and Gilbert Bernard displayed a 'stupefying credulity', attacked too impulsively, had not read Abelard's works thoroughly but relied upon the reports of friends.[2] J. Chatillon similarly finds that Bernard misunderstood the meaning of certain words and doctrines and accused Abelard rather too lightly of Arianism, Nestorianism and Pelagianism.[3] Abelard argued fiercely that the accusations were unjust. Were his protests made sincerely and in good faith[4] or were his explanations worthless?[5] The list of nineteen *capitula* does not consist of exact quotations from Abelard's writings and it is still imperfectly understood. How accurately does it convey Abelard's teachings? If the propositions were formulated with a proper appreciation of these and without misunderstanding, are the errors found in Abelard patently espoused falsehoods or the faults of omission? Are they the slips and exaggerations of a bold theorist or do they indicate the central points of Abelard's teaching?

To these questions answers can only be given by examining the charges in the light of Abelard's known teachings. It is important to know how accurately Abelard was criticized and condemned at the time of the council of Sens in order to be able to evaluate the discussions of other writers who did not participate in these proceedings. To concentrate in this and in following chapters upon the history of Abelard's condemned teachings is in fact to concentrate as well upon the influence of Abelard's principal theological opinions and indeed upon some of the most sensitive fields of debate developed in the whole twelfth century. Subsequent discussion of Abelard's teachings often unavoidably was the discussion of his condemned opinions and often this discussion was unavoidably controversy. There is moreover good

---

[1] 'S. Bernard théologien' in *San Bernardo*, pp. 30–41, here p. 37.
[2] 'San Bernardo nelle sue lettere' in *San Bernardo*, pp. 151–65, here p. 155. Otto of Freising, *Gesta Friderici*, I, 48 (ed. Waitz, p. 68), also thought Bernard credulous in his handling of the case against Gilbert.
[3] 'L'influence de S. Bernard sur la pensée scolastique au XIIe et aux XIIIe siècles' in *S. Bernard Théologien*, pp. 268–88, here pp. 284–5.
[4] Cf. T. Gregory, *Anima mundi*, p. 120.
[5] Cf. W. Meyer, 'Die Anklagesätze', p. 445.

reason to believe that the conflicts of Abelard's later years were themselves well remembered in the following decades,[1] for they were recorded by many writers and they were prominent in the numerous manuscripts containing the collected correspondence of Bernard of Clairvaux. There are also several manuscripts extant today which contain a small dossier of the principal documents concerning the trial of 1140. The dossier usually comprised Abelard's *Confessio fidei* '*universis*', one or more of the pertinent letters of Bernard and sometimes the *Apologeticus* of the frenzied Berengar or the list of the condemned *capitula*.[2]

The first of the condemned *capitula* was: *Quod Pater sit plena potentia, Filius quaedam potentia, Spiritus Santus nulla potentia*.[3] This has reference to Abelard's special attributions of power, wisdom and benignity or goodness to the persons of the Father, Son and Holy Ghost respectively.[4] The Father in a special sense is the power of God.[5] Wisdom is a sort of power, being the

---

[1] For example at Gilbert's trial at Rheims, see above, p. 34.

[2] Codd. Berlin, Staatsbibl. Phil. 1732 (twelfth century, at Rheims in the fifteenth century), London, British Museum, Cotton, Otto C. 14 (twelfth–thirteenth century), Oxford, Bodley Add. C. 271 (late fourteenth century, at Cambrai in the late fifteenth century), Paris, Bibl. nat. lat. 1896 (fourteenth century), 2923 (thirteenth–fourteenth century), nouvelle acquisition lat. 1873 (fifteenth century), Vienna, Nationalbibl. 998 (thirteenth century, from Gottweig, diocese of Passau). Other manuscripts containing the *Confessio fidei* '*universis*' are Heidelberg 71 (with Abelard's letter to his *socii*, ed. Klibansky), Cambrai, Bibl. municipale 27 (twelfth century, from Cambrai cathedral), Douai, Bibl. municip. 532 (thirteenth century), Paris, Bibl. nat. lat. 14,511 (thirteenth century, fragment), franc. 920 (translation of Jean de Meun). The documentation of the council of Sens was certainly influential upon Clarembald of Arras, John of Cornwall, Walter of St Victor and Matthew of Acquasparta.

[3] I cite the *capitula* from the critical edition newly made by J. Leclercq, 'Les Formes successives', pp. 103–4; this is an improvement upon the edition of L. Grill, 'Die neunzehn "Capitula",' pp. 236–7. The order and wording of the *capitula* in the list which was well conjectured by J. Rivière, 'Les "Capitula"', pp. 16–17, differ slightly from the list used here.

[4] *Theol*. '*Schol*.', I, viii–xii, II, xiii–xiv (PL. 178, 989C–998B, 1069C–1072C), *Theol. Christiana*, I, ii, IV (1124A–6D, 1288D *et seq*.), *Theol*. '*Summi boni*', I, ii–v, III, ii–iii (Ostlender, pp. 3–9, 86–105).

[5] *Theol*. '*Schol*.', I, viii (989C): 'Dei Patris vocabulo divinae majestas potentiae exprimitur specialiter'; *Theol*. '*Summi boni*', I, ii (Ostlender, p. 3): 'Patrem quidem secundum illam unicam maiestatis suae potentiam, quae est omni-

I

power of discernment.[1] Benignity is not a power nor wisdom but the effect of love, and to love something is not to have the power of achieving it but to have good will towards it.[2] Abelard always maintained that all the three persons are each fully powerful and fully wise and fully loving.[3] But there were deep Scriptural and Patristic roots for associating these three attributes with the three persons respectively. Works of power, such as the creation from nothing or the sending of the Son into this world are usually ascribed to the Father. The work of Christ, the Word of God, was, beside some miracles and other deeds which exhibited power, always educational. The Spirit who is the effect of divine love, is the giver of gifts such as regeneration in baptism and strengthening in confirmation.[4]

In 1136 or so Walter of Mortagne questioned Abelard's teaching. He appears to have encountered the first recension of the Theologia 'Scholarium' where Abelard argued that the wisdom

[1] Theol. 'Schol.' I, x (994): 'Est itaque divina sapientia quaedam divina potentia, per quam videlicet Deus cuncta perfecte discernere atque cognoscere habet'; II (1069C); III, vii (1109A).

[2] Theol. 'Schol.' II, xiv–xv (1072A–C): 'Benignitas quippe ipsa ... non est aliqua in Deo potentia sive sapientia, cum videlicet ipsum benignum esse non sit in aliquo esse sapientem aut potentem, sed eius bonitas magis secundum ipsum charitatis effectum sive effetus accipienda est ... ipse vero charitatis affectus magis ad benignitatem animi quam ad potentiam attineat'; Theol. Christiana, IV (1299C); Theol. 'Summi boni', III, iii (Ostlender, pp. 102–3).

[3] Theol. 'Schol.', I, x (992AB): 'Iuxta proprietates quippe trium personarum, quaedam specialiter ac tamquam proprie de aliqua earum dici vel accipi solent, quae tamen iuxta earum naturam, unionem singulis inesse non ambigimus, ut sapientia Filio, charitas Spiritui sancto specialiter attribuitur, cum tamen tam Pater ipse, quam Filius charitas dici possit. Sic etiam iuxta personarum proprietates, quaedam opera specialiter alicui personae attribuuntur, quamvis indivisa totius Trinitatis opera praedicentur, et quidquid ab una earum fit, a singulis fieri constet'; Theol. Christiana, IV (1274D–5B, 1282A, 1299A–C).

[4] Theol. 'Schol'., I, viii–xiv (989C–1004A); Theol. Christiana I, iii–v, IV (1126D–39A, 1279B–82C). Cf. particularly Augustine, De trinitate, VII, 2–3, XV, 17 (PL. 42, 936–9, 1079–82). Abelard's appropriation theory has to be understood in the light of his view of the similitudines between God and creation, cf. S. Otto, Die Funktion des Bildbegriffes in der Theologie, pp. 70–9.

potentia, qua scilicet efficere potest, quidquid vult, cum nihil ei resistere queat'; III, ii (Ostlender, p. 93): 'de generatione verbi ex deo patre breviter perstrinximus, hoc est divinae sapientiae ex divina potentia sive ex omnipotentia'.

of God is *quaedam potentia discernendi* which is *quasi quaedam portio . . . divinae omnipotentiae.* Thus Abelard was found to attribute to the Son an unequal or a lesser or a partial power.[1] In the second recension of the '*Scholarium*' the term *portio* suitably disappeared.[2] Nonetheless William of St Thierry felt that the relationship of the *potentia discernendi* to the *potentia* of the Father had been presented *quasi quiddam ad totum.* Although the ascriptions are sanctioned by Scripture and by convention, all three persons are—*sicut ipse solet dicere*—equally *omnipotentia, omnisapientia, omnibenignus* and the ascriptions must be made *secundum rationem fidei et intellectum pietatis.* They may be used to express the relations of the Trinity to men or the activities of the persons in cooperation with each other, but not to express the nature of the supreme essence which can only be done by using the proper names of Father, Son and Spirit. By ignoring this requirement, Abelard has come to ascribe *semipotentia* to the Son and *nulla potentia* to the Spirit; he has turned the divine persons into mere qualities of God.[3] Hence William formulated his *capitulum: Quod Pater sit plena potentia, Filius quaedam potentia, Spiritus Sanctus nulla potentia.*[4] Bernard of Clairvaux followed William in his criticisms and in addition seized upon Abelard's habit of making attributions to each person *proprie et specialiter.*[5] In his eleventh sermon on the *Canticle* Bernard had previously assigned power, truth

---

[1] *Epist. ad Abaelardum*, ed. Ostlender, pp. 35–6 *et in notis*; Ostlender, 'Die Theologia Scholarium', pp. 267–8. Cf. also *Theol. Christiana*, IV (1289B); *Theol.* '*Summi boni*', III, ii (Ostlender, pp. 86–7): 'sapientia, id est potentia discernendi, quasi quaedam, ut ita dicam, pars sit omnipotentiae divinae . . . '
[2] Ostlender, 'Die Theologia Scholarium', pp. 269–70.
[3] *Disputatio*, c. 2–4 (PL. 180, 252C–260C). Cf. *De erroribus Guillelmi de Conchis* (PL. 180, 336D–7C) and the *Aenigma fidei*, ed. M. M. Davy, pp. 140–4 (and in PL. 180, 421B–3D), where William seems to me to do no more than restate his position expressed in the *Disputatio*. An interesting example of the devotional use of the conventional attributions has been found by Dom J. Leclercq in an anonymous twelfth-century *De dilectione* contained in a Clairvaux manuscript; the author had been reading Abelard's *Theologia* (cf. *Theol.* '*Schol.*', I, ix (990AB), *Theol. Christiana*, I, ii (1126AB)), see 'Textes sur Saint Bernard et Gilbert de la Porrée' in *Recueil d'Etudes*, II, 341–71, here p. 347.
[4] William of St Thierry, *Epist.* 326 (PL. 182, 523B).
[5] *Tractatus de erroribus*, c. 1–3 (PL. 182, 1056A–61B). Cf. *Epist.* 330, 331, 332, 336, 338 (PL. 182, 536A, 537A, 538A, 540A, 543C).

and love to the three persons respectively,[1] but now he has to reassert against Abelard that the attributes do not constitute *propria* of the persons: *quod est commune amborum, non erit proprium singulorum*.[2] Bernard's objection is unfortunate since to the logician trained in the Porphyrian-Boethian language, *proprium* does not necessarily have an exclusive meaning[3] and it is clear that Abelard did not employ the term in its strictest sense.[4]

In the *Confessio fidei 'universis'* Abelard protested that the charge was malicious and he condemned the *capitulum* as diabolical and detestable.[5] He answered it in his fragmentary *Apologia* and there challenged Bernard to produce a text by Abelard which contained it.[6] He pointed out that it is one thing to say that the divine wisdom is a certain power of God, but another thing to say that the Son is a certain power of God; one thing to say that the love of God is not a power, but another thing to say that the Spirit is not a power. Two words with the same meaning can, when placed in identical sentences, produce two different meanings. For example, 'God' and 'divinity' have the same meaning but to say that God has suffered and to say that divinity has suffered is to say two different things. *Erras plane, frater, tamquam vim verborum nequaquam intelligens et illius expers discipline, que disserendi magistra est.* Abelard had said that wisdom is a sort of power, being the faculty of discerning all, and that the wisdom of God is the Son; he had not said that the Son is a certain power nor had he denied the Son's omnipotence. Similarly Abelard insisted, here in his *Apologia* and also in the fifth recension of his *'Scholarium'*, where he also defended himself against misinter-

---

[1] Here Bernard uses the term *assignare* and, writing as early as 1135–6, he cautions that these assignations should only be made 'ut nihil horum vel Patri, vel Filio, vel Spiritui Sancto subtrahatis, ne cui forte personarum aut plenitudinem minuat distinctio, aut proprietatem tollet perfectio', ed. Leclercq, *Opera Sancti Bernardi*, I, 58.

[2] *Tractatus de erroribus*, c. 3 (PL. 182, 1058D).

[3] *Boethii . . . in Isagogen Porphyrii Comment.*, rec. S. Brandt, pp. 275–6.

[4] See above, p. 116.

[5] 'Quae si quis in meis reperiat scriptis, non solum me haereticum, verum etiam haeresiarcham profiteor', PL. 178, 105–6.

[6] Ed. Ruf and Grabmann, pp. 12–17.

pretations,[1] that love or goodness is not power or wisdom and that the love of God is the Spirit, but not that the Spirit is not a power. On the contrary, each of the persons is equally powerful, wise and benign; the wisdom and the love of God are omnipotent, but it is not syntactically fitting to say as well that they are omnipotence. In reply to criticisms Abelard reveals his anxiety both to keep within the traditional framework of the faith[2] and to find the linguistically and logically most suitable formulas.[3]

Thomas of Morigny knew that in his *Apologia* Abelard denied the accusations against him and he believed that Abelard was still in the wrong, but he wholly failed to refute Abelard's defence.[4] He insisted that Abelard accept that his arguments were convertible: if the wisdom of God is the Son and if wisdom is a certain power, then it follows for Thomas that the Son is only a certain power and likewise if the love of God is the Spirit and is not a power, then it follows that the Spirit is not a power.[5] In other respects Thomas follows the pattern of criticism established by William and he quotes at length from Augustine and Hilary to show that the persons are equal.

Abelard was also condemned for teaching *quod adventus in*

[1] Cod. Balliol College 296, f. 37v, 40r–41r. Extracts are given by Ostlender, 'Die Theologia Scholarium', pp. 276–8.

[2] Cf. *Confessio fidei Heloissae* (PL. 178, 376c) where Abelard emphasizes his unqualified belief in the co-equality of the Father and the Son, saying that Arianism has no hold over him, and he stresses the co-equality of the Spirit 'utpote quem bonitatis nomine designari volumina mea saepe declarant'.

[3] J. Cottiaux underlined this aspect of Abelard's method with reference to the attributions of qualities to the persons in 'La Conception de la théologie', especially pp. 810–21.

[4] *Disputatio*, 1, ed. Buytaert, 'Thomas of Morigny', pp. 85–6; W. Meyer, 'Die Anklagesätze', p. 417 (fragment) and PL. 180, 283A–298B.

[5] After 1156 Clarembald, archdeacon of Arras and a former pupil of Hugh St Victor and Thierry of Chartres, continued the polemic in the course of a commentary on Boethius' *de Trinitate*, ed. W. Jansen, here pp. 48*–9*. He had read the *Theologia* but relied in the main upon Bernard's *Tractatus*. Like Thomas he tries to foist upon Abelard implications that Abelard would not have accepted. In this case he seized upon *Theol. 'Schol.'*, II, 13 (1070A): '. . . divina sapientia, quae est potentia discernendi, exigit quod sit divina potentia, sed non e converso' to show that Abelard would have to imply the proposition 'quod qui Filius est, Pater est, sed non e converso' and 'quod Filius est, Pater est, sed non e converso'. Clarembald may not have known Abelard's replies to such uncontrolled substitutions of the terms in an argument.

fine saeculi possit attribui Patri.[1] He protested in his *Confessio fidei 'universis'*[2] that this thought had never come into his head or into his writings and this we may believe for one reason why he specially associated wisdom with the Son was that it was the function of the Son to judge the world at the end of time.[3]

Abelard claimed in his *Confessio fidei 'universis'* that the proposition *Quod anima Christi per se non descendit ad inferos, sed per potentiam tantum*[4] was completely foreign to his words and meaning.[5] He taught in the *Theologia 'Scholarium'* that God, as a spirit, is neither circumscribed by location nor able to move from place to place. Space itself and what fills space is itself maintained by God who is therefore substantially present in it through the efficacy of his power.[6] When he wrote in his *Exposition* of the Apostles' Creed that, in view of the inability of any soul or spirit to move locally, the meaning of the descent into Hell of the soul of Christ is that his passion had a liberating effect upon the souls of the elect, it is clear that Abelard by no means minimized the reality of Christ's descent[7] and in neither passage did he deny

---

[1] Leclercq, 'Les Formes successives', p. 104, no. 16.

[2] 'Adventum Filii in fine saeculi posse attribui Patri nunquam (sciat Deus!) in mentem meam venit, nec se verbis meis inseruit', PL. 178, 107–8.

[3] *Theol. 'Schol.'*, I, x (995A) '... ea quae ad animi rationem vel sapientiam pertinent, sicut est judicare quod discretionis est. Unde scriptum est: "Pater omne judicium dedit Filio" '. Neither William of St Thierry nor Bernard makes this accusation. Thomas of Morigny tries to fasten upon Abelard the belief that the Son had less knowledge than the Father, but he can hardly be alluding to the condemned teaching: 'Sed dicet, quia Christus dicit in Evangelio, quod diem judicii neque angeli, neque Filius hominis scit, sed Pater solus (Matt. 24, 36). In maxima fuit Arianorum haereticorum calumnia, ne Filius haberet cum Patre aequalitatem, cum quo non haberet aequalem scientiam', *Disputatio*, I (PL. 180, 294B).

[4] Leclercq, 'Les Formes successives', p. 104, no. 18.

[5] 'Sic et animam Christi non per se ad inferos descendisse, sed per potentiam, omnino a meis verbis et sensu remotum est', PL. 178, 107–8.

[6] III, vi (1104–6c): '... Cum itaque Deus in Virginem venire aut aliquo dicitur descendere, secundum aequam suae operationis efficaciam, non secundum localem accessionem intelligi debet ... Quod tamen ubique esse per substantiam dicitur, juxta eius potentiam vel operationem dici arbitror ... Nam et ipsa loca, et quidquid est in eis, nisi per ipsum conserventur, manere non possunt; et per substantiam in eis esse dicitur ...' Cf. *Dialogus* (1664c–8B).

[7] PL. 178, 626CD: 'Ipsa quoque anima, quae in carne passa fuerat, ad inferos dicitur descendisse, quia passionis illius efficaciam justi senserunt antiqui, per

that Christ's soul descended *per se*, but he did exclude the idea of a local motion. Walter of Mortagne in his letter to Abelard reported that Abelard in a recent conversation had said some dubious things about the divine presence and the location of spirits, specifically that God is not essentially in the world or anywhere and that angels and souls are nowhere,[1] and in a letter which he wrote to one Master Thierry at an uncertain date he reported the thesis which he claimed was being taught in one school, which may be Abelard's, that God was omnipresent, not in essence but in power. Walter himself affirmed forcefully the essential omnipresence of God.[2] Abelard, however, in at least the fourth recension of his '*Scholarium*',[3] affirmed the omnipresence of the divine substance, with only the qualification that a terminology which implied the physical or local presence of incorporeal being should be avoided. Neither William nor Thomas nor the anonymous *Excerptor* discuss this teaching, although Bernard in *Epist.* 188 to the Curia wrote: '*Legite . . . quid sentiat de descensu Christi ad inferos.*'[4] The brief reference comes with a request to read Abelard's *Ethica* and *Liber Sententiarum* and since the teaching is not found in the former work, there is a strong presumption that it had been extracted from the *Liber Sententiarum* which is lost and of which Abelard himself does not appear to have been the author. If this is the case, a second presumption arises which is that the *Liber Sententiarum* presented a garbled form of Abelard's teaching. On the basis of Abelard's own writings, Dr L. Ott is surely right in considering this quarrel as a dispute over terminology in which Abelard was not heretical.[5]

The second *capitulum* in the condemned list reads: *Quod*

---

[1] *Epist. ad Abaelardum*, ed. Ostlender, p. 40.

[2] *Epist. ad Theodoricum*, ed. L. d'Achéry, *Spicilegium*, II, 462–6 and fully analysed by L. Ott, *Untersuchungen*, pp. 188–99.

[3] Namely the version printed in PL. 178 and the one which was not known to Walter at the time of his letter to Abelard.

[4] PL. 182, 353C.   [5] Ott, *Untersuchungen*, pp. 188–99.

---

eam a poenis liberati . . . Sicut ergo Deus, qui ubique est, descendere quoque dicitur secundum aliquem suae operationis effectum, ita et anima illa secundum efficaciam propriae passionis, quam habuit in electis, descendisse liberando dicitur.'

Spiritus Sanctus non sit de substantia Patris aut Filii. The accusation refers to Abelard's attempt in the *Theologia* to find the right way of relating the generation of the Son and the procession of the Spirit to the notion of the undivided substance of God. In the *Theologia Christiana* Abelard distinguished between the generation of the Son *ex ipsa Patris substantia* (wisdom being itself a certain power) and the procession of the Spirit which extends itself through love to another.[1] Peter Damian had raised the question why, if the Son and Spirit are *de substantia Patris*, there are not two Sons, but he left it well alone by professing that the difference between generation and procession is ineffable and incomprehensible.[2] In the third version of the *Theologia 'Scholarium'* Abelard developed an argument: while the Spirit is of the same substance as the Father and the Son (*eiusdem substantie ... cum patre et filio*), unlike the Son he is not *ex substantia patris ... aut filii* since this expression is reserved for generation (*quod esset ipsum ex patre vel filio gigni*).[3] In the fourth version of the work Abelard adds a cautionary element to this statement (*si proprie loquimur*).[4]

William of St Thierry, citing the third version of the *'Scholarium'*,[5] presented a straight bat to Abelard's argument by observing firmly that to proceed from the Father and the Son (*procedere ex ipsis*) is to proceed *ex eo quod sunt*. Abelard has made the procession *non tam substantialis ... quam affectualis*,[6] and William formulates a *capitulum: De Spiritu Sancto, quod non sit ex substantia Patris et Filii, sicut Filius est ex substantia Patris.*[7] Bernard rightly saw that Abelard had taught this proposition but proceeded to argue as if Abelard had denied that the Spirit is not *de substantia Patris*.[8] He quoted against this affirmations by Jerome and the pseudo-Athanasius.[9]

[1] IV (PL. 178, 1299D–1300A).   [2] *Opusculum* XXXVIII, c. 4 (PL. 145, 638C).
[3] Cited by Ostlender, 'Die Theologia Scholarium', p. 273.
[4] II, xiv (PL. 178, 1072CD); a better reading is given by Ostlender, 'Die Theologia Scholarium', p. 273.
[5] Ostlender, 'Die Theologia Scholarium', p. 273.
[6] *Disputatio*, c. 4 (PL. 180, 258A–265A).   [7] *Epist.* 326 (PL. 182, 532B).
[8] *Tractatus*, c. 1 (PL. 182, 1056A–7A). Cf. *Cap. Haeresum*, 2 (PL. 182, 1049BC).
[9] *Ibid.* (1057A). Cf. Jerome, *Epist.* 224 (PL. 22, 1072) and Pseudo-Athanasius (Eusebius of Vercelli), *De Trinitate*, I, xvii, ed. V. Bulhart, p. 7, ll. 147–50.

In the fifth version of the '*Scholarium*', written under the pressure of criticism, Abelard introduced defensive expressions (*quantum estimo, quantum arbitror*) and had recourse to a linguistic and logical *apologia*. He concedes that, since the Son and Spirit are both from the Father, it is meaningful to say that both are *de substancia patris*, although he does not appear to be altogether happy about the propriety of doing so (*non abhorremus sensum, quicquid verborum proprietas habeat.*) But he observes that the two prepositions *de* and *ex* (which Bernard had freely interchanged) sometimes have a different force in different contexts (cf. *loqui de spiritu sancto* and *loqui ex spiritu sancto*) and he will not concede that it is proper to say that the Spirit, like the Son, is *ex substantia patris*, although he recognizes that others are free to say *de substantia* or *ex substantia*.[1] In his *Apologia* he repudiates the charge that he has taught that the Spirit is not *de substantia patris*[2] and in the *Confessio fidei* he reaffirms his constant teaching that the Son and Spirit are of the same substance as the Father, but states, perhaps rather too strongly, that the actual charge made against him springs from either very great malice or very great ignorance.[3] Thus Abelard scrapes home to victory by the skin of his teeth, having faulted the draftsman of the *capitulum* over a two-letter word.

Did Abelard teach *quod Spiritus Sanctus sit anima mundi*?[4] Professor T. Gregory has demonstrated that there were some writers who identified the Holy Spirit with the world-soul, among them being Thierry of Chartres and, for some years of his life, William of Conches and also Arnold of Bonneval, friend and biographer of Bernard of Clairvaux. But Abelard was not strictly of their number.[5] Abelard certainly believed that he could show, principally from the *Timaeus* in the Latin translation of the fourth-century neo-platonist Chalcidius, that Plato had found

[1] Cited by Ostlender, 'Die Theologia Scholarium', pp. 276–8 from cod. Balliol College 296, ff. 39r–40r.
[2] Ed. Ruf, p. 18.   [3] PL. 178, 105–6.
[4] Leclercq, 'Les Formes successives', p. 103, no. 3.
[5] Gregory, *Anima mundi*, pp. 133–54. Further discussion of *anima mundi* teachings in Gregory, 'Nuove note sul platonismo medievale' and in L. Ott, 'Die platonische Weltseele in der Theologie'.

traces and prefigurations of the Trinity and that in the *Timaeus* the world-soul is like a third person coming from God and from the mind (*nous*) born of God.[1] But he strove throughout the successive versions of his *Theologia* to show how Plato and other philosophers spoke of God and the soul poetically and allegorically.[2] 'It is clear', he wrote referring to Macrobius's commentary on Cicero's *Somnium Scipionis*, 'that what the philosophers say of the world-soul must be interpreted allegorically. Otherwise we would have to censure the greatest of philosophers as the greatest of fools. What could be more ridiculous than to think that the whole world is one rational animal, unless this is said figuratively (*per integumentum*)?'[3] Their very words force upon one a mystical explanation, for human bodies have their animal life from their own individual souls and not from a world-soul. However, if Plato's doctrine of the world-soul is considered as an allegory it can be reasonably accepted without abandoning the faith.[4] The saints, and especially Augustine, have themselves commended Plato's teaching.[5] Thus Abelard interprets Plato to mean that the world-soul, like the Holy Spirit, confers the spiritual life upon human souls by his gifts; by locating this soul in the middle of the world Plato beautifully designates the grace of God which is offered to all in common. But the resemblance between the love of God, which is the Spirit, and the world-soul is only allegorical, for the Spirit in fact does not vivify all souls. Plato's doctrine

---

[1] *Theol.* 'Schol.', I, xvii–xx, II, xvi–xvii (PL. 178, 1012C–29D, 1080B–5A); *Theol. Christiana*, I, v, IV (1144A–66C, 1306D–1311A); *Theol.* 'Summi boni', I, v–vi, III, iv (Ostlender, pp. 13–23, 105–6).

[2] 'Semper philosophia arcana sua nudis publicare verbis dedignata sit, et maxime de anima et de diis per fabulosa quaedam involucra loqui consueverat', *Theol.* 'Schol.', I, xix (1022), *Theol.* 'Summi boni', I, iv (14).

[3] *Theol.* 'Schol.', I, xx (1023B), *Theol. Christiana*, I, v (1155A–56B), *Theol.* 'Summi boni', I, v (pp. 15–16). On the notion of *integumentum* and of *involucrum* see E. Jeauneau, 'L'usage de la notion d' "integumentum" ' and M. D. Chenu, 'Involucrum'.

[4] Cf. William of Conches, *Glosae super Platonem*, ed. Jeauneau, p. 211: 'Si quis tamen non verba tantum sed sensum Platonis cognoscat, non tantum non inveniet heresim sed profundissimam philosophiam integumentis verborum tectam. Quod nos, Platonem diligentes, ostendamus.'

[5] On Abelard's use of Augustine's *Confessions*, Bk. VII, cf. P. Courcelle, *Les Confessions de S. Augustin dans la tradition littéraire*, pp. 276–7.

that the world-soul consists of a divided and an undivided substance, of identity and of difference, is seen by Abelard as another allegory describing the Spirit whose essence is undivided and identical with that of the Father and the Son, but who is a different person, and who, though simple in himself, is multiple in his works, a sevenfold Spirit giving a sevenfold grace.

An obstacle to developing further the comparison between the allegory of the world-soul and the Spirit arises from the argument of the *Timaeus* that the world-soul was made and had a beginning, whereas Catholic teaching is that the three persons are coequal and coeternal. Abelard therefore notes the distinction between *spiritus*, the name of a nature, and *anima*, the name of a function which arises *quasi ab animando* or *vivificando nos donis gratiae suae per incrementa virtutum*. Plato is held to teach a spirit which is eternal in essence and which acquires animating functions, just as the Spirit is the gift of the Father and the giver of gifts, eternally proceeding from God and temporally proceeding with respect to creatures. In this way Abelard arrives at a comprehensive allegorical interpretation of the *anima mundi* as a prefiguration of the Spirit. His interpretation is mystical in the sense that he does not attribute to the *anima mundi* the physical, cosmological activities which were described by some of his contemporaries.[1] Nor does he reverse his arguments at any point to claim that the Spirit itself is a world-soul.

William of St Thierry was too definite in accusing Abelard of such an identification: *Quod Spiritus Sanctus sit anima mundi.*[2] In the *Disputatio*[3] he observes that Abelard's novelty has no support from Scripture and he effectively cites from Augustine against the notion that God is the soul of this corporeal world. He stresses against Abelard the dissimilarities between the world-soul and the Spirit, but in doing so he seems to have insufficiently appreciated that the effect of Abelard's spiritual interpretation of the allegory had itself been the removal of the cosmological interpretation by which the world-soul stood in relation to the

[1] Gregory, *Anima mundi*, pp. 133–54.
[2] *Epist.* 326, c. 5 (PL. 182, 532B).
[3] C. 5 (PL. 180, 265A–6B).

corporeal world as the human soul stands in relation to the body. William argued, what Abelard had denied, that the world-soul, if believed, and the universe would together constitute a rational animal and would have to be adored just as we adore in Christ the man joined in the unity of a single person. Bernard of Clairvaux makes only a brief and highly polemical allusion to Abelard's teaching in his *Tractatus*.[1] He believes that Abelard has taught that the Spirit is the soul of the world and has proved that Plato's world is a more excellent animal because in the Spirit it has a better soul. The more, says Bernard, that Abelard sweats to make Plato a Christian, the more he himself becomes pagan.

Thomas of Morigny objected particularly to Abelard's comparison of the Spirit offering grace to all men in common with the *involucrum* of the world-soul placed in the middle of the world. He objected that Abelard had introduced Plato, Macrobius and Virgil, *intonsos et illotos*, to the banquet of the supreme king and had imitated the use of allegory by John the Scot—*et ipse pro sua subtilitate de haeresi notatus est*. Like William, Thomas stressed the differences between the world-soul and the Spirit.[2] Against the insistence, however inaccurately this insistence was expressed in detail and the condemned *capitulum* did inaccurately present Abelard's teaching, that the differences between the *anima mundi* and the Spirit outweigh allegorical resemblances Abelard could have no answer. He passed over this accusation in silence in his *Confessio fidei 'universis'* and he turned upon his own teaching some sharp criticism in the *Dialectica*.[3] Here he observes, with a deceptive air of detachment, that some Catholics are too fond of allegory. The world-soul, *quam Platonici fingunt*, has only a creaturely origin in God, whereas the Spirit is consubstantial, coequal and coeternal with God. Plato's doctrine is now *ab omni veritate figmentum . . . alienissimum. De hac itaque Anima, quam nec fides recipit nec ulla rei similitudo sequitur, agere*

[1] C. 4 (PL. 182, 1062B): ' . . . Haec, inquam, omnia aliasque istius modi naenias eius non paucas praetereo: venio ad graviora.'

[2] *Disputatio*, III (PL. 180, 321C *et seq.*). Quotations from Abelard are taken from the *Theol. 'Schol.'*, I, xvii (1013B, 1018CD, 1019B).

[3] Ed. De Rijk, p. 558, *l.* 26, to p. 559.

supervacaneum omnino duximus. It is likely that Abelard wrote his *Dialectica* after the condemnation of 1140.[1]

The seventeenth *capitulum* reads: *Quod Deus nec debeat nec possit mala impedire*.[2] In his commentary on Romans Abelard, discussing the sense in which God is said to allow sins to occur without consenting to their occurrence, observes expressly that God could perhaps resist the sins of many but nonetheless he ought not to prevent them.[3] In a passage of the fifth and last version of his *Theologia 'Scholarium'*, where Abelard touches on the theme that it is good for evils to occur since God turns evil to good account, he says that it seems surprising that some events are said to displease him and how he prohibits sins when it is good that they occur.[4] In both passages Abelard seems to teach that God in his goodness ought not to prevent evils, but in neither does he suggest that God cannot prevent them. No criticism of Abelard's observations is advanced by William, Bernard or Thomas in their known writings. The only known critic is the anonymous *Excerptor* who cites an otherwise unknown passage which supports the condemned thesis but which is contrary to the teaching of Abelard's Commentary. The anonymous writer argues, as Abelard himself argued, that all that is done by God is done in the best possible way, but concludes that God neither ought nor can interfere with an arrangement which is the best possible arrangement in order to prevent evils.[5] This conclusion advances further than Abelard was himself prepared

---

[1] *Ibid.*, pp. xxii–xxiii.   [2] Leclercq, 'Les Formes successives', p. 104.

[3] 'Multorum enim fortasse Deus resistere peccatis posset, disturbando scilicet, ne fierent, nec tamen debet culpis nostris exigentibus, vel ipsis peccatis, melius utendo: ideoque consentire peccatis nullo modo dicendus est', PL. 178, 807C.

[4] 'Mala etiam ita bene ordinat ut etiam bonum sit mala esse, et quidquid evenit, bonum sit evenire; unde et mirabile videtur cur aliqua ex his quae eveniunt ei displicere dicuntur; aut quomodo peccare prohibeat, cum ipsa quoque bonum sit esse, tanquam aliqua nolit esse, quae tamen bonum est esse, atque ideo bonum, ut nonnulla etiam maxima peccata ita evenire approbet et dicat: (Matt. 18, 7) 'Necesse est enim ut veniant scandala; verumtamen vae illi per quem scandalum venit', ed. V. Cousin, *Opera Petri Abaelardi*, II, 149.

[5] '... Et ideo Deus a consensu malorum est alienus, qui nec debet, nec potest mala impedire...', *Cap. Haeresum*, 7 (PL. 182, 1052BA). The *capitulum* cited by the *Excerptor* lacks two words in this edition which are, however, found in cod. British Museum, Royal 8. F. XV, f. 2r.

to go in his *Theologia*.[1] There is a strong possibility that Abelard was condemned in this instance on mistaken evidence and perhaps as a result of a teaching contained in the anonymous *Liber Sententiarum*.

The tenth *capitulum*, *Quod in Christo non fuerit spiritus timoris Domini*, is not justified by Abelard's extant writings. In his Sermons Abelard several times refers to Christ knowing fear[2] and in the eleventh Sermon, in a passage which in the Migne edition unfortunately is somewhat corrupt,[3] Abelard appears to suggest that the fear felt by Christ before his passion pertains to the *persona suorum membrorum* and is not to be understood *iuxta litteram* of Christ himself. This is confirmed by Abelard's defence in his *Confessio fidei 'universis'* where he states that the spirit of fear, the fear that is of God and which is the beginning of wisdom, was not present in Christ's soul which had only a perfect love of God, but it was present in Christ's members.[4] Apart from a passing reference in Bernard's *Tractatus*[5] no critic either voiced an objection or cited a text in support of the condemned *capitulum*. Similar observations have to be made concerning the fourteenth *capitulum: Quod etiam castus timor excludatur a futura vita*, for Bernard is the only critic to mention the charge;[6] no text by Abelard is known to contain the teaching and in the *Confessio fidei* Abelard affirms that *castus timor*, the reverence of love, is present in the elect.[7]

The sixth *capitulum*, *Quod liberum arbitrium per se sufficiat ad*

[1] See above, p. 127, n. 4. Cf. *Confessio fidei 'universis'* (PL. 178, 107–8): 'Mala Deum impedire frequenter fateor . . . '

[2] Sermo XII, XXVII (PL. 178, 481B, 547CD). Cf. *Sic et Non*, c. 78, *Quod Christus servilem timorem habuisse videatur et non*, and c. 80, *Quod Christus nec secundum hominem passus fuerit aut timuerit, et contra* (1453B–5D, 1457B–65B).

[3] PL. 178, 468B–9C, here 469AB.   [4] PL. 178, 107–8.

[5] 'Omitto quod dicit spiritum timoris Domini non fuisse in Domino', c. 4 (PL. 182, 1062B).

[6] 'Omitto quod dicit . . . timorem Domini castum in futuro saeculo non futurum . . . ', *ibid.*

[7] *Confessio fidei 'universis'* (PL. 178, 107–8). Cf. *Sic et Non*, c. 152, *Quod timor Dei in sanctis perseveret et non* (1600B–D). On the early scholastic distinctions of kinds of fears see A. Landgraf, 'Die Lehre der Frühscholastik von der knechtischen Furcht' in *Dogmengeschichte*, IV, 276–371; D. Van den Eynde, 'Autour des "Ennarrationes" ', pp. 71–3; L. Ott, *Untersuchungen*, pp. 217–34.

aliquod bonum, appears to be a caricature of Abelard's teaching. In his commentary on Romans Abelard used the simile of an invalid having to be propped up by his doctor in order to take medicine and argued that man cannot receive grace unless he has grace.[1] But Abelard rejected the theory which envisaged a new grace preceding each good act in favour of a simpler model according to which an equal gift is offered to all which consists in the explanation and the promise of the happiness of God's kingdom; this itself suffices to fire a person with desire and this is prevenient grace, the grace of faith, which stimulates the elect to will the good but which the damned in their torpor inexcusably neglect.[2] Abelard's argument in the *Expositio* was not that man can earn merit by free will alone, but that successive enabling graces are not granted in addition to the prevenient grace of faith.[3] To will good is natural for we possess reason, but we lack the capability to achieve good without grace.[4] Justification without grace is impossible.[5] In the *capitulum* which William formulated he fairly objected that Abelard had abandoned *gratia adjuvans,*[6] but in his *Disputatio* he reproduced two passages of the *Liber Sententiarum* in which not only are continuing enabling graces eliminated, but a place is found for purely human achievements which earn merit from God. The author supposes that it is by the use of reason that the prudent man attaches himself to the grace offered by God.[7] William, complaining that this is

[1] PL. 178, 917CD. Cf. 840B.   [2] 917D–919A.
[3] Cf A. Landgraf, 'Die Erkenntnis der helfenden Gnade in der Früh-scholastik' in *Dogmengeschichte*, I, 1, 69–73; J. Gross, 'Abälards Umdeutung des Erbsündendogmas', pp. 27–33.
[4] *Expos.* (895D–6A).   [5] *Expos.* (917CD, 825B, 828CD).
[6] 'Quod libero arbitrio, sine adjuvante gratia, bene possumus et velle et agere', *Epist.* 326, c. 6 (PL. 182, 532B).
[7] ' " ... Si enim non potest ex se aliquid facere boni, et talis factus est, ut pronior sit ad malum quam ad bonum; nonne si peccat, immunis est a peccato? ... " Et post aliquanta, his similia: " ... Sed quia ita non est, sed longe aliter; dicendum est, prout veritas se habet. Dicendum est igitur quod homo per rationem a Deo quidem datam gratiae appositae cohaerere potest; nec Deus plus facit isti qui salvatur, antequam cohaereat gratiae, quam illi qui non salvatur ... Qui prudens est, per libertatem arbitrii sui cohaeret gratiae; piger et carnalis, quamvis per liberum arbitrium possit, negligit ... ", ' c. 6 (PL. 180, 267AB).

Pelagianism, asks where is predestination? or vocation?[1] The passage is unfortunately argued for in the references to the role of reason, no reference is made, as Abelard himself made,[2] to the doctrine of election. Bernard of Clairvaux contented himself with renewing the charge of Pelagianism[3] and the anonymous *Excerptor* presented two passages, neither known to be by Abelard, of which one is quoted by William but the second reveals verbal, though not doctrinal, variants from William's citations.[4] In his *Confessio fidei* Abelard re-affirms his faith in the necessity of grace to prepare the will and also to enable us to act and to persevere, but he does not adopt the terminology of a plurality of new and successive graces.[5] In a passage of the *Apologia* quoted by Thomas of Morigny, who believes that Abelard had not abandoned his Pelagianism, we see how Abelard elucidates the role of reason, but within the framework of predestination.[6]

The ninth *capitulum* concerns sins of ignorance: *Quod non peccaverunt qui Christum ignorantes crucifixerunt, et quod non sit culpae adscribendum quidquid fit per ignorantiam.* The latter clause accurately catches Abelard's teaching as it was expressed in the *Ethica*.[7] Defining sin as the contempt of God and consent to what one believes should not receive consent, he argues that a sin of ignorance, that is, of invincible ignorance *cui praevidere non valuimus*, is objectively a sinful deed which should not be done, but does not amount to a contempt of God. Unbelief in the Gospel or ignorance of Christ is sin and earns damnation, but only

[1] *Disputatio*, c. 6 (PL. 180, 267D).

[2] Cf. *Expositio* (918D–9A): 'Hanc autem gratiam tam reprobis ipse quam electis pariter impertit, utrosque videlicet de hoc instruendo aequaliter, ut ex eadem fidei gratia, quam perceperunt, alius ad bona opera incitetur, alius per torporis sui negligentiam inexcusabilis reddatur. Haec itaque fides . . . gratia Dei est quae unumquemque electum praevenit . . . '

[3] Cf. *Epist.* 192, 330, 331, 332, 336, 338 (PL. 182, 358D, 536A, 537A, 538A, 540A, 543C).

[4] C. 6 (PL. 182, 1051B–2A).   [5] PL. 178, 107–8.

[6] *Disputatio*, III (PL. 180, 321C–5B): ' " . . . Cum igitur Dominus tam electis quam reprobris rationem tribuat, et viam ostendat, qua perveniendum sit ad beatitudinem: et ad hanc percipiendum, quam omnibus offert, praeceptis et exhortationibus suis nos jugiter invitet . . . " ' (324A).

[7] C. 13–14 (PL. 178, 653C–7D).

the *contemptus Dei* is *culpa*.[1] *Culpa* in Abelard's terminology has
a very precisely defined usage and William of St Thierry was
wide of the mark in reporting that Abelard taught that no sin
is done through ignorance.[2] In his *Confessio fidei* Abelard acknowledged that deeds of ignorance acquire *culpa*, but he insists that this
is chiefly the case with negligent ignorance when we ignore
what we should know.[3]

Abelard certainly taught that Christ's crucifiers sinned. The
prayer on the Cross, *Pater, dimitte illis; non enim sciunt quid
faciunt* (Luke 23, 34), shows that the crucifiers were ignorant but
also that there are sins of ignorance which require forgiveness.
In their ignorance, the crucifiers did not offer that contempt
of God nor make that consent to evil which constitutes sin in
the proper sense; their ignorance excuses them from *culpa*.
The deed is objectively wrong and punishment would have been
reasonable, although Christ preferred to offer an example of
love and patience.[4] In *c.* 1125 Bernard of Clairvaux, in the *De
baptismo* which contains criticisms of teachings of Abelard or of a
member of his school, had taken the opportunity to stress the

---

[1] '... Ad damnationem quippe sufficit Evangelio non credere, Christum
ignorare ... quamvis hoc non (tam) per malitiam, quam per ignorantiam
fiat. De qualibus et Veritas ait: *Qui non credit, iam iudicatus est* (John 3, 18).
Et Apostolus: *Et qui ignorat*, inquit, *ignorabitur* (1 Cor. 14, 38). Cum autem
dicimus ignoranter nos peccare, hoc est, tale quid, quod non convenit facere,
peccare non in contemptu, sed in operatione sumimus ... quomodo ... culpae
debeat ascribi, non video ... quidquid per ignorantiam invincibilem ... Quem
tamen dum peccare per ignorantiam dicimus ... hoc loco non proprie pro
culpa ponimus, sed large accipimus, pro eo scilicet, quod nos facere minime
convenit' (656A–657C). On Abelard's teaching see R. Blomme, *La Doctrine du
péché*, pp. 275–88 and S. Kuttner, *Kanonistische Schuldlehre*, pp. 137–8.

[2] *Disputatio*, c. 13 (PL. 180, 282B): 'Dicit per ignorantiam nullum fieri
peccatum.'

[3] PL. 178, 107–8. On the two *capitula*, see R. Blomme, *La Doctrine du
péché*, pp. 275–88.

[4] '... Quod ergo dixit: *dimitte*, non ad culpam praecedentem, vel contemptum Dei, quem hic haberent, respexit sed ad rationem inferendae poenae,
quae non sine causa, ut diximus, subsequi posset, quamvis culpa non praeces-
sisset ... Quid itaque mirum, si crucifigentes Dominum ex illa iniusta actione,
quamvis eos excusat a culpa, poenam, ut diximus temporalem non irration-
abiliter incurrere possent ... illos, si persequebantur Christum vel suos, quos
persequendos credebant per operationem pecasse dicimus, qui tamen gravius
culpam peccassent, si contra conscientiam eis parcerent', *Ethica* (655B–657D).

K

sinfulness of the crucifixion, whatever the ignorance of its per-
petrators[1], and both William of St Thierry[2] and the anonymous
Excerptor[3] produce passages which are not by Abelard and which
expressly state what Abelard did not teach in the *Ethica*, that
Christ's crucifiers did not sin.

The remaining nine propositions condemned by Pope Innocent II fairly present Abelard's teaching. The thirteenth *capitulum*,
*Quod ad Patrem, qui ab alio non est, proprie vel specialiter attineat
omnipotentia, non etiam sapientia et benignitas*, is, however, somewhat misleading since it may give the impression that Abelard
excluded wisdom and benignity from the Father altogether.
In the *Confessio fidei* Abelard reiterated his constant belief that
no person of the Trinity differs from another in goodness or
dignity.[4] He had, however, associated omnipotence very closely
with the Father,[5] and Walter of Mortagne was disturbed by
reading in the first version of the *Theologia 'Scholarium'* a passage
where Abelard argued that power belonged specially to the
Father who alone has his being and his power from himself,
whereas the Son and Spirit have their power and being from the
Father.[6] Walter concluded that Abelard wished to accord a
greater power to the Father than to the Son. In the fourth version
of the *Theologia 'Scholarium'* Abelard made somewhat clearer
the omnipotence of each of the persons in the sense that each can
achieve all that he wills, but he finds that omnipotence is not
possessed in the same way by each person.[7] The major influence

---

[1] C. 4 (PL. 182, 1041C–2D). Cf. L. Ott, *Untersuchungen*, pp. 539–43.

[2] *Disputatio*, c. 13 (PL. 180, 282BC).   [3] *Cap. Haeresum*, 11 (PL. 182, 1053B).

[4] PL. 178, 107–8.   [5] See above, pp. 115–16.

[6] ' "Si potentiam tam ad naturam subsistendi quam ad efficaciam operationis referamus, inveniemus ad proprietatem personae Patris specialiter attinere
potentiam, quae non solum cum ceteris duabus personis aeque omnia efficere
potest, verum etiam ipsa sola a se, non ab altero existere habet; et sicut ex
se habet existere, ita etiam ex se habet posse. Ceterae vero personae, sicut ab
ipso Patre habent esse, ita et ab ipso habent posse, quod volunt, efficere" ',
cited by Walter in *Epist. ad Abaelardum*, ed. Ostlender, p. 35.

[7] PL. 178, 993A–4C: ' ... cum unaquaeque trium personarum inde omnipotens dicatur, quod quidquid earum quaecunque velit efficere possit complere,
non tamen necesse est eodem modo se penitus habere unam quo alteram, cum
in suis proprietatibus diversae sint. Solus quippe Pater potest esse Pater sive
ingenitus et solus Filius genitus sicut et solus Spiritus sanctus procedens. Quid-

upon Abelard's thinking was a remark of Maximus the Confessor that the Father is omnipotent through his unbegotten Godhead;[1] Abelard argued that the relationship of the persons within the Trinity affects the way in which each was omnipotent. Power properly belongs to the Father, not only in respect of what he does, but also because of his unbegotten nature or mode of existence. The other persons, who are equally omnipotent, do not have their power from themselves. Abelard did not abandon this teaching in the fifth and last recension of the 'Scholarium'.[2]

Bernard of Clairvaux, after objecting to the use of the adverb proprie,[3] suggests that if Abelard derives the omnipotence of the Father from his having being and power from himself, then wisdom and benignity should also be ascribed to the Father proprie for the same reason.[4] Bernard had no faith in the utilization of conventional assignations of properties to particular persons in analyses of the structure of the Trinity. Both Bernard and the anonymous Excerptor cite fairly from the 'Scholarium' in support of the capitulum.[5] Thomas of Morigny finds himself in agreement with Abelard's thesis that omnipotence belongs to the Father both because he is omnipotent and because he is unbegotten, but he rejects the additional terminology of proprie and specialiter, saying that in using it Abelard wished to avoid assigning omni-

[1] Homilia LXXXIII de traditione symboli (PL. 57, 433–4).
[2] Ostlender, 'Die Theologia Scholarium', p. 279.
[3] Cf. above, pp. 117–8.
[4] Bernard of Clairvaux, Tractatus de erroribus, c. 3 (PL. 182, 1058C–61B).
[5] Theol. 'Schol.', I, x (PL. 178, 993D). Bernard of Clairvaux, Tractatus, c. 3 (PL. 182, 1059A); Cap. Haeres., 14 (PL. 182, 1054BC).

quid itaque una persona facere potest, et alia potest, et ideo unaquaeque omnipotens dicitur; sed non quidquid una esse potest, necesse est alteram esse ... Ex his quidem verbis Hieronymi, cum profitetur nil plus in Patre quam in Filio, vel minus in Filio quam in Patre reperiri, excepto quod Filius a seipso non est, sicut et Pater profecto, videtur iuxta naturam vel modum existentiae, non operationis, hanc quasi propriam Patri ascribere potentiam, quod solus ipse per se subsistere queat, vel a se ipso existere habeat: hoc est non ab alio, caeteras vero duas in Trinitate personas ab ipso necesse sit esse, nec per se habeant subsistere ... Cum itaque de Patre Maximus dixerit quod per ingenitam deitatem sit omnipotens, id est per hoc quod cum sit Deus, sit etiam ingenitus, illa quoque propria Patris potentia qua solus ipse a se non ab alio subsistit, unde solus ipse ingenitus dicitur, in omnipotentia comprehenditur ... '

potence to the Son and Spirit; by ascribing omnipotence to the Father *specialiter, modo quodam, quantum ad subsistendi modum*, Abelard introduces inequalities into the Trinity.[1] Abelard's critics were perhaps clearer in finding Abelard's argument unacceptable than in stating why it was unacceptable. The crux of Abelard's discussion was that the relationship between the persons affects, not their equality in co-operation, but the manner in which they hold their attributes. The quotation from Maximus on which Abelard based his discussion was not given an alternative interpretation by Abelard's critics who essentially concentrated on declaring Abelard's terminology to be inadmissible.

Abelard was rightly charged with teaching the seventh *capitulum*: *Quod ea solummodo possit Deus facere vel dimittere vel eo modo tantum vel eo tempore quo facit, non alio.* In both the *Theologia Christiana*[2] and the *Theologia 'Scholarium'*[3] Abelard stressed the difficulty of the question whether God can do more and better than he does and whether God can abandon what he does. Whichever answer is given involves anxieties and will be unsatisfactory. If an affirmative answer is suggested, it will appear as a derogation of God's goodness that God can abandon what ought to be done and can do more or better than he does. Abelard himself offers a negative answer. The cornerstone of his argument is a passage of the *Timaeus*[4] which, Abelard claims, is Plato's proof that God could not have made the world better than he did, for he does everything as well as it can be done and everything that he does is necessarily done. To apply this thesis is difficult because faith teaches that God can make a good man better or save a man who would otherwise be damned and many testimonies affirm that God can do more than he ever does. Abelard examines one such testimony in the *'Scholarium'*, Matt. 26, 53, where Christ states that he could ask his Father for more

---

[1] *Disputatio*, 1, ed. Buytaert, 'Thomas of Morigny', pp. 85–6, W. Meyer, 'Die Anklagesätze', p. 417 (fragment) and PL. 180, 283A–298B.

[2] v (PL. 178, 1321A–30C).

[3] III, iv–v (PL. 178, 1091C–1104B). Also from the fifth and final version cf. V. Cousin, *Opera Petri Abaelardi*, II, 146–8. Cf. too *Logica 'Ingred.'*, ed. Geyer, pp. 429–31.

[4] 29D–30A, ed. Waszinck, p. 22, *ll.* 17–23.

than twelve legions of angels. But the passage signifies, not that God can do what he does not, but that he only does what he ought to do, for instead of asking for the angelic legions, Christ fulfils the Scriptures (Matt. 26, 54). Abelard offers his *estimatio*: God only and always does what he should do, therefore he only does what he does.[1] Abelard frankly admits that this opinion may have few or no supporters and that it appears to depart from tradition and, to some extent, from reason, but he answers several objections to it. The thesis does not limit God's freedom; it is a sign of glory, for example, that God can do no evil. The fact that God can save a man who would otherwise be damned arises from man's ability to consent to his salvation, not from God's saving a man who should otherwise be damned. Nor is it an objection to say that there is a variety of ways and means of which God chooses the most suitable, since this implies a possibility that God can choose a less fitting means of action. Perfect goodness consists in the will to act only in the most fitting way. As for the possibility that God can act at another time than he chooses, Abelard replies that God chooses only the most fitting time.

It is curious that neither William nor Bernard raised any objection whatsoever in their known writings to an argument which appeared in the '*Scholarium*' and in which Abelard freely granted that he was contradicting the saints. The condemned *capitulum* was merely supported by the anonymous *Excerptor* with five

---

[1] 'Quantum igitur aestimo, cum id tantum Deus facere possit quod eum facere convenit, nec eum quidquam facere convenit quod facere praetermittat, profecto id solum eum posse facere arbitror quod quandoque facit, licet haec nostra opinio paucos aut nullos habeat assentatores, et plurimum dictis sanctorum, at aliquantulum a ratione dissentire videatur', *Theol.* '*Schol.*' (PL. 178, 1098CD). The opinion cited in the question collection in cod. London, British Museum, Royal 9. E. XII, f. 255v is not found in Abelard's own writings: 'Item forte ex hoc (*cod*: hic ortum) illa m⟨agistri⟩ P⟨etri⟩ Haba ⟨iolardi⟩ oppinio, quod dicitur: nichil potest facere nisi quod facit. Dicebat enim, quod in Deo infinita erant exemplaria et unaqueque res in eo proprium habebat exemplar. Et ita, cum necessarium sit hoc exemplar demonstrato exemplari antichristi esse in Deo et esse exemplar, necessarium (*cod*: non tantum) est anti⟨christum⟩ fore. Et sic de quolibet.' Cf Landgraf, 'Beiträge', pp. 363-4 and also *Sententie Parisienses I*, ed. Landgraf, p. 28, *ll.* 12-17.

citations from the 'Scholarium'.[1] In his *Confessio fidei 'universis'* Abelard concedes that God can do many things which he will never do.[2] However, Thomas of Morigny cites passages from the lost part of the *Apologia* where Abelard apparently fully maintained his thesis.[3] Thomas himself thought that even if Abelard were right, it would have been better to be silent. He ventures some criticism with a distinction between, on the one hand, God's will and action *secundum id quod est* or *secundum essentiam* and, on the other hand, *secundum id quo se ad res conditas habet or secundum actionem id est rerum conditionem*. He argues, from the evidence of miracles, that God's power over creatures is unfettered and that with respect to nature many things can happen, if divine power so wills, which never in fact will happen. Abelard had, to some extent, attempted to cope with this problem in his example of the man who consents to salvation. In the last resort, Thomas's argument is somewhat similar to Abelard's for he insists on the immutability of God's designs with respect to his own nature.

The fifth *capitulum* was: *Quod neque Deus et homo neque haec persona quae Christus est sit tertia persona in Trinitate*. The teaching is not contained in the *Theologia* and William must therefore have formulated his own *capitulum*[4] after reading the *Liber Sententiarum* from which he quotes an offending passage: ' "Sciendum", ait, "est quod licet concedamus quod Christus tertia sit persona in Trinitate, non tamen concedimus quod haec persona, quae Christus sit, sit tertia persona in Trinitate".' To this William replies that the *assumptus homo* is the Son of God, although he agrees that the God-man is not a divine person *secundum quod homo est*; Christ is the Son of God in his humanity, but not by virtue of his humanity.[5] William, and after him Bernard,[6] accused Abelard of Nestorianism on the ground that he had excluded the *assumptus homo* from the Trinity. The

---

[1] *Cap. Haeres.*, 3 (PL. 182, 1049C–1050A). The citations are very similar to passages in the '*Scholarium*' but the last has an addition; cf. PL. 178, 1094D, 1095A, 1096C, 1098AB, 1101D.

[2] PL. 178, 107–8.   [3] *Disputatio*, III (PL. 180, 310D–321B).

[4] *Epist.* 326 (PL. 182, 523B).   [5] *Disputatio*, c. 8 (PL. 180, 276D–80B).

[6] *Epist.* 192, 330 (PL. 182, 359A, 536A).

anonymous *Excerptor* also cites the passage given by William as well as a passage from the same source which states that although Christ the Word is a person of the Trinity, it is not proper to say that 'God and man' is a person of the Trinity.[1] Thomas of Morigny produces quotations from Abelard's '*Scholarium*' which, without teaching the condemned proposition, make certain distinctions which are much less crude than the remarks of the *Liber Sententiarum*, for example that *homo res corporea* or *dissolubilis* is not God and that God is not, properly speaking, man or flesh.[2] Moreover, Thomas refers to a lost part of Abelard's *Apologeticus* where Abelard himself affirms that 'God and man' are not a person of the Trinity and the man assumed by the Word is not one of the three persons.[3] It seems clear from Thomas's quotations that Abelard taught what had been found in the *Liber Sententiarum*.

Abelard's critics successfully seized on the deficiency in his theory of the redemption. In his commentary on Romans Abelard, following Anselm of Canterbury, had rejected the view that Christ's death was a ransom paid to the devil who, upon receipt, surrendered his rights over mankind. Instead he taught that men, far from belonging to the devil by any right, had through the sin of Adam themselves entered into subjection to the devil. The only *ius* which the devil could be said to have gained by seducing men was by the permit of God who allowed him to act as torturer or gaoler. The price of blood was not paid to the devil but to God. Abelard believed that Christ's life and passion were an example of love; our redemption is the love which Christ showed in his passion.[4] In stressing the subjective and the psychological effect of the work of the passion, Abelard passed over in almost total neglect the objective aspects of the justification effected through the merits of Christ, and in a series of questions he challenged the wisdom of allowing the devil a

---

[1] *Cap. Haeres.*, 5 (PL. 182, 1051AB).
[2] *Disputatio*, II (PL. 180, 299A–310C). Cf. *Theol.* '*Schol.*', III, vi (PL. 178, 1107B).
[3] *Ibid.* (300D–1B).
[4] *Expositio in 'ad Romanos'*, II (PL. 178, 833D–6D). Cf. *Theol. Christiana*, IV (1278B–9A); *Theol.* '*Summi boni*', III, i (ed. Ostlender, p. 84).

central place in an explanation of the redemption. Nonetheless, the condemned *capitulum* is somewhat too categorical, at least when compared with Abelard's Commentary, for it charges Abelard with denying that Christ intended to liberate men from the devil's power.[1] The many references by Abelard to Christ bearing the penalty of our sins and bringing benefits to those already dead are not merely the casual survivals of traditional language based upon premisses which Abelard himself did not do much to trace,[2] but also a sign that when in argument Abelard one-sidedly developed the exemplarist thesis, he had not thereby deliberately rejected all other elements of the broader picture. Abelard did not fail to teach that Christ's death achieved the liberation of men from subjection to sin and their freedom as sons of God.[3] William of St Thierry corrected the disproportion in Abelard's theory by distinguishing three elements: the sacrament of the redemption, the example of humility and the incitement to charity.[4] Abelard had alighted upon the last alone, but William's heightened indignation is not only due to the seriousness of the issue; he is also contesting a passage from the *Liber Sententiarum* which altogether removed the notion of the liberation of men from the understanding of Christ's work.[5] The same unidentified passage, which conflicts with the argument in Abelard's commentary, was also reproduced by Bernard[6] and by the anonymous *Excerptor*.[7] Not one of Abelard's affirmations in the *Confessio fidei 'universis'*[8]—the liberation from slavery to

---

[1] *Quod Christus non assumpsit carnem ut nos a iugo diaboli liberaret*, Leclercq, 'Les Formes successives', p. 103, no. 4.

[2] Cf. J. Rivière, *Le dogme de la Rédemption*, pp. 113, 116–19, 124, who collects such references and describes them as orthodox fragments lodged in an alien and unorthodox system.

[3] 'Redemptio itaque nostra est illa summa in nobis per passionem Christi dilectio, quae non solum a servitute peccati liberat, sed veram nobis filiorum Dei libertatem acquirit . . . ', *Expos.* (PL. 178, 836B).

[4] *Disputatio*, c. 7 (PL. 180, 269C–76D), here 276AB. Cf. William's seventh *capitulum* (PL. 182, 532B).

[5] *Disputatio*, c. 7 (PL. 180, 269CD).

[6] *Tractatus*, c. 5 (PL. 182, 1062D–1072C, here 1062D–3A). Over half of Bernard's *Tractatus* is devoted to the debate on the redemption.

[7] *Cap. Haeres.*, c. 4 (PL. 182, 1050A–1A).   [8] PL. 178, 107–8.

sin and from the devil's yoke and the opening of the heavenly life—can be found denied in any previous extant writing by him.

The twelfth *capitulum*, *Quod propter opera nec melior nec peior efficiatur homo*, accurately summarizes Abelard's teaching, especially as it is presented in the *Ethica* where Abelard argued that human actions are in themselves morally indifferent and that a man's merit or guilt is determined not by what he does but by his intention. An action considered concretely or objectively adds nothing to merit or guilt which are earned by the will.[1] Walter of Mortagne asked Abelard whether he taught this[2] and William of St Thierry also charged Abelard with saying that sinful consent is not augmented by the sinful action.[3] The anonymous *Excerptor* produced two quotations, neither identifiable in the *Ethica*, but both consonant with Abelard's teaching.[4] In his *Confessio fidei* Abelard accepted the verdict of his critics.[5]

The nineteenth *capitulum*, *Quod neque opus neque voluntas neque concupiscentia neque delectatio quae movet eam peccatum sit, nec debemus eam velle extingui*, is both fair and unfair. Likewise Abelard's protest in his *Confessio fidei* that the charge is foreign to his writings and sayings is a half-truth.[6] He had written in his *Ethica* that all actions are in themselves morally indifferent[7] and that both natural pleasure[8] and concupiscence[9] are not sins. But he was there referring to sin in its strictest sense as contempt of God and consent to known evil and elsewhere, for example in his eighth sermon, he described sins of deed.[10] William[11] and

---

[1] *Ethica*, c. 3, 5, 7 (PL. 178, 640B, 644A, 647C–8C, 650B–651B). On Abelard's doctrine see R. Blomme, *La Doctrine du péché*, pp. 103–294.

[2] *Epist. ad Abaelardum*, ed Ostlender, p. 40.

[3] *Disputatio*, c. 12 (PL. 180, 282AB). Cf. *Epist.* 326 (PL. 182, 532B). Also Bernard, *Epist.* 188 (PL. 182, 353C).   [4] *Cap. Haeres.*, 10 (PL. 182, 1052D–3A).

[5] PL. 178, 107–8.   [6] PL. 178, 107–8.   [7] C. 7 (PL. 178, 650B).

[8] '. . . liquidum est nullam naturalem carnis delectationem peccato ascribendam esse . . . ', c. 3 (641B).

[9] 'Non itaque concupiscere mulierem, sed concupiscentiae consentire peccatum est; nec voluntas concubitus, sed voluntatis consensus damnabilis est', c. 3 (639A).

[10] PL. 178, 437AB. Also, *Ethica*, c. 14 (654B): 'Opera quoque peccati vel quidquid non recte scimus aut volumus, nonnumquam peccata dicimus . . . '

[11] *Disputatio*, c. 12 (PL. 180, 282A). Cf. *Epist.* 326 (PL. 182, 532C) and R. Blomme, *La Doctrine du péché*, pp. 262–72.

the anonymous *Excerptor*[1] quoted against Abelard texts that may have come from the *Liber Sententiarum*, but they do not misrepresent the challenged aspect of Abelard's teaching.

Abelard also taught the eighth *capitulum*: *Quod non contraximus culpam ex Adam, sed poenam tantum*. In his *Confessio fidei*[2] he retracts this thesis which in the commentary on Romans he had offered as an opinion rather than as a universally acceptable interpretation.[3] Here, probing the concept of sin, Abelard had been insistent that *culpa* could only ensue from a deliberate contempt of God by the free will. Such contempt cannot be offered by new-born children nor has all mankind consented to Adam's own *culpa*. Original sin in us is therefore the debt of damnation with which we are bound because of the fault (*culpa*) of our first parents. William countered by saying that it is the *culpa* which is forgiven in baptism while the *poena* survives in the tribulations of life.[4] The anonymous *Excerptor* presented two unidentified quotations which fairly present the teaching of Abelard's commentary.[5]

Behind the eleventh *capitulum* lay a complicated doctrine: *Quod potestas ligandi atque solvendi apostolis tantum data sit, non etiam successoribus eorum*. In the *Ethica*[6] Abelard suggested that this power was given specially to the apostles but not generally to all bishops because many lack religion and discretion. He notes that various promises were given at various times by Christ to the apostles and he believes that the gift of the Spirit to remit or retain sins (John 20, 22–3) was addressed exclusively to the apostles and to those successors who share their worthiness.

---

[1] *Cap. Haeres.*, 13 (PL. 182, 1054AB). Cf. Blomme, *La Doctrine du péché*, pp. 272–4.

[2] PL. 178, 107–8.

[3] *Expositio*, II (866A–73D): 'non tam pro assertione quam pro opinione' (873D). Cf. J. Gross, 'Abälards Umdeutung des Erbsündendogmas', pp. 14–27.

[4] *Disputatio*, c. 11 (PL. 180, 281D–2A), also c. 7 (275C–6A). Cf. *Epist.* 326 (PL. 182, 532B).

[5] *Cap. Haeres.*, 8 (PL. 182, 1052B).

[6] C. 26 (PL. 178, 673C–8A) continued in cod. Balliol College 296, f. 79r–v. Abelard's teaching is analysed by P. Anciaux, *La Théologie du sacrement de pénitence*, pp. 286–93. Also by L. Hödl, *Geschichte der scholastischen Literatur*, pp. 79–86.

He collects support from Jerome, Origen and Gregory to show that the power of the keys is tied to a power of discernment, to merit and to justice and he also argues that the power of the keys granted to Peter can mean merely the power, granted to all bishops, of excommunicating and readmitting into the present church. But in respect of the gift of the Spirit to remit or to retain sin, Abelard is more hesitant; he does not wish to oppose those who interpret the New Testament texts so that this special grace is extended equally to all bishops, both worthy and unworthy, and in the *Confessio fidei 'universis'*[1] he concedes that the power of binding and loosing was so extended to all successors of the apostles, although he does not here specify in what he thinks the power of binding and loosing consists. This is Abelard's only retreat from frankness and openness in this argument. Apart from a very brief reference by Bernard,[2] the only critic was the anonymous *Excerptor* who presents passages not found in the *Ethica* but which support its teaching.[3]

The last *capitulum* which remains for consideration, the fifteenth, provides an anti-climax: *Quod diabolus immittat suggestiones per appositionem lapidum sive herbarum.* Abelard ignored it in his *Confessio fidei* although his guilt was glaring; in the *Ethica* he had clearly taught that demons, the *scientes*, experts in the natural powers of things, can use herbs and seeds, stones and trees to influence and sway our minds and for example, *Deo permittente*, to induce languor.[4] William knew, not this passage of the *Ethica*, but an equivalent passage of the *Liber Sententiarum* which taught that when the devil wishes to suggest lust or anger he produces a stone or a herb which contains the power of exciting the required passion. William commented that Abelard must have taught this flippantly.[5] Nonetheless, William booked it.[6]

It is clear from this examination that much contemporary criticism of Abelard's teaching was thwarted by being founded upon statements taken from the *Liber Sententiarum* even when

[1] PL. 178, 107–8.   [2] *Epist.* 188 (PL. 182, 353C).
[3] *Cap. Haeres.*, 12 (PL. 182, 1053C–4A).
[4] C. 4 (PL. 178, 647A–C).   [5] *Disputatio*, c. 10 (PL. 180, 281A–C).
[6] *Epist.* 326 (PL. 182, 532B). Cf Bernard, *Tractatus* (PL. 182, 1062B).

they contradicted Abelard's own thought as it is found in his writings. Moreover, Abelard's critics were not uniformly successful in finding replies to the teachings which they criticized. Judged by the standard of accuracy the list of condemned *capitula* is an unfortunate piece of work. Nonetheless, for all the raggedness of of battle William and Bernard between them brought the anxieties of many into a sharper focus and managed to highlight and to challenge forcefully what seemed to be the weaknesses and eccentricities of Abelard's teaching. They drove him to abandon some ground. They also drove him to take refuge in syntactical arguments which, however right in themselves, were something of a 'blind alley' allowing of no further development. Some of Abelard's teachings simply disappeared from subsequent writing and discussion, but many remained to preoccupy and to challenge other disciples and critics. The council of Sens had not wholly cleared the air nor was its verdict wholly convincing.

CHAPTER V

THE THEOLOGICAL WRITINGS
OF ABELARD'S
CLOSEST DISCIPLES

The circle of Abelard's followers or of those scholars who actually wrote treatises or commentaries under Abelard's impulsion and who closely followed his teaching was small. As a productive force in the literature of the twelfth century it ceased to exist within a decade or a little more of Abelard's death. It is probably realistic to distinguish between those students of Abelard who wrote up his teaching while in his school or shortly after leaving it and other clerics or monks who drew upon Abelard's material and who even did so after his departure from the schools and after his final condemnation. In spite of the size of Abelard's following in his lifetime, no term was coined in the twelfth century in corporate designation of these disciples as was the case with the *porretani* and it is possible, though undemonstrable, that the need for such a classification was greatly lessened by Abelard's death and by the effects of the condemnation. In the following pages the fortunes of Abelard's most controverted opinions will be traced through the writings of his closest disciples as well as of other authors outside his school or formed by other traditions of teaching than that of Abelard alone but who gave a full consideration to Abelard's thought. The posthumous influence of Abelard's teaching is, however, too diffuse to be discussed at all adequately by this means; particular aspects can best be appreciated by the attentive study of the history of single ideas or themes as they have been treated already in many cases by such doctrinal historians as O. Lottin in numerous chapters of his *Psychologie et Morale*, and L. Ott on many pages of his admirable *Untersuchungen*. One such doctrinal historian, P. Anciaux, has justly observed that the multiplicity and complexity of the relationships between different masters of different schools who copied each other, even unscrupulously, is such that attempts to classify them or to summarize the thought of particular authors run the risk of distorting proper perspectives.[1]

The term 'follower' is itself a multiple equivocation: *plurimi professi sunt Abaielardum*. Some defended his theses, but others abused them and Abelard may well have thought unkindly of the author of the *Liber Sententiarum*. To many, no doubt, Abelard was a passing event in their scholastic career, the most controversial of a variety of masters who were heard prior to a life spent in perhaps ecclesiastical administration or in the cloister. The scholastic firmament was filled with numerous competing masters and the pace of development was, in the decades from the 1130s to the 1150s, accelerated. Those who remained in the schools had to continue to follow the development of thought. The conventional description of a Roland or an Omnebene as disciples of Abelard is a historical simplification. The rubricators of Omnebene's Sentences thought that he had collected the opinions of 'diverse authorities',[2] even of 'all the masters'.[3]

A distinction can be made between, on the one hand, those writers who exclusively depend upon the lecturing or writing of Abelard and do so either directly or through the intermediary of the *Liber Sententiarum* which Dr Ostlender posited as the source of some of the Abelardian sentence collections and, on the other hand, those authors whose writings rest upon material taken from other masters as well as from Abelard. The *Sententie Parisienses I, Sententie Hermanni, Sententie Florianenses* and *Commentarius Cantabrigiensis* have no other contemporary source than Abelard and are the work of close disciples who had presumably been taught by Abelard. But Abelard's opinions as they are found in his writings and as they are found in the *Liber Sententiarum* differ, and so these close disciples are most important for the evidence they offer of the way in which Abelard's teachings were understood or misunderstood in his entourage and hence too outside his circle. It is most difficult to give an exact date to

[1] Anciaux, *La Théologie du sacrement de pénitence*, p. 5.
[2] Clm. 19,134, p. 151.   [3] Cod. Naples, VII, C. 43, f. 1r.

any work by a close disciple. Suggestions can only be of the most general kind since these authors are anonymous and have contributed scarcely any personal or topical allusions, and since evidence of dating is to be gleaned only by textual or doctrinal analysis. As in the foregoing chapter we shall not attempt to assign dates rigidly to any texts but to indicate what can be stated about their literary precedents and their place in the succession of Abelardian writings.

THE 'COMMENTARIUS CANTABRIGIENSIS'

The *Commentarius Cantabrigiensis* on all the Epistles of St Paul was written before 1153, the year of the death of Bernard of Clairvaux who is mentioned in the work favourably but also rather pointedly: 'illam mirabilem gratiam loquendi et alios instruendi spiritu Dei assecutus est potius quam subtilitate ingenii.'[1] Dr Landgraf moreover believed that it was written before or not long after Abelard's final condemnation.[2] The author knew something of the activities of Count Theobald of Champagne and a joke concerning the canons of St Martin of Tours.[3] His language betrays some Germanisms[4] but the only manuscript of his work comes from Buildwas in England; it is often barely legible and Dr Landgraf's edition in four volumes of over 800 pages is a fine feat of endurance. The anonymous commentator expounded the words of Paul in literal-historical glosses and in many places used the text of Paul as a stimulus to brief argument and to the introduction of the opinions of Abelard. He was interested in logical modes of expression; the words 'significatio', 'predicatio', 'genus', 'predicabile' and 'iunctura' appear in his examination of original sin[5] and in a joke he scoffed at backward dialecticians: 'quomodo etiam, ut aliquid ludicri interseramus, veteres dialectici refullari debent, ut novi fiant'.[6] He never mentions Abelard's name but he has found a title for him which

---

[1] Ed. Landgraf, IV, 729.   [2] *Ibid.*, I, introduction, pp. xiv–xvi.
[3] *Ibid.*, III, 460–1, IV, 685–6. See *ibid.*, introduction, pp. xiv–xvi.
[4] *Ibid.*, I, introduction, pp. xvi–xvii.
[5] *Rom.* 1, 76. I cite by volume and page according to Landgraf's edition, and I prefix the name of the epistle which is commented.   [6] *Heb.* IV, 685.

he employs again and again: 'Philosophus.' In the later commentaries he omits even this and simply introduces quotations with the word 'inquit'.[1] He thought of Abelard as the great innovator in dialectic: 'dialectica, ut quidam ait, que cum sub illo et illo magistro alia et alia habuerit vestimenta adveniente philosopho omnino remotis veteribus nova accepit indumenta.'[2] But the words 'philosophus' and 'philosophia' had not yet acquired a purely secular and academic significance.[3] For Abelard not only Plato but also Christ were philosophers,[4] and for this commentator Abelard the dialectician is also the master of theology. The opinions of Abelard which are adopted and cited concern marriage,[5] the degrees of love,[6] justice,[7] the angels' joy on the conversion of a sinner,[8] the divine will,[9] mortal and venial sin.[10] Moreover many of the disputed theological opinions of Abelard are presented.

Abelard's only surviving New Testament commentary is his exposition of Romans. The Cambridge Commentary on all the Pauline epistles offers, however, good evidence for believing that Abelard had lectured on these epistles in general and Dr Landgraf has shown that this commentator had himself heard Abelard.[11] By reporting Abelard's *lectura* the commentator does not offer the security that he was always correctly reporting or interpreting his master. But the comparison of the teachings of this commentary with passages in Abelard's own writings provides a valuable opportunity of comparing, if not Abelard's spoken teaching and his writing, at least his writings and reports of his teaching.

The commentator claims to quote the spoken words of Abelard ('Philosophus:... inquit, dico') touching the properties of the divine persons. The Father is omnipotence; 'Filius est quedam potentia, quia est sapientia, id est potentia discernendi'; the Spirit has benignity specially assigned to him and benignity is no

---

[1] See *ibid.*, I, introduction, pp. xi–xiii.   [2] 2 *Cor.* II, 287.
[3] See J. Leclercq, 'Pour l'histoire de l'expression "philosophie chrétienne"'.
[4] *Theol.* 'Schol.', II, xiii (PL. 178, 1071D). Cf. *Comment. Cantabrig.*, Col. III, 490: 'philosophi huius temporis monachi sunt, qui vitam philosophicam ducunt, unde de Johanne dicitur, quia philosophatur in heremo'.
[5] I *Cor.* II, 241 *et seq.*   [6] *Gal.* II, 376; *Eph.* II, 431–2; I *Tim.* III, 587.
[7] 2 *Cor.* II, 295.   [8] *Phil.* III, 449–50.   [9] I *Tim.* III, 556.
[10] *Heb.* IV, 836.   [11] *Ibid.*, I, introduction, pp. xvii–xxxviii.

power.[1] Abelard did not himself write that the Son is *quedam potentia* and in reply to criticism he most vigorously objected that if such a teaching could be found in his writings, he would be not only a heretic but a heresiarch.[2] In his defence he wrote that the *sapientia Dei* is *quedam potentia Dei* but that it is not proper to say that the Son, who is the wisdom of God, is a certain power of God. There is a strong possibility that the commentator has here simplified Abelard's argumentation and also that he was unaware of the heightened need of precision in statement which was felt by Abelard in around the year 1140.

The Commentator also reports the *Philosophus* teaching that the Spirit shares the substance of the Father and the Son but is not from (*de*) the substance of the Father or the Son: 'Spiritus vero Sanctus, cum sit omnino eiusdem substantie cum Patre vel Filio, non est tamen de substantia Patris vel Filii, cum benignitas potentia omnino non sit nec benignum esse sit potentem esse, sicut sapientem esse est potentem esse.'[3] Once again the Commentator reports what Abelard in his *Confessio* strongly denied having written[4] and once again there is a strong possibility that the Commentator is somewhat loosely reporting Abelard or alternatively that Abelard had lectured less carefully than he wrote. The evidence for this judgment comes from the way in which the Commentator goes on to report Abelard's observations on a supposed (but now unidentified) quotation from St Ambrose saying that the Spirit is *de substantia Patris*. Abelard is here found saying that the expression *de substantia Patris* can be understood of the procession of the Spirit and of the generation of the Son. But according to the Nicene Creed, which refers to the Son as *ex Patre natum*, only the Son is *ex substantia Patris*.[5]

---

[1] *Col.* III, 483. Cf. *Rom.* I, 22; also Landgraf's introduction, I, xii–xiii.

[2] *Conf. fidei*, PL. 178, 105–6, and cf. above, pp. 115–19.

[3] *Col.* III, 483. Cf. Landgraf's introduction, I, xii–xiii.

[4] PL. 178, 105–6 and cf. above, pp. 122–3.

[5] 'Obicitur de beato Ambrosio qui dicit Spiritum Sanctum esse de substantia Patris. Philosophus: De substantia, inquit, Patris esse intellexit sive per processionem quod ad Spiritum Sanctum spectat, sive per genituram, quod Filii est, cuius gigni est. Unde natum ex Patre Filium cum in simbolo habeatur, Nicenum Concilium exponit ex substantia Patris esse, id solum ad Filium applicans', *Col.* III, 483–4.

L

This reported teaching corresponds to the teaching of the *Theologia* where it is clear that Abelard was trying to describe the procession of the Spirit in terms other than those which he reserves for the description of the generation of the Son.[1] The Commentator, however, also gives the impression that Abelard did not actually object to Ambrose's description of the Spirit as *de substantia Patris*.

The Commentator mentions Plato's knowledge of God, of the *nous* or *mens nata a Deo* and of the *anima omnia replens*. He believes that the ancient pagan philosophers came to know not only the distinction between the divine persons but also the processions, and he cites the image of the bronze seal used by Abelard.[2] He does not provide evidence that Abelard ever taught that Christ's soul did not descend into Hell *per se*. He discusses the impossibility of spirits moving locally and the meaning of the divine omnipresence as Abelard had done, although without referring to Christ's descent into Hell. The incarnation of Christ is called a descent with respect to the humiliation, not to movement in space,[3] and the last coming of Christ is explained either as an unusual event upon earth or also as a local and real coming of Christ from the heavens.[4] The divine omnipresence is an omnipresence of power.[5]

There are repeated echoes in the *Commentarius* of Abelard's insistence that Christ's passion and death were both an exhibition of God's love for mankind and an inspiration which liberated men from the yoke of sin.[6] Christ was an offering for sin and the

---

[1] Cf. above, pp. 122-3.   [2] *Rom.* 1, 21-3.

[3] *Eph.* II, 411, 416.

[4] 'Dominum de celo ad nos descendere non est aliud, ut sepe diximus, nisi eum in terra aliquod inusitatum operari. Vel descendet de celo, quia localiter etiam Christus de illa eminentia celorum usque ad nos veniet, cui obviam in aera occurremus', *Thess.* III, 525. The first opinion, considered singly, might suggest that Abelard conjectured that Christ at the last coming would not be corporeally present.   [5] *Eph.* II, 413.

[6] *Rom.* I, 102-4. Cf. *Titum* III, 628; 2 *Cor.* II, 292-3; *Gal.* II, 344; *Heb.* IV, 695-9, 785, 845. In *Heb.* IV, 695-9 the Commentator dwells descriptively on Christ's sufferings and in *Heb.* IV, 664-5, he refers directly to Abelard's *Theologia* on the purpose of Christ's incarnation: 'quemadmodum enim in theologia habetur philosophi'.

memory of his passion drives out that carnality 'que etiam diu a mundo abscessisset, si predicatores essent, quales oporteret, qui et verbo et exemplo instruerent, qui iustitie rigorem tenerent nec Dominum venderent, quem etiam pro minori pretio vendunt, cum nummum accipiant'.[1] The justice of God is *dilectio Dei et proximi*.[2] In addition there are in the *Commentarius* clear references to our liberation by Christ from servitude or captivity under the devil[3] and to Christ's battle on earth against the devil to free us from his power.[4] The latter remark is somewhat against the spirit of Abelard's argument, for Abelard stressed that Christ himself permitted what the devil had over mankind and suggested that his work on earth, far from being orientated towards the devil was orientated towards the instruction of mankind.[5] It is possible that these phrases in the *Commentarius* were introduced by Abelard's disciple, but although Abelard demoted the devil from an exaggerated place in the interpretation of Christ's work, he had never gone as far as to deny that Christ also liberated men from the servitude to the devil to which this Commentator refers.

In his written commentary on Romans, 9, 21 Abelard, like this Commentator, argued the freedom of God to bestow his grace where he pleases; on earth a man may present a horse to another man without being obliged to give horses to all and sundry.[6] The Commentator continues to discuss grace with the aid of a different selection of analogies than those used by Abelard in his writing but perhaps coined by him in his lecturing. He does not use the simile of the patient who is too weak to

---

[1] *Rom.* I, 103.   [2] *Rom.* I, 104.

[3] 'At vero miserum est, imo miserrimum, creatorem suum relinquere et diabolo servire. A qua servitute sive captivitate nos Christus liberavit', *Eph.* II, 415.

[4] '. . . de Christo adhuc agonizante et pro suis in terra dimicante contra diabolum, ut ab ipsius potestate eos erueret et a iugo peccati liberaret', *Heb.* IV, 688. Cf. the Commentator on excommunication: 'Cum aliquis iuste sit excommunicatus ita satane traditus est, ut cum voluerit, in eum manum ponat et, quocumque modo placuerit, eum tractet. Sed quamdiu quis quantumcumque pessimus est in unitate ecclesie . . . non habet diabolus in eum potestatem', I *Cor.* II, 232.   [5] Cf. above, pp. 137–9.

[6] *Expositio*, IV (PL. 178, 916C–9A). Cf. *Comment. Cantabrig., Rom.* I, 129–30.

take his medicine without support, but a simile of the carpenters who, if they lack tools, cannot be blamed for not doing their master's will, or of the chariot which cannot move without oxen to pull it or of the men who are offered food from an inaccessible pinnacle. These illustrations, which would suggest that without grace men can do nothing ('subtracta gratia ex se nichil possunt, quantuncunque conentur') are considered unfitting.[1] Instead the Commentator offers the simile of two men who are offered a prize for going to Jerusalem. The poorer of the two has the ability and the greater incentive to win the prize but he is also lazy; the richer, who is also the weaker of the two, sets out and wins the reward.[2] The Commentator argues that no new or additional grace is given to either of these men; he claims to be quoting Abelard's own words and he makes it clear that the discussion only concerns those men who already have faith. The incitement offered to men by God is the promise of eternal beatitude; by the gift of reason and of faith men are moved to love. Some say that between faith and love a new grace is necessary to produce the will which strives for the reward—'quod utique philosophus non recipit'.[3] The Commentator provides a valuable insight into the way in which Abelard reasoned his denial of the theory of enabling graces; in essence Abelard was attempting to establish that God does not resort to 'pressure' but uses the better means of teaching the goal and of providing the instruments—reason and faith—for achieving it: 'Deus vero non solum non impellit vel non cogit, verum etiam viam pertingendi ad bravium docet et instrumenta, quibus pertingi potest prestat, rationem et fidem.'[4] Since reason and faith are clearly seen as gifts from God, it cannot be said that Abelard was attempting to undermine human indebtedness to God for the ability to seek the reward, but the uncompromising way in which further

---

[1] *Rom.* 1, 131–2.   [2] *Ibid.*, p. 132.

[3] 'Sed inquiunt quidam, quod inter fidem et dilectionem necessaria est quedam nova gratia, que videlicet ipsum velle in nobis efficiat . . . ut ad illud scilicet bravium velimus tendere, que, quo nomine appelletur, omnino ignorant. Quod utique philosophus non recipit', *ibid.*

[4] *Rom.* 1, 133.

cooperation between God and man is ignored can be appreciated clearly in the Commentator's account.

The Commentator teaches, with Abelard, that original sin in the descendants of Adam is not *culpa* or sin in the proper sense of a fault which we have committed, but a debt of punishment incurred with the sin of Adam. Sin, in the sense of *culpa*, cannot be committed by little children who do not consent to evil or offer contempt to God; but the penalty for Adam's sin is incurred unless the sacraments intervene.[1] The Commentator is fully in accord with Abelard's insistence that sin is a consent to disobey conscience. He uses the example of the crucifixion of Christ and Abelard's example of the persecutors of the early martyrs, who thought they were doing good and serving God, but their intentions were not good for they were mistaken, nor was their action good because their intentions were bad, but provided good faith or sincerity was present, their consciences were pure and they did not sin.[2] The *Philosophus* is quoted explicitly affirming that what is done in ignorance is not against conscience; where there is no contempt of God there is no sin. But Abelard also taught that in another sense, but not as contempt of God, ignorance can be called sin. Similarly the Commentator says both that the ignorant do not sin and that ignorance can be called a sin in the sense of being the penalty for previous sins.[3] It is not surprising that critics should have misunderstood Abelard's teaching.

The Commentator frequently finds occasion to state emphatically that *opera* are never sins and can earn neither merit nor damnation. Merit lies in the will.[4] The author offers Abelard's examples of murder and adultery which are not sins; they may be committed by mistake.[5] Only where there is a contempt of the mind, in the sense of contempt offered to God by the mind, is there sin and with it a consent to evil.[6] Sin is consent, not will. A desire to fornicate is not sin, but a natural will.[7] Of the three

---

[1] *Rom.* 1, 75–8. Cf. Abelard, *Expositio in 'ad Rom'.*, II (PL. 178, 866c *et seq.*).
[2] *Rom.* 1, 179, 203. Cf. above, pp. 131–2.   [3] 2 *Tim.* III, 601–2; 1 *Tim.* III, 521.
[4] *Rom.* 1, 179; 2 *Cor.* II, 290, 311.   [5] *Gal.* II, 366; 1 *Tim.* III, 571–2. Cf. above, p. 139.   [6] *Gal.* II, 359.   [7] 1 *Thess.* III, 520–1.

parts of temptation—suggestion, pleasure and consent—only the latter, the consent to the suggestion and the pleasure, is sin.[1] The Commentator is aware that Abelard's views, e.g. that murder or adultery is not a sin, have to be instantly explained if they are not to be scorned,[2] and he quotes a remark of Abelard which is not found in his writings, that there still persists a Judaical attitude of mind which thinks of murder and adultery as sins in the way that Jews thought of the touching of lepers or corpses as sins although they are merely deeds. This is not, however, true of those who have heard Abelard ('nisi qui me audierint') who teaches that only contempt by the mind is sin.[3]

On the power of the keys the Commentator teaches like Abelard that priests can declare a presumed divine sentence but do not themselves have the power of opening or closing heaven, and he uses the authorities—Jerome, Gregory and the example of Lazarus—discussed by Abelard to show that sinners are first reconciled to God and then loosed by the priests.[4] The Com-

---

[1] I Cor. II, 256–7.

[2] 'Veluti si aliquis statim diceret occidere hominem, concumbere cum uxore alterius non esse peccatum, sed contemptus mentis, quemadmodum astruit philosophus, non audiretur, nisi pedetentim rationes premitteret', Gal. II, 366.

[3] 'Philosophus: . . . tangere leprosum vel tangere mortuum . . . nullatenus peccata erant, que ipsi tamen pro peccatis reputabant. In quo iudaismo nonnulli etiam hodie sunt, qui ipsa facta, ut hominem occidere, adulterari, astruunt esse peccata, nisi qui me audierint, qui solos mentis contemptus peccata esse arbitror.' Heb. IV, 775.

[4] I Cor. II, 232–3. Cf. above, pp. 140–1. Two other Pauline commentaries have been supposed to adhere to Abelard. Dr Landgraf, 'Zur Lehre von der Gotteser-kenntnis', p. 272, and more recently Z. Alszeghy, 'Nova Creatura', p. 20, describe the commentary on Romans found in cod. Paris, Bibl. nat. lat. 567, ff. 36r–66r (twelfth century) as influenced by Abelard. Alszeghy, pp. 43–4, thought that the image of the doctor dispensing medicine to the sick and thus exemplifying the action of divine grace upon the soul, was borrowed from Abelard. Cf. f. 41r: ' . . . ut vester medicus valuus imperfectionis vestre curaret'. Also f. 51r: 'Adhuc alio modo ostendit quod super omnes est iusticia [Alszeghy: gratia] Dei. Vere super omnes quoniam omnes peccaverunt, omnes in uno et morte vitiorum dormientes ad iusticiam Dei consequendam imbecilles facti sunt, et nullus fuit sibi sufficiens ut, quando vellet, per se decutere posset hanc infirmitatem, id est et egent gloria Dei; in se non habent, unde propellent hanc peccatorum infirmitatem. Non plus possent Iudei quam gentes; omnes indigent iustitia et sanitate anime, qui sunt impotentes sibi mediri in sua infirmitate.' The image, is, however, adumbrated in the earlier Glossa ordinaria:

mentator does not discuss Abelard's suggestion that not all prelates have received the powers of binding and loosing given to the Apostles; he simply affirms that they were given to both the Apostles and to their vicars.

The *Commentarius Cantabrigiensis* provides valuable complements to the evidence of Abelard's teaching found in his own writings. On grace, on the nature of sin and possibly on the redemption the Commentator helps us to understand better what Abelard wrote. On the divine attributes, the procession of the Spirit, the sin of ignorance and, again, grace, the Commentator helps us to appreciate better the anxieties of Abelard's critics. He allows us to approach very near to the actually spoken teaching of Abelard and offers a report that is in the main accurate but occasionally mistaken—or apparently so.

THE 'SENTENTIE FLORIANENSES'

The author of the Sentences contained in the manuscript of Sankt Florian intended to summarize concisely theological doctrine in accordance with Abelard's division of theology into the three parts of faith, sacrament and charity.[1] The surviving text, however, breaks off before the end of the discussion of the sacraments and charity is wholly missing. What survives is a

---

[1] 'Tria sunt in quibus summa nostrae salutis consistit: fides, caritas, sacramentum, de quibus, si ad plenum disseramus, sufficere credimus', ed. Ostlender, 1. Cf. Abelard, *Theol. 'Schol.'* (PL. 178, 981c). On the features of the *Sent. Florianenses* see Ostlender's introduction to his edition, pp. v–vii and *idem*, 'Die Sentenzenbücher', p. 218; also Grabmann, *Geschichte*, II, 224 and an attentive study by E. Bertola, 'Le "Sententie Florianenses".'

'Sed voluntas nostra ostenditur infirma per legem, ut sanet gratia voluntatem et sanata voluntas impleat legem non constituta sub lege nec indigens lege' (PL. 114, 480B). There is no other sign of dependence upon Abelard. Dr Landgraf, *Introducción*, p. 111, and Alszeghy, *op. cit.*, p. 22, mention an exegetical fragment concerning *Romans* 8, 28–31 and found in cod. Paris, Bibl. nat. lat. 2,800, f. 55r–v (twelfth century) and supposed to depend upon St Bruno the Carthusian and Abelard. There are in fact no parallels with Abelard that cannot be found in the commentary uncertainly ascribed to Bruno (PL. 153, 75B–76B) and in the *Glossa ordinaria* (PL. 114, 498A–C). The fragment is identical with cod. Paris, Bibl. nat. lat. 15,601, ff. 13r–14v which is ascribed to the circle of Ralph of Flaix (cf. W. Affeldt, 'Verzeichniss der Römerbriefkommentare', p. 400).

brief, crisp and rapid presentation of the outlines of Abelard's thinking about God, the redemption and some of the sacraments. The author reflects Abelard's teaching as it stood before Walter of Mortagne wrote to Abelard and before a mounting tide of opposition caused Abelard to revise some of his opinions. The *Sententie Florianenses* are shocking. The brevity of the work does not render it more innocuous but the more potent for being a distillation. In a few lines the author can deliver without any sign of caution or hesitation several of the most controverted and most personal theses of Abelard. His work does not seem to have been composed for general circulation. The style has in places been left unpolished and one has the impression of a private compilation made primarily for personal purposes.[1] The actual sources of the work cannot be determined.[2]

The author writes that the Father, Son and Spirit designate respectively power, wisdom and benignity;[3] wisdom is a part of power ('quaedam potentia', 'pars potentiae') and benignity is not a part of omnipotence or of omnisapience.[4] However, the author also interchanges the names of the persons and of their attributes in a manner which Abelard himself, under the pressure of criticism, strenuously repudiated. He not only writes that wisdom is a part of power but also that the Son is *ex portione Patris* and designates *quaedam potentia*.[5] The term *portio* is used by Abelard only in the first version of his *Theologia 'Scholarium'*, written before the letter of Walter of Mortagne.[6] It is possible that his disciple, in teaching what was to be condemned by Pope Innocent II, namely that the Son is *quaedam potentia*, had taken a step which Abelard himself never took, but it is also possible

---

[1] Ostlender, 'Die Sentenzenbücher', p. 218.   [2] *Ibid.*
[3] C. 8 (4). References to the text of the *Sent. Flor.* are by chapter number and page as found in Ostlender's edition.   [4] C. 15 (6–7).
[5] 'Pater designat omnipotentiam et ideo quasi stipes dicitur. Filius dicitur, quod est ex portione Patris. Filius autem omnem sapientiam designat. Omnis autem sapientia est quaedam potentia; sed quia Filius designat quandam potentiam, Pater omnem potentiam, ideo dicitur Filius esse genitus, quasi ex portione Patris exsistens. Nam Filius, ut dictum est, designat quandam potentiam. Sapientia enim quae ipse (est), est quaedam potentia et pars etiam potentiae', c. 15 (6).   [6] Cf. above, p. 117.

that in the early to middle 1130s Abelard had himself not yet learned to avoid such statements.

A further indication that the *Sententie Florianenses* were influenced by the terminology which Abelard used at the time of writing the first version of his *Theologia 'Scholarium'* is provided by the teaching concerning the divine omnipotence. Although all the divine persons are omnipotent,[1] the Nicene Creed names the Father omnipotent; omnipotence belongs to the Father *proprie*; he is *maxime omnipotens* for unlike the Son and Spirit he derives his existence from himself.[2] Likewise in the *'Scholarium'* Abelard claimed that the power of God 'ad personam Patris maxime pertinere' for the Father, in addition to being able to fulfil his will, derives his power and his being from himself alone.[3] On the procession of the Spirit the *Sententie Florianenses* teach like Abelard that the Spirit is not begotten 'quia non est ex substantia Patris et Filii'.[4] The author also distinguishes two processions of the Spirit, 'una in affectu, alia in effectu'. The first is eternal for the Spirit is eternally benign; the other is temporal and relates only to creation. In his doctrine of the created world-soul Plato understood that the Spirit is the beginning of the life of things in time.[5]

The *Sententie Florianenses* hold with Abelard that God cannot do what he does not do nor more than he does nor can he have another or a better will than he has. He can do nothing without reason. Each man can be saved because his nature can be changed;

---

[1] C. 12 (5–6).　　　　　　　　　　　[2] C. 8–9 (4).

[3] Landgraf in his edition of the *Commentarius Cantabrigiensis*, III, 483n. citing from cod. Fritzlar, f. 97r: 'Unde, quod ait Maximus episcopus per omnipotentiam Patrem esse, tale est acsi dicat ipsam divinam potentiam ad personam Patris maxime pertinere, non quod ipse solus est omnipotens, id est omnia, que vult, efficere possit, sed quod insuper ipse solus ex se habeat posse, sicut ex se habet esse, non ex alio.' The passage continues: '. . . Per Filium quippe divinam intelligimus sapientiam. Sapientia autem, cum sit quedam potentia, discernendi scilicet, quasi quedam est portio divine omnipotentie, cum sit ipsa quoque quedam potentia, sicut quilibet filius quedam proprii patris portio esse dicitur. Quasi-portionem quidem non vere portionem dicimus, cum in ipsius divine nature simplicitate nulle penitus partes existere queant, nulla omnino rerum multitudo, nichil penitus, quod non sit ipse.'

[4] C. 8 (4).　　　　　　　　　　　[5] C. 17 (7).

God cannot save everyone for his will is immutable.[1] The author comes close to seeming to teach what is the seventeenth *capitulum* in J. Leclercq's list of condemned propositions,[2] when he writes that God, whose reason determines every happening and who cannot act against reason and who knows why evil ought to occur, cannot disturb an evil event.[3] On the other hand, the author does not teach the eighteenth *capitulum*, that Christ's soul did not descend into Hell *per se*; to the word 'descend' he applies the meaning of ceasing to vivify the body.[4] With Abelard he teaches that God is essentially omnipresent.[5]

Abelard was accused of teaching that the person of Christ was not a person of the Trinity.[6] The *Sententie Florianenses* do not contain expressions which are seriously compromising. They stress that in Christ a human and a divine nature combine in one person without humanity becoming divinity or vice versa. In expressions such as 'God is man' and 'man is God' the part stands for the whole and the phrases are therefore not proper. The human Word is naturally the Son of God and is *de substantia Patris*; but the *homo assumptus*—soul and body—is not the Son of God naturally or by generation because the *homo assumptus* is not *de substantia Patris*.[7] On the manner of our redemption the author argues that Christ was not bound by the existence of rights belonging to the devil to choose the method which was adopted. If God gave to the devil a power to punish men, he could reclaim it justly without assuming flesh and he could redeem men without paying a price.[8] In this sense the *Sententie*

---

[1] C. 23 (11).   [2] See above, p. 127.

[3] 'Illi dicuntur consentire malo, cum sciant aliquem aliquod malum velle facere, et possunt disturbare et ad eos pertinent et non disturbant. Deus non videtur consentire malo; cum sciat, quare illud debeat fieri, non potest disturbare. Nam ratio est, quare nec ipse contra rationem facere potest', c. 25 (12).

[4] 'Quod descendit, desinit vivificare', c. 22 (10).

[5] C. 22 (9–11).   [6] See above, pp. 136–7.   [7] C. 34–6 (16–18).

[8] 'Dicunt quidam, quod homo se subiecerat diabolo propter primum peccatum. Unde inquiunt Deum non posse ei auferre hominem, nisi quadam redemptione, nisi iniuriam ei faceret . . . Dicunt etiam, quod homo non valeret ad redimendum . . . Nos vero dicimus, quod haec ratio non est valens. Nam Deus poterat condonare peccata homini et poterat liberare eum instauratione, etsi carnem non assumpsisset . . . ', c. 30 (14–15).

Florianenses teach what was condemned by Pope Innocent, namely that liberating men from the devil was not the reason why Christ assumed flesh; the purpose of the incarnation was to demonstrate the love of God.[1] Nonetheless, the purposes of the redemption also include the redemption of men from their slavery to sin. The way in which this redemption comes to us is explained either by saying that the memory of Christ's example and love leads us to abstain from sin or by saying that Christ's example leads us to consent to reason and therefore to extract ourselves from the grip of the suggestions of the devil to whom we previously belonged.[2] In the *Sententie Florianenses* the devil is excluded from the explanation of the manner of the redemption chosen by God and is retained in one of two alternative explanations of the workings of the redemption in ourselves. But it would be wrong to attach a too rigid meaning to the way in which the author appears to hesitate about the place of the devil in the redemption, for the work survives in an unpolished condition. It is perhaps just to conclude that in this account the rejection of the theory of devil's rights does not imply a total rejection of the devil from any place in the interpretation of the redemption.

The *Sententie Florianenses* subscribe to Abelard's rejection of enabling graces and do so by attacking the concept of *adiutrix gratia*; when William of St Thierry wrote to Bernard, it was against the denial of *gratia adiuvans* that he protested.[3] The *Sententie Florianenses* assert that man receives the power in free will and reason with which to seek to obtain the grace of God.[4] Original sin is here described as Abelard described it in terms of a penalty incurred by Adam's sin and not as *culpa*.[5] Since the

---

[1] C. 31 (15).

[2] 'Ad quid fuerit iste modus redemptionis. Dicendum est: ad redimendum, scilicet a peccato cuius eramus servi ... haec redemptio talis facta est a Deo in persona Filii, ut quotienscumque reminisceremur dilectionem, quam nobis exhibuit, a peccatis abstineamus nos. Vel potest dici, quod fueramus diaboli, quia eius suggestionibus occumbebamus, a quibus nosmetipsos retraximus propter admirabilem dilectionem, quam nobis exhibuit, et propter dolores, quos pro nobis tulit, suggestiones diaboli spernemus et rationi, quae contra appetitus corporis resistit, potius (quam) diabolo consentiremus', c. 33 (16).

[3] See above, p. 129.   [4] C. 27 (13).   [5] C. 54 (26).

third part of the Sentences, that which concerns charity, is missing the author's teaching on actual sin is not given. However, an incidental remark in the surviving portion of the work suggests that the author held with Abelard that external actions are not sins and that sin resides in the internal will.[1]

These Sentences are wholly Abelardian, but their usefulness as a guide to Abelard's teaching as it stood perhaps before the mid-1130s is somewhat limited by the brevity and the awkwardness of the author's presentation. In summarizing Abelard's positions, he may have violated some of the arguments by which they were supported. Historically the work has a significance as an example of the impulsion given by members of Abelard's school to the production of small, systematic *summae* of theology. But to any contemporary reader outside Abelard's own circle, it must have seemed extraordinarily provocative.

THE SENTENCES OF HERMANN

The Sentences of Hermann were first edited in 1835 by F. H. Rheinwald under the title *Petri Abaelardi Epitome Theologiae Christianae*. But whereas the *Theologia Christiana* did not complete even the discussion of the Trinity, the *Epitome* which was also incomplete nonetheless possessed chapters on Christ and the redemption, the sacraments (baptism, confirmation, the eucharist, unction and matrimony) and charity by which is meant the nature of charity, the virtues and vices, sin and merit. The work was clearly a valuable source of Abelard's teachings, but belief in Abelard's authorship was challenged first by H. Denifle, who assigned the work to an unknown disciple of Abelard,[2] and finally by H. Ostlender who in 1936 convincingly demonstrated from the internal evidence of self-references that the name of this disciple was Hermann.[3] His work is not to be confused with the lost *Liber Sententiarum* combated by William and

---

[1] 'Filius ... docuit non esse peccata exteriora opera, sed interiorem voluntatem', c. 32 (15-16).
[2] Denifle, 'Die Sentenzen Abaelards', pp. 420-2.
[3] Ostlender, 'Die Sentenzenbücher', pp. 210-13.

Bernard.[1] Although the first eleven chapters of Hermann's Sentences are virtually excerpted from the second version of Abelard's *Theologia 'Scholarium'*,[2] the model for the work appears to have been the anonymous *Liber Sententiarum*.[3] In addition Hermann's Sentences may bear the traces of slight reaction to the criticisms made against Abelard's teaching and the date of composition may be not before 1139.[4]

Whereas the *Sententie Florianenses* are brief and unpolished in style, the *Sententie Hermanni* are lengthier, more comprehensive and more thorough. The work is still quite short but it presents the main features of a larger selection of problems, and solutions are worked out in more detail. Hermann's opinions are always pronounced opinions, and his definitions and propositions are clearly articulated. There is no sense of mystery or of hestitation in either this work or in the *Sententie Florianenses*. Of course Hermann is essentially reporting a master's teaching, but if we wish to recapture the sense of novelty, the freshness of Abelard's teaching and the confident spirit which underlay it as well as the stimulus of bold, unsparing and efficient criticism, and the rapid movement of Abelard's arguments, then Hermann's Sentences should be read as well as the more spacious *magna opera* of Abelard, the heavier, repetitious and meandering *Theologia 'Scholarium'*. or the very fine and intricate analyses of the *Ethica*.

Like the *Sententie Florianenses* Hermann's work is full of the controversial opinions of Abelard. The attributions of power, wisdom and will are made to the persons of the Godhead,[5] although Hermann appears to omit deliberately a discussion of the *sapientia Dei* as *quaedam potentia Dei*; he announces it inadvertently

---

[1] *Ibid.*, pp. 229–30.   [2] *Ibid.*, p. 217.
[3] *Ibid.*, pp. 230–42.
[4] *Ibid.*, pp. 213–14.
[5] ' . . . potentia genus est sapientiae et scientiae . . . potentia divina continet sapientiam . . . Quod etiam similitudine generis ad species, vel materiae ad materiatum, facile videri potest . . . ideo translatum est hoc nomen Pater ad significandam divinam potentiam, Filius ad significandam sapientiam, quia ut diximus, sapientia discernendi est ex potentia illa. Sed potentia non est ex sapientia . . . voluntas non est potentia, ideo non continet sapientiam', c. 15 (PL. 178, 1716D–7C).

but does not include it.[1] In a similar way Hermann omits the
controversial simile of the bronze seal, but he inadvertently
refers to it as if he had already discussed it.[2] However, apart from
these two instances which perhaps indicate the author's unease,
the work is Abelardian to a fault. Power belongs to the Father
proprie and *quasi proprie et specialiter*; the Father is omnipotence,
not only because nothing can resist his will, but also because he
has his power and his being from himself.[3] Although the Spirit
is of the same substance as the Son, he is not from the same
substance and Hermann employs the much criticized phrase
'non . . . de eadem substantia cum Filio'[4] which Abelard himself
did not employ, at least in his *Theologia*.[5] Hermann, like Abelard,
teaches that Plato believed in a created world-soul, known through
his effects, but that Plato did not perceive the eternal procession
of the Spirit from the Father; the temporal procession of the
anima mundi means the procession of the sevenfold Spirit to
creation.[6]

Hermann teaches that God cannot do more or otherwise than
he does. He claims Plato's support for the proposition 'optimus
optimum facit'; everything that God does is done wisely and
rationally and to do otherwise would be to act against an immutable wisdom. A man may become better by God and through
God, but God cannot make him better, for possibility lies in the

---

[1] '. . . cum ipsa scilicet quaedam potentia sit, sicut posterius ostendemus', c.
10 (1708C). Cf. Ostlender, 'Die Sentenzenbücher', p. 214.
[2] '. . . sicut in praemissa similitudine videri potest. Vere siquidem sunt
istae, hoc aes est sigillum et hoc sigillum est aes, et hoc sigillabile est sigillum
vel etiam est aes et hoc sigillum vel hoc aes est sigillabile', c. 17 (1720BC). Cf.
Ostlender, 'Die Sentenzenbücher', pp. 213–14.
[3] C. 5–8 (1700A, 1701C–2A, 1702D–3A, 1703C).
[4] C. 17 (1719D).   [5] See above, pp. 122–3.
[6] 'Animam vero mundi, per quam Spiritum vivificantem cuncta intellexit,
creaturam esse dixit et mundo infusam . . . Videamus igitur sensum eorum,
ut tandem eum bene dixisse sentiamus . . . Spiritus sanctus in se secundum
affectum coaeternus est Patri et Filio, divisos habet effectus . . . Secundum igitur
hunc septiformem effectum, per quem effectuum cunctorum universitas desig-
natur, quae in creaturis efficiuntur, Spiritus sanctus anima mundi dictus est,
quia anima et creata censetur, quia ipse Spiritus creaturas vivificat . . . licet
(Plato) non aeternam processionem, temporalem tamen assignavit, quomodo
videlicet ad cuncta vivificanda procedas . . . ', c. 18 (1720D–1D).

things which God has made in the wisest and most rational way, not in God himself.[1] Hermann imposes the same argument of divine invariability upon God's knowledge, disposition, predestination, prescience, providence and goodness.[2] Like Abelard, Hermann does not compromise the reality of Christ's descent into Hell but argues that the soul of Christ did not move locally but descended 'per efficaciam infernum spoliandi'.[3]

The incarnation of the wisdom of God was designed to enlighten men and to exhibit love which would effect the redemption of men from the yoke of sin.[4] Hermann questions what some say, that the redemption is from the power of the devil who subjugated man and held him *iure* so that God had to humble himself if he was not to offer *iniuria* to the devil. Hermann attacks the notion that the devil had a power over man. If a servant leads his under-servants away from the service of their common master, he forfeits his *potestas*. The argument pursued by Hermann appears to assume a purely juridical view of power and to attack the possibility that the devil had a rightful power over men, but Hermann's terminology is ambiguous and he concludes that man was not under the devil's power and was not redeemed from his service, because no price was paid to the devil nor did the devil will the reconciliation of God and man.[5] It is hard to see why a *de facto* relationship between men and the devil is not posited; moreover Hermann does not mention such a relationship even obliquely, although he does comment that the better the man-Christ was, the more envious and therefore the more worthy of punishment the devil became.[6]

---

[1] C. 20 (1724A–6B). [2] C. 20–2 (1726A, 1729C, 1730A).

[3] C. 19 (1724A). Cf. c. 17 (1737D–8D).

[4] '... pro dilectione siquidem, quam erga nos habuit, ut nos a iugo peccati redimeret, carnem assumpsit', c. 23 (1730C).

[5] 'Ego vero ... dico, et ratione irrefragibili probo, quod diabolus in hominem nullum ius habuerit ... constat hominem sub potestate diaboli non fuisse nec de eius servitute redemptum esse. Venit ergo Filius Dei, non ut hominem de potestate diaboli redimeret, cum nec ipse diabolus pretium aliquod inde reciperet, imo hominem nunquam reconciliatum Deo vellet, sed ut eum a servitute peccati dilectionem suam ei infundens, redimeret, seipsum pretium et hostiam puram Patri offerendo et solvendo,' c. 23 (1730C–1A). Cf. J. Rivière, *Le Dogme de la rédemption*, pp. 172–9. [6] C. 23 (1731B).

Hermann assuredly did not wish to compromise the divinity of Christ, and like the *Sententie Florianenses* he did not use phrases which gravely compromised the divinity of Christ's person.[1] He explains the presence of the Word in Christ, which is not the presence of a person in another person, by means of the simile of body and soul which is employed in the pseudo-Athanasian Creed: the Word is the third person of the Trinity, but when the Word is present in Christ, just as when the soul is joined to the body, it is not a person *per se*, for the whole union is one person.[2] With Jerome and against Augustine, Hermann considers that the divine and human natures of Christ may be called parts of Christ. He also qualifies certain *locutiones* as improper, e.g. that God is man, for the Creator cannot be a creature nor the eternal temporal; in such expressions the whole is made to stand for a part.[3] Hermann has nothing to say on the nature of the fear possessed by Christ, except that Christ really suffered physically.[4]

Hermann's presents Abelard's thesis on grace by means of expressions which confer upon human initiative a greater autonomy than is found in Abelard's *Expositio*.[5] Merit lies in the will and God searches the wills of men,[6] but when St Paul says that what is achieved by (purely human) merits is not of grace,[7] must it be inferred that the role of grace altogether excludes purely human capacity? Hermann claims that there would be no merit to be earned unless we say that men of themselves, through free will and of their own nature, can love and belong to God.[8] He adds that man's will is naturally prone to good.[9] Free will

---

[1] C. 24 (1732B–4A).

[2] 'Quamvis enim ibi sit Verbum, quod est tertia persona in Trinitate, non tamen ibi est persona per se, quia sic persona iam esset in persona, et ita duae personae essent in Christo, sicut anima separata a corpore persona est, non tamen corpori iuncta persona potest dici', c. 24 (1732B).

[3] C. 24 (1733D–4A).   [4] C. 25 (1734–5).

[5] See above, p. 129.   [6] C. 34 (1754C, 1755B).

[7] 'Si ex meritis, iam non ex gratia', *Rom.* 11, 6; *Sententie* of Hermann, c. 34 (1755D).

[8] '. . . nisi dicamus quod homo ex se etiam per liberum arbitrium ex natura sua habeat diligere, et ei adhaerere, non possumus vitare, quin gratia meritis nostris praeiudicare probetur . . . ', c. 34 (1755D–6A).

[9] 'Velle autem bonum unicuique naturale est', c. 34 (1756A).

and the natural inclination to will good are not presented by Hermann as gifts of God; Hermann's expressions appear to establish a purely human capacity in the will which appears to restrict the action of grace as such.

Hermann does not discuss original sin which may have been fully treated in a commentary on Romans which he is thought to have written.[1] He does, however, say that children and natural idiots cannot act against conscience and therefore cannot incur a fault or offer contempt to the Creator. Sin is present in them only in a transitive sense and as penalty.[2] Hermann also presented Abelard's thesis that sin lies in the will and that human actions are in themselves morally indifferent.[3] On the power of the keys, these Sentences teach that priests do not themselves save or damn a man but open or close the church to sinners. The authorities, Jerome, Gregory and the example of Lazarus, are presented as in Abelard's *Ethica*.[4] The question whether all the successors of the Apostles receive the power of the keys does not appear, perhaps because of the unfinished condition in which the work is found in the manuscripts.

The *Sententie* of Hermann invite mixed conclusions. It is possible that on the Trinity Hermann felt a need to be cautious and therefore omitted to follow his source in explaining the divine wisdom and the simile of the bronze seal. But in other respects he fully adheres to Abelard's teachings, and on grace Hermann does much to justify the accusations of Pelagianism made by Abelard's critics. Hermann followed, according to Dr Ostlender, the *Liber Sententiarum* which in several ways simplified Abelard's teaching and rendered it more rigid and untra-

---

[1] 'quod quidem quia in epistola ad Romanos super eum locum: Iacob dilexi etc. diligenter expressi, hoc quasi notum praetereundum existimo', c. 34 (1756A). Cf. Ostlender, 'Die Sentenzenbücher', pp. 214–15; but it is also possible that Hermann was slavishly reproducing his source, presumably the *Lib. Sententiarum*.

[2] C. 33 (1753D).   [3] C. 34 (1754C, 1755A).

[4] The passage does not appear in the printed ed. and is only found in cod. Carpentras, Inguimbertine 110, f. 65v which carries the text of Hermann beyond the point where all other manuscripts end. It is printed below, Appendix I.

M

ditional than in fact it was.[1] As a guide to Abelard's opinions, Hermann must, therefore, be received with caution.

The *Sentences Parisienses I* are so called because they are the first of two collections of Abelardian sentences now preserved in the Paris MS., Bibl. nat. lat. 18,108. The work is anonymous, although a very slight indication that the author knew the Parisian scene is that he illustrated the distinction between *fides* and *cognitio* by distinguishing between the act of thinking that the king is in Paris and the act of seeing him there.[2]

In respect of length these Sentences stand between the *Sentence Florianenses* and *Sentence Hermanni*. Like those two collections, the *Sentence Parisienses I* are completely dependent upon a version of the theological teaching of Abelard and are systematically structured according to a logical plan.[3] Both features are in effect announced in the words with which this, like other works of the school, begins: 'Tria sunt que ad humanam salutem sunt necessaria: fides, sacramentum, caritas'. The author first discusses faith in God and Christ and then proceeds to the sacraments of which he mentions five: baptism, confirmation, the eucharist, marriage and unction. Finally he considers charity: virtues and vices, sin, merit and grace.[4] Particularly in the opening pages the work appears to be represented in only a rough draft;[5] the phrasing is even less polished than in the *Sentence Florianenses* and the work can scarcely be relied upon to represent Abelard's teachings with verbal accuracy. There are many resemblances with the Sentences of Hermann, but also many dissimilarities so that it is reasonable to assume that both works depend upon a common source. Dr Ostlender believes that this source is the

[1] See above, pp. 121, 129–30, 136–7, 138.
[2] Ed. Landgraf, p. 3.
[3] The planning of theological treatises in Abelard's school and in those of his contemporaries is studied by H. Cloes, 'La systématization théologique'.
[4] See Landgraf's introduction to his edition where (pp. xxvi–xxvii) a fuller analysis of the contents is offered.
[5] *Ibid.*, p. xxviii.

Liber Sententiarum[1] and the editor, Dr Landgraf, accepted this hypothesis with the qualification that the very imperfect passages with which the work opens may be the direct report of Abelard's lectures.[2]

The *Sententie Parisienses* are very scholastic and school terms—*queritur, solutio, opponitur, responsio*—are frequently employed. The dialectical spirit of the author is evident; the Scriptures and the writings of the Fathers are incorporated in fast moving, if often rather too brief, arguments which are themselves generally integrated into the overall systematic structure. The author is disputatious: brief expositions of doctrine are followed by a multitude of debating performances and logical skirmishes. This is strictly scholastic theology written down by a questioning mind.

The author applies the divine attributes of power, wisdom and love to the explanation of the generation and procession of the Son and the Spirit. The Son is the wisdom of God and wisdom, being the power of discerning, is born of the substance of power like a species from its genus. Love is not born of power because it is will which is different from power. Baptismal regeneration is attributed *proprie* to the Spirit and this signifies that grace is received by the goodness of God the Father and Son, for it is granted by means of the power and wisdom of God. In all the operations of God, his power, wisdom and goodness are signified. The name, Father, indicates that God is omnipotent.[3] However, the anonymous author does not say that the Father is omnipotent by reason of having his power and being from himself alone, whereas the Son has his power and being from the Father. Nor does he say that the wisdom of God is *quaedam potentia*. He indicates that will is differerent from power[4] but not that the will of God is not the power of God. He argues that the Spirit proceeds from power and wisdom, because being a rational will, or so the author reasons, he has to have the power to do what he

---

[1] Ostlender, 'Die Sentenzenbücher', pp. 231, 241. Dr Ostlender did not exclude the possibility that a direct influence of Abelard's *Ethica* was also felt.
[2] Landgraf, introduction, pp. xxxviii–xxxix; also p. xxxvi.
[3] Ed. Landgraf, pp. 7–13, 19–20.
[4] 'Aliud voluntas, aliud potentia', *ibid.*, p. 10.

wills and he also has to be able to discern in order to be rational; but he does not argue that the Spirit is not *ex* or *de substantia Patris*. In fact he writes that God is better called essence than substance.[1] It is possible to see in these 'omissions' a reaction to adverse criticism from outside Abelard's school,[2] but whereas Hermann has left signs suggesting that he may have thought better of certain doctrines of Abelard, the silence of the present author concerning similar opinions may simply represent his lack of interest in or affection for such doctrines and it need not necessarily imply that the author was writing in the troubled period immediately before the council of Sens.[3]

It is interesting, in view of the attacks made upon Abelard, that none of his four closest disciples went beyond Abelard's teaching on the Platonic world-soul to the point of identifying the Spirit with the world-soul. The *Sententie Parisienses I*, like Abelard, compare the created world-soul of Plato, the vivifier of all temporal things, with the Spirit as understood by his effects in time.[4] The author is also to be compared with his fellow disciples in his teaching that God cannot do otherwise or more or better than he does,[5] and he writes that Christ's soul did not descend into Hell by moving locally but by bearing the sufferings of Hell in order to liberate men. He remarks that Christ's soul did not possess feet.[6]

On the person and natures of Christ, the *Sententie Parisienses I* do not differ much from the *Sententie Florianenses* and *Sententie* of Hermann. He presents the analogy of the soul, which ceases to be itself a person when joined to a body, in order to state that the soul of Christ, which is always joined to the Word, was joined to a human nature as one person.[7] None of his

---

[1] Ed. Landgraf, p. 6.
[2] Cf. Ostlender, 'Die Sentenzenbücher', pp. 220–1.
[3] Landgraf, introduction, pp. xxxix–xl conjectured 1139–41; Ostlender, 'Die Sentenzenbücher', p. 221, confirmed this conjecture.
[4] It would be wrong to take out of context a phrase such as the following: 'Illud vero vocavit animam mundi, que omnium rerum vivificatrix est, Spiritus Sanctus est', ed. Landgraf, p. 6; cf. *ibid.*, pp. 5–6, 16–18.
[5] *Ibid.*, pp. 20–6.   [6] *Ibid.*, pp. 13–16; cf. 36–7.
[7] *Ibid.*, pp. 29–30.

expressions could be construed to imply that the person of Christ is not a person of the Trinity. He also argues that such expressions as 'Christ is God and man' are improper, for in them the part is signified by the whole; with Jerome and against Augustine, he thinks that there are parts in Christ.[1] There is no discussion of the redemptive work of Christ because it is dealt with in a *lectio* on Romans, 5, 6;[2] Abelard had similarly in his *Expositio*[3] discussed the same subject, but whether the anonymous author is referring to Abelard's lectures or to his own exposition or that written by the author of his source cannot be determined.

The author puts Abelard's question whether men are capable of raising themselves to receive God's gifts and answers: 'Hanc questionem quomodo solvere possim, non video, nisi dixero, quod iste aliquid ex se habuit, unde assurgere potuit ... Et ita dicimus, quod omnes homines ex se habent, unde assurgere possint, sed alii solliciti sunt ad appositam gratiam accipiendam, alii vero negligentes et pigri ad appositam gratiam accipiendam.'[4] The text of the Sentences breaks off in the course of this discussion, but the author had earlier stated that human merits themselves come from grace since faith and love are themselves gifts of grace[5] and in this respect his exposition is more faithful to Abelard's thought than was Hermann.[6] Like Hermann, this author does not discuss original sin; neither sentence-work is truly a *summa* for both rely upon biblical commentaries to handle some topics. The *Sententie Parisienses I* do, however, affirm that *culpa* is not present in children who cannot commit a contempt of the Creator.[7] On actual sin, the author indicates that sin, a contempt of God, resides in the will; works are judged to be good or bad according to the intention of the agent.[8]

The *Sententie Parisienses I* are incomplete and several of Abe-

---

[1] *Ibid.*, pp. 31–2.
[2] 'De qua satis in lectione dictum, ibi: *Ut quid* etc.', *ibid.*, p. 29.
[3] PL. 178, 860. At *Romans* 3, 26 (PL. 178, 833D–6D) Abelard discusses the redemption more exhaustively. Landgraf, *op. cit.*, p. xxxix, thought that the anonymous author was referring to a version of Abelard's written *Expositio*.
[4] Ed. Landgraf, pp. 59–60, here p. 60.
[5] *Ibid.*   [6] See above, pp. 162–3.
[7] Ed. Landgraf, p. 56.   [8] *Ibid.*, pp. 25, 57, 59.

lard's most characteristic opinions are absent from the work on that account. None of the doctrines we have mentioned is sufficiently argued for an informative comparison with Abelard's own work to be made or for omissions in the arguments to be satisfactorily explained. But if the Sentences are a somewhat untrustworthy account of Abelard's teaching, like other similar works of Abelard's school they witness powerfully to the provocative character of the thought of Abelard and his school.

THREE MINOR PIECES

Abelard's theory of the redemption was curiously, not to say surreptitiously, introduced into a series of Augustinian fragments found in a twelfth-century manuscript now in Florence, Laurenziana, Aedilium CXLII.[1] An anonymous compiler has here brought together passages which resemble Augustine's *Tractatus* LI–LII on St John,[2] but where Augustine treated of the domination of Satan in our hearts, the compiler inserted, without indication of his purpose and probably deliberately, a passage which is very similar to one found in Hermann's Sentences[3] and which contains Abelard's argument that the devil possessed no rights over mankind and that Christ redeemed man by the example of his love.

Also remarkable is the way in which Abelard's doctrine of sin entered an anonymous homiletic and ascetical *Enchiridion* on confession which is found in a twelfth-century manuscript Clm. 7698, ff. 43r–73v.[4] This work was written for priests with the purpose of exhorting them to repent and especially to confess their sins orally.[5] A few echoes of the schools can be

---

[1] On what follows see J. Rivière, 'De quelques faits nouveaux sur l'influence théologique d'Abélard', or *idem*, *Le Dogme de la rédemption*, pp. 186–90. On the manuscript see above, pp. 87–8.

[2] They are printed among Augustine's writings in PL. 47, 1211–19.

[3] C. 23 (PL. 178, 1730–1).

[4] The work was first discussed by H. Weisweiler, 'Eine neue Bearbeitung', pp. 369–71. On the manuscript see above, p. 82.

[5] The eulogy of public confession is warm: 'O bonum neglectum, immo improvisum, immo vero a nullis vel paucissimis intellectum, bonum bonorum,

found[1] and in addition Abelard's teachings are much used. The author cites Abelard's definition of sin in a passage strongly reminiscent of Hermann's Sentences and of the *Sententie Parisienses I*; sin is a contempt of the creator, an act of will against conscience and against the will and precept of God.[2] Mortal and venial sin are distinguished with phrases which also recall Hermann and the *Sententie Parisienses I*. An unwitting offence or slip, however grave, is a venial sin; a deliberate offence against conscience, however small in itself, is a mortal sin meriting damnation.[3] The distinction is supported with examples employed by Abelard.[4] A criticism of priests who impose insufficient penalties upon sinners is presented in a further passage which can only be paralleled in Abelard's *Ethica*,[5] and the author also agrees with Abelard that priests who think that they can bind and loose men, with insufficient regard for what they have actually done, mis-interpret Christ's commission to Peter. God heeds the state of the man, not the verdict of priests.[6] Moreover, will is here considered

---

[1] E.g. perhaps in the distinction between reason and authority ('videtur namque clarius luce auctoritate probatum, ratione confirmatum', f. 52r; 'rationis duce . . . ', f. 63r). More important is a possible trace of the teaching of the Laon school on the natural propensity of the human will to sin: 'quod (homini) arbitrium liberum et possibilitatem sive ad bonum per gratiam sive ad malum per se de casu in casu declinandi attribuit', f. 53r. Cf. O. Lottin, *Psychologie et morale*, I, 27.

[2] Weisweiler, 'Eine neue Bearbeitung', pp. 369–71; Clm. 7698, f. 68v ('ut ait quidam'); *Sententie* of Hermann, c. 33 (PL. 178, 1753D); *Sent. Paris. I*, ed. Landgraf, p. 56. Also, Abelard, *Ethica*, c. 3 (PL. 178, 639D).

[3] Weisweiler, 'Eine neue Bearbeitung', pp. 369–71; *Sententie* of Hermann (1753D–4A), *Sent. Paris. I*, ed. Landgraf, p. 56. Also Abelard, *Ethica*, c. 15 (PL. 178, 658C–9A).   [4] *Ethica*, c. 15 (PL. 178, 658C–9A).   [5] *Ibid.*, c. 25 (672C).

[6] 'Notandum vero est quod Petro dictum est, et in Petro ceteris: "quodcunque ligaveris super terram, etc." (Matt. 16, 19) . . . Hec verba episcopi multi et

---

sacramentum sacramentorum, salvatio salvationum', Clm. 7698, f. 71v. The relative value of public or oral confession and private confession to God is discussed: 'Due nimirum sunt confessiones, una privata, altera publica, sicut duo genera peccatorum quedam venaalia [!], quedam mortalia . . . ', f. 67r. Many attempts were made in the twelfth century to harmonize the roles of inner contrition (to which Abelard attributed a remissive value) and public confession. The latter had been in decline in reaction against the custom of imposing long and severe penances; cf. A. Teetaert, *La Confession aux laïques*, pp. 85 *et seq.*

to be the principal factor in man which earns for him guilt or merit, and the author now makes his first acknowledgement of the inspiration of these theories: '... spiritualiter peccatur amplius quam corporaliter atque frequentius, et, sicut probat ille summus peripatethicus, voluntas salvat vel dampnat, quoniam, ita voluntas, quia perpetua est, [et] perpetuam meretur remunerationem vel dampnationem, sicut locutio vel actio, quia transitorie sunt, temporalem.'[1] The use of the title 'peripatethicus' suggests that the author had moved in or near to Abelard's circle.[2] His *Enchiridion* is an unusual example of Abelard's influence upon devotional writing and upon theological writing outside the schools.[3] It is a clear witness to the fact that Abelard's teaching on the remissive value of inner contrition was not linked with an accompanying neglect of the place of confession in penance.[4]

Dr Landgraf noticed[5] a sermon in cod. Paris, Bibl. nationale, lat. 13,582, ff. 41vb–42va[6] which contained Abelard's teaching on

---

[1] F. 71v. By the word 'voluntas', where first used, another hand has added in the margin 'voluntate'. Cf. *Ethica*, c. 3 (PL. 178, 636B); *Sententie* of Hermann, c. 34 (1755A). Weisweiler, 'Eine neue Bearbeitung', pp. 369–71, does not note this passage nor that concerning the power of the keys.

[2] John of Salisbury often names Abelard the *Peripateticus Palatinus* in his *Metalogicon*; cf. the rubricator of the manuscript containing Abelard's *Introductiones parvulorum* (ed. M. Dal Pra, *Scritti filosofici*, p. xv).

[3] For another example, see above, p. 117, n. 3.

[4] P. Anciaux, *La Théologie du sacrement de pénitence*, pp. 176–82, presents Abelard's own teaching as an academic discussion in which the necessity of confession is maintained but in which also a will to confess is not made an essential complement of the act of inner contrition which itself secures the remission of sin.   [5] *Introducción*, p. 111.

[6] The manuscript is of unknown origin but formerly belonged to St Germain des Près. The Sermons found on ff. 1–70 are discussed by B. Hauréau, *Notices et extraits*, II (1891), p. 294, and are also found in cod. Paris, Bibl. nat. lat. 12,413 where they bear an attribution to Chrétien, abbé of St Pierre. Hauréau rejects this attribution. The sermon under discussion is found on ff. 63vb–64vb. The MS. 13,582 also contains sermons by Peter Manducator, see M. M. Lebreton, 'Recherches sur les manuscrits contenant les sermons', p. 26.

---

sacerdotes male intelligunt, putantes sive noxios sive innoxios ligatos quos ligant, solutos quos solvunt. Sed neminem possunt solvere vel ligare nisi quem Deus propter vite sue ac fidei meritum solvit vel ligat, cum Deus non sacerdotum sententiam sed cuiusque penset vitam', f. 69r. Cf. *Ethica*, c. 26 (PL. 178, 673C–8A).

free will and grace. Twelfth-century sermons have sometimes the character of a lecture and here the anonymous preacher argues against an excessive belittling of the role of free will in the earning of merit. Before the Fall man had a freedom of will which sufficed to earn merit, but subsequently grace is necessary to strengthen the will in order that it may cooperate with the divine purpose. The preacher introduces an analogy of a lord with two servants who are required to move a mill-stone and who are offered a reward for their pains. The lazier of the two servants does not, however, cooperate. The difference between the servants is a difference in their use of free will. Both have received the same impulse of grace, which is the promise of a reward, and with grace an active will can earn merit.

Many other writers made incidental borrowings from Abelard's works. A notable example is Anselm, bishop of Havelberg from 1129–55 and theological envoy to Byzantium, who reveals in his *Dialogues* that he had produced against the Greeks Abelard's defence of Latin teaching on the procession of the Spirit.[1] Our main concern here is, however, with Abelard's closest disciples and particularly with the literature of the schools.

The works of Abelard's closest disciples do not depend upon an identical common source. The *Sententie Parisienses I* and *Sententie Hermanni* may report Abelard only at second hand through the medium of the *Liber Sententiarum* which cannot be trusted to have presented all Abelard's arguments fairly. The *Sententie Florianenses* present Abelard's thought at a stage when it was singularly vulnerable to criticism and the *Commentarius Cantabrigiensis* raises the question whether in his oral teaching Abelard put forth formulae which he was to handle more carefully at a later time. However, none of these disciples is creative and all are more or less servile. The sentence-collection form was adopted by some of them for reasons which are probably associated with the way in which Abelard organized his school. A book of sentences was also swift and convenient for pupils to prepare and to handle, but

[1] *Dialogi*, II, 24, 25, 26 (PL. 188, 1202D–3, 1205, 1206D–7A). Cf. Abelard, *Theol. 'Schol.'*, II, 14, *Theol. Christiana*, IV (PL. 178, 1077A–8, 1079D; 1302C–5, 1306BC).

in such a book Abelard's argumentative *excursus* and his analytical and experimental probes were unfortunately abbreviated and 'potted'. With the advantage of hindsight it is easier for us to see that the appropriate response to some of Abelard's initiatives was to explore them creatively as Robert of Melun was later to do. Contemporaries knew the danger of discrepancies appearing between the teaching of a master and the reports of his pupils;[1] in view of the much superior argumentative ability displayed by Abelard in his own writings, it is surely wise not to see in these works full confirmation of the criticisms made by Abelard's critics.

[1] Cf. Walter of Mortagne, above, p. 106, n. 1. Also Gilbert of Poitiers: 'Fateor me plures habuisse discipulos, qui me quidem omnes audierunt, sed quidam minus intellexerunt', John of Salisbury, *Hist. Pont.*, c. 10 (ed. Chibnall, p. 22).

CHAPTER VI

THE SCHOOL OF LAON

In the lifetime of Anselm (d. 1117) the cathedral school of Laon was without a peer as a centre of theological instruction.[1] In 1113 Abelard, already a celebrated teacher of dialectic and past his thirtieth year, himself went to Laon to learn theology under Anselm. He found that Anselm was revered by his hearers and had a considerable verbal facility, but he thought that in his lectures Anselm did not say anything which could not be as well learned from books.[2] The surviving productions from the school of Laon support Abelard's criticisms in the sense that the school was characterized by a great, even extreme, fidelity to patristic teaching and to the text of the sacred page and also in the sense that the more speculative areas of Christian theology, such as the Trinity and the person of Christ, were largely by-passed in favour of more practical subjects, such as the evaluation of moral experience and the sacraments, and of historical-biblical subjects such as the creation, the fall and the redemption.[3] From the doctrinal viewpoint the school in general made little progress, although in relation to the organization of studies in the twelfth century the school was of very great importance. It was the first theological school since the great days of Bec

[1] A general survey with a bibliography is made by J. de Ghellinck, *Le Mouvement théologique*, pp. 133–48, and a convenient summary of the literature on the school is given by A. Landgraf, *Introducción*, pp. 89–103.

[2] 'Accessi igitur ad hunc senem, cui magis longevus usus quam ingenium vel memoria nomen comparaverat ... Mirabilis quidem in oculis erat auscultantium, sed nullus in conspectu questionantium. Verborum usum habebat mirabilem, sed sensum contemtibilem et ratione vacuum ... Saluberrimum quidem huius lectionis esse studium ubi salus anime cognoscitur, sed me vehementer mirari quod his qui litterari sunt ad expositiones sanctorum intelligendas ipsa eorum scripta vel glose non sufficiunt, ut alio scilicet non egeant magisterio ... ', *Hist. Calam.*, ed. Monfrin, *ll.* 164–70, 191–5.

[3] On the mentality of Anselm and the features of his teaching see O. Lottin, *Psychologie et Morale*, v, 443–4, and E. Bertola, 'Le critiche di Abelardo ad Anselmo di Laon ed a Guglielmo di Champeaux'.

which could boast a high reputation and a large following and, unlike Bec, it was a school of clerics. Anselm and his brother Ralph and their followers fostered the production of the *Glossa* on the Bible[1] and they stimulated the systematic arrangement of theological sentence-collections which lay at the base of the theological movement of the twelfth, even of the thirteenth, centuries. Moreover, Anselm and his school were not averse to the introduction of the *quaestio* to biblical exegesis or to the re-appraisal and supplementation, when need arose, of patristic tradi-tion. It is Anselm, not Abelard, who directed the first 'scholastic' school of theology which enjoys a historical importance.

Anselm's disciples were active and seemingly ubiquitous throughout the whole of the first half of the twelfth century and no doubt most of them reacted in neutral and negative ways to Abelard's teaching as it developed. But their own teachings formed the immediate background to that of Abelard as well as to that of the other Parisian theologians and the force or the pervasiveness of the Laon tradition affected the reception of Abelard's work.[2]

In comparison with the relative neglect by Anselm of Trinitarian thought, Abelard's speculations seem precocious, although some speculation was promoted in a 'wing' of the school by the dia-lectician William of Champeaux.[3] The teaching of Anselm on the redemption insisted that the devil did not rule men by any right after the fall; although men were justly under his power, the devil himself had usurped this power which should rightly

[1] The understanding of the exegetical work of Laon owes more to the work of Miss B. Smalley than to any other historian; see especially her 'Gilbertus Universalis'.

[2] A. Landgraf in *Zeitschrift für kathol. Theologie*, LIV (1930), p. 361, n. 1, and F. Bliemetzrieder in *RTAM*, III (1931), p. 290, have pleaded for a com-prehensive comparison of the teachings of Laon and of Abelard.

[3] See the Sentences of William, nos. 236–9, ed. O. Lottin, *Psychologie et Morale*, V, 190–8. From Anselm's teaching comes an anonymous Trinitarian sentence collection, *Filius a patre gigni*, ed. Lottin, *op. cit.*, V, 338–42. Both this author and William use the attributions to the divine persons of power, wisdom and goodness or love. The *Sententie divine pagine*, ed. Bliemetzrieder, *Anselms systematische Sentenzen*, here (4–10) have a short section on God and also make the attributions just mentioned (7).

have been forfeited without injury to himself. Anselm and his followers viewed Christ's work on earth as a *causa inter Deum et diabolum*, although Anselm had himself followed his earlier namesake in rejecting the theory of the devil's rights.[1] In the school of Laon the love and example offered by Christ to men held such a small place in discussion that Abelard's forceful emphasis of these aspects of Christ's work is more readily appreciated.

It is also noteworthy that Anselm debated the place which confession occupied in penance.[2] P. Anciaux has written that already in the school of Laon there developed a split between those who described penance chiefly with respect to the external behaviour of the penitent and those who emphasized his inner disposition.[3] The so-called *Sententie Anselmi* may have used, or alternatively may coincide with, Abelard's own emphasis on the remissive value of contrition in the heart;[4] at the same time the *Sententie Anselmi* resist any consequent devaluation of the place of confession in the remission of sin.[5] In another Sentence of the school the primacy of the role of contrition and of intention in penance is affirmed.[6] Similarly the school came to see

[1] *Liber Pancrisis, Sent.*, no. 48, 54, ed. Lottin, *Psychologie et Morale*, v, 46–7, 50–1. In the *Sententie Atrebatenses* of Anselm's school (ed. Lottin, *op. cit.*, v, 416) and in the Sentences of Ralph, no. 231, 232 (*ibid.*, pp. 184–6), the theory of the devil's rights is maintained.

[2] *Liber Pancrisis, Sent.*, no. 64, ed. Lottin, *Psychologie et Morale*, v, 56–7.

[3] Anciaux, *La Théologie du sacrement de pénitence*, p. 145.

[4] 'Cum multis modis fiat commissum illicitum, scilicet, cogitatione, verbo, opere, quibus quasi quedam vulnera inferuntur anime, totidem remedia eidem anime vulnerate per vitia adhiberi debent. Voluntas namque est quasi gladius ipsam animam consensu et delectatione vulnerans, et proximi vulneris dolor quasi emplastrum est, quia interior cordis contritio commissorum est ablutio. Secundum quasi emplastrum est oris confessio. Tertium est iniuncte satisfactionis diligens expletio', ed. Bliemetzrieder, *Anselms systematische Sentenzen*, 121. Cf. the same text in *Sententia* 533, ed. H. Weisweiler, *Das Schrifttum*, p. 217. For discussion see Anciaux, *op. cit.*, pp. 183–4. Lottin, *op. cit.*, iv, 47, dates the *Sent. Anselmi* to the 1130s.

[5] 'Sciendum est penitentiam non sufficere sine confessione, quamvis quidam dicant, compugitionem cordis solam esse necessariam, non confessionem', ed. Bliemetzrieder, p. 124.

[6] 'In omni opere nostro discutiamus qua intentione illud incipiamus, velut in penitentia ... ', *Sent.* 383, ed. Lottin, *Psychologie et Morale*, v, 280. Cf. Abelard, *Ethica*, c. 18–19 (PL. 178, 661–5) and Anciaux, *La Théologie du sacrement de pénitence*, p. 157 and note. The Sentence has not been dated.

intention as the most important factor determining the gravity of a fault before God.[1] Some writers of the Laon school considered that concupiscence was not itself a sin,[2] although the weight of the Laon tradition bore in favour of accepting that *delectatio*, both avoidable and unavoidable, which is experienced in the course of temptation is sin.[3] The thesis that the fleshly appetites considered in themselves were morally indifferent is asserted in a sentence in cod. Bamberg Patr. 47, f.15v, although Dr Landgraf rightly taught us to beware of assuming an actual dependence upon Abelard.[4] A reference in the *Sententie Anselmi* to those who advocate the moral indifference of human actions is more clearly a reference to Abelard's thesis.[5] When the same work mentions an opinion held by others that on the union of body and soul in man, the soul does not contract the stain of sin, Abelard may have been in mind, although the opinion presented is not an adequate summary of his teaching that men are born bearing the penalty for Adam's sin but without con-

---

[1] Cf. a sentence perhaps by Anselm, no. 213, ed. Lottin, *Psychologie et Morale*, v, 137: 'Non attendit Deus peccatum quantum ad rerum quantitatem, sed quantum ad intentionem facientis . . . ' See also R. Blomme, *La Doctrine du péché*, especially pp. 68–85.

[2] Cf. *Sent.* 451, ed. Lottin, *Psychologie et Morale*, v, 304.

[3] Cf. Anselm, *Liber Pancrisis*, *Sent.* 85; also, the school of Anselm, *Sent.* 450, ed. Lottin, *Psychologie et Morale*, v, 74, 303.

[4] *Cit.* Landgraf, 'Beiträge', p. 365. Cf. Abelard, *Ethica*, c. 3 and *Expos. in* 'ad Romanos' (PL. 178, 642C–3A, 894). As recently as 1947–8 R. Silvain, 'La tradition des Sentences d'Anselme de Laon', p. 20, erroneously believed this to be a unique instance of Abelard's influence in texts from the Laon school. The Bamberg collection also contains a question concerning the mobility of the soul (f. 22: 'An anima moveatur et si movetur, quomodo movetur'; Landgraf, 'Beiträge', p. 366) and Dr Landgraf was again rightly uncertain whether it was due to the interest of Abelard in this problem (*Sic et Non*, c. 43, *Theol.* 'Schol.', III, vi, PL 178, 1404D–5D, 1104B–6C).

[5] 'Sunt qui aliter de peccato sentiant; nam dicunt omnes actus per se indifferentes esse, id est neque bonos neque malos, formatos autem bonos vel malos esse, et quidem actus tam corporis quam anime intelligunt. Verbi gratia. Concumbere cum muliere actus est indifferens per se; accepta forma, coniunctus intentioni facientis, bonus est vel malus,' *Sent. Anselmi*, ed. Bliemetzrieder, p. 71. Cf. Lottin, *Psychologie et Morale*, IV, 47, but also II, 421, n. 2. A very similar passage is found in the anonymous *Prima rerum origo* and is produced by Lottin, 'Aux origines de l'école théologique d'Anselme', p. 120. Cf. Abelard, *Ethica*, c. 3 (PL. 178, 643B, 644A, 650B).

tracting the fault itself.[1] William of Champeaux was a particularly interesting precursor of Abelard. He defined original sin in the newborn child as being present not because the child has sinned nor even because he has material concupiscence, but because he has the spiritual sin of Adam.[2] Concupiscence is not a sin but the effect of sin.[3] In this development, which one writer has named revolutionary,[4] William modifies the pessimism of the ruling Augustinian view of men being born as sinners. Moreover, in his analysis of grace William also sets the scene for Abelard's discussions with his distinction between prevenient grace which prepares nature to discern good and evil and to have a natural appetitite and will for good, and helping grace which enables men to fulfil their good desires.[5]

In a collection of theological questions of the school, perhaps written as late as 1150 and found in cod. Zurich, Zentralbibl. C. 61, an explicit reference is made to *Magister Petrus* and his opinion is quoted concerning the power of the keys.[6] This reference and those other clear references to Abelard's teachings

---

[1] 'Alii autem dicunt animam in corporis unione nullam prorsus peccati maculam suscipere, sed quia statim egressa nichil in eo meruit, gloria tamen carere', *Sent. Anselmi*, ed. Bliemetzrieder, p. 77. Cf. Abelard, *Expos. in 'ad Romanos'*, II (PL. 178, 866CD).

[2] 'Dicitur puer, quam cito habeat animam, habere originale peccatum, non quia aliquid peccasset, sed quia illud spirituale peccatum per quod ... Adam peccavit, imputatur ei. Ideo vero imputatur quia ex pena illius peccati generatus est. Peccatum autem illud est prevaricatio; pena, concupiscentia ... ', *Sent.* 247, ed. Lottin, *Psychologie et Morale*, v, 204.

[3] 'Concupiscentia ergo, que non peccatum quidem sed fomes peccati et quedam possibilitas est peccandi ... ', *Sent.* 259; 'illa autem infirmitas non est peccatum, sed est effectus peccati et causa aliorum peccatorum', *Sent.* 257, ed. Lottin, *Psychologie et Morale*, v, 210, 208.

[4] J. Gross, 'Die Ur- und Erbsündenlehre der Schule von Laon', p. 25.

[5] *Sent.* 240, ed. Lottin, *Psychologie et Morale*, v, 199. Caution should perhaps be exercised over the extent of the resemblance between Abelard's teaching on free will and a sentence, possibly of Anselm of Laon, ed. Lottin, *Psychologie et Morale*, v, 124 (no. 172). See *ibid.*, I, 24 and Abelard, *Expos. in 'ad Romanos'*, II (PL. 178, 867D).

[6] F. 46, cited by Weisweiler, *Das Schrifttum*, p. 169: 'Magister vero Petrus dicit, quod una tantum clavis est, scilicet potestas. Quod dicitur hic contingit propter diversos effectus, quos habet scilicet et ligando et solvendo; et quod discretio dicitur clavis, hoc ideo dicitur, quia uti discretione in ligando et solvendo (debet)'. Weisweiler confirmed the reference to Abelard by com-

found in the *Sententie Anselmi* occur in later productions of the Laon school.[1] When Anselm died, Abelard had only just begun his theological career and the slight influence of his teaching upon Anselm's followers is found, not in their biblical exegesis, but mostly in moral discussions in the later sentence collections.

Abelard was not viewed with any greater favour by those followers of Anselm whom we can name, and it is difficult to determine the occasions when his teachings may have been employed by them. Dr Landgraf noticed that Hugh of Amiens is like Abelard in describing the Word and the Spirit as being *proprie* wisdom and charity.[2] Hugh uses the word *proprie* only in passing and without discussion and the passage occurs in his *Dialogi* which were completed by 1126 when he was abbot of Reading in England, but revised in 1130–4 when he was archbishop of Rouen. It is the revised form that we know[3] and Abelard's influence cannot be excluded from it on chronological grounds, but the attributions of power, wisdom and love to the persons of the Trinity were common and the word *proprie* so convenient that there is little reason in the years before Bernard stigmatized Abelard's discussions to assume that it was exclusively a hallmark of Abelard's teaching, particularly in the case of a writer who was not otherwise in Abelard's debt. A few years later it was Hugh who bade Thomas of Morigny write his

[1] N. M. Haring found superficial resemblances in the use of patristic authorities between the *Sic et Non*, c. 54, 73, 123, 125, 128 and the *Sententie Magistri A.* found in cod. Vatican, lat. 4361 and containing sentences of Anselm; Haring did not conclude that the *Sic et Non* (of which only one version is printed) was a source of the sentences, 'The Sententiae Magistri A', pp. 3–4.

[2] 'Verbum Dei proprie dicitur sapientia . . . Spiritus quoque sanctus proprie charitas dicitur', *Dialogi*, II (PL. 192, 1154); Landgraf, *Dogmengeschichte*, I, i, 225.

[3] This dating is suggested by D. Van den Eynde, 'Nouvelles précisions chronologiques', pp. 74–7. On Hugh see F. Bliemetzrieder, 'L'oeuvre d'Anselme de Laon et la littérature théologique contemporaine, II.'

paring the *Sententie* of Roland and the *Sententie* of Omnebene, ed. Gietl, p. 265 and n. The same teaching appears in the hitherto inedited fragment of the *Sententie* of Hermann in cod. Carpentras, Inguimbertine 110, f. 65v; see Appendix I.

Disputatio after the appearance of Abelard's *Apologia*.[1] Another master, John of Tours, was quoted in later years saying that the divine persons are distinguished by their properties.[2] John had been a pupil under Anselm,[3] and Dr Landgraf suggested that his opinion is very close to Abelard's thinking. However, Abelard, in attempting to ground the distinction between the persons in their possession of properties, did not himself develop the analysis between paternity and sonship nor did he use the simile of the duke and the bishop.

The theological style of Anselm had a firm hold over the educated clergy of the first half of the twelfth century.[4] The prevailing climate of thought was not created by him but it was preserved by his disciples. Much of the public opposition to Abelard is explained by the theological temper of the school of Laon and was led by its devotees. The condemnation of 1121 was initiated by Anselm's leading disciples, Alberic of Rheims and Lotulph of Novara.[5] In return Abelard continued to criticize the surviving devotees of Anselm. He attacked Gilbert the Universal, a master at Auxerre or Nevers in Burgundy, later bishop of London from 1128 to 1134. Whether or not Gilbert had attended Anselm's school, he shared in its tradition.[6] Abelard accused him of erecting the properties of paternity, sonship and procession into three essences separate from God and the three persons.[7] Anselm and Ralph of Laon as well as

[1] See above, p. 50.

[2] 'Dicebat magister Johannes Turonensis, quia divina essentia Pater pater-nitate, Filius filiatione, nec tamen divina essentia his proprietatibus distingitur, sed ille due persone. Et hoc, inquit, ostendebat per simile: esto, quod idem sit dux et episcopus. Iste est dux ducatu, episcopus episcopatu. Ecce hec persona non distingitur a se his proprietatibus, que significantur his nominibus: dux, episcopus, sed illa duo officia inter se distinguntur. Sic divina essentia Pater est paternitate, Filius filiatione, nec tamen distingitur his proprietatibus, sed ille due persone. Sic ille.' Cited by Landgraf, 'Zwei Gelehrte aus der Umgebung des Petrus Lombardus', p. 158.

[3] Landgraf, 'Zwei Gelehrte', pp. 157–60, collected the little information that he could find concerning John of Tours.

[4] Cf. Lottin, *Psychologie et Morale*, v, 445–6; Weisweiler, *Das Schrifttum*, pp. 244–7. [5] See above, p. 104.

[6] See B. Smalley, 'Gilbertus Universalis', especially pp. 235–45.

[7] Abelard refers to a master in Burgundy without mention of name, but

N

Alberic of Rheims also upheld Gilbert's doctrine.[1] Abelard further accused Gilbert of denying that Christ grew in human stature[2] and of advocating freedom for religious to enter matrimony.[3] Gilbert is one of four theologians of whom Abelard expressed his disapproval in the *Theologia*. All of them were friends of Bernard of Clairvaux.[4]

The antagonism between the school of Laon and Abelard also partly underlay Abelard's second trial for heresy. Hugh Métel (1080–1157), a regular canon at Toul and a great admirer of his former master, Anselm, joined the epistolary campaign for Abelard's condemnation. He was not personally acquainted with Abelard and did not know what his errors were, but he imitated the letters of Bernard.[5] More important is Walter of Mortagne, a critic of Alberic at Rheims but from within the traditionalist standpoint of the Laon school which he attended prior to coming to Paris in the 1130s and which he later ruled as bishop of Laon from 1155 till his death in 1174.[6] Walter's teaching had a future for his writings on the Trinity and on marriage were adopted by

---

[1] According to Robert de Bosco whose words spoken in defence of Gilbert of Poitiers in 1148 are related by John of Salisbury in the *Historia Pontificalis*, VIII (ed. M. Chibnall, pp. 18–19). On the doctrinal issue see A. Hayen, 'Le Concile de Reims', pp. 45–9.

[2] '. . . in tantam prorupit insaniam, ut corpus Dominicum ejusdem longitudinis seu grossitudinis in utero Virginis fuisse astruat, cuius et in provecta aetate exstitit', *Theol. Christiana*, IV (PL. 178, 1286B); *Theol. 'Schol.'*, II, 7 (1056D–7A).

[3] *Theol. 'Schol.'*, II, 7 (PL. 178, 1057A).

[4] Smalley, 'Gilbertus Universalis', p. 243.

[5] In 1140 or so Hugh wrote to Pope Innocent II and to Abelard, *Epist.* IV and V, ed. C. L. Hugo, *Sacrae Antiquitatis Monumenta*, II, 330–4. Cf. Vacandard's true judgment: 'bel esprit du temps, en quête de thèmes a déclamations, (il) saisit cette occasion pour faire montre de style, en dénonçant Abélard au souverain Pontife', *Vie de S. Bernard*, II, 140. The best account of Hugh's life and letters is by L. Ott, *Untersuchungen*, pp. 47–56.

[6] See above, pp. 105–6.

---

cf. Smalley, 'Gilbertus Universalis', p. 243. 'Alter quoque totidem erroribus involutus, tres in Deo proprietates, secundum quas tres distinguntur personae, tres essentias diversas ab ipsis personis, et ab ipsa divinitatis natura constituit, ut scilicet paternitas Dei, vel filiatio sive processio, res quaedam sint tam ab ipsis personis, quam ab ipso Deo diversae', *Theol. 'Schol.'*, II, 7 (PL. 178, 1056D); also *Theol. Christiana*, IV (1285B).

the compiler of the *Summa Sententiarum* and by Peter Lombard.[1] Another critic of Abelard, also dependent upon the letters of Bernard, was Clarembald who perhaps taught dialectic at Laon in the early 1140s.[2]

The persistence and strength of the conservative but also very productive and organized tradition of Laon is evident at the end of Abelard's life and after his death as much as at the outset of his theological career. The repeated instances of tensions between him and members of the school over a period of thirty years arose from disagreements over particular opinions as well as from more basic differences in outlook. Abelard's final condemnation, for which the blame or credit is still assigned too generously to Bernard, represented in part another round in a series of quarrels between Abelard and the members of the school of Laon or their heirs and successors.

The followers of Anselm scarcely attempted to assimilate Abelard's thinking. An exception, however, is provided by the *Sententie Varsavienses* which appeared in the later 1120s or early 1130s. This work is an amalgam of sentences from the school of Laon together with extracts from the *Tractatus de trinitate* of Walter of Mortagne and from Abelard.[3] Many minor traces of the *Theologia 'Scholarium'* in its first or second redaction are found. Faith is defined as *existimatio* but also rather as *certitudo rerum non apparentium*. Power and wisdom and love or goodness are ascribed specially to the Father, Son and Spirit respectively, although the author attacks those who make each of these attributes exclusively belong to one of the persons. No use is made of Abelard's more personal theses, on omnipotence for example or on pagan witnesses to the Trinity and for this reason the work is not to be seen as the product of a close disciple of Abelard but of a mind formed essentially within the Laon tradition

---

[1] See L. Ott, 'Walter von Mortagne und Petrus Lombardus' and *idem*, 'Der Trinitätstraktat Walters von Mortagne als Quelle der Summa Sententiarum'.

[2] See above, p. 119, n. 5; also H. Vaupel, 'Clarembaldus von Arras'.

[3] This work was discovered and edited by F. Stegmüller, 'Sententiae Varsavienses'. Cf. *idem*, 'Die Quellen der "Sententiae Varsavienses"'. I am grateful to Professor Stegmüller for kindly sending to me copies of these two articles.

but open also to influence from another quarter. The *Sententie Varsavienses* are a pointer to the future for, in spite of Abelard's condemnation and of the intellectual ostracism with which his public career closed, the attempt to assimilate Abelard's thinking within more widely acceptable cadres of thought was to be made. Moreover copyists of manuscripts and their directors ensured that Abelard's writings often entered into the same volumes as those which contained texts from the school of Laon so that students read Abelard as they read the works of the school.[1] Nowhere was this reading more thoroughly done than at the house of St Victor in Paris.

[1] See above, pp. 100–1.

CHAPTER VII

HUGH OF SAINT VICTOR

Abelard claimed to have had a part in the foundation of the house of Saint Victor in Paris by William of Champeaux in 1108. He claimed to have put William to flight from the schools to seek the shelter of the cloister.[1] The scorn which he poured upon William's conversion could not have been quickly forgotten in that quarter, although in time it was matched by the ravings of Walter against his Minotaur.[2] The main features, however, of the Victorine reaction to Abelard's teaching were not merely impatience or violence. No two Victorine masters are wholly alike, but the group of thinkers who were in the house between the 1120s and 1160s undertook patiently to censor, amend, absorb and surpass Abelard's theological production. A readiness to censure defects was graced with a striving to provide alternative theses by means of a scholarship which rivalled that of Abelard himself.

The abbey's rapid rise to fame was stimulated by its situation close to the schools of Paris and by its own opening of a school for students who were not themselves canons of the house. Among the canons there developed a remarkably distinguished circle of scholars. St Victor was a vital centre[3] for the promotion of the *vita communis*, the canonical ideal which, if less spectacular than the new monastic initiatives, was still so fertile an element in the life of the eleventh and twelfth centuries. The spirituality of the regular canons of St Victor rivals that of the early Cistercians; Hugh and Richard, as masters of spiritual thought and writing, enjoyed a fame comparable with that of Bernard of Clairvaux and William of St Thierry.

[1] *Hist. Calam.*, ed. Monfrin, *ll.* 70-6. On the foundation of Saint Victor see also Fourier Bonnard, *Histoire de l'abbaye royale . . . de S. Victor*, I, 1-17.
[2] *Contra Quatuor Labyrinthos Franciae*, II, ed. Glorieux, pp. 219-45. See also Glorieux, *ibid.*, introduction, pp. 187-95 and *idem*, 'Mauvaise action et mauvais travail'.
[3] Cf. J. C. Dickinson, *The Origins of the Austin Canons*, pp. 85-6; also Fourier Bonnard, *op. cit.*, I.

Hugh was the greatest of the Victorine masters and a leader of thought in the 1130s. He became a canon towards the end of the second decade of the century and remained at St Victor until his death in February 1141.[1] Unlike Abelard he gained no known enemies. His influence was felt not only in the early scholastic theological movement but also in grammar, chronicle writing, exegesis, canon law and spirituality.[2] But for his theological thought the Lombard's Sentences would never have been written. Among the great masters of the thirteenth century Alexander of Hales, Albert the Great and above all Bonaventure[3] were notably in his debt. The school of St Victor was the school of Hugh, and succeeding Victorines each owed something to Hugh. In comparison Abelard was a much weaker direct influence upon the masters of the twelfth and thirteenth centuries.

At St Victor Hugh both knew current developments in thought and kept in touch with men who were promoting such developments. In correspondence he prepared arguments of his own and received those of others.[4] Bernard's *De baptismo* was a reply to a letter of Hugh and it was inserted into the *De sacramentis*. A letter to Walter of Mortagne became the *De sapientia animae Christi*. The *De arca morali* was conceived in the course of sedentary conversations in the house when companions raised questions with him.[5] As a teacher of theology Hugh was influenced by the Laon tradition and by Abelard, though it should not be pretended that his doctrinal work was commensurate with all his thought or all his theological writing. Hugh, the *lector sacer*, is not easily separable from the exegete and the *homo interior*. Like Anselm of Laon he ploughed an Augustinian furrow. There is evidence that some of the early theological teaching of Hugh found its

[1] On Hugh's life see R. Baron, 'Notes biographiques'; also J. Taylor, *The Origin and Early Life of Hugh*, and R. Baron, *Etudes sur Hugues*, pp. 9–30. A. M. Landgraf, *Introducción*, pp. 121–131 provides a bibliographical survey.
[2] See R. Baron, 'L'influence de Hugues'.
[3] 'Anselmus in ratiocinatione, Bernardus in predicatione, Richardus in contemplatione—Hugo vero omnia haec', *Opusculum de reductione artium ad theologiam* (*S. Bonaventurae Opera*, v, 321).
[4] On Hugh's theological letters see the thorough study by L. Ott, *Untersuchungen*, pp. 348–495.   [5] *Prologus* (PL. 176, 617–18).

way into the sentence collections of the Laon school. Hugh's *Questiones* are the link between the Laon school and the *De sacramentis*.[1] Although the growth of Hugh's teaching and the precise order and date of his works are difficult to trace, it seems clear that in the main his thought moved forward steadily without great changes and without great hesitations in the face of contemporary developments which were, however, closely followed.[2] In the second half of the 1120s one of his students, Lawrence, wrote down his lectures, the *Sententie de divinitate*, so that copies could circulate among fellow students. Once a week Hugh personally reviewed Lawrence's *reportatio* as it proceeded and these lectures were the basis of the *De sacramentis christianae fidei*[3] 'in quo nonnulla quae antea sparsim dictaveram ... inserui'.[4] The *De sacramentis*, written between 1130/1 and 1137,[5] amounts to more than an arrangement of insertions and to more than a review of teachings, old and new.[6] Its movement and structure—mature, personal and original—transcend those of a mere sentence collection and the work does not reflect contemporary controversies very sharply. In this and in many of his other writings, Hugh's relationship to Abelard's teaching is an important but not an overriding consideration.

Underlying Hugh's definition of faith in the *De sacramentis*[7]—

[1] See O. Lottin, 'A propos des sources de la *Summa Sententiarum*', pp. 44–5; *idem*, 'Questions inédites de Hugues', (1959) p. 184, (1960) pp. 42–66. R. Baron, 'Etude sur l'authenticité de l'oeuvre de Hugues', p. 220: 'On ne peut guère douter que (Hugues) fut l'héritier légitime de l'Ecole d'Anselme de Laon et de Guillaume de Champeaux.'

[2] See D. Van den Eynde, *Essai sur la succession et la date des écrits de Hugues*, pp. 208–9.

[3] Only Lawrence's prefatory letter has been edited; see B. Bischoff, 'Aus der Schule Hugos', pp. 246–50, here 250. See also H. Weisweiler, 'Zur Einflußsphäre der "Vorlesungen" Hugos'. On the date of the *Sententie* see Van den Eynde, *Essai*, pp. 74–7, 207 and Table I. On their utilization in the *De sac.* see Weisweiler, 'Die Arbeitsmethode Hugos', pp. 256–66.

[4] PL. 176, 173. On the preparation of this work see in addition to the articles mentioned in the foregoing note, Weisweiler, 'Hugos von St Victor Dialogus de sacramentis'. Also Van den Eynde, *Essai*, p. 37.

[5] Van den Eynde, *Essai*, pp. 100–3, 207, Table I. R. Baron, *Science et sagesse chez Hugues*, pp. xliv–xlv: after 1130.

[6] Hugh's systematic plan is evaluated by R. Baron, *Science et sagesse*, pp. 136–42; also *ibid.*, pp. xlvii–xlviii. [7] 1, 10, 2 (PL. 176, 331).

'fides est certitudo rerum absentium supra opinionem et infra scientiam constituta'—scholars[1] have generally found a deliberate intention of improving upon Abelard's definition with its perilous equivocation: 'existimatio rerum non apparentium'.[2] Hugh had earlier attacked Abelard's attitude to the development of faith and in particular his belief that such events as the Incarnation and virgin birth of Christ had been occasionally as well known before as after Christ's coming. Abelard's opinion stemmed from his enthusiasm and zeal to discover among the ancient pagan writers the elements of true religion.[3] In c. 1125 Hugh had transmitted Abelard's opinion to Bernard of Clairvaux for comment. Hugh's letter is lost, but Bernard's reply, the De baptismo,[4] survives. Neither writer had mentioned Abelard by name; indeed it is arguable that a pupil of Abelard rather than Abelard himself is the subject of the exchange.[5] Bernard approved of Hugh's criticism,[6] and in the De sacramentis[7] Hugh reproduced, without acknowledgement, Bernard's own arguments against the quidam who do not allow sufficiently for the development of faith in history. Here Hugh distinguishing between faith itself and

[1] Cf. M. D. Chenu, 'La Psychologie de la foi', pp. 165–74; R. Baron, 'Le Sacrement de la foi'. I have been unable to obtain M. Grabmann, 'Hugo von St Victor (†1141) und Peter Abaelard (†1142)' in Theologie und Glaube, xxxiv (1942), pp. 241–9.

[2] Theol. 'Schol.' I, 1 (PL. 178, 981C).

[3] Cf. Theol. 'Summi boni', I, v et seq. (ed. Ostlender, pp. 11 et seq.), Theol. Christiana, I, v (PL. 178, 1139C–66B) and Theol. 'Schol.', I, 15–25 (1004D–34D).

[4] Epist. 77 (Opusc. X) (PL. 182, 1031–46). On the date c. above, p. 26n.

[5] 'Is ergo, cuius me respondere assertionibus iubes, et nomen taces, tibi noverit a me super consultis quod sentio dictum, non sibi contradictum, etiamsi quid aliter ab ipso sapimus . . . non quaerimus pugnas verborum . . . Patrum tantum opponimus sententias, ac verba proferimus, et non nostra', Bernard, De baptismo, Praefatio (PL. 182, 1031AB).

[6] Ibid. c. 3 (PL. 182, 1038B–41C, here 1038C): 'Verum ad refellendum tu tanta in tua epistola posuisse videris (al. tu tantum in tua epistola enituisti), ut nil addendum penitus putem; et pene quid addi possit, non inveniam'. Nonetheless 'hoc addidi, ne intactum quid praeterirem ex omnibus quae petisti' (1041BC).

[7] I, 10, 6–7 (PL. 176, 335–41). Cf. Dialogus de sacramentis (PL. 176, 37AB) and L. Ott, Untersuchungen, pp. 527–39. On Hugh's use of the De baptismo, see also Weisweiler, 'Die Arbeitsmethode Hugos', pp. 63–4. This exchange of views is a good example of Bernard's influence upon scholastic theology; cf. J. Châtillon, 'L'influence de S. Bernard sur la pensée scholastique au XIIe et au XIIIe siècles' in S. Bernard Théologien, pp. 268–88, here pp. 279–80.

knowledge of the faith, affirms that the latter has increased since the Incarnation and he disagrees with Abelard that the details of the redemption were foreknown by pagan writers. Nonetheless Hugh himself did trust in the ability of the human mind to rise to a knowledge of the Trinity and to achieve 'clara demonstratio' and 'manifesta declaratio'. His own argument is constructed upon the *simulacra* of the Trinity in the human soul which is made in the image of God and which is composed of *mens, sapientia* and *amor*, three *vestigia* of the triune God.[1]

Hugh accepts, like Abelard, the traditional use of the ternary of power, wisdom and goodness (or benignity or love or will) in discussion of the Father, Son and Spirit.[2] The divine will would not be perfect with goodness or wisdom but without power.[3] In the human mind is a power from which wisdom is born and the mind loves wisdom and proceeds to it. Rising from this trinity in the human soul to the supreme Trinity of persons, man attributes power to the Father, wisdom to the Son and love to the Spirit; he distinguishes the truth through the image by which he found the truth.[4] Hugh never alludes overtly to

[1] *De sacramentis*, I, 3, 21 (PL. 176, 225CD). Cf. Baron, *Science et sagesse*, pp. 24–5: 'Enfin de compte, la *demonstratio* consiste beaucoup plus à mettre en lumière qu'à faire une déduction rationelle rigoureuse, à montrer qu'à démontrer.'

[2] *De sac.* I, 3, 26–9 (PL. 176, 227C–231B); *De tribus diebus*, c. 1 and 21 (PL. 176, 811CD, 831D–2A). In the *Tractatus de trinitate* ascribed to Hugh and ed. R. Baron, p. 112, the properties of justice, wisdom and *misericordia* are applied to the three persons respectively. Van den Eynde, *Essai*, pp. 68–9, 207, considers Hugh's triad *potentia–sapientia–benignitas* to show the influence of Abelard since Augustine (*De trinitate*, VII, 2–3, XV, 17 (PL. 42, 936–9, 1079–82)) used *caritas*, not *benignitas*, and on this account he suggests that the *De tribus diebus* was written shortly after 1123 or *c*. 1125. R. Baron, *Science et sagesse*, p. 26, n. 114 had thought Hugh's triad traditional. I wonder whether the appearance of *benignitas* itself marks the influence of Abelard. The *Filius a patre gigni* from the school of Laon uses *bonitas* and, adverbially, *benigne* (see above, p. 174, n. 3). Walter of Mortagne, surely an uncompromising critic of Abelard, wrote: 'procedit ab utroque amor et benignitas, id est Spiritus sanctus' (*Tract. de trinitate*, c. 9 (PL. 209, 585D)).

[3] *De sac.*, I, 2, 5 (PL. 176, 208AB). Cf. I, 2, 6 (208B–D): 'non est posse illud quod scire, neque scire illud quod velle; et tamen Deo unum sunt posse, scire et velle'.

[4] *De sac.*, I, 3, 27 (PL. 176, 228D–30B). Hugh's inspiration in this is Augustine *De trin.*, 15, 1 (PL. 42, 1064).

Abelard. He does not analyse Scriptural and Patristic evidence concerning the features of the separate persons; here Abelard excelled. He does not use these attributes to explain the generation and procession of the Son and the Spirit, but to help men to know the perfection of God through his image in the soul, the most perfect creation of God.[1] He does not dispute with contemporary masters and he avoids the Sabellian flavour which others detected in Abelard. He offers back-handed conjectures in order to show the suitability of the attributions: if the Father is not only powerful but also omnipotent, he will not be mistaken for an aged and infirm person; if the Son is wise, he will not be thought immature; if the Spirit is benign, he will not seem rigorous or cruel.[2] Yet in the *Sententie de divinitate* Hugh had also taught that gentile philosophers, such as Plato, had by natural reason found the Trinity[3] and he had also said that power, wisdom and benignity were attributed *specialiter* to each of the persons.[4] In other writings Hugh virtually identified wisdom, not with the Word or the Son of God, but with Christ and his identification was perhaps a more felt or more persuasive commitment than Abelard offered.[5]

In the *Didascalicon*, written before 1125,[6] Hugh appears to have been deeply concerned over the identification by some of his contemporaries of the Spirit with the world-soul. There is no evidence which suggests that Hugh had Abelard more in his mind than other like-minded contemporaries. He argues that pagan philosophical texts which refer to the entelechy formed

[1] Cf. J. Hofmeier, *Die Trinitätslehre des Hugo*, pp. 227, 243–4.

[2] *De sac.*, I, 2, 8; I, 3, 26 (PL. 176, 208B–9A, 228CD).

[3] Cod. Breslau, Stadtbibl. Rehdiger 61, f. 146r, cited by J. Hofmeier, *op. cit.*, p. 219, n. 2, p. 220, n. 1. Hofmeier (p. 220, n. 2) also believes that the inedited sentences of the school of Laon, *Deus summe*, make this point about pagan philosophers and are here the link between Abelard and Hugh. According to Hofmeier (p. 226) the *Sententie de divinitate* reveal how indebted to Abelard Hugh is when he uses the three attributions.

[4] Cod. Breslau, Rehdiger 61, f. 149v, cited by Hofmeier, *op. cit.*, p. 242, n. 1.

[5] *De arca morali*, III, 6 (PL. 176, 651D), *De sapientia animae Christi* (PL. 176, 848CD). Cf. Baron, *Science et sagesse*, pp. 155–7.

[6] Van den Eynde, *Essai*, pp. 45–51, Table I.

out of divided and individual substance, out of identity and difference, indicate that the rational mind of man, formed out of all things and imprinted with the likeness of all things, possesses a marvellous power, but, stupefied by bodily sensations, it needs to be restored through instruction and through the pursuit of wisdom.[1] It is possible that Hugh, by offering a man-centred interpretation of texts which inspired some of his contemporaries to establish parallels with the third person of the Trinity, was consciously standing apart from fashion.[2] Hugh certainly deplored an excessive preoccupation with pagan lore and he classified purely literary works as mere *appendicia artium*.[3] He wrote of the philosophers and of their teaching about God that they concealed behind an attractive and shining surface of eloquence and behind a semblance of truth, the clay of error.[4] But instead of rejecting philosophical testimony outright, he appears to have tried to devalue its usefulness for others by considering it as rhetorical ornamentation, by insisting on the disparity between the *Timaeus* and Christian truth,[5] and by offering an alternative interpretation which interfered less with theology.

In the *De sacramentis* as well as in other earlier and later writings, Hugh left no doubt of his animosity against Abelard's teaching on the power of God. He attacks the thesis that God cannot alter his actions without qualifying his prescience and immutability, that God can only do what he does and that he cannot do better than he does.[6] His feelings were strong: 'Eant ergo nunc et de

---

[1] *Didascalicon*, I, I and 3, trans. J. Taylor, pp. 46–7, 48–50. I follow here the interesting interpretation of J. Taylor, given in his introduction to his translation, pp. 24–7, and in his notes on pages 178–80. I have been unable to obtain the edition of C. H. Buttimore, *Hugonis de S. Victore Didascalicon de Studio legendi* (Washington, 1939). For textual discussion of this edition see J. Châtillon, 'Chronique de Saint Victor', pp. 153–4.

[2] In the *De tribus diebus*, 19 (PL. 176, 828BC) Hugh considers that the Creator Spirit fills the world in a quite different way from that in which the soul fills the body.

[3] Cf. Taylor's introduction to his translation of Hugh's *Didascalicon*, pp. 19–21, and also *Didascalicon*, III, 4 (*ibid.*, pp. 87–9).

[4] *Ibid.*, IV, I (trans. Taylor, p. 102).

[5] Cf. *ibid.*, Taylor's introduction, pp. 22–3.

[6] *De sac.*, I, 2, 22 (PL. 176, 214A–16D). The argument is the same, word for word, in the *Explanatio in Canticum Beatae Mariae* (PL. 175, 425A–7A) and similar,

suo sensu glorientur qui opera divina ratione se putant discutere, et eius potentiam sub mensura coarctare.'¹ To say that God can do this much and no more (except of actions which would injure himself and denote impotence rather than omnipotence) is to restrain and moderate and contain an infinite power. 'Aiunt enim: Non potest Deus aliud facere quam facit, nec melius facere quam facit'² and they reason that if God could do other than he does, he could do what he has not foreseen and his providence would be mutable. 'Sed hoc pia mens in Deum dici non sustinet.'³ Hugh half-apologizes for replying to their argument which he does not wish to reject without showing cause and which he does not wish the credulous to accept.⁴ He argues that although everything that occurs has been eternally foreseen, what seems able to occur and yet does not occur has not been foreseen. This does not mean that some things are prevented from occurring; a different future is possible under God's power but not under his providence.⁵

Hugh also disputes Abelard's 'optimistic' thesis that nothing can be better done than it is done: 'Hic illi nostri scrutatores qui defecerunt scrutantes scrutationes, novum aliquid et vere novum, nec tam verum quam novum afferre se dicunt.'⁶ Hugh argues that if creation cannot be made *melior*, either it is supremely good and therefore is equal to the Creator, which is impossible, or it is incapable of sustaining improvement in which case it is defective. But what has been made by God can be made *melior*, although *quantum ad se* God cannot do what he does *melius* than he does it.⁷ In comparison with Thomas of Morigny,⁸ Hugh's criticism is more deft and more succinct; he tries to agree with Abelard that God's will is immutable and his goodness supreme while removing expressions which appear to impose a necessity upon a

¹ *De sac.*, I, 2, 22 (PL. 176, 214BC).   ² *Ibid.* (214C).
³ *Ibid.* (214D).   ⁴ *Ibid.* (215B).
⁵ *Ibid.* (215BC). Cf. R. Baron, *Science et sagesse*, pp. 22–3.
⁶ *De sac.*, I, 2, 22 (PL. 176, 215D).
⁷ *Ibid.* (216AB).   ⁸ See above, p. 136.

but less finished, in the *Sententie de divinitate*; cf. L. Ott, *Untersuchungen*, p. 518, n. 59, referring to cod. Breslau, Rehdiger 61, f. 141vb.

supremely free will and a limitation upon omnipotence. But he may have felt that in the *De sacramentis* he had not done enough to show that unlimited power is compatible with the divine will for he later wrote a *Libellus de potestate et voluntate Dei* in which he asked whether the divine power or the divine will is the greater of the two.[1] This is the question put by Abelard when he asked whether God can do more than he wills to do and Hugh's answer had been in the *De sacramentis* that God can do more than he wills to do. Here he makes clear that God can do more than he wills to do, not in the sense that he can do things against his will, but in the sense that what he does not will to do, he could do if he wished and in the sense that if he were to do what he does not will, he would will to do it.

Hugh nowhere in his *De sacramentis* considered the view attributed to Abelard that Christ's soul did not descend into Hell *per se* but only through his power.[2] However Abelard's position was derived from his argument concerning the omnipresence of God and the inability of spirit to be contained *in loco*. Hugh chastized *quidam insipientes* who maintained, as Abelard did not, that God is not present everywhere essentially[3] and also, as Abelard did maintain,[4] that created spirits are not present *in loco*.[5]

---

[1] PL. 176, 839–42. Cf. Van den Eynde, *Essai*, pp. 128–9.

[2] The descent into Hell is discussed in the *De sac.*, II, 1, 11 (PL. 176, 401B–403C). For Abelard see above, pp. 120–1.

[3] 'Id quod quidam insipientes, imo solam carnem sapientes et quae carnis sunt solum considerantes, existimant quasi corporalium sordium et pollutionum inquinationes Deum contingere possint si rebus omnibus essentialiter vel substantialiter inesse dicatur; tam frivolum est ut nec responsione sit dignum cum et ipse Spiritus creatus corporeis sordibus inquinari non possit . . . Postremo respondeant utrum potius concedendum de Deo existimant, quod nusquam sit Deus, an quod ubique sit', *De sac.*, I, 3, 17 (PL. 176, 223BC). Cf. R. Baron, *Science et sagesse*, p. 21.   [4] *Theol. 'Schol.'*, III, 6 (PL. 178, 1105BC).

[5] 'De spiritu creato . . . fatemur, ut non solum in loco esse, sed localem esse pronuntiemus sine dubitatione . . . Non ignoro tamen quosdam ab omni spiritu locum universaliter removere voluisse . . . Sed horum consideratio nimis a communi existimatione et possibilitate recessit', *De sac.*, I, 3, 18 (PL. 176, 224B–D). Among the *quosdam* may be counted the earlier Hugh who in a *Questio* taught that created spirits are not found in places, but were local or rather circumscriptible, see O. Lottin, 'Questions inédites de Hugues' (1959), p. 185, no. 3. Hugh may have been influenced by Abelard and may have been more open to this influence in the earlier years of his teaching.

Hugh disliked the description of the Word as a part of Christ.[1] This thesis is not found in Abelard's own writings but is contained in some of the Sentence collections of his school,[2] and Hugh may have had the Abelardians in his mind. He taught that the Word assumed a human nature (body and soul) into his person as a person of the Trinity; the *homo assumptus* became the person of God by whom this nature was assumed, and to talk of the separate parts of Christ is to destroy a divine and human unity.[3] Hugh's argument includes a strongly worded attack on the dialectical theologians of the day. They chiefly examine what is to be said and not what is to be believed. No characterization of Abelard's methods, even those of J. Cottiaux and J. Jolivet, surpasses in its accuracy what Hugh says here: 'Quaerunt an locutio illa bona est et an locutio illa recipienda est, et an probanda est locutio illa.'[4]

In Hugh's account of the redemption, the devil has a large place in the cause between God and man.[5] Hugh followed Anselm of Laon and agreed with Abelard and Anselm of Canterbury in denying that the devil possessed rights over fallen man. Man has freely consented to the devil's yoke and is justly held although the

---

[1] 'Fortassis ergo cogitas quasi tria quaedam: divinitatem, animam et carnem Christum composuisse: divinitate et carne et anima. Ergo tertia pars Christi Verbum est? Absit! Non enim pars Christi Verbum est, sed ipse Christus Verbum est', De sac., II, I, 11 (PL. 176, 402D–3A).

[2] See above, p. 25.   [3] De sac., II, I, 9 (PL. 176, 394A–C).

[4] 'Quaerunt hi quotidie homines quid dicendum sit, et quid credendum raro. Quaerunt an locutio bona est, et an locutio illa recipienda est, et an probanda est locutio illa. In moneta verborum positi sunt, et concurrit multitudo magna sermonum, et infinita perplexio . . . Nesciunt enim quia opus litteram judicare debet, non littera spiritum. Sicut scriptum est: "Spiritualis judicat omnia, et ipse a nemine judicatur" (I Cor. 11). Laborant ergo in judicio dicendi, quia spiritum non habent intelligendi . . . Quaerunt quid sit persona, et adducunt deinde definitionem personae, sicut a quibusdam facta est et probata, quia persona est individuum rationalis substantiae', De sac., II, I, 11 (PL. 176, 405CD). L. Ott, 'Hugo und die Kirchenväter', p. 293 suggested that Hugh himself searched for a freer form of expression than the tight dialectical method of Abelard.

[5] De sac., I, 8, 4 (PL. 176, 307D–9C). Cf. Dialogus de sacramentis: 'Quid Verbum incarnatum dixerim, nisi regem qui hunc mundum intravit per assumptam humanitatem cum diabolo bellaturus, et eum exinde, quasi tyrannum et violenter in alieno dominantem, expulsurus?' (PL. 176, 31D).

devil does not justly hold man and his dominion is not of right.[1]

On the subject of grace Hugh resembles Abelard in the nature of his questions, although there is no overt doctrinal or literary relationship between them and there are significant differences between their arguments. Both Abelard and Hugh put the problem of human responsibility in its relationship to the necessity for grace, but whereas Abelard searches to define the area in which human will, which is endowed by God with faith and love, can naturally be said to do good and in which the will earns merit by responding to the goodness of divine preaching,[2] Hugh, starting from man's loss of his natural will for good and from the depression and inclination of his will to evil, asks how man has the ability to avoid evil. He finds that the freedom of the will enshrines a certain power of consenting and attaching itself to grace if it is offered and of cooperating with grace. Grace in this way resuscitates the fractured will and provokes it towards action.[3]

Hugh is quietly opposed, in his *De sacramentis* at least,[4] to Abelard's theory of the nature of original sin in us. He admits the difficulties involved in defining original sin and is reluctant to broach them.[5] He adheres to Augustine's doctrine of the imputation of original sin and adds a sharper emphasis on ignorance as a fault caused by Adam's sin.[6] He defines original sin as the corruption or vice which we acquire by our birth in mental ignorance and in fleshly concupiscence.[7] This double corruption in us is 'culpa simul et poena originalis'.[8] It is true that unlike

---

[1] 'Nullam diabolus iustam causam habuit quare sibi ius in homine vindicare debuit', *De sac.*, I, 8, 4 (PL. 176 308B). Cf. Hugh's *Questiones* 28 and 29, ed. O. Lottin, 'Questions inédites de Hugues' (1959), pp. 202–7; also *Dialogus de sacramentis* (PL. 176, 29A–30D, 31CD). [2] See above, pp. 129–30.

[3] *Questio* 19, ed. Lottin, 'Questions inédites de Hugues' (1959), p. 198.

[4] I, 7, 25–28 (PL. 176, 297D–9A).

[5] *De sac.*, I, 7, 25 (PL. 176, 297D–8A).

[6] Cf. J. Gross, 'Die Ur- und Erbsünde bei Hugo', p. 52.

[7] 'Corruptio sive vitium quod nascendo trahimus per ignorantiam in mente, per concupiscentiam in carne', *De sac.*, I, 7, 28 (PL. 176, 299A).

[8] 'Hoc autem vitium originis humanae duplici corruptione naturam inficit; ignorantia scilicet mentem et concupiscentia carnem. Haec duo mala in primo quidem parente poena fuerunt praecedentis culpae et culpa actualis; in nobis autem culpa subsequentis poenae, et culpa simul et poena originalis', *De sac.*, I, 7, 26 (PL. 176, 298B).

Adam we do not sin actually but what was imputed to Adam on account of his action descends to us through our nature.[1] Earlier in his *Questiones* Hugh stated that Adam has transmitted sin and the penalty of sin to his whole succession, excepting Christ who did not bear the sin but freely bore the penalty of original sin.[2] Hugh nowhere overtly criticizes Abelard's thesis, but it is possible to detect that in his choice of words, in his insistence that original sin is both *poena* and *culpa* and that although this sin is not present in us by our action, it is imputed to our nature, Hugh resists the error of his contemporary.

Hugh does not, in his *De sacramentis*, overtly criticize Abelard's theory of the moral indifference of human actions, but he does ask why, since merit wholly lies in the will, actions are necessary to earn merit and whether they increase the merit earned by the will.[3] These questions are strikingly similar to those of Abelard,[4] although the answer given is a contrary one. Hugh believes that, when the opportunity to act is present, there can be no meritorious will which does not proceed to act. Moreover, in action, will and therefore merit are increased. It is possible to say that both the action and the will secure a reward since the action is the occasion and the cause of the reward.

When Hugh wrote to Bernard, he raised the question of sins of ignorance. Bernard in his reply, the *De baptismo*, mentioned Hugh's argument and gave it his support, stressing that the persecutors of Christ had sinned, whatever their ignorance.[5] Abelard

---

[1] 'Nos autem qui ab illo nascendo originem traximus, quod illi actuale fuit, originale habemus, quia in nos per solam nativitatem descendit quod in illo per actionem fuit. Natura enim nostra corruptionem quam in illo per ipsius actionem concepit, per nostram solum ad nos nativitatem traduxit. Et ideo nos nascendo peccatum concipimus, quod ille non nascendo sed agendo habuit, a quo per nativitatem venimus', *De sac.*, I, 7, 27 (PL. 176, 298CD).

[2] *Questio* 20, ed. Lottin (1959), p. 199. Also: '(Adam) peccatum et penam peccati in omnem posteritatem suam traduxit . . . Infans etenim, licet actu non concupiscat, neque ignorantiam aliquo effectu ostendat, tamen nec caret concupiscentia nec caret ignorantia . . . qua ratione vero anima . . . licet ex se naturaliter actualiter nichil commiserat tamen statim ab ipsa adiunctione originali reatu teneatur penes Deum . . . apud nos autem insolubile est', in Lottin, 'A propos des sources', pp. 50–1.

[3] *De sac.*, II, 14, 6 (PL. 176, 560C–4A).   [4] Cf. above, p. 139.

[5] C. 4 (PL. 182, 1041C–2C). Cf. L. Ott, *Untersuchungen*, pp. 539–43.

himself would have agreed provided that the term 'sin' was not understood in its strict sense of a contempt of God.[1] But it seems from the later writings of William of St Thierry as well as of Bernard that Abelard was believed by his critics to have taught that Christ's crucifiers did not sin.[2] Some of Hugh's remarks about concupiscence bear an affinity with Abelard's thought. He teaches that vice becomes a *culpa* when consent is given to it[3] and that concupiscence is the *pena primi peccati* which becomes sin if consent is given to it.[4] It is possible, however, that Hugh was here influenced by the thought of William of Champeaux.[5]

On the power of the keys Hugh affirms[6] that priests have a power to forgive sins and he disputes with those, no doubt the Abelardians, who consider that priests have merely a declaratory power to indicate in confession that absolution has been obtained from God through inner contrition.[7] Hugh thinks that the mistake of his opponents is not to realize that a sinner is bound both by obduracy of mind and by the debt of future damnation. He does not believe that every priestly sentence is ratified by God; what Scripture says of the power of binding and loosing shows that

---

[1] Cf. above, p. 131.   [2] Cf. above, p. 132.

[3] *De sac.*, II, 13, 1 (PL. 176, 525A–C).

[4] *Questio* 20, ed. Lottin (1959), p. 199; cf. *Questio* 21, ed. Lottin (1959), p. 200: 'concupiscentia que peccatum est, id est fomes peccati, et pena peccati ...'. Also Lottin, 'A propos des sources', pp. 50–1: 'concupiscentia naturalis motus est, nec peccatum, si infra terminum suum temperetur; sed si extra augetur, culpa est et dicitur tunc concupiscentia mensuram excedens'. But also cf. *De sac.*, I, 7, 20 (PL. 176, 296AB): 'haec necessitas concupiscendi non ideo culpa non est, quia necessitas est, quia ut esset haec necessitas, non necessitas causa fuit sed voluntas'.

[5] Cf. above, p. 177.   [6] *De sac.*, II, 14, 8 (PL. 176, 564C–70B).

[7] 'Potestatem remittendi peccata quidam soli Deo ita ascribere conantur, ut in ea hominem participem fieri posse nullo modo concedant. Et ad confirmationem huius assertionis adducunt mundationem illius leprosi quem Dominus prius per semetipsum sanitati restituit, ac sic deinde ad sacerdotes misit; non ut eius mundatio virtute illorum perficeretur; sed ut tantummodo testimonio illorum confirmaretur. Simili modo nunc in praesenti Ecclesia dicunt ministeria sacerdotum nihil amplius virtutis habere, nisi quaedam tantummodo signa esse, ut ille videlicet qui prius per contritionem cordis intus a Domino absolvitur, postmodum in confessione oris ab eis absolutus esse ostendatur', *ibid.* (564CD, 565B). Cf. P. Anciaux, *La Théologie du sacrement de pénitence*, pp. 295 et seq.

O

God can, not that he must, accept the judgment of priests.

In his writings Hugh emerges as one who dissociated himself generally from the teaching of Abelard. Not infrequently he attacks or appears in effect to attack Abelardian positions, such as those concerning pagan foreknowledge of the Incarnation, the nature of the divine power and of original sin, the morality of actions and the power of the keys. The lost letter to Bernard appears to be a sign of his anxiety in the mid-1120s, and Hugh then communicated to Bernard his misgivings on teachings which some fifteen years later were still associated with Abelard. Hugh's part in the conflicts of the later 1130s and shortly before his death is wholly unknown, but his manner in all his writings was to formulate criticism precisely and, as it were, quietly. The letter to Bernard, in which no name was mentioned, was not a broadside. Hugh's mistrust of Abelard has to be pieced together from implicit indications. Hugh did not seek a Bernardine conflict with Abelard. The absence of any criticism of Abelard's exemplarism is even surprising. Moreover, Hugh did learn from Abelard. If in the *Sententie de divinitate* he allowed himself a fractionally greater latitude with regard to Abelard's opinions than was his later custom, throughout all his writing there is evident a real concern to formulate his teaching in a way that takes into account Abelard's views and passes beyond them. The conjecture may also be advanced that sometimes Hugh sought to destroy an objectionable thesis by deflecting it and by reinterpreting its significance in an altered way. If Abelard and others found the Spirit in the doctrine of the *anima mundi*, Hugh found references to the human soul; if Abelard found the attributions of power, wisdom and love useful in the understanding of the generation and procession of the persons of God, Hugh found them useful as correctives of possible misapprehensions of the characters of each of the persons. Above all, Hugh left no doubt in the minds of his hearers and readers concerning why as well as where he thought Abelard was wrong and he equally has left no doubt concerning his opinion of dialectical theologians and lovers of *Sprachlogik*.

In the *Didascalicon* Hugh had perhaps something to say of Abelard's personality which may suggest that he felt a cultured distaste towards him or at any rate towards a certain kind of schoolman.[1] The passage contains a highly generalized description of a whole class of students who boast of having read or heard great men but who do not see what they lack, as well as of masters who are peddlars of trifles. But some of Hugh's remarks can be read, if we wish to do so, as thinly veiled criticisms of men like Abelard who accuse their forefathers of simplicity, who wrinkle their noses and purse their lips at lecturers in divinity, who can sufficiently penetrate to the hidden treasures of truth by their own mental acumen and who find the divine utterances so simply expressed that they do not need to study under the guidance of masters. Hugh was writing shortly after the council of Soissons and perhaps while Abelard was teaching at Quincey: 'it is not my advice that you imitate men of this kind'.

[1] III, 13 (trans. Taylor, pp. 94-7). Cf. Taylor, *ibid.*, p. 215, n. 68 and G. Paré *et al.*, *La Renaissance du XIIe siècle*, p. 67, n. 5.

CHAPTER VIII

THE 'SUMMA SENTENTIARUM'

Among the works of Hugh of St Victor in Migne, PL. 176, 41–174, is found a compact sentence work, there ascribed to Hugh and known to students of the theological literature of the early twelfth century under the title of *Summa Sententiarum* (= SS). Much of the work is a summary of sentences, a review and critique of opinions and as such it takes us inside a theological school. In some ways the SS is the *Place de l'Etoile* of early twelfth-century theological literature, the point of arrival and of departure and the centre of circulation for many other writings and teachings. For historians also the SS has assumed a central place in enquiries into the history of the period and one which corresponds to its influence in its own day. To the student of Abelard's influence the SS appears as a Gordian knot.

Who wrote the SS? Those manuscripts which offer an attribution do so variously: 'Magister Odo', 'Odo episcopus de Luca', 'Odo ex dictis magistri Hugonis', 'iuxta magistrum Anselmum et magistrum Hugonem', 'Magister Hugo'.[1] Historians have offered even more varying suggestions. Against the many who have attached the work to Hugh of St Victor, there has been another stream of opinion which has advocated in turns Hugh of Mortagne, Odo of Soissons, Odo of St Victor, Otto, perhaps of Lucca, and even Hildebert of Lavardin.[2]

The least unsatisfactory candidate seems to be Otto, the friend of Peter Lombard and from 1138 till his death in 1145 or 1146 bishop of Lucca. Recently, however, there has been a move away from the well worn search for the single author of a work which

---

[1] R. Baron, 'Note sur l'énigmatique *Summa Sententiarum*', pp. 37–8.

[2] J. de Ghellinck summarized the history of this question up to 1923 in his introduction to M. Chossat, *La Somme des Sentences, oeuvre de Hugues de Mortagne vers 1155*, pp. 1–19; also see de Ghellinck's note in *Le Mouvement théologique*, pp. 293–5. Perhaps the most effective contribution was made in 1926 by B. Geyer, 'Verfasser und Abfassungszeit'; Geyer favoured Otto of Lucca.

is known to be more complex than its printed version suggests.[1]
Several differing versions of the work are presented in the
manuscripts.[2] In its fullest form the SS also contains the treatise
on order by Ivo of Chartres and the treatise on marriage by Walter
of Mortagne. It underwent at least two redactions[3] and it does
not appear to have been issued directly by an author in a definitive form. The SS is, moreover, a compilation, disputatious,
critical and inquisitive, from a number of sources. It is firmly
rooted in the tradition of the school of Anselm of Laon and of
William of Champeaux. In its teaching on free will and on original
sin it follows the Augustinian furrow ploughed by Anselm[4]
and it borrows from the so-called *Sententie Anselmi* on the subjects of the creation, angelology and the fall of man.[5] The inscription in the Rouen MS. 553 reads 'ex tractatu magistri
Othonis iuxta magistrum Anselmum et magistrum Hugonem'.[6]
Above all the SS is closely related to the *De sacramentis* and to other
writings of Hugh and to the Sentences of Peter Lombard. Although
it is no longer believed[7] that it is posterior to the Lombard's
Sentences, scholars have remained in a quandary over the question
whether it is anterior or posterior to Hugh's *De sacramentis*.

R. Baron explains[8] the relationship of the SS to the *De
sacramentis* in terms of literary leap-frogging: an original version
of the SS, based upon the early teachings of Hugh, was compiled
from his sentences by his disciples. Later Hugh wrote the *De
sacramentis* and formulated a maturer expression of his thought.
One of his disciples was able to give a freely circulating com-
pendium of Hugh's Sentences a more rigid structure by using
for the purpose the newer *De sacramentis*, but at the same time

---

[1] See R. Baron, 'Note' and *idem*, 'Etude sur l'authenticité de l'oeuvre de
Hugues', pp. 214–15; also O. Lottin, 'A propos des sources de la Summa
Sententiarum'.

[2] Baron, 'Note', pp. 33–5.

[3] J. de Ghellinck, 'A propos de l'hypothèse des deux rédactions'.

[4] Lottin, 'A propos des sources', pp. 44–5.

[5] SS, II, 1–2, III, 5 (PL. 176, 79C–82C, 96BC). Cf. H. Weisweiler, 'La Summa
Sententiarum', pp. 143–8, 153, and *idem, Das Schrifttum, fere passim*.

[6] Baron, 'Note', pp. 37–8; Lottin, 'A propos des sources', p. 43.

[7] Principally since the time of Geyer's article, cited above, p. 198, n. 2.

[8] 'Note'.

incorporating criticisms of his master. This evolutionary hypothesis represents an attempt to do justice to the existence of
varying versions of the SS. The principal disadvantage of the
hypothesis would appear to be that it has not yet been thoroughly
tested by reference to the varying manuscript versions themselves.[1]
Nonetheless, stimulated by R. Baron's theory, the late Dom O.
Lottin searched for and found instances where the SS drew
upon some scattered sentences of Hugh concerning free will
and original sin and contained in two florilegia which principally
contain sentences from the Laon school.[2]

So R. Baron considers that, whether or not the SS was compiled
and written by Otto of Lucca, it was not written by Hugh but
was nonetheless Hugonian: 'lorsqu'on fait la part belle à Théo-
phraste on doit se souvenir d'Aristote'.[3] In its *ur*-form the SS
would represent the earlier thought of Hugh when he was,
perhaps, open to the influence of Abelard's methods and certainly to that of the Laon tradition. Later a maturer Hugh leaves
his mark upon the work, inspired by the opposition of Bernard
of Clairvaux to Abelard.[4] This codicil to Baron's hypothesis,
referring first to Abelard and then to Bernard's opposition to
Abelard, has not been tested by consulting the attitude of the SS
to Abelard, nor can such an examination be satisfactorily made
until a critical edition of the SS is made. The question of the
relationship of the SS to Abelard's teaching can at present only
be discussed with reference to an inadequate printed edition.

Among the first to broach the question was E. Portalié who,
arguing against Hugh's authorship, pointed to the presence of
Abelardian elements in the SS which contradicted Hugh's own

---

[1] Van den Eynde in his *Essai* on the writings of Hugh, pp. 101–2, is firmly
persuaded that the SS is posterior to the *De sacramentis*, although his judgment
would appear to refer to the printed version of the SS alone.

[2] 'A propos des sources', pp. 46–50.

[3] Baron, 'Etude sur l'authenticité', pp. 214–15.

[4] Baron, 'Note', pp. 39–40. Van den Eynde, *Essai*, p. 209, found no evidence
of changing opinions in Hugh's work and did not believe that the SS rested
upon unpublished notes of Hugh, but see above, pp. 188, 191n., 196, for
suggestions that Hugh made minor alterations in his views, correcting an
earlier, but very limited, openness to Abelard's teaching.

teachings. For Portalié the SS represented the fusion of the schools of Abelard and of Saint Victor.[1] Claeys-Boúúaert, writing in 1909[2] and following E. Kaiser,[3] claimed that the SS both borrowed Abelard's systematic plan for the composition of a sentence work and used extracts from Abelard's *Theologia*. In 1922 F. Vernet found in the SS a considerable use of Abelard's opinions and even of his errors, but attempted to cast a doubt over the view of Claeys-Boúúaert that the plan of the SS was Abelardian.[4] However, in 1923 M. Chossat accepted the thesis of Portalié and Claeys-Boúúaert, arguing that the SS depended verbally on passages from Abelard's *Ethica* and *Sic et Non* and from the Sentences of Abelard's school which are now ascribed to Hermann.[5] This fusion of Victorine and Abelardian currents is 'une caractéristique sensationelle dans le mouvement dogmatique du XIIe siècle'.[6] J. de Ghellinck, in the second edition of *Le Mouvement théologique*, accepted the interpretation of the majority of his predecessors: 'l'oeuvre tient de très prés à la double source des productions abélardiennes et victorines, si bien qu'on peut la considérer comme le confluent des deux courants. Bien des matériaux sont abélardiens. Dans mainte conception, dans mainte doctrine et même dans quelques erreurs, l'on peut retrouver sans peine la marque abélardienne. Le plan aussi nous rapproche sensiblement de l'école d'Abélard.'[7] The SS is 'le point de convergence du courant victorin et du courant abélardien'.[8] Vernet's criticism had been ignored and some recent and novel remarks by other scholars have been made without, it would seem, a clear recognition of the weight of previous opinion concerning Abelard's influence on the SS. Thus R. Sylvain, in an attempt to

---

[1] 'C'est précisément la comparaison de cette somme avec les sommes abélardiennes qui manifeste la fusion des deux écoles', 'Pierre Abélard', col. 51.

[2] 'La Summa Sententiarum', especially pp. 710–19.

[3] The purpose of E. Kaiser's *Pierre Abélard critique* was, in its third part, pp. 237–325, to show, against S. M. Deutsch and E. Vacandard, that Abelard rather than Hugh was the author of a theological movement in the twelfth century.

[4] 'Hugues de S. Victor', cols. 255, 284–5, 294.

[5] Chossat, *La Somme des Sentences*, p. 69.

[6] *Ibid.*, p. 1.

[7] De Ghellinck, *Le Mouvement théologique*, pp. 197–8.

[8] *Ibid.*, p. 201.

win back the SS for Hugh, described it as a reply, written about 1127, to Abelard's *Theologia*.[1] D. Van den Eynde noted the servile use made of Abelard's teaching in the period before the conflict initiated by William of St Thierry in 1138/9.[2]

These authorities conflict; accordingly their references to the SS and to points of comparison with Abelard's works deserve to be examined.

The notion that the SS was written in dependence upon Abelard's division of theology into faith, charity and sacrament is an error. Claeys-Boúúaert affirmed this and sought confirmation in an examination of the second chapter of the SS which concerns faith, hope and charity, and in which extracts from Abelard's *Theologia* are found.[3] But he did not investigate the overall plan of the SS nor compare it with any of the sentence works which were written according to Abelard's plan, such as the Sentences of Hermann or of Roland which were both in print in 1909. He confused the three theological virtues of faith, hope and charity, which are discussed by the SS but not because they offer a schema for the composition of the work, with Abelard's own different division of the *necessaria ad salutem* into their dogmatic, moral and sacramental aspects.[4] Had Claeys-Boúúaert looked in the SS for a section on charity, such as Abelard proposed, he would have found none, for charity is there inserted into a consideration of the sacraments of the Old Testament and in particular of the commandments to love God and one's neighbour.[5] It is curious that so much credence should

[1] 'La tradition des Sentences d'Anselme de Laon', pp. 21–31.
[2] 'Précisions chronologiques', pp. 228–9; *Essai*, p. 102.
[3] Claeys-Boúúaert, 'La Summa Sententiarum', pp. 710–19. Cf. SS, I, 1–2; IV, 8 (PL. 176, 43A, 44A–45A, 126A) and *Theol. 'Scholarium'*, I, 2; I, 1–2, 3; II, 3; I, I (PL. 178, 984C, 981C, 984D–6C, 1051A, 981D–2D).
[4] Cf. Abelard, *Theol. 'Schol.'*, I, I, 2: 'Tria sunt . . . in quibus humanae salutis summa consistit, fides videlicet, charitas et sacramentum . . . tribus supra positis breviter assignatis atque descriptis, scilicet fide, charitate et sacramento, de singulis diligentius est agendum' (PL. 178, 981C, 984B).
[5] For further criticism of the so-called Abelardian plan of the SS see Vernet, 'Hugues de S. Victor', cols. 284–5, and H.Cloes, 'La systématization théologique', pp. 299–301, although even Cloes regards a few extracts from Abelard as traces of an Abelardian *plan*. For the dependence of the SS in the plan of the

have been given by a whole series of historians[1] to a demonstration which was so manifestly incomplete.

The SS could quote extensively from contemporary authors, lifting even lengthy passages out of their writings or inserting here or there a few borrowed lines without acknowledgment of the source or even of the fact that there is a source. Abelard is less often used in this manner than Hugh or Walter of Mortagne, but he furnishes the SS with some lengthy considerations on the nature of faith and hope and especially on the question whether faith embraces what is visible. Claeys-Boúúaert has collated these passages in the SS with their equivalents in the Migne version of Abelard's *Theologia 'Scholarium'*. Much later in the work the SS reproduces almost verbally the definition of charity which Abelard gives in the opening of his *Theologia*.[2]

The SS also appears to have borrowed from Abelard patristic texts. Dr Ott discovered, by reference in the main to the *Sic et Non*, *Theologia Christiana* and '*Scholarium*', that both authors present similar abbreviations of texts and similar variants from original materials, and that they adopt the same order in the presentation of some authorities.[3] Moreover the SS appears to have been influenced by Abelard's argument against Gilbert the Universal on the relationship of properties to the divine persons and on the question whether God generated himself or

---

[1] Cf. de Ghellinck, *Le Mouvement théologique*, p. 197; Chossat, *La Somme des Sentences*, p. 69: 'La Somme s'inspire du plan général de l'Introduction' (= *Theol. 'Schol.'*).
[2] Claeys-Boúúaert, 'La Summa Sententiarum', pp. 711-14; see above, p. 202, n. 3.
[3] Ott, 'Der Trinitätstraktat Walters von Mortagne als Quelle der Summa Sententiarum', p. 237, collects several examples which together make his conclusion credible. Among the more striking examples are: 1. a row of three texts of Bede and Augustine in SS, I, 6 (PL. 176, 52A), cf. *Theol. Christiana*, IV (PL. 178, 1309CD), *Theol. 'Schol.'*, II, 17 (1082D–3A); 2. two texts of Augustine and Ambrose in SS, I, 9 (56A), cf. *Sic et Non*, c. 5 (1358C), *Theol. Christiana*, I, (1123A).

---

work upon Fulgentius see A. Grillmeier, 'Fulgentius von Ruspe, De Fide ad Petrum'.

another,[1] and also by Abelard's analysis of the different applications of the names of the Trinity.[2]

In addition to these unacknowledged quotations and borrowed materials there is evidence that the SS accepted individual opinions taught by Abelard. In particular the SS looks to Abelard for his refutation of Hugh's thesis on the reviviscence of pardoned sins. Hugh taught that if a man falls into mortal sin, he will be punished for this sin and also for all those earlier sins for which he had made a repentance which was in the event not lasting.[3] But the SS, after quoting this opinion, introduces a contrary one: 'alii, quibus magis videtur assentiendum, dicunt . . . ' According to this teaching God does not punish the same fault twice once satisfaction has been made, but a later lapse by a sinner who has once repented merits punishment on account of the ingratitude shown in respect of a grace which has been spurned.[4] On this the SS reminds one of the Sentences of Hermann which themselves reflect the lost *Liber Sententiarum* which had circulated in Abelard's school.[5] Both the SS and Hermann similarly present Hugh's argument together with the supporting authorities and they both reply to Hugh by invoking an opinion of Gregory. It is also possible, though not definite, that the SS turned to Abelard in order to advance beyond an uncertainty expressed by Hugh on the question whether Christ's prayer in the garden

[1] Ott, 'Der Trinitätstraktat Walters', p. 238. SS, I, 11 (PL. 176, 58D et seq.); cf. *Theol. Christiana*, III (PL. 178, 1254 et seq., 1240) and above, p. 179.
[2] Ott, 'Der Trinitätstraktat Walters', p. 238. SS, I, 9 (PL. 176, 56AC); cf. *Theol. 'Schol.'*, I, 6 (PL. 178, 988C) and more strikingly the *Sententie* of Hermann, c. 4 (PL. 178, 1699B). The *Sententie* of Hermann, if written after 1138, may be posterior to the SS which was written before 1140 and perhaps before 1138 (Van den Eynde, 'Précisions chronologiques', pp. 223–9 and 'Nouvelles précisions', pp. 83–6). But the *Sententie* of Hermann may be closely dependent upon the lost *Liber Sententiarum*.
[3] SS, VI, 13 (PL. 176, 150C–1A): 'Dicunt aliqui quod ille qui habet cordis contritionem et condignam facit satisfactionem pro praeteritis peccatis vere consequitur remissionem . . . sed si postea ad mortem peccat redeunt omnia, et si tunc moreretur de omnibus puniretur . . .' Cf. Hugh, *De sac.*, II, 14, 8–9 (PL. 176, 570B–8A).   [4] SS, VI, 13 (PL. 176, 151A–C).
[5] *Sententie* of Hermann, c. 37 (PL. 178, 1758BD). Cf. Abelard, *Expos. in* '*ad Romanos*', II (864D); Portalié, 'Pierre Abélard', col. 53; Vernet, 'Hugues de S. Victor', col. 254.

of Gethsemane ('Father, let this chalice pass from me') was heard.[1]

When, however, further evidence is sought of doctrinal agreements between the SS and Abelard, difficulties appear. The SS distinguishes four meanings of the divine will ('idem cum Deo', 'beneplacitum vel dispositio,' 'praeceptio vel prohibitio', 'operatio vel permissio')[2] and this suggested to M. Chossat[3] that the author had read Abelard.[4] But the SS may be compared more closely with the *De sacramentis*[5] and O. Lottin found the source of the SS among the collections of *questiones* stemming from Hugh and contained in the manuscripts Troyes 1174 and Châlons-sur-Marne 72.[6] Hugh himself may have been inspired by Abelard, but at best the SS would have been influenced by Abelard indirectly.

The SS also teaches that certain names which pertain to the unity of the divine substance are sometimes used to distinguish the persons, and he illustrated the point with the attributes of power, wisdom and goodness.[7] L. Ott has demonstrated[8] that the SS is here inspired by the *Tractatus de trinitate* of Walter of Mortagne[9] and by Hugh.[10] The SS does not borrow any characteristically Abelardian argument concerning these attributions which he did not find in Walter or Hugh.

E. Portalié thought that the SS turned to Abelard to modify without wholly rejecting Hugh's attribution, not only of the uncreated knowledge of the Word, but also of omnipotence to Christ.[11] Portalié referred to the Sentences of Hermann who taught that the soul of Christ, separated in death, did not have the knowledge possessed by the Word. Hermann did not mention

---

[1] I, 17 (PL. 176, 76AB). Cf. Abelard, *Expos. in 'ad Romanos'* (PL. 178, 865C) and *Theol. 'Schol.'*, III, 5 (1097 *et seq.*). On this question, see L. Ott, *Untersuchungen*, pp. 392–7.

[2] I, 43 (65AC).   [3] *La Somme des Sentences*, p. 142, n. 7.

[4] *Theol. 'Summi boni'*, III, 2 (ed. Ostlender, p. 99).

[5] I, 4, 2–11 (PL. 176, 235A–239A).

[6] 'A propos des sources', pp. 49–50.   [7] SS, I, 10 (PL. 176, 56D–57D).

[8] *Untersuchungen*, pp. 585–6; 'Der Trinitätstraktat', p. 236.

[9] C. 8 (PL. 209, 583–4).

[10] *De sac.*, I, 3, 26, 28, 29 (PL. 176, 227–8, 230–1).

[11] 'Pierre Abélard', col. 53; SS, I, 16 (PL. 176, 74D–5A). Cf. Hugh, *De sac.*, II, 1, 6 (PL. 176, 383D): 'ex ipsa divinitate humanitas accepit per gratiam totum quod divinitas habuit per naturam... ex illa ineffabili unione divinitatis

the question of the power of Christ.[1] The SS, however, in rejecting Hugh's notion that Christ had omnipotence, also supported Hugh's notion, rejected by Hermann, that the soul of Christ had omnisapience.[2] Portalié wrote that the SS mentions a semi-donatist opinion found in Abelard's circle, namely that excommunicate or heretical priests cannot validly consecrate, since consecration, unlike other sacraments, is an offering by the whole church and cannot be made outside the church.[3] But apart from the *Confessio fidei*, to which Portalié refers and which does not mention any such opinion,[4] only Roland can be adduced in support and he wrote some twenty years later.[5] The link between the SS and Abelard's circle in this matter is as tenuous as their references are brief. Portalié further wrote: 'Hugues avait très sagement démontré que l'extrême-onction peut être réitérée comme l'eucharistie . . . La *Summa* emprunte à l'école d'Abélard l'erreur contraire.'[6] But, as Vernet later remarked,[7] the SS and Hugh conclude their differing arguments by agreeing with each

---

[1] C. 27 (PL. 178, 1737BC): 'Quaeritur etiam utrum eamdem scientiam habuerit anima illa, quam Verbum habebat. Quidam dicunt quod eamdem . . . Aequalis ergo erat creatura illa in hoc Creatori suo, quod irrationabile esse videtur. Non itaque dicimus quod eamdem habuerit scientiam.'

[2] 'Dicunt quidam quod non habuit (anima Christi) omnem scientiam nec omnia scivit quae Deus scit; quod ita volunt probare: Anima illa creatura est, sed in nullo aequatur creatura Creatori; non ergo scit quidquid Verbum, non tamen aequatur ei in scientia, quia illi inest per naturam illa scientia, animae per gratiam' (PL. 176, 74AB) . . . Sed quamvis supradictis respondere nesciant, adhuc tamen nobis opponunt: Si anima illa scit omnia quia unita est scienti omnia, ergo debet dici omnipotens, quia unita est omnipotenti. Ad hoc dici potest quod naturaliter anima est capax scientiae . . . sed cum idem sit esse Deum quod omnipotentem esse, non potuit illud conferri creaturae' (74D-5A).

[3] 'Pierre Abélard', col. 53; also Vernet, 'Hugues de S. Victor', col. 286. SS, VI, 9 (PL. 176, 146B).

[4] PL. 178, 107–8; presumably this was cited because here Abelard affirmed that the power of binding and loosing was transmitted to all the successors of the Apostles.

[5] Ed. Gietl, p. 218. Roland teaches that priests who have been *exauctorati*, and not merely deposed, lack the power to consecrate.

[6] 'Pierre Abélard', col. 54.   [7] 'Hugues de S. Victor', col. 286.

---

plenam et perfectam sapientiam, et potentiam et virtutem et bonitatem accepisse credimus'. Also, Hugh, *De sapientia animae Christi* (PL. 176, 845–56); this work was sent to Walter of Mortagne. Cf. R. Baron, *Science et sagesse*, pp. 157–60 and L. Ott, *Untersuchungen*, pp. 374–5.

other. The SS affirms that a person can receive these sacraments more than once[1] and Hugh argues that neither the oil nor the host is consecrated twice.[2] In the Sentences of Hermann it is expressly stated, moreover, 'de iteratione ... non videtur prohibere quin repetatur'; Hermann also distinguishes between the non-reiterability of the consecration of a host and the reiterability of receiving the body of Christ.[3] Portalié suggested that the SS may have been directly influenced by Abelard in teaching 'an error strange to St Victor', that faith without love is not a virtue, but with love is a virtue;[4] but Abelard's own remarks on faith do not concern virtue.[5]

It appears that the SS adopted only on a most limited scale opinions taught by Abelard. The SS borrowed passages from Abelard concerning faith, hope and charity, his arguments against Gilbert the Universal, and his analysis of the different applications of the names of the Trinity. The SS also used Abelard's thesis on the non-reviviscence of previously pardoned sins to reject the contrary thesis of Hugh and similarly may possibly have inclined to Abelard rather than to Hugh on a question concerning the human will of Christ. But other possible examples of doctrinal agreement with Abelard have not been established. It is therefore an exaggeration to say with Claeys-Boúúaert:[6] 'Souvent, en quittant le De Sacramentis, l'auteur de la Summa se rapprochait de l'école abélardienne'; or with Vernet:[7] 'La Somme, dans son plan, dans maintes opinions, et même dans quelques erreurs porte l'empreinte abélardienne', 'un peu partout .... des emprunts lui sont faits'; or with de Ghellinck:[8] 'dans

---

[1] VI, 15 (PL. 176, 154AB): 'de sacramento altaris vel unctionis, licet iteratio fiat quantum ad personam quae iterum suscipit sacramentum, tamen, quia non iterum benedicitur eadem hostia vel idem oleum, non iteratur sacramentum'.

[2] De sac., II, 15, 3 (PL. 176, 578B–80B).   [3] C. 30 (PL. 178, 1745AB).

[4] 'Pierre Abélard', col. 53; Vernet, 'Hugues de S. Victor', col. 286. SS, I, 2 (PL. 176, 45AB): 'Solet quaeri de fide utrum sit virtus ... sane potest dici quod fides per dilectionem operans sit virtus, sine dilectione non est virtus.'

[5] Theol. 'Schol.', II, 3 (PL. 178, 1051A): 'nunquam si fidei nostrae primordia statim meritum non habent, ideo ipsa prorsus inutilis est judicanda, quam postmodum charitas subsecuta, obtinet quod illi defuerat'.

[6] 'La Summa Sententiarum', p. 719.

[7] 'Hugues de S. Victor', cols. 255, 294.   [8] Le Mouvement théologique, p. 197.

mainte conception, dans mainte doctrine et même dans quelques erreurs, l'on peut retrouver sans peine la marque abélardienne'; or with Chossat:[1] 'souvent même (la Somme) s'approprie les conclusions et les preuves d'Abélard'. These writers are as dependent upon each other as any series of writings from a twelfth-century school. Their common source is easier to identify than the source of the *Summa* itself or of the sentence books of Abelard's school, for it is Portalié whose arguments rested upon weak foundations. Abelard did contribute in a positive sense to the SS, but his theses were only occasionally adopted, his plan not at all. His patristic scholarship was also found occasionally helpful.

On the other hand there are numerous occasions when the SS takes issue with Abelard's teachings. Abelard's name is never mentioned, but under the anonymity of *quidam* frequent references are made to Abelard and to his school. Moreover, the hostility of the SS is sometimes fierce. 'Quidam . . . calumniatores veritatis dicunt (Deum) per potentiam et non per essentiam ubique esse' writes the SS in criticism of an opinion which was ascribed to Abelard's school by several contemporaries.[2] 'Plane dicit Ambrosius quod angeli locales sunt': thus the SS in reply to Abelard's doctrine that created spirits are not localized.[3] 'Quidam tamen de ingenio suo praesumentes dicunt se non nescire'; the SS is critical of those, perhaps Abelardians, who presume to know how the Son is engendered and who invoke Isaiah, 53, 8 ('Generationem eius quis enarrabit?') as an invitation to solve a difficulty

---

[1] *La Somme des Sentences*, p. 69.

[2] '. . . eum contingere possent inquinationes sordium si ubique esset essentialiter. Quod ita frivolum est, ut nec responsione dignum sit, cum etiam spiritus creatus sordibus corporis (etsi leprosi vel quantumcunque polluti) inquinari non possit . . . Auctoritas Augustini quam solent inducere, illorum errorem potius quam iuvet destruit: Haec scilicet qua dicit Deum ubique esse non locis, sed actionibus ut errorem foveant, fures veritatis efficiuntur. Sic namque est in auctoritate illa. Deus ubique est, cui non locis, sed actionibus appropinquamus. Fatendum est itaque Deum in omni loco veraciter et essentialiter esse, nec tamen loco comprehendi ullo, quoniam incircumscriptibilis est . . . ', 1, 4 (PL. 176, 48C–50B). Cf. Hugh, *De sac.*, I, 3, 17 (PL. 176, 223B–4A). Cf. above, pp. 120–1.

[3] I, 5 (PL. 176, 50B–D). The text of Augustine quoted here (50C) is also found in the *Sententie* of Hermann, c. 19 (PL. 178, 1723D). Cf. above, pp. 120–1.

concerning the Trinity and not, as did St Jerome, concerning the Incarnation.[1] The SS follows Hugh in arguing against 'quosdam scientia inflatos' who argue that God can only do what he does.[2] The Abelardians say that what God does not do, he ought not to do, 'sed ut mihi videtur sub hoc verbo (sc. debet) latet venenum.'[3] Abelard had argued from a remark of Augustine that God could not engender a better Son to the thesis that God cannot do anything better than he does,[4] but the SS fairly observes that the Son is born of the divine substance and is equal to the Creator, but creation is inferior.[5] The Abelardians say that Christ did not possess omniscience, but 'Fulgentius multa opponit contra illum errorem.'[6] The Abelardians say that Christ could sin: 'quid absurdius quam quod Filius Dei (qui erat homo ille) damnari posset!'[7] The Abelardians do not consider original sin in us to be

[1] SS, I, 7 (PL. 176, 53D–4A). Cf. Sic et Non, c. 18 (PL. 178, 1376D–7A), but also cf. Theol. Christiana, I, v (1135C), Theol. 'Schol.', I, 13 (1001A), II, 3 (1054D–5B), and the Sententie of Hermann, c. 10 (PL. 178, 1708B). Cf. Ott, 'Der Trinitätstraktat', p. 234.
[2] I, 14 (PL. 176, 68C–70B). Cf. above, pp. 134–5, 189–91.   [3] Ibid. (69C).
[4] Lib. Quaestionum LXXXIII, c. 50 (PL. 40, 31–2). Cf. Abelard, Theol. Christiana, v (PL. 178, 1326D), Theol. 'Schol.', III, 5 (1094C).
[5] I, 14 (PL. 176, 69D–70A).
[6] I, 16 (PL. 176, 74A–D) and cf. above, pp. 205–6. Cf. the Sententie of Hermann, c. 27 (PL. 178, 1737BC), Sent. Florianenses, c. 43 (ed. Ostlender, 20). Also Claeys-Boúúaert, 'La Summa Sententiarum', pp. 715–17 and L. Ott, Untersuchungen, pp. 372–5, 368–71. Ott, Untersuchungen, p. 374, observes that in the use of Fulgentius the SS may have drawn upon Sic et Non, c. 73 (PL. 178, 1445C).
[7] I, 18 (PL. 176, 78AB): 'Solet quaeri utrum Christus peccare potuerit. Quod quidam volunt probare auctoritate illa: "Potuit transgredi et non est transgressus; malum facere et non fecit" (Eccli. 31, 10). Sed hoc non putamus dictum de Christo, sed de sanctis hominibus. Item oppunt: Christus habuit liberum arbitrium, ergo in utramque partem poterat flecti. Sed hoc non valet cum etiam angeli habeant liberum arbitrium et tamen ita sunt confirmati per gratiam quod peccare non possunt ... Item opponunt: Ille homo poterat non esse Verbo unitus, et si non esset unitus Verbo, peccaret sicut alii homines .... Sed hoc non negamus ... sed postquam fuit unitus Verbo, peccare non potuit. Si enim potuit peccare, et damnari potuit.' Cf. Abelard, Expos. in 'ad Romanos', I (PL. 178, 823B–4C): 'Forte quaeritur si homo in Christo unitus divinitati mentiri aut peccare potuerit ... Nemo autem ambigere debet hominem illum Deo unitum, postquam ei unitus est, aut dum ei unitus est, nullatenus peccare posse, sicut eum qui praedestinatus est, postquam praedestinatus, vel cum praedestinatus sit, damnari non posse. At vero si simpliciter dicitur hominem illum, qui unitus est, nullo modo peccare posse, potest

a sin, 'sed plane contra Apostolum loquuntur isti'.[1] The Abelardians will not admit baptism by desire and in order to assure that believers are saved they argue that God would not allow a believer to die, except by martyrdom, before he could receive baptism. 'Sed, ut mihi videtur, cum ipsi non sint consiliarii Dei, stultum est et temerarium eos hoc affirmare.'[2]

Less passionately, but no less firmly, the SS disputes other theses of Abelard. The SS is not satisfied with Abelard's depreciation of the propriety of such phrases as 'homo est Deus' used in description of Christ.[3] The SS rejects the view that Christ was partly

[1] III, 11 (PL. 176, 106B–D): 'Quidam dicunt quod originale peccatum sit debitum quo tenentur omnes pro peccato primi hominis . . . Isti dicunt quod originale peccatum non sit peccatum; sed si Scriptura quandoque vocat illud peccatum, astruunt quod ibi peccatum pro poena peccati accipitur . . . et ita secundum istos in anima pueri nullum peccatum est . . . et tamen concedunt quod in ea est originale peccatum quia tenetur debito peccati . . . Apostolus vocat eos peccatores antequam regenerentur (Rom. 5, 19); sed si tantum esset poena et non culpa in istis, ut ipsi aiunt, non peccatores essent.' Cf. above, p. 140.

[2] v, 5 (PL. 176, 131C–2C): 'dicunt non posse esse ut aliquis habeat fidem et charitatem et moriatur sine baptismo. Non enim, ut dicunt, permitteret eos mori sine baptismo'; v, 7 (133D): 'Non enim alligavit Deus sacramentis potentiam suam; et quamvis per sacramenta salutem dare decreverit, potest tamen et dat sine eis salutem.' Cf. Abelard, Expositio in 'ad Romanos', II (PL. 178, 837B): 'Nos autem cum dicimus omnem, qui Dominum sincere et pure propter ipsum iam diligit, praedestinationem ad vitam, nec unquam praeveniendum morte, donec ei vel per praedicationem vel per Spiritum sanctum Dominus revelet quidquid ei de sacramentis fuerit necessarium, et insuper facultate hoc percipiendi tribuit'; also 845D. Cf. L. Ott, Untersuchungen, pp. 507–20; also Grillmeier, 'Fulgentius', pp. 560–1, on the use made by the SS of the Sic et Non.

[3] I, 15 (PL. 176, 71CD): 'Homo est Deus sic exponitur, id est unitus Deo; Deus est homo, id est unitus homini. Quam expositionem ego non improbo;

quilibet ambigere. Si enim penitus peccare non potest . . . quod meritum habet, cavendo peccatum quod nullo modo potest committere . . . Scriptum praeterea est in laude iusti: "Qui potuit . . ." Et hoc quidem ad liberum hominis arbitrium pertinet, ut in eius sit potestate agere bene et male. Quod si Christus non habuit libero videtur privatus arbitrio . . . Videtur itaque nobis ut in hac quoque, sicut in caeteris rebus, vires propositionum diligenter attendamus . . . Verum quippe est si simpliciter dicatur, quod eum qui praedestinatus est, et qui salvandus est, possibile est damnari, cum omnino possibile sit eum fuisse non praedestinatum nec salvandum, non tamen cum determinatione verum est dicere, quod eum possibile est damnari, cum sit praedestinatus, vel cum sit salvandus . . . fortasse non est absurdum nos concedere simpliciter, quod cum hominem, qui Deo unitus est, possibile sit peccare, non tamen postquam unitus vel dum unitus est.'

God and partly man[1] and that after death Christ's divinity was separated from his body.[2] Abelard's thesis that human acts are in themselves morally indifferent is similarly rejected.[3] The relationship of the SS to Abelard's teaching is clear. With relatively rare exceptions, this author's overriding intention with regard to Abelard is to provide a far reaching, thorough and very conspicuous refutation of a host of Abelardian theses. This was probably achieved earlier than the intervention of William of St Thierry.[4] Often the SS follows Hugh's own criticisms of

[1] I, 18 (PL. 176, 77D–8A). Cf. above, p. 25, and L. Ott, *Untersuchungen*, pp. 170 *et seq.*
[2] I, 19 (PL. 176, 78D–80B). Cf. the *Sententie* of Hermann, c. 27 (1737AB), *Sent. Florianenses*, c. 44 (ed. Ostlender, p. 20), *Sent. Paris. I* (ed. Landgraf, p. 35).
[3] III, 15 (PL. 176, 113A–C): 'Quidam dicunt quod omnes actus indifferentes sint, ut nec boni nec mali dicantur quantum ad se; sed dicitur bonus actus, quia fit bona intentione, malus quia mala intentione. Ut occidere hominem zelo iustitiae bonum est, ex odio malum est: per se nec bonum nec malum. Unde Ambrosius: Affectus tuus operi tuo nomen imponunt. Cui sententiae sic opponitur: Si omnis actus indifferens est, tunc adulterari et pejerare actus indifferentes sunt . . . Quod ita ipsi solvunt: Adulterari et pejerare, nec tamen actum notant sed et vitium . . . actus illi [Migne: ille], scilicet agere cum muliere et jurare, indifferentes sunt . . . Nec ideo dicitur occidere hominem malus actus peccatum sit: sub hoc sensu occidere hominem peccatum est, id est actus peccati. Duo enim, ut Augustinus dicit, considerantur in peccato: actus et reatus. Actus in opere, reatus in voluntate. Ut in hoc peccato quod homicidium est reatus est ipsa voluntas, vel vitium voluntatis: qua manente homo reus est sive sit actus sive nondum fuerit, sive iam praeteritus fuerit; et utrumque appellatur homicidium consuetudine loquendi et usu Scripturae; nec duo sunt peccata, vel duo homicidia, sed unum et idem, licet diversis modis, scilicet voluntate et actu. Duobus namque modis malum dicitur, substantive et adjective . . . Actio dicitur mala non quod sit ipsum malum, sed mali exhibitio.' Cf. above, p. 139.
[4] Cf. above, p. 202. The reason for suspecting that SS is anterior to William's intervention is that it does not appear to be influenced by the disputes of William or Bernard; firmer evidence is wanting. One can nonetheless say that

sed tamen mihi videtur quod plus in istis verbis contineatur. Si enim nihil aliud dicitur his verbis, homo est Deus, nisi homo unitus est Deo, quare non potest dici caro est anima, cum sit unita animae? . . . Itaque ideo dicitur, homo est Deus, Deus est homo; quia ille idem qui est homo, est Deus; et ille idem qui est Deus est homo.' SS, I, 15 (72AB) controverts the thesis of Walter of Mortagne's letter (ed. L. d'Achéry, *Spicilegium*, II, 462–6) that *homo assumptus non est Deus* and is here perhaps guided by Abelard's insistence that terms used in different constructions acquire different significances; cf. L. Ott, *Untersuchungen*, pp. 178–9.

P

Abelard. The author also, as L. Ott has demonstrated,[1] relied upon another critic of Abelard, Walter of Mortagne, for much of his Trinitarian thought. Already before ecclesiastical authority was summoned to condemn Abelard academic opinion in the school of St Victor had arrived at a comprehensive formulation of objections to Peter Abelard. The place of the SS in the history of Abelard's school is also clear and we must considerably qualify Portalié's judgment that the SS represents 'la fusion des deux écoles'[2] as well as that of Chossat ('la fusion du courant victorin et du courant abélardien')[3] and that of de Ghellinck ('le point de convergence du courant victorin et du courant abélardien').[4] The SS, according to the available printed version, did not turn to Abelard to controvert Hugh as much as it turned to Hugh and to Walter of Mortagne to controvert Abelard. The SS made more use of Abelard's writing and teaching than did Hugh, but it also expressed greater opposition to Abelard than appears in the surviving writings of Hugh. The SS, at least in its printed version, represents the hardening of opinion in the school of St Victor against Abelard.

Hugh and his disciple prepared the case against Abelard in advance of the council of Sens.[5] The public campaign led by William of St Thierry and Bernard of Clairvaux and resulting in the condemnation of Abelard by Pope Innocent II is undeniably an important episode. But underlying and probably preceding that campaign was the less vociferous but more comprehensive criticism of the school of Hugh. Compared with Bernard, Hugh and the SS have failed to 'hit the headlines', but their criticisms were the actual basis for subsequent thinking in the schools of

[1] 'Der Trinitätstraktat'.   [2] 'Pierre Abélard', col. 51.
[3] La Somme des Sentences, p. 1.   [4] Le Mouvement théologique, p. 201.
[5] Van den Eynde, Essai, pp. 102–3 writes that all the attacks of the SS upon Abelard concern doctrines already incriminated before the intervention of William. This is difficult to accept, except in the sense that the SS reflects thought at St Victor.

the criticisms of SS, whether anterior or posterior to William's, are independent of his. To this extent Baron's hypothesis (cited above, pp. 199–200) that the SS came to reflect the later Hugh's response to Bernard's criticisms of Abelard is not proven.

Paris. Bernard, William and Thomas paraded a large number of
texts against Abelard; in this respect Victorine criticism was
restrained. Abelard's monastic critics were often penetrating
but also often inaccurate; the Victorines were on the whole
more accurate in their work and Hugh's ability to transcend
polemic by converting Abelard's errors into improved teachings
was admirable. No doubt in the 1120s and 1130s Hugh and his
school had superior opportunities and more need to reflect on
Abelard's thought, whereas Bernard worked hastily. But at
bottom Bernard and the school of St Victor were united.

In time Abelardian and Victorine thought did merge and draw
closer together. If 'fusion' did not occur in the SS, something
more like fusion can be found in the work of Robert of Melun,
Peter Lombard and Richard of St Victor. Moreover, Abelard's
own followers, no doubt feeling the pressure of Victorine criticisms but also anxious to keep abreast of developments in
general, took up the SS and treated it as a major source alongside
the teachings of Abelard. The interaction of Abelardian and
Victorine thought is perhaps the salient fact of theological
development in the years following Abelard's final condemnation.

CHAPTER IX

ABELARD AND THE
'DECRETUM' OF GRATIAN

In his *Decretum* Gratian not only utilized previous canonical collections but also applied hermeneutic principles in the task of reconciling the contradictions which appeared to exist in the masses of received *auctoritates*. The achievement of a *concordia* between the *discordantes canones* was a fundamental purpose of the *Decretum*; if previous canonical collectors had used rules of reconciliation to remedy the difficulties in the sources which they used, Gratian made such rules the central principle of his whole edifice. Like Gratian Abelard in his *Sic et Non* made the task of reconciliation the cornerstone of his work and, as S. Kuttner observed, it is a stupendous fact of medieval history that within a decade or two such a synchronism and parallelism should occur in this respect and generally too between the birth of scholastic theology in northern France and the rebirth of jurisprudence in Bologna.[1] F. Thaner in the year 1900 went so far as to state that Gratian, particularly in the first part of the *Decretum*, was directly influenced by the *Sic et Non* of Abelard.[2] But Thaner's thesis has usually been judged to be too absolute since Abelard was, like Gratian, himself much influenced by earlier reconcilers such as Bernold of Constance, Ivo of Chartres and Alger of Liège.[3] P. Fournier and G. Le Bras considered that the *Sic et Non* was only possibly influential upon Gratian when he decided upon the method and the approach to be adopted in the *Decretum*,[4]

[1] 'Graziano: l'uomo et l'opera' in *Studia Gratiana*, I, 24.
[2] *Abälard und das canonische Recht*. Similarly, G. Robert, *Les Ecoles*, pp. 170–9.
[3] The state of this question is set out by A. Van Hove, 'Quae Gratianus contulerit', pp. 22–3, and by H. E. Feine, 'Der Deutschsprachige Forschungsanteil zum Dekret Gratians' in *Studia Gratiana*, II, 465–82, here 478–81. E. Bertola, 'I precedenti storici del metodo del *Sic et Non*' has drawn attention to biblical exegetes prior to Abelard.
[4] *Histoire des collections canoniques*, II, 334 *et seq.* and 359: 'Ce qu'Yves a fait pour les canonistes, Abélard le fait pour les théologiens.' A. Amanieu, 'Alger de

yet J. de Ghellinck—'le meilleur guide pour la préparation théologique du Décret de Gratien'[1]—insisted that the specifically Abelardian injunction to examine the various meanings given to the same words by various authors marked an epoch and, by being adopted in the *Decretum*, gave that work an immediate superiority over all previous collections.[2] De Ghellinck's opinion is persuasive but in view of Thaner's failure to deduce convincingly from the study of Gratian's *dicta* any certain traces of Abelardian influence, the problem must surely be deemed to be still unsolved, if not unsolvable.

Discussion of the possibility of Abelard's influence upon the *Decretum* has centred mostly on the question of the methods employed by the two masters; their doctrines and their repertories of materials also merit attention. Between the canonists and the theologians there existed, in de Ghellinck's phrase, 'une vraie communauté des matières'. Gratian himself is the point of convergence and of departure for many developments in both canon law and in theology and G. Le Bras has appealed to historians to ascertain his theological sources and background.[3] In discrediting the likelihood of Gratian having used the theological sentences of the Laon school, S. Kuttner brought into sharp focus the possible contributions of source materials by Abelard and by Hugh of St Victor,[4] but a major obstacle still prevents the precise study

[1] Fournier and Le Bras, *Histoire des collections canoniques*, II, 315.
[2] *Le Mouvement théologique*, pp. 65, 490-4. Cf. Abelard, *Sic et Non, prolog.*: 'facilis autem plerumque controversiarum solutio reperietur, si eadem verba in diversis significationibus a diversis auctoribus posita defendere poterimus' (PL. 178, 1344D).
[3] 'Il appartient aux historiens de la théologie d'insérer le Décret et les décrétistes dans la trame du développement doctrinal: de reconnaître les sources et de relever la trace des influences ... Nous pensons que toute la littérature théologique, surtout entre 1090 et 1140, devra passer au crible', 'Inventaire théologique du *Décret* et de la Glose ordinaire. Etres et Monde invisibles' in *Mélanges J. de Ghellinck*, II, 603-15, here 611.
[4] 'Zur Frage der theologischen Vorlagen Gratians'. Recently Mme J. Rambaud has brought precise proof that the *Sententie Magistri A.* were at most an extremely slight source of the *Decretum*; in respect of possible parallels Ivo's

Liège' gives examples of *dicta* in the *Decretum* in which reconciliations occur and which are borrowed from Alger.

of possible literary relationships between Abelard and Gratian: we have in print only one version of the *Sic et Non* and an unsatisfactory text of the *Decretum*.[1] At the present time only a few tentative observations can be advanced, particularly with respect to the doctrinal resemblances which appear between the two writers.

Towards the end of his work in the *De Consecratione*, Gratian[2] incorporates three Trinitarian texts. On account of their novel arrangement, which was not suggested to Gratian by any previous model, G. Le Bras suggested[3] that he thereby intended to make an assertion of orthodox faith in reply to Abelard's trouble-making in the very year of the council of Sens.[4] The conjecture is stimulating, but it is surely more likely that these texts, which have no special relevance to the arguments of Abelard or of his critics, were simply reproduced from Ivo, Gratian's favourite recent source,[5] under Ivonian inspiration. One of them, an extract from Augustine's *De Trinitate*, I, 4, is introduced with the rubric used in the *Panormia*,[6] and the other two, texts of Didymus and Cyrill, which elaborate on the theme of the unity of the Trinity in truth, were brought together by Ivo in the

[1] The problem of the sources utilized by Gratian has often led scholars to make negative findings (Rambaud, *loc. cit.*, pp. 51, 53) particularly since 'comme pour la plupart des oeuvres médiévales, il n'y a pas un texte du Décret, il y a des manuscrits du Décret et chacun a sa forme propre, sa personnalité' (Rambaud, 'L'Etude des manuscrits du Décret de Gratien conservés en France' in *Studia Gratiana*, I, 119–45, here 144).

[2] Rambaud in *L'Age classique*, pp. 90–9 finds it impossible to determine definitively the origin and authorship of the *De Consec.*

[3] 'Inventaire théologique' in *Mélanges J. de Ghellinck*, II, 606.

[4] P. Fournier's thesis that the *Decretum* appeared in 1139–40 has, after much debate, been powerfully vindicated, see Rambaud in *L'Age classique*, pp. 57–8. The *Decretum* may have been begun even in the first quarter of the century but it was not completed before 1140.

[5] Finding the parallel does not always establish the source and I regret not having been able to consult C. Munier, *Les sources patristiques du droit de l'Eglise, du VIIIe au XIIIe siècle*, Mulhouse, 1957, who (see Rambaud in *L'Age classique*, pp. 61–3) has demonstrated the central place among Gratian's sources of the Ivonian collections which provided some three-quarters of Gratian's patristic texts.

[6] *De Consec.*, D. III, c. 30 (*de fide Trinitatis et Unitatis inviolabiliter servanda*). Cf. Ivo (or rather Ivo's disciples), *Panormia*, I, 7 (PL. 161, 1048A–C); also

Panormia is much more significant, see G. Le Bras *et al.*, *L'Age classique*, pp. 63–4.

Sermon on Pentecost.[1] Ivo himself offered the important precedent of including the theology of the Trinity in a canonical collection by including in his *Decretum* a whole book entitled *De Fide*.

In *Causa XI*, q. 3, Gratian discusses the power of the keys and with the aid of patristic and conciliar authorities he argues that an unjust sentence of excommunication promulgated against an innocent victim is not confirmed by God; it is, however, to be feared, that is, it is not to be proudly condemned, and if it was sincerely imposed by a well-meaning judge, it is to be obeyed. Abelard also argued that an unjust sentence is not divinely binding; in a lengthy analysis of both patristic and particularly New Testament sources, he suggested that the keys are a power of excommunication, not of imputing sin, and a power, not of remitting sin, but of loosing the sinner from the penalties of sin. Ecclesiastical authority, while it has to be obeyed, does not always pronounce the sentences of God.[2] Gratian and Abelard agree on the relationship of ecclesiastical to divine power, although Gratian shares none of Abelard's speculative interest in the basis and justification of episcopal use of the power of the keys; Gratian's interest bears more practically upon the distinction between a valid and an invalid use of this power.[3] The influence of Abelard cannot be considered impossible, but it is much less directly felt than that of Ivo whose *Decretum*[4] provided him with many of the materials required and who was also concerned with establishing the differences between a just and an unjust sentence of excommunication and with practical questions concerning the occasions and methods of excommunicating.

[1] *De Consec.*, D. v, c. 39, 40 (*Quod Spiritus sanctus procedit a Patre et Filio; De eodem*). Cf. Ivo, *Sermo* XX (PL. 162, 594). Abelard also juxtaposes the two texts but only in part in *Theol. Christiana*, IV (PL. 178, 1302D–3B) and *Theol. 'Schol.'*, II, 14 (PL. 178, 1077B).
[2] *Ethica*, c. 25, 26 (PL. 178, 669–678) and cod. Balliol College, 296, ff. 78v–79v. Cf. P. Anciaux, *La Théologie du sacrement de pénitence*, pp. 286–92; also L. Hödl, *Geschichte der schol. Literatur*, I, 79–86.
[3] Cf. Anciaux, *op. cit.*, pp. 302 *et seq.*
[4] XIV, 3, 8–15, 23, 24, 28, 30, 35, 43, 45, 46, 48, 50, 74, 80, 81, 95.

Decretum, 1, 2 without the rubric (PL. 161, 60C–61A). The summarizing *tituli* of Gratian were taken from the *Panormia*, see Rambaud in *L'Age classique*, p. 72.

Twelfth-century doctrines of penance are the classic example of the intimate connection then existing between speculative theology and canonistic study and the *De Poenitentia* in Gratian's *Decretum* bears the clear marks of being influenced by scholastic theological thought. The *De Poenitentia* constitutes a sort of annexe in Gratian's work which Gratian himself may have modestly started but which may have been expanded by his followers.[1] The famous first *Distinctio* of the *De Poenitentia*, for which Gratian himself may be mostly responsible, asks the question whether the sinner can make satisfaction to God by contrition of heart and by secret satisfaction without recourse to oral confession. The question witnesses to the contemporary interest in the speculative problem of the relationship between the elements constitutive of penance.[2] Abelard raised the question in the *Sic et Non*, c. 151, but his short chapter cannot be certainly considered to have provided texts for Gratian.[3] In other passages in his writings Abelard supported the thesis that true penance is the contrition of heart which, inspired by God in the soul of a sinner, obtains pardon for his sins, but he was also struck by the apparent antinomy between patristic texts relating to the necessity of confession.[4] Of St Peter's tears in repentance for having denied Christ Abelard says that this event was so unusual that it cannot itself be used as an argument against oral confession.[5] Hugh of St Victor also saw that contrition and the inner working of divine grace removes the darkness and obduracy of the mind,

---

[1] Kuttner, 'De Gratiani opere noviter edendo', p. 127, found that nothing in the question of authorship was agreed, and Le Bras, 'Inventaire théologique', p. 606, conjectured that the *De Poen.* may have been the re-working of a theological sentence-work. Rambaud in *L'Age classique*, pp. 82–9, considers no definitive solution possible but there are serious reasons for thinking that q. 3 of *Causa* 33 originally contained D. I of the *De Poen.* (but without c. 6–30), d.a.c. I and c. I of D. V, D. VI and D. VII. The c. 6–30 D. I and c. 2–8 D. V were first added, then D. II–IV, and they appear in manuscripts of the second half of the twelfth century.

[2] Anciaux, *La Théologie du sacrement de pénitence*, pp. 196–208, and earlier A. Debil, 'La première distinction du *De Poenitentia* de Gratien'.

[3] Cf. c. 1, 2, 38, 39 of Gratian with Abelard's *Sic et Non*, c. 151.

[4] Cf. Anciaux, *op cit.*, pp. 140–63, 176–85.

[5] *Ethica*, c. 25 (669BC).

but in a violent reaction to Abelard he affirmed the need for the penitent to approach the priests to be loosed from the bond of sin which is the debt of damnation.[1] Gratian reports alternative theses for and against the necessity of confession, but offers no solution to the divergences of the *auctoritates*.[2] He presents an enormous documentation, in all likelihood reflecting contemporary interest in the debate but not obviously or certainly drawn from Abelard or from Hugh who scarcely attempts to reproduce such texts. Gratian's dossier was subsequently utilized by Roland and Omnebene and by Peter Lombard.

Distinctiones II, III and IV of the *De Poenitentia* move further into the realm of speculative theology and may not be the work of Gratian himself. They concern the reiterability of penance, the reviviscence of pardoned sins and the alienability of charity. The question put in the second *Distinctio*, whether charity can desert a man, was topical among theologians[3] and is here joined to the question of the reiterability of penance. Several of the authorities presented by Abelard in the *Sic et Non*, c. 138 are

---

[1] *De sacramentis*, II, 14, 1; II, 14, 8 (PL. 176, 549–554, 564–570). Cf. Anciaux, *op. cit.*, pp. 186–96.

[2] D.p.c. 37: '... Non ergo in confessione peccatum remittitur quod iam remissum esse probatur. Fit itaque confessio ad ostensionem penitenciae, non ad inpetrationem veniae, sicut circumcisio data est Abrahae in signum iusticiae, non in causam iustificationis, sic confessio sacerdoti offertur in signum veniae acceptae, non in causam remissionis accipiendae. Alii e contra testantur, dicentes sine confessione oris et satisfactione operis neminem a peccato posse mundari, si tempus satisfaciendi habuerit. Unde Dominus per prophetam ait: "Dic tu iniquitates tuas, ut iustificeris" (Esa. 43, 26).' D.p.c. 89: 'Cui autem harum potius adherendum sit, lectoris iudicio reservetur. Utraque enim fautores habet sapientes et religiosos viros.' The Gdansk abbreviation (Mar. F. 275) of the *De Poen.*, printed by K. Wojtyła in *Studia Gratiana*, VII, 359–72, does not have this indecision and concludes: 'Concluditur ergo ex premissis quod nullus ante confessionem oris et satisfactionem operis peccati abolet culpam', but the thesis that this abbreviation reflects an earlier version of Gratian's work is not proven.

[3] D.a.c. 1: '... diversorum sentencias certis auctoritatibus munitas in medium proponentes. Alii dicunt penitenciam semel tantum esse utilem. Unica enim est, nec reiterari potest. Si vero reiteratur, precedens penitencia non fuit ...' D.p.c. 40: 'Eligat adversarius e duobus quod vult, optionem damus ... Evidenter itaque ex premissis apparet, nonnullos karitatem habere, quam postea criminaliter delinquendo amittunt.'

used too by the author of the *De Poenitentia*[1] who does not appear to have been much guided here by earlier canonical collections. Hugh, who does not on the whole argue by means of manipulating tests, insists on the mutability of human nature which can fall and repent and fall again.[2] The argument of *Distinctio* II, however, is based upon a distinction between perfect charity, which never fades, and imperfect charity, which can appear and fade,[3] and the author relishes a welter of Scriptural examples of repentent sinners. *Distinctio* II is a highly individual piece of work, topical, but not evidently under the direct influence of Abelard.

In *Distinctio* III, a continuation of the previous *Distinctio*, the question is whether penance, unlike baptism, can be reiterated. A large collection of authorities is presented and a distinction is made between perfect penance, which like perfect charity lasts for ever, and imperfect penance which need not endure. The question was also raised by Abelard in the *Sic et Non*, c. 116 and 146, with particular reference to some difficult passages of St Jerome which are also partly used in the *De Poenitentia*. Hugh of St Victor, moreover, mentions, without accepting, an opinion also referred to by the author of the *De Poenitentia*, namely that patristic references to an unrepeatable penance concern the imposition in the early days of the church of a solemn form of penance.[4]

In *Distinctio* IV the author asks whether forgiven sins can return and whether a previously forgiven sin can, if it recurs, be punished again. The author once more indicates the existence of diverse opinions on the question which both Abelard and Hugh had raised and had argued seriously.[5] But only one of the authorities presented by Abelard in the *Sic et Non*, c. 116 and 146 appears in this *Distinctio*.[6] The author distinguishes between two kinds

[1] C. 2, 3, 4, 7, 8, 25, 41; cf. *Sic et Non*, PL. 178, 1578A, 1577C, 1578B, 1574C, 1577B, 1580C, 1581A, 1580C.

[2] *De Sacramentis*, II, 13, 11; II, 14, 4 (PL. 176, 539–45, 556–9).

[3] D.p.c. 14.

[4] D.p.c. 21. Cf. Hugh, *De sacramentis*, II, 14, 4 (PL. 176, 559BC).

[5] 'Huius questionis diversorum varia est sentencia, aliis asserentibus, aliis econtra negantibus, peccata dimissa ulterius replicari ad penam', d.a.c. 1. Cf. Abelard, *Expositio in 'ad Romanos'* (PL. 178, 864, 872D–873); Hugh, *De sac.*, II, 14, 9 (PL. 176, 570–8), I, 7, 38 (304–6).

[6] C. 13; cf. *Sic et Non*, c. 116 (PL. 178, 1518).

of remission of sins, *secundum iusticiam* and *secundum praescientiam*,[1] but then baldly concludes that since a larger number of authorities and more evident reason affirm that sins do return, the affirmative thesis is right.[2]

There are many other properly theological issues in the *Decretum*; there are three more *Distinctiones* in the *De Poenitentia* concerning the nature of satisfaction, the ministry of penance and the moment of penance and there are elsewhere many other questions, for example concerning angels[3] and divine prescience,[4] but in none of these questions does Gratian come as obviously near to contemporary French theological discussion. Gratian does appear occasionally in his *Decretum* to have been aware of the theological questions which were being raised in northern France in the second quarter of the century and possible parallels do exist between some of his authorities and opinions and some of those employed by Abelard and by the Victorine school. But a direct utilization of their writings is not proven and their influence always appears somewhat remote. The somewhat slight similarities which are found are thematic and concern the topics raised as well as the general trends of discussion more than they concern the details of argument and exposition. Gratian could have owed more to oral reports by French visitors or other teaching theologians in Bologna than to a direct acquaintance with contemporary French writings. Gratian has never led his modern students to credit him with great theological originality or depth. G. Le Bras has found in the *Decretum* a less imposing use of Scripture than one might have expected[5] and, one may add, than was shown by either Abelard or Hugh. He inaugurates the age of the masters of canon law rather than ends that of the theologian-canonists. On the other hand, his two

---

[1] D.p.c. 7.

[2] D.p.c. 14: 'quia pluribus roboratur auctoritatibus et evidentiori ratione firmatur'.   [3] *De Poen.* c. 45 D. II.

[4] Q. 4 C. XXIII, d.a.c. 20 and d.p.c. 23. The subject matter may be compared with Abelard, *Sic et Non*, c. 26–31, and *Theol.* '*Schol.*', III, 7 (PL. 178, 1109–14), but the arguments and the handling of the authorities are very different. In the use of Augustine, Gratian resembles Ivo, *Decretum*, XVII, 32.

[5] 'Les Ecritures dans le Décret de Gratien.'

disciples, Roland[1] and Omnebene, were most conversant with contemporary French theological teaching and to an extent that led A. Landgraf to wonder whether the way in which canonist writers formed schools could be correlated with their affinities with individual theological schools.[2] Yet, if we could only judge Roland and Omnebene, as we have to judge Gratian, by their canonical writings, we should similarly know little about their interest in contemporary theological thought or about Abelard's influence in the schools of Bologna.

Contributions by Abelard to the canonistic movement of the twelfth century may sometimes be more clearly ascertained with respect to Gratian's successors. S. Kuttner has established[3] that Abelard's distinction between *peccatum* and *crimen* found an echo among decretists such as Huguccio[4] and the author of the *Summa Coloniensis*. Abelard was almost alone among his contemporaries in distinguishing offences against God and offences against God and the church. Not all sins are such as murder and infidelity which scandalize the church and are knowable from their effects and Abelard discussed the various ways in which God and the church respectively judge sin, for God probes the hearts of sinners while the church can only know and judge the effects of sin. A second example of a possible contribution by Abelard to the canon lawyers is his use of the term *ius positivum*,[5] which has its roots in the Chalcidian version of the *Timaeus* and which influenced Anglo-French canonists such as Odo of Doura,[6] but the credit for popularizing this usage does not pertain to Abelard alone.[7] Stephen of Tournai provides a somewhat clearer

[1] Since Gratian's disciples appear to have collaborated in the composition of the *Decretum*, Rambaud in *L'Age classique*, p. 49, does not exclude the possibility that Roland helped in this work.

[2] 'Diritto canonico e teologia nel secolo XII' in *Studia Gratiana*, I, 371–413, here 380.

[3] *Kanonistische Schuldlehre*, pp. 4–6, 19–21.

[4] Huguccio's indebtedness in theological matters was normally to the later generation of French masters including Peter Lombard, Peter Comestor, Odo the Chancellor; see Landgraf, 'Diritto canonico', in *Studia Gratiana*, I, 371.

[5] 'Ius quippe aliud naturale, aliud positivum dicitur', *Dialogus* (PL. 178, 1656).

[6] Kuttner, *Repertorium der Kanonistik*, I, 172 et seq.

[7] S. Gagner, *Studien zur Ideengeschichte der Gesetzgebung*, pp. 210–13, 228.

case of Abelardian influence.[1] He became a Victorine canon at Orleans after a period of study at Bologna in the later 1140s and like Roland and Omnebene he was a theologian-canonist, although he expressed his view of the differences between the two disciplines in terms of the differences between the tastes of sugar and salt. From Abelard the theologian Stephen learnt how not to consider as faults sinful acts committed involuntarily or the unexpected evil effects of voluntary acts. Then as a canonist Stephen applied this understanding to specific moral questions by intervening on behalf of a Cistercian who had in childhood accidentally killed a playing companion and, on another occasion, on behalf of a Spanish cleric who had in good faith committed a simoniacal act.[2] These three examples show the influence of a French theologian among the French canonists, but both Gratian and Huguccio and also, as theologians, Roland and Omnebene offer evidence that the Italian canonists too were sometimes sensitive to French theological discussion.

[1] For what follows see P. Delhaye, 'Morale et droit canonique dans la "Summa" d'Etienne de Tournai', in *Studia Gratiana*, I, 435–49.

[2] *Epist.*, 51, 170, 189 (ed. Desilve, pp. 65, 198–9, 235–6).

CHAPTER X

ABELARD'S DISCIPLES AND THE SCHOOL OF ST VICTOR

Simultaneously preeminent in the Parisian scholastic scene of the 1130s, Abelard and Hugh of St Victor jointly influenced succeeding writers and even shared disciples such as Zachary, the *scholasticus* of Besançon from 1131–8 and later Praemonstratensian canon of St Martin's, Laon. Zachary wrote before 1161 an introduction to the Gospels which achieved popularity[1] and which imparted an Abelardian flavour in respect of the Trinity, the example of Christ and the power of the keys. Several passages in this *Super Unum ex quattuor*[2] strikingly resemble the Sentences of Hermann and others betray the marks of Victorine influence.[3] But Hugh's school was also a powerful rival to that of Abelard and the originator of a mass of criticisms directed against Abelard which exceeded in their variety and number the criticisms of those monastic writers who attempted to refute Abelard's errors. Since the doctrines of Abelard and Hugh were often contrary, they had to be juxtaposed and collated and, finally, evaluated. This need was recognized in the *Concordia discordantium canonum* and also within Abelard's school. The circle of writers who made Abelard's thought the basis of their own compositions included several scholars who were ready to employ and to evaluate ideas and material produced in the school of St Victor.

'ABAELARDI EXPOSITIONIS IN EPISTOLAM AD ROMANOS ABBREVIATIO'

One of Abelard's followers abbreviated Abelard's exposition of Romans. A mere fragment of the work survives and it has been

---

[1] Cf. Landgraf, *Introducción*, pp. 113–14.   [2] PL. 186, 11–620.
[3] Cf. S. Deutsch, *Peter Abaelard*, pp. 463–6, D. Van den Eynde, 'Les "magistri" du Commentaire "Unum ex quattuor" ', L. Hödl, *Die Geschichte der scholastischen Literatur*, pp. 98–102, P. Anciaux, *La Théologie du sacrement de pénitence*, pp. 214–16, 318–21. Also, P. Glorieux, 'Les "Deflorationes" de Werner de S. Blaise'.

edited by Dr Landgraf from the unique manuscript, Paris, Arsenal 1116.[1] The abridgement is well-enough executed; there is no pronounced bias affecting the omissions and contractions of passages found in the *Expositio*. Some teachings for which Abelard was condemned are present and the work is, therefore, more likely to have been prepared before than after the council of Sens.[2] In the lower margin of f. 83v of the Arsenal manuscript, at the point where Abelard's teaching on the redemption is summarized, the word *Magistreli* is found and Dr Landgraf entertained the conjecture that this might be the name by which Abelard was known to some of his followers, *magistrellus* or *parvus magister*.[3] This follower knew more of Abelard's teachings than can be found in the *Expositio* itself. He occasionally diverges from Abelard's opinions and makes slight additions;[4] these developments may be personal contributions by the abbreviator or may be due to his acquaintance with Abelard.[5] Some additions, however, are borrowed from the *De sacramentis* of Hugh. The abbreviator also reserves some questions for treatment elsewhere: 'Sed de his alias.'[6] The date of this abbreviation cannot be precisely established; the *De sacramentis* has been assigned to the years between 1130/1 and 1137[7] while the *Expositio* was written

[1] On this MS. see above, pp. 66, 101. Landgraf's edition of the *Abbreviatio* is prefaced by a short study of the work, pp. 3–7. The abbreviation breaks off at the word 'utatur' just before the end of the second of Abelard's five books (*Rom.* 6, 13; PL. 178, 878D ll. 3–4). The author up to this point abridges the *Expositio* by an approximate factor of three.

[2] Cf. Landgraf's introduction to the *Abbreviatio*, p. 7.

[3] *Ibid.*, pp. 7 and 43. Abelard was described in the *Vita Gosvini*, I, 4 (Bouquet, *Recueil*, XIV, 443) as small in stature: 'exilis corpulentiae et staturae non sublimis'.

[4] Landgraf (pp. 7, 29) noticed in particular that the author moderated Abelard's insistence upon the necessity of real baptism 'propter fixam Domini sententiam de baptismo' (*Expos.*, II; PL. 178, 838A) by substituting 'ne de contemptu precepti Domini de baptismo reus statuatur'. On this question see above, p. 210.

[5] Cf. the prologue (Landgraf, pp. 7–8) and various passages on pp. 8, 11, 17, 33 and 34 of the text.

[6] Landgraf, pp. 19, 43. Landgraf, p. 7, suggested rather curiously that the author wished his work to be read aloud. These references to other discussions are not the same as Abelard's own references in the *Expos.* to his other writings; these latter references are omitted by the abbreviator.   [7] Cf. above, p. 185.

at the time when Abelard had completed two books of the *Theologia 'Scholarium'* on which he was engaged in the 1130s.[1] In all likelihood the *Abbreviatio* was prepared in the middle or later 1130s, but there is no cogent reason why a somewhat later date should be ruled out.

St Paul's remarks on the revelation of God in creation (Rom. 1, 18 *et seq.*) furnished Abelard with an occasion to consider the knowledge of God that could be acquired by natural reason.[2] The abbreviator reproduces Abelard's reflections.[3] The writings of the ancient pagan philosophers witness to the Trinity; they clearly perceived from the visible world the power, wisdom and benignity of God; in these attributes the distinction of the Trinity consists. Power is specially suggested by the name Father. Wisdom is the divine Word of the Gospel or the Platonic *mens* born of God. The Trinity may also be illustrated by similes such as a bronze statue or the sun.[4] Abelard was condemned for supposedly teaching that God cannot and ought not to prevent evils. The abbreviator concurs with the *Expositio* in teaching the contrary: God permits evils to occur, although he could prevent them.[5]

Abelard's opinion, ridiculed in the *Summa Sententiarum*,[6] that the soul of Christ could be said, simply, to be peccable is here reproduced. The text in *Ecclus.* 31, 10 ('Potuit transgredi et non est transgressus') is here also applied to Christ.[7] However the abbreviator omits prominent elements in Abelard's explanation of the redemption, in particular Abelard's series of questions concerning the devil's rights over mankind.[8] He teaches nonethe-

---

[1] Cf. Sikes, *Peter Abailard*, p. 266. Ostlender and Buytaert and Van den Eynde have described the various recensions of the *'Scholarium'* but although one manuscript (Douai 357) contains only the first two books, they are agreed that in developing the *'Scholarium'* Abelard produced only a first book in the first two recensions, and in all the following recensions three books. Presumably, therefore, the *Expos.* was composed while Abelard was engaged in writing or in expanding the third recension which is usually dated to the years 1133–8.

[2] *Expos.*, I (PL. 178, 802B–5A).   [3] Landgraf, pp. 15–17.

[4] Landgraf, p. 17. Cf. *Expos.*, I (804D); the simile of the sun is only found in the *Theol. 'Schol.'*, II, 13 (1071AB).

[5] Landgraf, p. 18; also p. 25. Cf. *Expos.*, I (807C); also above, p. 127.

[6] Cf. above, p. 209.

[7] Landgraf, pp. 24–5. Cf. *Expos.*, I (823B–4B).   [8] *Expos.*, II (834–5B).

less that Christ bore the penalty of our sins and offered us his teaching and the example of his life; the love displayed in that life moves man.[1]

In the *Expositio* Abelard taught that the man to whom justice is offered cannot receive it of himself; he also discussed, without rejecting, the image of the doctor who has to help his patient to take the medicine which he offers to him.[2] The abbreviator similarly presents this image and he does so without criticism.[3] Other disciples of Abelard, however, rejected the simile as part of their rejection of the theory of succeeding, enabling graces.[4] The abbreviator refers several times to Abelard's doctrine of intention and merit: works are morally indifferent in themselves, God rewards or punishes the will of the doer and examines his intention rather than the quality of his action. The abbreviator accepts what was condemned by Pope Innocent, that external actions cannot earn merit or blame for man.[5]

Abelard's arguments concerning original sin are maintained in the *Abbreviatio*: infants do not sin in Adam *absolute* because they cannot exercise free will or reason and therefore cannot transgress. Original sin in us is a debt, a liability to eternal punishment on account of the fault or *culpa* which lay in the first parents.[6]

On circumcision the abbreviator quotes, without acknowledgement, from Hugh's *De sacramentis* as well as from the *Expositio* of Abelard. His purpose, seemingly, was to introduce some supplementary considerations beside Abelard's own fulsome treatment of circumcision. He cites Hugh's description of three circumcisions, of the flesh, the mind and the whole body, and also his answers to the questions why only males were circumcised and why they were circumcised on the eighth day after birth.[7]

[1] Landgraf, pp. 27-8, 38. Cf. *Expos.*, II (833C-6D, 859AB).
[2] *Expos.*, II (840B): ' "Fert iustitiam" (*Rom.* 4, 6), quia ipse, cui offertur, sumere per se non poterat.' Also, IV (917D).
[3] ' "Fert" tamquam medicus egro medicinam, etiam in ore instillat, quam ipse, cui affert, per se sumere non poterat', Landgraf, p. 30.
[4] Cf. above, p. 167. Also *Sent. Florianenses*, c. 27 (ed. Ostlender, p. 13) and *Sent. Hermanni*, c. 34 (PL. 178, 1755D-6A).
[5] Landgraf, 15, 19, 20, 22. Cf. *Expos.*, I (800A, 801B, 810A, 812A).
[6] Landgraf, pp. 40-3. Cf. *Expos.*, II (866A-C, 871AB, 866D-8D, 870, 872).
[7] Landgraf, pp. 32-3. Cf. *De sac.*, I, 12, 2 (PL. 176, 350A-C).

Q

To the last question in fact the abbreviator offers two answers. The first is Hugh's: the number eight signifies the time of resurrection or the time of grace.[1] The second ('vel ideo') is Abelard's: circumcision is effected in the very young to remind adults that they will not achieve enlightenment ('illius octave claritatem') unless they become like little children.[2] The abbreviator does not express a preference for either opinion. Hugh is also quoted for the sake of his view that the sin of the original fault of Adam is transmitted to the whole of mankind through carnal concupiscence.[3] This was the type of statement to which Abelard was himself opposed and on another page the abbreviator reproduced Abelard's own theory of original sin.[4] The abbreviator does not advert to the disagreement between Abelard and Hugh. His work is interesting, therefore, by reason of its confirmation of the teachings of the *Expositio*. If it curiously omits Abelard's rejection of the theory of devil's rights, it does not modify Abelard's other controversial theses. In turning to Hugh the abbreviator seems to be motivated by reasons of convenience, if not by fancy; he adumbrates further developments within Abelard's school but his juxtaposition of the teachings of Abelard and Hugh is not an attempt to integrate them into a single framework or to discriminate between them.

THE 'SENTENTIE PARISIENSES II'

When in 1934 Dr Landgraf edited *Sententie Parisienses I* he noted[5] the identification by J. Trimborn of a second sentence collection from Abelard's school contained in the same manuscript, Paris, Bibl. nat. lat. 18, 108 on ff. 170r–7v.[6] The promised

---

[1] Landgraf, p. 33. Cf. Hugh, *De sac.*, I, 12, 2 (PL. 176, 350AB).

[2] *Ibid*. Cf. *Expos.*, II (845A).

[3] 'Maxime autem in genitali membro, quo per carnalem concupiscentiam culpe originalis peccatum una cum prole propagatur, hoc sacramentum (*sc.* circumcisionis) fieri oportuit', Landgraf, p. 32. Cf. Hugh, *De sac.*, I, 12, 2 (350B).

[4] See above, p. 140.   [5] *Ecrits théologiques*, pp. xi–xii, xxiv.

[6] *Inc.* 'Quoniam misso nobis omnipotentis Patris Filio ad salutem vocati . . .' *Exp.* '. . . doctrina autem quia similitudine quandoque sit per naturalia quandoque per artif⟨iciosa⟩'. On the manuscript see above, pp. 67–8, 101.

study of this work by Trimborn has not subsequently appeared and the work therefore needs some introduction. It appears without title or name of author in a mid twelfth-century copy made on a palimpsest. The scribe is capable of making elementary mistakes and his version is undistinguished but clear. The folios contain no notes or additions of any kind and the text breaks off unfinished through loss of folios at the bottom of f. 177v.[1]

The work belongs to the class of sentence collections from Abelard's school which have adopted Abelard's division of theology into three parts, faith, charity and sacrament and which embark upon a comprehensive survey of theological teaching in a systematic manner and in direct, but not unique, dependence upon Abelard. The stated intention of the author is to present the 'summa humane salutis', that is the knowledge needed for salvation,[2] but other purposes are included within this general framework. In particular the author selects from the sum of essential knowledge problematical topics.[3] He subjects the principal contents of the Christian faith to a dialectical analysis. For example, he strives to achieve terminological precision and he examines the various meanings attached to the words 'faith',[4] 'person' and 'individual'.[5] He insists upon definitions, of faith for instance, and hope, charity, love and sacrament.[6] The treatment of patristic authority is marked by a similar questioning procedure.[7] The author also employs Abelard's apologetical argu-

---

[1] A typed edition is contained in my Dissertation in King's College Library, Cambridge, pp. 137–82.

[2] '. . . in quibus maxime nostra salus consistat videamus. Tria sunt, ut arbitror, in quibus humane salutis summa consistit, scilicet fides, caritas et sacramentum', f. 170r; cf. Theol. 'Schol.', I, I (PL. 178, 981c). 'Nunc ea consideremus sine quibus salus esse non potest hoc tempore. Ei enim qui de fide ad edificationem loquitur ea sola sufficit docere que si non credantur dampnationem pariunt. Hec autem sunt que ad fidem pertinent catholicam', f. 172v; cf. Theol. 'Schol.', I, 3 (986c), and Sententie of Hermann, c. 2 (1697c).

[3] 'Nunc tribus supra positis breviter assignatis atque descriptis, scilicet fide, caritate et sacramento, de singulis diligentius agendum est et de his precipue que maioribus implicita questionibus videntur', f. 170v; cf. Theol. 'Schol.', I, 2 (PL. 178, 984B), and Sententie of Hermann, c. 2 (1696A).

[4] Ff. 170v–171r.   [5] Ff. 174rv.

[6] Ff. 170rv. Cf. Theol. 'Schol.', I, 1–2 (PL. 178, 981CD, 982C, 984B).

[7] Notably on the question (cf. Summa Sent., I, 3 (PL. 176, 46B–7C)) whether salvation is possible without revelation, f. 172rv.

ment; he is ready to present and answer objections and to resort to similes.[1] He searches for evidence of belief in the Trinity of divine persons among the writings of the pagan philosophers as well as in the law and among the prophets of the Old Testament.[2]

These Sentences have a place in the history of early scholastic theological literature by reason of their attachment to the teaching of Abelard, their significance in the early history of the systematization of works of theology and their supplementation of Abelard's teaching with that of the Victorine *Summa Sententiarum*. Doctrinally the work is of little independent importance for its teaching is found in Abelard and in the *Summa*. But to the historian *Sententie Parisienses II* are instructive for they reveal an inadequacy in Abelard's legacy to his followers and they shed light upon a development in the transmission of theological thought in the first half of the twelfth century.

The dependence upon Abelard is unmistakable. The manuscript text does not present even a completed account of the Trinity, but the greater part of this closely resembles the printed version of the *Theologia 'Scholarium'* and in many places appears to be an abbreviation of Abelard's work. After the introductory definitions of faith, charity and sacrament, faith is neatly divided into two parts, the first concerning God and the Trinity and the second concerning the divine gifts to man.[3] Throughout the examination of the nature of the Trinity, the dialectical preoccupations of Abelard are manifest in his follower who analyses closely the relationships of the three persons in one God[4] and

---

[1] 'Nunc autem fidei summa circa Trinitatem ac Unitatem divinam a nobis proposita, superest ut adversus inquisitiones dubitantium congruis eam similitudinibus et exemplis defendamus atque astruamus. Quid enim ad doctrinam loqui proficit, si quod docere volumus, exponi non potest ut intelligatur?' ff. 174v–175r. Cf. *Theol. 'Schol.'*, I, 6 (988D); the *Sententie* of Hermann, c. 5 (1699CD). 'Sciendum est autem quod cum diversis modis sit doctrina, scilicet similitudine, exemplo (quod idem est diffinitione), divisione, precepto, tamen convenientius sit similitudine', f. 177v.

[2] Ff. 177rv. Cf. *Theol. 'Schol.'*, I, 6–14, 16, 22–23 (998C–1004D, 1009C–10A, 1032D–3B); the *Sententie* of Hermann, c. 9–10 (1705D–11A, 1712A).

[3] F. 173r. Cf. *Theol. 'Schol.'*, I, 4 (986CD).

[4] Ff. 173rv, 175v–176r. Cf. *Theol. 'Schol.'*, I, 5–6, 9–10 (987A–8D, 991A–2C).

distinguishes the divine names into the categories of personal and natural.[1] A particular emphasis is laid upon the sense in which the word 'person' can be applied to the Trinity.[2] Until the author turns to consider ancient literature concerning the Trinity, he is subjecting the Trinity to a dialectical analysis and reflecting sharply the attraction of this subject for a dialectician such as Abelard. In this Abelard and his school were separated by a wide gulf from the theologians of the school of Laon, with the striking exception of William of Champeaux who was himself a dialectician.

The Abelardian method of systematizing theology according to a logical plan and with emphasis upon problems of particular interest to the dialectical mind did not lack strong rivals. Much of theology, being historical and biblical, was customarily expounded according to a historical and biblical plan which allowed a writer to explain the historical content as well as the historical development of faith. The *De sacramentis* of Hugh proceeds historically as does the *Summa Sententiarum* which reaches back to the Laon tradition to preserve a historical basis.[3] The author of *Sententie Parisienses II* in turning to the *Summa Sententiarum* seeks to maintain this other approach by way of reaction against the logical plan of Abelard. On completing a dialectical analysis of the word 'faith' he takes from the *Summa* ('Supradictis addendum est . . .') some historical considerations concerning the development in knowledge of the faith through the major historical epochs.[4] This is followed by a disagreement with Abelard's thesis that faith in Christ was in all ages essential to salvation; it was because Abelard believed that knowledge of Christ had always been available that he was less concerned to trace the development of this knowledge. His disciple continues to follow the *Summa* which had opposed Abelard on the ground

---

[1] Ff. 173v–174r.   [2] Ff. 174rv.

[3] On the varying plans of construction used by twelfth-century writers of systematic sentence works, see H. Cloes, 'La systématization théologique'.

[4] 'Supradictis addendum est de cognitione fidei quam antiqui habuerunt et quomodo aucta sit per legem Moysi et per legem Evangelii . . .', ff. 171v–2r. Cf. *Summa Sent.*, I, 3–4 (PL. 176, 45C *ll.* 1–2; 45D *l.* 1–46A *l.* 14; 47C *l.* 1–47D *l.* 4; 46A *l.* 14 *et seq.*).

that the Incarnation was not foreseeable by human reason except under a veil of mystery, since removed, nor was a revelation of the Incarnation imparted to all the ancients.[1]

In spite of this use of the *Summa* the author's adherence to Abelard's other controversial opinions was unshaken. He reproduces Abelard's definition of faith: 'existimatio rerum non apparentium',[2] and he subscribes fully to Abelard's teaching[3] on the divine attributes of power, wisdom and goodness which are assigned respectively to each of the divine persons 'specialiter ac tamquam proprie', although it is recognized that all the persons have all the attributes equally. Although the wisdom of God is not stated to be *quaedam potentia* nor the love of God *nulla potentia*, the author goes as far as Abelard dared in isolating the singular feature of the omnipotence of the Father: 'Quedam ei secundum subsistentie modum propria maneat potentia ut cum videlicet ipse omnia Pater facere possit que Filius aut Spiritus sanctus, hoc insuper habet, ut a se ipso solus ipse queat existere.'[4] The omission from these Sentences of Abelard's simile of the seal and the wax and of his denial that the Spirit is from the substance of the Father is explained by their appearance in the *Theologia* after the point where these Sentences break off.[5]

The Sentences are closely related to the fourth (and printed) version of the *Theologia* '*Scholarium*'. There are, however, several

---

[1] Ff. 172rv. Cf. *Summa Sent.*, I, 3 (46B–47C). *Sent. Parisienses II* later omit pertinent passages of Abelard's *Theol.* '*Schol*'., I, 15 (PL. 178, 1004–9). Abelard's teaching had been previously controverted by Bernard, *De baptismo*, c. 3 (PL. 182, 1038–41); the question is fully discussed by L. Ott, *Untersuchungen*, pp. 527–39. On two other occasions *Sent. Parisienses II* introduce into Abelardian material notes taken from the *Summa*: 'Notandum vero quia... in causa fides... precedit spem et caritatem...' (ff. 170rv. Cf. *Summa Sent.*, I, 2 (43C *l.* 13–43D *l.* 3)); 'Notandum quoque quia non est ⟨idem⟩ ingenitum ⟨dicere, quod patrem⟩ dicere...' (f. 174r. Cf. *Summa Sent.*, I, 11 (59C *l.* 13– 60A *l.* 1)). There are a few further examples of short borrowings from the *Summa*, the most curious concerning the question whether faith embraces the visible; here the *Summa* (f. 171r; I, 2 (44B *l.* 13–44C *l.* 1)) had itself abridged the *Theol.* '*Schol.*', I, 2 (985A *l.* 15–985B *l.* 3).
[2] F. 170r. Cf. *Theol.* '*Schol.*', I, 1 (981C).
[3] Ff. 175v–7r. Cf. *Theol.* '*Schol.*', I, 10–12 (991C–8B).
[4] F. 175v. Cf. *Theol.* '*Schol.*', I, 10 (992C).
[5] *Theol.* '*Schol.*', II, 13 (1068C–9C, 1072C).

passages and phrases not found in the *Theologia* but which recur in other sentence works of the school. These are of small moment in themselves and the place where they should be identified is in the apparatus of an edition; it is sufficient to note here that such resemblances occur between the *Sententie Parisienses II* on the one hand and on the other the Sentences of Hermann, Roland and Omnebene, *Parisienses I* and the *Ysagoge*. A small residuum of the text bears no resemblance to other known contemporary literature; it may constitute the author's own meagre contribution or it may derive from his untraced source. This source could be an unknown version of Abelard's *Theologia* or the lost *Liber Sententiarum*; the Sentences are sufficiently close to the written *Theologia* to exclude the likelihood that Abelard's oral teaching is their main source; the assimilation of sources is impressive and the weaving together of Abelardian passages and of even quite short passages from the *Summa* is diligently effected.

In the absence of clear knowledge of the author's main Abelardian source it is difficult to be precise about the date of composition of these Sentences. The affinities with the fourth version of the *Theologia* '*Scholarium*', which is very similar to the third version of the same work, lead us to the middle or late 1130s;[1] similarly the *Summa Sententiarum* appears to be a work produced in the middle or later years of the same decade.[2] *Sententie Parisienses II* in no way appear to react to the criticisms of Abelard's teachings which intensified at the end of the decade. The city of Paris is twice cited in examples;[3] this could possibly indicate that the work was produced in or near Paris as were its main sources. However, the author may have slavishly copied an intermediary source[4] while not himself residing there.

---

[1] On the dating of the *Theologia* '*Scholarium*', see Van den Eynde, 'La "Theologia Scholarium"', p. 241; Buytaert, 'An Earlier Redaction', p. 495. On the similarity between the third and fourth redactions see Buytaert, 'Critical Observations', pp. 403–4.

[2] See above, chap. VIII.

[3] 'de fide . . . supradicte diffinitioni opponitur: iste existimat quod rex sit Parisius sive quod non sit' (f. 170v): 'fides autem est de Deo et quibuslibet rebus, ut credimus regem esse Parisius' (f. 171v).

[4] The same example appears in *Sent. Paris. I*; see above, p. 164.

'BERNARDI ABBATIS SENTENTIE'

Of the abbot Bernard whose name appears at the head of the sentence work found in the Munich MS., Clm. 4,600[1], nothing is known beyond the bare attribution and this single surviving composition. These Sentences are curious. They are divided into three books, the first treating of the Trinity, the second of Christ and the third concerning the 'teaching of the Lord'. Of these the first two books are largely an amalgam of shortened extracts from Abelard's *Theologia 'Scholarium'* and from the Victorine *Summa Sententiarum*. Bernard's method of compiling from these sources has been revealed by H. Weisweiler who first identified the nature of this work.[2]

The *Sententie* begin by abbreviating the *Theologia 'Scholarium'*, I, 5–16.[3] The subjects are the nature of the Trinity, the distinction of persons, the divine attributes of power, wisdom and love, Scriptural evidence of the Trinity and the evidence of pagan philosophers. But Bernard inserts a note that the knowledge of the Trinity obtained in Old Testament times was not clear knowledge. This, as Weisweiler observed,[4] seems to be inspired by the controversy over Abelard's belief that the Trinity was perceived before the coming of Christ by some pagan philosophers.[5] Moreover, although Bernard accepts the traditional attributions of power, wisdom and love, even when made *proprie*, he does not reproduce the more controversial applications of this teaching to the explanation of generation and procession. Bernard's use of Abelard's *Theologia* appears to be cautious and it is confined to the first book.

Soon, however, Abelard is abandoned in favour of his opponent, the author of the *Summa*. Like the writer of *Sententie Parisienses II* Bernard uses the *Summa* not only to supplement Abelard's discussions but also as a stick with which to beat

---

[1] On this manuscript see above, pp. 86, 102.
[2] 'Eine neue Bearbeitung', pp. 346–66. Weisweiler's edited transcriptions are somewhat faulty.
[3] PL. 178, 987–1009.
[4] 'Eine neue Bearbeitung', p. 353.
[5] Clm. 4,600, f. 68v. Cf. *Theol. 'Schol.'*, I, 12 (998BC).

Abelard. He abbreviates the *Summa*, I, 6–11[1] in a similar manner to that used in abbreviating the *Theologia* and the subject matter is not wholly different: the nature of the Trinity, the divine names, the equality of the persons and their properties. Where the *Summa*, discussing divine omnipresence, attacks the *calumpniatores veritatis* among whom some of Abelard's followers may have been found, Bernard omits the denigratory reference and writes simply *quidam*.[2] But he stands firmly opposed to the pseudo-Abelardian notion that the divine omnipresence is merely potential.[3]

Bernard's Sentences are unsatisfactorily arranged. After some abbreviated extracts from the *Summa*, I, 4–5, outlining the mystery of the Trinity and discussing the location of God, Bernard turns to the Incarnation in what appears to be the beginning of a second book.[4] The *Summa* remains his source and the constitution of Christ, his soul and his sadness are discussed in dependence upon chapters 15 to 17.[5] Then Bernard reverts to chapters 13 and 14 of the *Summa* to discuss the will and power of God and to reproduce the strong and thorough refutation of Abelard's theses concerning the divine power.[6] First he argues against the opinion that God can only do what he does and not more, and then he attacks the *quidam* who deny that God can do better than he does.

When Bernard returns to the consideration of Christ he continues from chapter 17 of the *Summa* to explain the two wills of Christ.[7] He abbreviates chapter 18 on the questions whether Christ is a creature and whether he is the natural or adoptive son of God. Christ's faith and his impeccability are also described.[8] On the last point Bernard reproduces from the *Summa* the argument against Abelard who attributed peccability to the human soul of Christ.[9]

The third book[10] concerns the 'teaching of the Lord' and dis-

---

[1] PL. 176, 50D–61B.
[2] Weisweiler, 'Eine neue Bearbeitung', p. 358. Cf. *Summa Sent.*, I, 4 (48C).
[3] On this see above, pp. 120–1.
[4] Clm. 4,600, ff. 69vb–70ra. Cf. *Summa Sent.* (47C–50).
[5] Ff. 70va–11ra. Cf. *Summa Sent.* (70B–75D).
[6] F. 71ra. Cf. *Summa Sent.* (64D–70A).
[7] F. 71rb. Cf. *Summa Sent.* (76A).   [8] F. 71rb–va. Cf. *Summa Sent.* (76C–78C).
[9] Cf. above, p. 209.   [10] Ff. 71va–2v.

cusses the creation, angels, the prophets and Paul. The whole work is of uneven quality and its material is rather untidily arranged. However, Bernard's attitude to Abelard and to the Victorine *Summa* is instructive. Bernard leans to the school of St Victor rather than to that of Abelard. But he follows the lead set by the *Summa* itself in making use of the material which is contained in the first book of the '*Scholarium*' and he did so to a greater extent than the author of the *Summa*. The *Summa* was more preoccupied with criticizing Abelard's positions than with appropriating his material; Bernard developed the latter initiative, in particular in his reproduction of a part of Abelard's collection of pagan philosophical texts concerning God. It is surely probable that just as certain writers were ready to amalgamate Abelardian and Victorine materials, so too some students in Paris attended the teachings of both Abelard and Hugh.

THE 'YSAGOGE IN THEOLOGIAM'

In the broad lines of its plan the *Ysagoge* owes nothing to Abelard[1] and it is not another of the sentence books produced by his followers. Of the three books into which it is divided the first concerns man, the second Christ and the sacraments, the third the angels and God. One of the purposes of the work is polemic against the Jews and Scriptural citations are given in Hebrew as well as in Latin.[2] When Dr Landgraf edited the *Ysagoge*, this direct recourse to the Hebrew language seemed a very singular initiative for a twelfth-century theologian; this impression should now partly give way to an acknowledgement of the flourishing interest in Hebrew exhibited by a number of Latin scholars. The author of the *Ysagoge* lived in a period when Hebrew

---

[1] On the *Ysagoge* see Landgraf's introduction to his edition in *Ecrits théologiques*, pp. xl–lv, and specifically on the plan of the work, pp. xlvi–xlviii, li. Also on the plan see H. Cloes, 'La systématization théologique', pp. 285, 303–4, 313.

[2] These Hebraic citations have been studied by J. Fischer, 'Die hebräischen Bibelzitate des Scholastikers Odos' and also in notes accompanying Landgraf's edition.

scholarship, if still very rare among Christian theologians, could be pursued with enthusiasm.[1]

Dr Landgraf placed the *Ysagoge* among the writings of Abelard's school since the work contains many Abelardian features.[2] Abelard's influence is observable in the definition of friendship[3] and of charity,[4] and in the discussion of the nature of Christ[5] and of the sacraments in Book II. The *Ysagoge* borrows Abelard's collections of prophetic and philosophical texts which support belief in the Trinity.[6] The author is also under the influence of Abelard's theories of sin[7] and of the redemption.[8] But, as Dr Landgraf also found,[9] there is no general and overall community of doctrine between Abelard and the author of the *Ysagoge*. The latter borrows more from the *Summa Sententiarum*[10] than from Abelard and could with good reason be claimed for the school of Hugh as well as for that of Abelard. The documentation and the arguments of the *Summa* are found in abundance in the *Ysagoge*.

Nonetheless, in his acceptance of three of the leading condemned doctrines of Abelard the author shows that he was peculiarly in debt to Abelard, and not wholly converted to the school of Hugh. He retains Abelard's insistence on the similarity between Christian knowledge of the Spirit as the goodness of God and pagan perception of the world soul.[11] The parallelism

---

[1] On Andrew of St Victor, see B. Smalley, *The Study of the Bible*, chapter 4; on Herbert of Bosham and English Hebrew scholarship see *idem*, 'A Commentary on the *Hebraica*'; R. Loewe, 'Herbert of Bosham's Commentary' and 'The Medieval Christian Hebraists of England'. Also R. W. Hunt 'The Disputation of Peter of Cornwall'. G. I. Lieftinck has rediscovered a 'Psalterium Hebraycum from St Augustine's, Canterbury'. On the *Altercatio Synagogae et Ecclesiae* see B. Blumenkranz and J. Châtillon, 'De la polémique antijuive à la catéchèse chrétienne'. On Gilbert Crispin, abbot of Westminster, see especially the edition of his *Disputatio* by B. Blumenkranz.

[2] Ed. Landgraf, pp. xlix–lii.

[3] *Ibid.*, p. 76. Cf. Cicero, *De inventione*, II, 53. The *Ysagoge* may be influenced here by the *Moralium Dogma Philosophorum*, ed. J. Holmberg, pp. 23 *et seq.*; P. Delhaye, 'Une adaptation du *De Officiis*', believes it to be anterior to the *Ysagoge*.   [4] Ed. Landgraf, p. 85.   [5] *Ibid.*, pp. 163 *et seq.*

[6] *Ibid.*, pp. 257 *et seq.*   [7] *Ibid.*, pp. 106 *et seq.*

[8] *Ibid.*, pp. 155 *et seq.*   [9] *Ibid.*, p. l.

[10] 'Cet ouvrage ... est la source principale de l'*Ysagoge*', Landgraf in his introduction, p. li.   [11] Ed. Landgraf, pp. 257–8.

is supported by the suggestion that there is no great difference between the notion of spirit and that of soul. Virgil's phrase, *Spiritus intus alit*,[1] even diminishes this difference. With the aid of the documentation assembled in Abelard's *Theologia*,[2] but without reference to Abelard's careful argument that the world-soul must be allegorically interpreted and related only to the temporal activity of the Spirit, this author juxtaposes Solomon ('Spiritus Domini replevit orbem terrarum')[3] and Plato ('Deus animam per omnem globum equaliter porrigi iussit').[4]

Abelard is again most clearly followed in the account of the redemption. Here Abelard appears in the context of anti-Judaic apologetic. Imaginary Jews are given the task of raising objections to traditional Christian explanations of the redemption such as Abelard himself opposed. The author writes that Christians like to believe that Christ redeemed man from the devil or from the anger of God or from sin, but none of these versions is sound and none probable, for Christ did not liberate the unjust from Satan nor were the elect ever subject to the *ius diaboli*. The Jews are here made to criticize the notion of devil's rights, not by using Hugh of St Victor but by using Abelard. The author employs the analogy of the slave who abandons his master to serve another; the second master, who signifies Satan, does not thereby gain just or rightful possession of the deserter, who signifies fallen man. Similarly, if a senior servant seduces an under-servant away from a common master and enslaves him to himself, he does not earn any right over his former fellow servant. Man was justly tormented by the devil and God justly permitted this, but the devil had no rights and God had no obligation to send his Son to be the man over whom the devil could not rightfully rule. According to these criticisms, God did not strike a bargain with the devil; he could have terminated the devil's affliction of mankind at any moment; there was no necessity for Calvary nor did Christ's death redeem man from the devil. Objection is also made to the idea that Christ redeemed man from sin; the paralytic

[1] *Aen.* VI, 726.
[2] *Theol. Christiana*, I, 5 (PL. 178, 1150); *Theol.* 'Schol.', I, 20 (1027).
[3] *Sap.* I, 7.   [4] *Timaeus*, 34B (ed. Waszinck, p. 26).

and the penitent sinner were justified without the crucifixion.[1] It is clear that the author of the *Ysagoge* is formulating an objection, not to the fact that men were liberated from sin by Christ, but to the view that the death of Christ was a necessary means of this liberation.

The author of the *Ysagoge* intends to answer these objections with the reasons given by the Fathers. His reply is a series of deductions made from the premiss that divine purposes would be frustrated if fallen man were not restored to eternal glory. Man had been given natural reason to discern good and evil and he had been made in order to enjoy supreme good. Before the Fall God willed that man should achieve eternal good and this will could not be contradicted even after the Fall. Being omnipotent, God can achieve his will. But man was bound by the stain of sin and an expiator was needed to achieve the necessary beatification and to assure that the satisfaction which must follow a fault is rendered. No sinner could suffice for this expiation, nor could an angel nor a mere man free of sin; before the Fall man had been second only to God and he would not regain this position if he became indebted to a liberating angel or man. Since, however, man owed expiation, God alone could not effect it nor could God alone be born and die. God and man were both needed in a union of natures. So Christ's death had a necessary and a reasonable cause. The reconciliation of God and man could have occurred solely by an act of power, but the fault of Adam should be removed by one who is greater than all men and in an act of expiation. Moreover Christ had to teach men by his word and example lest justice be driven away from them under pressure; the example given was a death.[2] The argument of the *Ysagoge* consists of a chain of necessary reasons designed to prove to Jews that the incarnation and crucifixion of Christ were necessary means to the restoration of man. The words *debet* and *oportet* are prominent in the vocabulary of this argument. Here, as

[1] Ed. Landgraf, pp. 155–8. Cf. above, pp. 137–9.
[2] *Ibid.*, pp. 158–62, 176–7. Landgraf's impression (p. l) that the *Ysagoge* does not adhere to Abelard's teaching on the purpose of the redemption seems to me to be an oversimplification.

elsewhere in the *Ysagoge*,[1] the influence of Anselm of Canterbury is felt. Moreover, Abelard's exemplarist thesis is fitted into an account of the redemption which, while it neglects the devil, acknowledges that man is liberated from the consequences of Adam's sin by divine justice.

Abelard's analysis of sin is fully accepted. Sin is the contempt of God, an opposition of the will to the knowledge of what is commanded or prohibited. A fault therefore can only lie in the will and not in the flesh, unless consent is given, nor in actions, which are indifferent. Perjury and adultery seem to be actions which can only occur unjustly, but actions are transient and sin does not lie in a deed which has been perpetrated; nor does it lie in the limbs or the senses, which are instruments of the will, but in the will of the sinner himself.[2]

In other matters, however, the *Ysagoge* often resists Abelard's influence. The author attributes power, wisdom and love to the three divine persons respectively,[3] but he declares it inexpedient to search for or to teach the reasons underlying individual attributions when all persons possess all the divine attributes equally.[4] In the *Ysagoge* omnipotence is treated as a name signifying unity of substance and not as a ground for distinguishing any of the persons.[5] When the author writes of the *propria* of the persons he refers not to their power, wisdom and love, but to the unbegotten nature of the Father, the begotten nature of the Son and the procession of the Spirit in which is found the true distinction between the persons.[6] Hugh is the principal influence: the *Ysagoge* follows him in finding in the power, wisdom and love of the human mind the image of the Trinity.[7] As in the *Summa Sententiarum* those who rely upon their own wits and claim to know how the Son is engendered are castigated.[8] Hugh's reasons for accepting the attributions are given.[9] In addition, the *Ysagoge*

---

[1] Cf. Landgraf's edition, pp. 93–5, 117, 189.
[2] *Ibid.*, pp. 91–2, 106–8; also, introduction, p. l.
[3] *Ibid.*, pp. 242, 257, 263.
[4] 'Cuius rei causam nec querere nec querentem docere expedit', p. 263.
[5] *Ibid.*, p. 258.   [6] *Ibid.*, p. 258.
[7] *Ibid.*, pp. 241–3. above, p. 187.   [8] *Ibid.*, p. 251. Cf. above, pp. 208–9.
[9] *Ibid.*, pp. 256–7. Cf. above, p. 188.

finds that the sensible world is a book in which creatures are the letters which describe divinity. The notes or signs of divine power are the immensity and complexity of the world; wisdom is found in its beauty and goodness in its usefulness.[1] Throughout Abelard is ignored. On divine power and will and on the question whether God can do more or better or other than he does or wills to do, Abelard is refuted with the arguments of the *Summa*.[2]

The Christological thinking of the *Ysagoge* is also largely that of the *Summa* which is followed where it controverts Abelard. The *locutiones*, such as 'Deus est homo', are defended because he who is God is also man; thus such a proposition is not similar to the proposition 'anima est caro'.[3] God and man are, moreover, not to be considered parts of Christ;[4] the soul of the *homo assumptus* is to be considered equally knowledgable with the divine Word;[5] *Ecclus.* 31, 10 ('Potuit transgredi et non est transgressus') refers to just men and not to the soul of Christ.[6]

Hugh is the model for the teaching of the *Ysagoge* on original sin. Men are born with *culpa*.[7] However, the author is aware of his need to reconcile this teaching with what he also accepted from Abelard concerning *culpa* and the will.[8] Little children cannot exercise their wills, but ignorance or impotence does not excuse their nature which is devoid of justice; sin cannot lie in the flesh, but corruption can.[9] The author distinguishes between

---

[1] *Ibid.*, pp. 235–41. Cf. Hugh, *De tribus diebus*, c. 1–14 (PL. 176, 811–22).

[2] 'De hac re cum apud omnes constet, de illo, utrum scilicet plura possit Deus quam velit vel faciat, controversia est', pp. 265–8, here 265. Cf. above, p. 209.

[3] *Ibid.*, p. 165. Cf. above, p. 210.   [4] *Ibid.*, p. 165. Cf. above, pp. 210–11.

[5] *Ibid.*, pp. 168–70. Cf. above, pp. 205–6, 209.

[6] *Ibid.*, pp. 174–6. Cf. above, p. 209.

[7] 'Originale ergo peccatum est culpa humani generis a primis traducta parentibus . . . Nascitur ergo in filiis Ade natura humana cum culpa'; 'homo . . . sine culpa non nascitur', pp. 116, 118.   [8] Cf. above, p. 240.

[9] 'Sed dices. Quomodo parvulus concupiscentiam mali habet, cum nondum velit aliquid vel nolit? Ad quod dicimus, quod licet actum non habeat, vicio tamen non caret', p. 116. 'Hec obicere poteris: Pueros scilicet pro culpa alterius persone puniendos non esse, maxime cum careant intelligentia qua bonum comprehendere, vel potentia qua illud complere valeant . . . dicimus pueros nequaquam pro peccato Ade puniri, sed pro suo . . . Ignorantia autem vel impotentia ideo non excusant naturam . . . ', p. 117. 'Oppones etiam de eo, quod cum solam carnem a primis parentibus traducamus, culpa autem, ut

conserving grace, operating grace and cooperating grace.[1] He is influenced by Abelard to the extent of writing that the act of willing good (as distinct from deeds or a merely good will which is a natural power) earns merit.[2] Abelard had concentrated his discussion of merit upon the action of the will, endowed with faith and love, in choosing good or evil and the *Ysagoge* resembles him in finding merit in the consent to good. Operating grace, which corresponds to the prevenient grace of which Abelard wrote, raises a man from evil to willing good by preparing his will and by stirring his heart. But the *Ysagoge*, unlike Abelard, posits conserving grace, which assures that a man will not incline from good to evil, and cooperating grace, which helps a man to use the grace which he has accepted. It is possible that the *Ysagoge* has superimposed upon an Abelardian analysis of merit and will a more conventional appraisal of the various kinds of graces.

Abelard is again rejected by means of Victorine arguments in a discussion of the power of the keys. The author asks what is the function of confession or satisfaction if remission comes through inner contrition. He reports the Abelardian opinion that priests do not bind or loose sins but show who is bound or loosed, just as the priests of the Old Testament merely discerned who were and who were not lepers. With Hugh the *Ysagoge* teaches that the sinner is bound in two ways, by blindness of mind which is removed in compunction and by the debt of future damnation which remains until satisfaction is rendered and until the priest looses the penitent.[3] From the *Summa* the author takes a reply to Abelard's thesis that not all priests have the power of the keys.[4]

The *Ysagoge* is a work with an individual flavour and it would be wrong to characterize it, like *Sent. Parisienses II*, merely as an example of the fusion of Abelardian and Victorine currents.

[1] *Ibid.*, pp. 92–3. [2] *Ibid.*, pp. 91–2. Cf. above, p. 139.
[3] *Ibid.*, pp. 210–13. Cf. above, p. 195 [4] *Ibid.*, pp. 215–16 and nn.

monstravimus, non sit nisi in voluntate anime, non videmur a patribus originalem contrahere culpam ... Ad hec dicimus, quod quamvis in carne nullum sit peccatum, tamen corruptio inest, per quam anima peccatum trahit', p. 118. It is hard to agree with Dr Landgraf that Abelard's influence is here unfelt: 'Pas même une allusion!', introduction, p. l.

Nonetheless many of the most interesting moments in the work are best understood by relating them to their sources in the teaching of Abelard and Hugh. While adhering to Abelard's theses on the world-soul, sin and the redemption, the *Ysagoge* looks to the school of St Victor not only for much material but also for many criticisms of other controversial theses of Abelard. The *Ysagoge* is not especially faithful to Abelard, but neither does it display animosity in criticism of him. The integration of Abelard's exemplarist thesis into an account of the restoration of man by the expiation of his sin on the Cross is particularly original.

The date of the *Ysagoge* is not known. The *Summa Sententiarum* constitutes a *terminus a quo* and it had appeared by 1140.[1] P. Delhaye has argued that the *Moralium dogma philosophorum* was also used by the author[2] but the date of the *Moralium dogma* is not agreed. The most helpful indication may be provided by the dedicatory letter which prefaces the unique manuscript of the *Ysagoge*. This is from Odo to Gilbert Foliot while he was abbot of Gloucester between 1139 and 1148;[3] whether or not this letter announces the *Ysagoge* and informs us of the name of its author is, however, difficult to decide.[4]

A rearrangement of a large part of the *Ysagoge* has been found in two manuscripts of the British Museum by Dr E. Rathbone.[5] The manuscripts are Royal 10. A. XII, ff. 117v–123r and Harley 3038, ff. 3r–7v[6] and they contain virtually identical texts which may be divided into two parts. In the first part (ff. 117v–121r of the Royal MS. and ff. 3r–6v of the Harleian MS.) pp. 69–103 in the edition of Dr Landgraf are reproduced. These concern man, the sciences, virtues, faith, hope, charity, merit, grace and free will. The Harleian text is slightly closer to the unique full text of the

---

[1] Cf. above, pp. 202, 211–12.   [2] 'Une adaptation du *De Officiis*'.
[3] The letter of Odo is printed by Landgraf in his edition of the *Ysagoge*, pp. 287–9.
[4] An article on 'The Authorship of the *Ysagoge in theologiam*' is forthcoming in the *AHDLMA*; the evidence appears to me to point in favour of attaching the dedication to the *Ysagoge*.
[5] Dr Rathbone very kindly allowed me to use transcripts in her possession.
[6] See above, p. 92.

R

Ysagoge found in the Cambridge MS., Trinity College B. 14. 33, but both copies contain minor and usually short omissions which reflect a moderate desire to abbreviate. The extract was probably made with an appreciation of its whole source, for link-phrases (e.g. 'ut sequentia nos docebunt') which are inapplicable here have been omitted. The abbreviator had no special interest in Abelard's teaching, although an informed reader will find here Abelard's definition of charity and his siting of merit in the will alone. The second part of these extracts (Harley, ff. 6v–7v; Royal, ff. 121v–123r) depart more readily from pp. 103–9 of the text of the *Ysagoge*. The subject is sin and the writer describes the vices at a greater length than the author of the *Ysagoge*. He reproduces Abelard's definition of sin as *Dei contemptus* but ignores the passages where the *Ysagoge* teaches that *culpa* lies in the will and that acts are morally indifferent; he returns to the *Ysagoge* only briefly to present the distinction between venial and mortal sin.

THE SENTENCES OF ROLAND BANDINELLI

The Sentences of Roland are the outcome of teaching at Bologna, although Roland may have completed the work elsewhere. It was finished in the year that he became a cardinal, about a decade after Abelard's condemnation.[1] The hall mark of Abelard's school appears in the opening of the work where Roland divides theology into the three parts of faith, charity and sacrament and where he proceeds to construct his work according to this classification.[2] In his method of writing Roland differs from other disciples of Abelard by being more exhaustive and more thorough. The set pattern of his discussions, which contrasts markedly with Abelard's own freer compositions, with their digressions and

[1] Ed. A. M. Gietl. On Roland see above, pp. 15–16.; on the manuscript of the Sentences see above, p. 86. On the date of the work, see D. Van den Eynde, 'Nouvelles précisions chronologiques', pp. 100–10.

[2] Cf. Gietl, pp. XXI *et seq.*, 1, 154–5, 313. Gietl believed that Roland's work was derived from Abelard's *Theologia* with which there are many close parallels. Ostlender, 'Die Sentenzenbücher', p. 219, preferred to see the lost *Liber Sententiarum* as the source. On the plan of the Sentences see H. Cloes, 'La systématization théologique', pp. 304–7.

polemics and their cultivation of style, is also quite different from that of other sentence works of the school which are briefer and more summary. Roland divided each subject into its parts and carefully and systematically discussed each in turn. Each division would be briefly introduced, definitions would be formulated and a series of questions would be put.[1] These questions would be answered singly. First the authorities and then the reasons supporting one solution would be listed; then would follow separate lists of contrary authorities and reasons. The conclusion, if a conclusion was formulated, would comprise a methodical reconciliation of opposing authorities or a repudiation of certain opinions or arguments. This formal and rigid manner is the technique of the *quaestio* applied in a systematic *summa*. The work echoes the schoolroom where one master presides and the *determinatio* or conclusion contains the *verba magistri*: *Nos vero dicimus*. In view of the later history of scholasticism, the formality of these Sentences would, of course, be hardly worth mentioning for its own sake. But in the context of twelfth-century theology it represents the arrival of a standardization of writing such as was more familiar to a Bolognese lawyer reading Gratian than to a theologian in France. It would be inadequate to describe Roland's method as that of the *Sic et Non*.

Roland placed great reliance upon Victorine thought.[2] The plan of the Sentences betrays Victorine influence in the way in which the discussion of God is followed by a more historical presentation of angels, the creation, the fall and the restoration of man, whereas the sentence works of Abelard's closest disciples pass immediately from God to the *beneficia Dei* beginning with the Incarnation.[3] In his teaching Roland often considers Abelard and St Victor as twin but antithetical sources of authorities and reasons. At the beginning of the work Roland asks whether

---

[1] A good example is Roland's discussion of the divine will, Gietl, pp. 60–79.

[2] Cf.Gietl, pp. XXXIV–XLIX; Gietl, pp. XXXIV–XLI, attributed the *Summa Sententiarum* to Hugh. Roland also used the *De sacramentis*; Gietl, p. XLIX.

[3] Cf. Cloes, 'La systématization théologique', pp. 304–7. It should be remembered that although Abelard's closest disciples reflected in their works an inattention to many aspects of theology, the *Sic et Non* is arranged according to a much broader framework.

salvation is possible without faith in Christ.[1] He presents two
opinions, for and against the possibility. The first is Hugh's
and had been formulated in opposition to Abelard.[2] The second,
that salvation is impossible without faith in Christ, is Abelard's.[3]
Roland does not attempt to mediate between the two views.
He passes to another question, whether salvation is possible
without real baptism or without martyrdom.[4] Roland presents
an affirmative thesis which is again one which Hugh had formulated against Abelard.[5] Next he presents the negative thesis of
Abelard.[6] Here too Roland offers no solution or preference,
although later in his work he inclines to the Victorine view.[7] In
his examination of the nature of faith Roland first quotes the
Victorine definition: '... infra scientiam ... quia plus est scire
quam credere ... Supra opinionem, quia plus est credere quam
opinari'.[8] Roland then writes: 'Magister vero Petrus aliam fidei
ponit diffinitionem dicens: "fides est certa existimatio rerum
absentium" ... "Certa existimatio" dicitur ad remocionem
opinionis.' Hereby Roland, whether authentically or not, presents Abelard's definition with a helpful and well-justified qualification not present in his *Theologia*.[9] Roland reveals, more directly
as well as more fully than Gratian, the tension existing between
Abelard and Hugh. Within Roland's school the same antithesis
also appears and is reflected in a legal question concerning secret
marriages. In this instance Roland's unnamed disciple prefers the
opinion of Hugh.[10]

[1] Gietl, pp. 5–7. Cf. L. Ott, *Untersuchungen*, pp. 527–39.
[2] Cf. *De sacramentis*, I, 10, 6–7; *Summa Sent.*, I, 3 (PL. 176, 335 *et seq.*, 45
et seq.). Also Bernard, *De baptismo*, c. 3 (PL. 182, 1038–41).
[3] Cf. *Theol. Christiana*, IV; *Theol. 'Schol.'*, I, 15; II, 6 (PL. 178, 1285, 1008,
1056); *Problemata Heloissae*, 13 (696).
[4] Gietl, pp. 7–9. Cf. L. Ott, *op. cit.*, pp. 507–27.
[5] Cf. *De sac.*, I, 9, 5; II, 6, 7; *Summa Sent.*, V, 5 (323 *et seq.*, 452 *et seq.*, 132).
Also Bernard, *De baptismo*, c. 2 (PL. 182, 1034–8).
[6] Cf. *Theol. Christiana*, II; *Expos. in ad Rom.*, II (PL. 178, 1173 *et seq.*, 1204D,
1205, 836D–8C). Also *Sic et Non*, c. 106.
[7] Gietl, p. 209.
[8] Gietl, pp. 10–11. Cf. *Summa Sent.*, I, 1 (43) and above, pp. 185–6.
[9] Gietl, pp. 11–12. Cf. *Theol. 'Schol.'*, I (981): 'Est quippe fides existimatio
rerum non apparentium ...'
[10] 'Dicit Petrus Baiolardus ... Magister ergo Hugo beatae recordationis

Roland wishes in his Sentences to dissociate himself from the condemned opinions of Abelard.[1] He shares with the *Summa Sententiarum* and with Hugh a thorough-going opposition to Abelard's doctrine that God cannot do otherwise or more than he does. Roland's handling of this thesis is exhaustive and long.[2] Unlike the *Sententie Bernardi* he does not merely reproduce the arguments of the school which he supports and in his *determinatio* he proceeds step by step and without polemic towards a solution. Abelard is undoubtedly in his mind as one of those who 'dissent from the reason of the church' by denying that God can do more than he does and asserting that he can only do what he wills.[3] Roland offers the example of a rich man who can give money to the poor when he wants to, but when he does not want to, his power to do so remains. Roland agrees that God cannot move a stone when he does not move it because it does not suit him to do so; but God can make it fitting to move the stone which he is not moving and in this event he could move it. God cannot act against his disposition, but he can change his disposition.

Roland expands his rebuttal of Abelard's thesis with considerations of a like kind concerning the will of God—the divine disposition, predestination, pleasure (*beneplacitum*) and permission —and also concerning the prescience and knowledge of God.[4] He mentions Abelard by name: 'Secundum magistrum Petrum non potuit plura predestinare quam predestinaverit; secundum nos vero plura potuit predestinare quam predestinavit.'[5] Again: 'Dicebat enim magister Petrus, quod Deus non potest plura scire quam sciat ... Nos vero dicimus Deum plura posse scire quam sciat.'[6] Roland's treatment of Abelard's opinions is thus broader than that of Hugh and the *Summa*.

[1] The third part of Roland's Sentences, on charity or moral theology, has not wholly survived and Roland's teaching on, for example, free will and merit and the nature of sin is lost.
[2] Gietl, pp. 49–60. Cf. above, pp. 134–6, 189–91, 209.
[3] *Ibid.*, p. 54.   [4] *Ibid.*, pp. 63, 65, 66–7, 68, 71, 80–4.
[5] *Ibid.*, p. 65.   [6] *Ibid.*, pp. 81–2.

videtur in contrarium allegare', *Incerti auctoris quaestiones*, p. 25 (ed. F. Thaner, *Die Summa Magistri Rolandi*, p. 274).

The question whether Adam's sin is found in all men provides an occasion for a no less firm repudiation of Abelard's thesis on the nature of original sin in the descendants of Adam. Some, in fact the Abelardians, deny that sin is in children. Sin is a word with many meanings; it can signify a stain, action, guilt, fault or penalty. Sin may be present in the child as the guilt (*reatus*) or the penalty of the sin committed by Adam, but the action, fault or stain are not present. An analogy, not found in Abelard's writings, makes this clear: if a man commits treason, his family and heirs suffer and contract infamy for the crime and are held to be guilty of it although they did not perform the act of treason. Similarly the children of Adam contract guilt for Adam's sin although the act of that sin cannot be imputed to them.[1] This argument is immediately opposed by a second view which is that original sin is actually present in the child ('actu in pueris esse') without being actual sin ('non est eis actuale') because it is not committed by them. Original sin is 'fomes peccati seu carnis concupiscentia quod idem est'. Rolands accepts this view on the ground that Augustine support it.[2] It is Victorine although it is not an exact reproduction of the Victorine viewpoint for Hugh called original sin ignorance as well as carnal concupiscence and he wrote that original sin is present in us through our nature rather than *actu*.[3] On this occasion Roland does not proceed to a step by step critique of the Abelardian thesis.

Roland disputes Abelard's thesis that there is only one key, namely the power of binding and loosing, and that discretion is not a second key. He agrees that not all priests are discreet, but they ought to use discretion in binding and loosing and it is a key.[4] He seems to envisage Abelard in affirming that all priests indifferently have the keys; unworthy priests lack merit and

---

[1] Gietl, pp. 132-4. Cf. above, p.140.

[2] *Ibid.*, pp. 134-5. Cf. also Roland's considerations on the effect of baptism: 'Sunt quidam tamen qui dicunt, quia parvulis non remittitur (in baptismate) aliquod peccatum, quia nullum habent ... actu. Habet tamen aliquod reatu ... est in eo quedam obnoxietas, quia obnoxius est eterne pene, que quidem peccatum non est, sed tamen pena peccati ... Nos vero dicimus, quod peccatum est in puero nedum reatu, sed etiam actu', *ibid.*, pp. 201-2.

[3] Cf. above, pp. 193-4.   [4] *Ibid.*, pp. 264-7. Cf. above, p. 177n.

those authorities which deny to such priests the keys refer to their not meriting the keys, not to their failure to have them by virtue of their office.[1] Roland does not offer a declaratory interpretation of the nature of this power; he thinks that even in the case of a mistaken judgment by a priest, the fact of the binding or loosing, although not the supporting reasons, pleases God.[2]

Roland's acceptance of other teachings by Abelard is extensive but prudent. He accepts the attributions of power, wisdom and goodness or benignity to the persons of the Trinity,[3] but he is far from using the appropriations as the basis for probing the generation and procession. He turns to Hugh for reasons with which to justify the attributions.[4] He passes over without use Abelard's proof that Jews and pagans had a knowledge of the Trinity. However, Roland accepts that the attributes belong to individual persons *specialiter*.[5] His reasons for distinguishing three persons in God are those of Abelard: power, wisdom and goodness together form the perfection of God; fear, which is roused by power and wisdom, and love, which is roused by benignity, persuade men of religion; the attributes demonstrate the perfection of divine works.[6] Abelard's arguments against the Greeks on the procession of the Spirit are reproduced.[7] Roland also uses similes to illustrate the relationships between the persons; these include the sun, soul, fountain, cithara and also Abelard's much disputed simile of the seal. Roland objects that the simile of the seal does not denote the diversity of persons and he offers, as an alternative which seems to be his own invention, a simile of a triangular stone. One angle has a seal bearing the image of a man, another has a seal with the image of a lion and the third has the image of an eagle. No two seals are confused and the separateness of the persons is demonstrated. Roland believes that this contains what is less understood in Abelard's simile, but his argument is uninteresting.[8]

Roland attempts to save what he felt to be worthy in Abelard's

[1] *Ibid.*, pp. 267–8. Cf. above, pp. 140–1.
[2] *Ibid.*, pp. 268–9. Cf. above, pp. 152, 169.   [3] *Ibid.*, p. 21.
[4] *Ibid.*, p. 22. Cf. above, p. 188.   [5] *Ibid.*, p. 22.
[6] *Ibid.*, pp. 23–5. Cf. *Theol. 'Schol'.*, I, 7–9 (989–91).   [7] Gietl, pp. 33–8 and nn.
[8] *Ibid.*, pp. 25–9. Cf. *Theol. 'Schol'.*, II, 13 (1068–9).

theory of the redemption.[1] He presents the exemplarist thesis: God wished to redeem man by the sacrifice of his Son in order to stimulate men to humility and to veneration of him. Moreover Roland agrees with Abelard that the devil did not possess rights over man and he uses Abelard's example of the two servants. These were the two main features of Abelard's position. However Roland also affirms, as Abelard had unnecessarily neglected to do, that God did deliver man from Satan; the devil had dominion over man and the human race was once subject to his power, but *dominium* is a different thing from *ius* in its proper sense and Abelard, unlike Roland, had not distinguished clearly between them nor shown to which he was objecting. The rejection of the theory of devil's rights meant the removal of conventional reasons for the Incarnation and passion of Christ. If *iniuria* could not be suffered by the devil, there seemed to be no reason why the redemption should not have been effected by a divine word of command. Yet Christ's life and death were facts and they required explanation. Abelard contributed the exemplarist thesis and in effect if not in intention proceeded to ignore what happened to the devil. Hugh, who also denied the devil's rights, ignored the exemplarist thesis and continued to give the devil a large place in the consideration of Christ's mission. The author of the *Ysagoge* set the example and teaching of Christ within an interpretation of his life as a necessary act of expiation and of justice to God. Roland stressed Christ's example but also retained, as Hugh had done and as Abelard could have done, an emphasis upon Christ's work of liberating men from subjection to the devil.

Abelard's Christological thought greatly occupied Roland. He considered the Abelardian opinion that Christ had parts and was partly God and partly man.[2] He distinguished the divine and human natures of Christ and found the latter composed of two parts, body and soul.[3] But are the two natures also parts of

---

[1] Gietl, pp. 158–62. Cf. J. Rivière, *Le Dogme de la rédemption*, pp. 179–81.

[2] Gietl, pp. 172–4.

[3] 'Dicimus: Christus secundum quod homo partes habet, secundum quod Deus omnino partibus caret', p. 173.

Christ? Roland found *prima facie* support for this view in the authorities; just as body and soul are parts of man, it seems that God and man are parts of Christ. But Roland rejects this after the example of the *Summa*.[1] The parallel between a man's body and soul and Christ's natures is not complete. Roland also asks the question, debated in the schools of Abelard and Hugh, whether the soul of Christ knew as much as the Word.[2] Some, including Hugh,[3] argue affirmatively, but they are opposed by Roland: 'Nos vero contrariam partem munientes animam Christi non tantum quantum et Verbum scire dicimus.' He draws a parallel with an angel united to a man in a personal union. The man knows as much as his own soul and also as much as the angel, but the soul does not have as much knowledge as that of which it is the soul.

Abelard had not been content with certain *locutiones* which seemed to him to confuse the divine with the human and the eternal with the temporal.[4] He was condemned on the ground that he had denied that Christ is the third person of the Trinity[5] and this condemnation is clearly in the front of Roland's mind when he seeks to do justice to the difficulties which Abelard had raised.[6] He contrasted Christ, a mortal, visible and passible creature, with the divine persons who are the immortal, invisible and impassible creator. He wished to say and did say that Christ is a third person of the Trinity, but with the qualification that Christ is a third divine person as God, not as man.[7] All the theologians of the schools agreed that the human nature of Christ was not a person. Roland wrote that Christ, who is truly God and truly man, is not, as man, a person. He developed the thought until it became one of the most disputed statements of the century: Christ as man is nothing at all. He was man in a fashion, but that man was not a divine person.[8]

[1] 'Dicimus, divinam et humanam naturam partes Christi minime esse', p. 174. Cf. above, pp. 210–11.   [2] *Ibid.*, pp. 166–71.
[3] Cf. above, pp. 205–6.   [4] Cf. above, pp. 137, 156, 162, 167.
[5] Cf. above, pp. 136–7.   [6] Gietl, pp. 174–9.
[7] 'Dicimus, Christum terciam personam esse in Trinitate, sed secundum quod Deus, nec secundum quod homo', pp. 175–6.
[8] '... cum secundum quod homo non sit persona, et ut verius loquamur nec menciamur, nec aliquid; non enim ex eo, quod Christus homo est, aliquid, sed potius, si fas est, dici potest alicuius modi', pp. 176–7.

This is the thesis which possesses the name of Christological nihilism.[1] In later years John of Cornwall wrote and sent to Roland, now Pope, a treatise in which he informs us of the opposition offered to this thesis by Maurice of Sully and Robert of Melun.[2] At the council of Tours in 1163, while Roland was pope, the thesis was discussed at length before several hundred cardinals, bishops and abbots. It loomed large in the debates at Sens in 1164 where, or so we are told, three thousand schoolmen witnessed Alexander's prohibition of 'omnes tropos et indisciplinatas quaestiones in theologia'. In 1170 Alexander wrote to the prelates of Bourges, Rheims, Tours and Rouen seeking to prohibit the teaching of Christological nihilism. In 1177 Alexander finally issued to William, archbishop of Rheims, a definitive condemnation of the proposition 'Christus non est aliquid secundum quod homo': 'sicut verus Deus, its verus est homo ex anima rationali et humana carne subsistens'.[3]

Whether or not it was Roland, or indeed any single person, who was most responsible for the popularity of this thesis, by the sixties and seventies of the century Roland had become its highest ranking critic. The parentage of Christological nihilism is usually ascribed to Abelard.[4] But Abelard is not known to have taught that Christ as man is nothing. Roland built upon a foundation laid by Abelard, but in order to maintain effectively that Christ was a person of the Trinity, he restricted, unlike Abelard, the humanity of Christ.

Roland's editor, A. M. Gietl, concluded from his study of Roland's teaching that since he disagreed so frequently with Abelard, he could not be considered a member of Abelard's school: 'die Verschiedenheit der Ansichten erweist sich als eine so bedeutende, dass wir Roland nicht einen Schüler Abälards nennen können'.[5] On the other hand all subsequent scholars

---

[1] The history of the nihilist thesis has been outlined by J. de Ghellinck, *Le Mouvement théologique*, pp. 251–63, who provides the basis of the following summary.

[2] *Eulogium quod Christus sit aliquis homo ad Alexandrum III*, ed. N. M. Haring.

[3] 'Cum Christus', Mansi, *Concilia*, xxi, col. 1081.

[4] Cf. de Ghellinck, *Le Mouvement théologique*, p. 253.

[5] Gietl, p. XXX.

have included his Sentences among the writings of Abelard's followers and Gietl himself knew, of course, that their plan was in the main Abelardian. For all his dependence upon the Victorine legacy and for all his avoidance and denial of Abelard's condemned teachings, Roland, even more than the author of the *Ysagoge*, was also engaged in the task of accommodating what was useful in Abelard's teachings within the framework of an acceptable structure of theological thought.

THE SENTENCES OF OMNEBENE

The Sentences of Omnebene remain inedited.[1] Roland's editor, A. M. Gietl, who discussed briefly their relationship with the Sentences of Roland,[2] gave in the notes to his edition many extracts from the Munich copy (= M) of Omnebene's work. In the following pages reference is also made to the Neapolitan (= N) and to the Cassinese (= C) copies.[3]

Omnebene's Sentences are constructed according to the Abelardian plan. The opening words announce the usual division of theology: 'Tria sunt in quibus humane salutis summa consistit, scilicet, fides, sacramentum et dilectio.'[4] But there are features of Omnebene's plan which are common to Roland and not to Hermann or to the *Sententie Florianenses* or *Sententie Parisienses I*. The opening passages on faith and its necessity for salvation include material taken from the *Summa Sententiarum*.[5] Moreover, Omnebene, like Roland, divides faith into two parts, the first concerning the divine essence and the second concerning the

---

[1] Prof. C. Ottaviano wrote to me in 1960 that he hoped to publish an edition speedily. Cf. J. de Ghellinck, *Le Mouvement théologique*, p. 159n: 'l'édition d'Omnebene avait été entreprise vers 1932 par M. C. OTTAVIANO pour la *Reale Accademia d'Italia*, ce qui avait ralenti l'exécution de l'ancien projet du Spicil-(egium) sacr(um) Lovan(iense).' See now C. Ottaviano, 'Prolegomeni all' edizione critica delle "Sententiae" del Magister Omnibonus'.

[2] *Op. cit.*, pp. L–LVI.

[3] On these three manuscripts see above, pp. 83, 88. The Cassinese manuscript is incomplete at the beginning and commences with questions on predestination.

[4] M, p. 151; N, f. 1r. On the plan cf. H. Cloes, 'La systématization théologique', pp. 296, 300, 304–8.

[5] Cf. Gietl, pp. XLIV–XLV, LIV.

opera Dei which here comprise the angels, their creation and that
of the elements, the creation and fall of man and the commandments.[1] The second part of the treatise on faith, common to
both Roland and Omnebene, represents an addition in comparison
with the sentence works of Abelard's closest disciples; as in
Sententie Parisienses II, Roland and Omnebene have expanded
the framework for the discussion of faith by recourse to Victorine
models.[2]

Gietl examined the difficult question of the relationship of the
Munich copy of Omnebene's Sentences to those of Roland.[3]
Omnebene and Roland were contemporaries and Gietl argued
that Omnebene used Roland's work as his model and source.
Whereas Roland was gifted enough to be able to leave a personal
stamp upon the Abelardian and Victorine materials which were
his inspiration, Omnebene was a more servile compiler and much
of his work, like *Sententie Parisienses II* and *Sententie* of Bernard,
consists of excerpts, taken not only from Roland, but also inde-
pendently of Roland from Hugh's *De sacramentis* and from the
Summa Sententiarum.[4] However, there are many occasions when
Omnebene and Roland differ in their opinions.[5] The two most
striking features of Omnebene's Sentences are their resemblance
to Roland's plan and text but also their fidelity to the condemned
opinions of Abelard in contradiction to the teaching of Roland's
Sentences.

Omnebene accepts that power, wisdom and charity are
attributed 'proprie' to the Father, Son and Spirit.[6] Unlike Roland,
Omnebene describes the generation of the Son in terms of these
appropriations.[7] He explicitly prefers Abelard's image of the seal

[1] 'Postquam diximus de illa parte fidei que spectat (N: pertinet) ad
cognitionem divine essentie . . . restat tractare de illa parte fidei que spectat
ad opera dei, in quibus fides a nobis exigitur . . . ', M, p. 173, N, f. 43v. I cite
from M without noting minor variants from the other copies. Cf. Gietl, p. 85
l. 1n.
[2] Cf. Gietl, pp. XLVI–XLVIII and 85–154 *in notis passim*.
[3] *Ibid.*, pp. LI–LVI.   [4] *Ibid.*, pp. XLIV–XLIX.
[5] Cf. *Ibid.*, pp. 25 *l.* 18n., 29 *l.* 26n., 54 *l.* 5n., 60 *l.* 18n., 63 *l.* 11n., 65 *l.* 13n.,
68 *l.* 14n., 71 *l.* 9n., 82 *l.* 7n., 173 *l.* 5n., 234 *l.* 11n.
[6] M, pp. 158, 162, 166; N, ff. 11rv, 25v–26r, 31r. Cf. Gietl, p. 21 *l.* 10n.
[7] M, p. 161; N, f. 16r. Cf. Gietl, p. 29 *l.* 26n.

which he uses to demonstrate the generation of the Son in terms of the relationship of wisdom to power, wisdom being the power of discerning just as the bronze seal is a certain bronze ('quoddam es'). Divine wisdom has its being 'ex divina potentia'. The Spirit does not denote power but benignity.[1]

Omnebene's teaching that God cannot do more than he does is directly contradictory to that of Roland, although the two texts are otherwise very similar.[2] Omnebene disagrees with the 'quidam' who affirm *with the church* that God can arrange or order ('disponere') more than he has arranged. His phrase is so blunt that one wonders whether the text of the Neapolitan manuscript, which alone contains it, is corrupt.[3] Like Roland, Omnebene includes divine predestination in his treatise on the divine will; Abelard and his closest disciples considered it under wisdom.[4] Nonetheless Omnebene teaches an opposite opinion to Roland: God cannot predestine more than he does.[5] He adds that God cannot permit, know or foreknow more than he does,[6] although he agrees with Roland that God can be more pleased than he is.[7]

On questions concerning Christ Omnebene once more crosses the floor of the House to separate himself from Roland. Roland refuted the Abelardian teaching that there were parts in Christ.[8] Omnebene affirms it.[9] Roland affirmed that Christ was a third

[1] M, pp. 159–61; N, ff. 14r–16r.

[2] M, pp. 167 *et seq.*; N, ff. 32r–35v, 37rv.

[3] 'Non potuit plura disponere quam disposuit. Quidam dicunt quod potest plura disponere, et hoc dicit ecclesia, sicut diximus de potentia', N, f. 38v. The phrase, 'et hoc dicit ecclesia' interrupts the sentence. Cf. M, p. 170 (and Gietl, p. 63 *l.* 11n.): 'Non potuit plura disponere quam disposuit, sicut diximus de potentia.'

[4] *Theol. 'Schol.'*, III, 7 (PL, 178, 1112B–1114). *Sententie* of Hermann, c. 21 (1728B–9C), *Sent. Paris. I* (ed. Landgraf, p. 27), *Sent. Florianenses* (ed. Ostlender, pp. 11–12).

[5] M, p. 170 (cf. Gietl, p. 65 *l.* 13n.); N, f. 39v. C, p. 57a.

[6] M, pp. 171, 172 (cf. Gietl, pp. 68, 71 and 82 *in notis*); N, ff. 40v, 41r, 42v; C, pp. 57a, 58a.

[7] M, p. 171 (cf. Gietl, 66 *l.* 23n.); N, f. 40r; C, p. 57a is here barely legible in film.

[8] Cf. above, pp. 250–1.

[9] M, pp. 187–8 (cf. Gietl, p. 173 *l.* 5n.); C, p. 68b. This question is missing in N, as are other questions relating to Christ and the redemption.

person of the Trinity. Omnebene reports two opinions, one affirming this thesis and the other controverting it. He does not decide between the two, although he remarks that those who deny that Christ is a third person of the Trinity prove their thesis by means of the theory, which Omnebene accepted, that Christ has parts.[1] Omnebene does not consider the argument which led Roland to adopt Christological nihilism. He follows Abelard, and not the Victorines, in considering the *locutiones*, for example 'homo est Deus' and 'Deus est Christus'; he writes that if we have to speak properly, we should not accept them, but the authorities utter them and the church adheres to them and therefore they should be accepted but only in part.[2] Omnebene follows Abelard on the redemption: the devil had no right to rule man just as a servant has no right to subject another servant to himself; the manner of our redemption was chosen by God because it was the fitting way of exhibiting love. Omnebene does not raise the further issues debated by Roland.[3]

Roland rejected Abelard's definition of original sin as it is transmitted to the descendants of Adam in favour of the Victorine opinion. Omnebene embraced Abelard's view: the new born contract only the penalty of Adam's sin.[4] Omnebene is also in favour of Abelard's analysis of actual sin; he defines vices as consent (to evil) or as contempt of God.[5] Only the will is rewarded by God; works do not earn merit for man.[6] On this issue Roland's

[1] M, p. 188 (cf. Gietl, p. 174 *l.* 25n.); C, p. 69a.

[2] 'Si proprie deberemus loqui, non concederemus sed quia auctoritates dicunt et ecclesia tenet concedenda est, sed pro parte', M, p. 188 (cf. Gietl, p. 176n.); C, p. 69ab. Cf. above, pp. 156, 162, 167, 210.

[3] M, p. 185 (cf. Gietl, pp. 158 *l.* 6n., 159 *l.* 5n.); C, p. 67ab.

[4] M, p. 181 (cf. Gietl, p. 132 *l.* 5n.); N, f. 57v; C, p. 64a. Cf. also among the questions which follow Omnebene's Sentences in M, pp. 217–28, here pp. 217–18: 'Queritur si peccatum sit in puero isto qui non est baptizatus . . . peccatum Ade est mala voluntas vel commestio pomi sed nullum horum est in puero isto'; only the *pena peccati* or *debitum eterne pene* is present in the unbaptized child. On these question see Gietl, pp. L–LI.

[5] 'Vicia . . . dicimus malum motum vel etiam consensum vel dei contemptum', M, p. 216; N, ff. 79v–80r. Cf. Abelard, *Ethica*, c. 3 (PL. 178, 636A). Sin as contempt is referred to in M, p. 180 (cf. Gietl, p. 125 *l.* 9n.) and N, f. 56r and in the questions following Omnebene in M, p. 226 (cf. Gietl, p. L n. 1).

[6] 'Opera meritum non habent . . . sic habemus quod sola voluntas remuner-

teaching does not survive owing to the incompleteness of the text of his Sentences. Omnebene also mitigated the guilt of those who crucified Christ and seemingly on the ground that the crucifiers of Christ were not motivated by evil intentions as were the Jews who prosecuted Christ.[1] On the other hand, Omnebene departs somewhat from Abelard in teaching that not all actions are morally indifferent; a good action can be performed with evil intent or an evil action with a good intent.[2] Nor does he advocate the condemned opinion that the power of the keys was not conceded to all successors of the Apostles. On the nature of this power he offers an interpretation, rejected by Roland, which in another source[3] is attributed to Abelard. According to this Abelard appeared to teach that the two keys do not signify power and discretion, for ordination evidently does not endow all priests with discretion. In reality there is only one key, namely the power of binding and loosing, although Christ used the plural to indicate the two effects of this power, namely binding and loosing men.[4]

Omnebene's work is unquestionably as much a work from the

[1] 'Item magis adtribuitur mors Christi Iudeis quam illis qui occiderunt ipsum . . . Istis auctoritatibus et rationibus probatur quod sola voluntas remuneratur', M, p. 217; N, f. 80r.

[2] 'De operibus videamus quare quedam dicuntur indifferentia, id est, nec bona nec mala; quedam solummodo mala, quedam tantum bona . . . ' 'Queritur si bona possunt fieri mala intentione vel mala bona. Ita.' M, p. 217; N, f. 80rv. Omnebene's teaching on grace is not wholly available; Gietl, pp. 93, 94 and 119 in notis gives citations from M, pp. 174, 178 (cf. N, ff. 45v–46v, 52v–31r) concerning grace in angels and in man before the fall. In one of the questions following the Sentences in M, p. 219, Abelard's teaching on prevenient grace is presented.

[3] Cf. above, p. 177n.; also p. 248.

[4] 'Quidam sunt qui dicunt quod claves ille sunt discretio et potestas (cf. Roland's Sententie, ed. Gietl, pp. 264–7; Summa Sent., VI, 14 (PL. 176, 152AB)). 'Quod non videtur . . . dicendum est quod non sunt claves ille nisi potestas qua potest ligare et solvere [et hoc tenendum est, add. N] et propter diversos effectus dixit (Dominus) "claves" et non "clavem" cum tantum (tamen, M) sit una clavis', M, p. 205 (cf. Gietl, p. 265 l. 26n.); N, ff. 63rv. Cf. also among the questions following Omnebene in M, p. 218 (cf. Gietl, p. L, n. 2) and p. 223.

atur', M, pp. 216–17, here p. 217; N, ff. 80v–1r. Also in the questions found in M, pp. 218–19: 'Utrum opera remunerentur eterno bono . . . Non remunerantur opera ex se sed ex voluntate. Sola voluntas remuneratur ex se.'

school of Abelard as are the *Sententie Florianenses*, *Sententie Parisienses I* and *Sententie* of Hermann, although we have no means of determining whether Omnebene belonged to Abelard's school in a physical or institutional as well as in a literary and intellectual sense. Unlike the three works just mentioned, Omnebene borrows material from the *Summa Sententiarum*, but, unlike the *Ysagoge* and the Sentences of Bernard and Roland, this fact does not affect his acceptance of many of the most plainly controversial opinions of Abelard. The *Summa* is used in the main to supplement Abelard, on faith for example and especially on angelology and the creation.

Gietl's suggestion[1] that Omnebene's work possesses the marks of literary dependence upon the Sentences of Roland was based upon a comparison with one of the three manuscripts of Omnebene's work and it must await confirmation or modification by means of a critical edition of Omnebene's text. The hypothesis creates difficulties. Roland's work appeared in 1150, although it no doubt was prepared over many years. If Omnebene used a version of these Sentences, it follows either that he modelled his work upon Roland's and reversed, without further arguments, the latter's criticisms of Abelard or that Roland, after influencing Omnebene, proceeded to change many of his views. The multiplication of inextant hypothetical texts is often the last resort of the bewildered, but the question must be raised whether Roland and Omnebene both employed a common source resembling perhaps the *Sententie Parisienses II* in the sense of being an amalgamation of Victorine and Abelardian material in which Abelard's more objectionable opinions were nonetheless presented; a common source, to which Omnebene adhered more slavishly than Roland, would perhaps explain the many resemblances between the two Bolognese masters.[2] It is clear, nonetheless, that Omnebene and Roland are like two factious twins, possessing many traits in common, who have fallen out with each other.

[1] Pp. L–LVI.
[2] Ostlender, 'Die Sentenzenbücher', pp. 222–3, demonstrated that Omnebene did make some use of Roland's teaching, but the supposition that Omnebene's work generally depends upon Roland's is open to doubt.

The writers just considered were all active in developing and, in some instances, in criticizing Abelard's thought. Roland and the author of the *Ysagoge* produced works which were, if not of the very first importance in their day, at the front of the second rank. None was content merely to reproduce Abelard's teaching or what they thought was Abelard's teaching. Omnebene, the Abbreviator and the author of *Sententie Parisienses II* supplemented Abelard's material by recourse to Victorine writing, but without showing much willingness to abandon Abelardian theses in the light of Victorine criticism. Roland, Bernard and the author of the *Ysagoge* followed the Victorines in a number of their criticisms of Abelard. In this way Abelard's extremes of insufficiency and of exaggeration were trimmed. Roland's Sentences and the *Ysagoge* apart, these writings do not possess an independent significance in the history of ideas. Their influence upon other writings is unknown. But all are important to the historian by reason of the revelation which they provide of the movements of thought during and after Abelard's last years. How far their authors were guided or not guided by the council of Sens and by Abelard's condemnation it is almost impossible to say. Only Roland can be certainly said to have written after this condemnation. The criticisms of Bernard of Clairvaux were no doubt known to those who wrote subsequently and it would be surprising if the Abbreviator and Omnebene wrote after 1140. The main interest of these works lies therefore less in what they reveal concerning the readiness of their authors to resist or to accept the criticisms of a Bernard of Clairvaux or a William of St Thierry than in their readiness to turn to St Victor when they abandoned or opposed Abelard. In so doing the disciples of Abelard began to fuse the achievements of Abelard and of Hugh. They showed how the extensive corpus of Victorine teaching, which had in many respects been elaborated in opposition to Abelard, could be fertilized and even expanded further by direct use of Abelard's teachings. Some of Abelard's followers, for example Roland at Bologna, perhaps saved Abelard from the possibility of being spurned by his successors. At the least the most unfavourable criticisms of Abelard prior to the council of Sens did not establish

S

themselves as a common estimation of Abelard. His followers certainly discovered a way of continuing to promote fruitful discussion of his thought and in particular Roland and the author of the *Ysagoge* contributed valuable discussions of the redemption. When Peter Lombard came to write his Sentences, in which he continued to juxtapose the thought of Abelard with that of Hugh, he succeeded to an example set by Abelard's own disciples.

CHAPTER XI

PETER LOMBARD

No longer a young man, Peter Lombard left Bologna for France in perhaps 1134,[1] armed with a recommendation from the bishop of Lucca.[2] He went first to Rheims where Alberic taught until 1136 and also probably Lotulph, who, like the Lombard, had come from Novara. Soon, perhaps even in the same year, Peter moved to St Victor in Paris where he was recommended by Bernard of Clairvaux.[3] He did not become a canon there but did become a master in the cathedral school of Notre Dame.[4] By staying first at St Victor he must have come into contact with Hugh; perhaps too he came into contact with Abelard[5] and he surely would have been well informed of Abelard's last struggles.

In Paris Peter Lombard undertook an expansion of the gloss upon the Psalms made by Anselm of Laon. Our source of information is Herbert of Bosham who later and at the instigation of Thomas Becket corrected and re-edited the Lombard's commentary.[6] It fills over a thousand columns in the *Patrologia*

[1] D. Van den Eynde, 'Essai chronologique', pp. 52–3. If the Lombard did not come in 1134 he did so before the end of the decade. Cf. L. Ott, 'Pietro Lombardo: Personalità e Opera', pp. 11–12 (and *idem*, 'Petrus Lombardus. Personlichkeit und Werk', pp. 99 *et seq.*). On the Lombard's career and work see also J. de Ghellinck, 'Pierre Lombard'. G. Le Bras, 'Pierre Lombard, Prince du droit canon', noting the resolute exploitation of Gratian and Ivo of Chartres by the Lombard in his Sentences, suggested that he had possibly studied under Gratian.

[2] Either U(m)berto (1128–37) or Otto (1138–46), the latter being the strongest candidate for the authorship of the *Summa Sententiarum*.

[3] *Epist.* 410 (PL. 182, 618C–19B). Ott, 'Pietro Lombardo', pp. 11–12, regarded Bernard's letter as undatable; Van den Eynde, 'Essai chonologique', pp. 52–3, suggested the date 1134.

[4] I. Brady, 'Peter Lombard: Canon of Notre Dame', suggests that he became a canon of Notre Dame at least by 1145.

[5] Abelard is known to have been in Paris in 1136 and again, though after an absence, in 1140; cf. J. G. Sikes, *Peter Abailard*, pp. 25–6.

[6] 'Nequaquam, sicut ipsomet referente didici, ipsi venit in mentem, quod in scolis publicis legerentur, solum ob id facta, ut antiquioris glosatoris, magistri videlicet Anselmi laudunensis brevitatem elucidarent obscuram', cited by J. de Ghellinck, 'La carrière de Pierre Lombard', col. 98.

latina[1] and Herbert also tells us that it was not designed for reading
in the schools. The commentary was finished before 1142 and
perhaps between 1135 and 1137.[2] Between 1139 and 1141[3] he
also wrote a commentary upon the Epistles of Paul which, in its
strictly exegetical parts, refashioned the interlinear notes and
marginal texts of the Laon glosses into a continuous work.[4]
The commentary was filled with biblical and patristic illustrations
and references and the occasional disagreement was registered
with the teachings of Gilbert, later bishop of Poitiers.[5] The
commentary earned a phenomenal success. Throughout the middle
ages it was known as the *Magna Glossatura*, to be distinguished
from and preferred to the *Glossa parva* of Anselm and the *Glossa
media* of Gilbert.[6]

The publication of the four books of Sentences occurred much
later, between 1150 and 1157 and perhaps between 1154 and
1157.[7] They offer a very full presentation of patristic and biblical
texts and a mosaic of pickings from the writings of immediate
predecessors.[8] The Lombard was a cautious, sober and apparently
dull expositor, but his work, now one of the least read of the
world's great books, was destined to become for centuries the
basis of theological teaching. For all his apparent self-effacement,
it is becoming increasingly recognized that Peter Lombard
engaged fully in the disputes of his time, particularly concerning
the teachings of Gilbert.[9] But he also leaned heavily upon the

[1] PL. 191, 55–1296.
[2] Van den Eynde, 'Essai chronologique', pp. 45–6; Ott, 'Pietro Lombardo',
p. 13.   [3] Van den Eynde, 'Essai chronologique', pp. 53–5.
[4] PL. 191, 1297–1696 and PL. 192, 9–520. Cf. Van den Eynde, 'Essai chronologique', p. 47. J. Leclercq, 'Les deux rédactions du prologue de Pierre Lombard', has found two redactions of the prologue to this commentary.
[5] Leclercq, 'Les deux rédactions', p. 110. Peter Lombard also made use of
the *De coniugio* of Walter of Mortagne in this Commentary as he did later in
the fourth Book of the Sentences, cf. L. Ott, 'Walter von Mortagne und Petrus
Lombardus', pp. 653 *et seq.*   [6] J. de Ghellinck, 'Pierre Lombard', col. 1956.
[7] Van den Eynde, 'Essai chronologique', pp. 55–8; *idem*, 'Nouvelles précisions chronologiques', pp. 110–18; Ott, 'Pietro Lombardo', p. 15.
[8] 'Egregius multarum et diversarum ecclesiasticarum et scholasticarum
tam antiquarum quam et novarum sententiarum collector', Gerhoh of Reichersberg, *Lib. de gloria et honore Filii hominis*, c. 19 (PL. 194, 1143D).
[9] The 'modernity' of the Sentences is witnessed by their use of the new

work of Hugh and upon the *Summa Sententiarum*.[1] The Victorine criticisms of Abelard reappear in the Sentences, although Peter also incorporated numerous other borrowings from Abelard's writings. In this way Abelard's thought and writing remained available to scholastic masters in later centuries and in this way too Abelard became, however much the fact lacked acknowledgement, one of the *fontes* of later scholastic teaching.

The Lombard followed Hugh and the *Summa Sententiarum* in associating power, wisdom and love with the persons of the Father, Son and Spirit respectively.[2] But he also introduced into his account Abelard's terminology: the Spirit is *proprie* the love of the Father and the Son and the Word is *proprie* the divine wisdom.[3] Charity is sometimes assigned *specialiter* to the Spirit.[4] The Lombard also borrowed Abelard's demonstration, from the power, wisdom and love of God, of the supreme perfection and goodness of God.[5] He overtly criticizes no part of Abelard's Trinitarian thought, although when he affirms that the Son, who cannot engender a Son, does not lack a power possessed by the Father and when he affirms that no divine person has more power than another and that the Son is omnipotent although his existence comes from the Father, he may have had Abelard much in mind.[6]

[1] 'Nous en venons toujours à la même conclusion: l'oeuvre du Lombard se compose manifestement d'extraits du *De Sacramentis* et de la *Summa Sententiarum*; ce qu'elle emprunte à celui-là correspond presque exactement à ce que celle-çi n'a pas', H. Weisweiler, 'La Summa Sententiarum, source de Pierre Lombard', p. 160. Cf. also L. Ott, 'Die Trinitätslehre der *Summa Sententiarum* als Quelle des Petrus Lombardus'.

[2] (*Sententiarum Lib.*) I, (*distinctio*) 34, (*cap.*) 4 ((*ed. secunda*, ad Claras Aquas 1916), p. 218).   [3] I, 10, 1-3 (pp. 73-7).

[4] I, 10, 1 (p. 74); I, 10, 3 (p. 76).

[5] I, 34, 3 (pp. 217-18). Cf. Abelard, *Theol.* 'Schol.', I, 9 (PL. 178, 989D-990A).

[6] I, 7, 2 (pp. 56-7); I, 20, 1-3 (pp. 137-40). That Abelard's teaching on omnipotence was remembered after the mid century is clear from an anonymous gloss on the Sentences, I, 7, 2 (pp. 56-7), cited by I. Brady, 'Peter Manducator and the Oral Teachings of Peter Lombard', pp. 467-8: 'Magister Petrus Abaia(lardus) concedebat conclusionem, scilicet aliquam potentiam esse in Patre que non est in Filio. Hoc autem visum est ei ex quodam sermone Maximi episcopi qui legitur in Pascha, ubi specialiter videtur attribuere omnipotentiam Patri.' On Abelard's teaching see above, pp. 132-4.

Latin version of St John Damascene's *De orthodoxa fide*; cf. E. Buytaert, 'St John Damascene, Peter Lombard and Gerhoh of Reichersberg'.

Peter Lombard ignored Abelard's comparisons of the Spirit with the Platonic world-soul. Whereas Abelard zealously uncovered in ancient philosophical writing the evidence of belief in the Trinity, the Lombard denied that natural knowledge can achieve *sufficiens notitia* of the Trinity and he declared that what the ancient philosophers knew of God was perceived *per umbram et de longinquo*.[1] Yet while he dissociated himself from the cult of classical philosophy, he borrowed from Abelard's *Theologia* almost the entire collection of Old Testament evidence for belief in the Trinity.[2] He ignored Abelard in teaching that the Spirit is from (*de*) the substance of the Father, although, unlike the Son, the Spirit proceeds and is not generated.[3] But he reproduces, almost *in extenso*, Abelard's argument against the Greek interpretation of the *Filioque* clause in the Nicene Creed,[4] and he uses too Abelard's discussion of the question whether the Spirit proceeds principally from the Father.[5]

Thus the Lombard repeatedly uses Abelard's Trinitarian thought and in particular he exploits Abelard's rich documentation. His purpose was largely to supplement what he had found in the *De sacramentis* and the *Summa Sententiarum* and J. de Ghellinck observed that in the scale of his attention to the subject of the Trinity in the first book of the Sentences he resembles Abelard rather than Hugh.[6] He dissociated himself from Abelard's condemned or controversial teachings but he did not attack them, perhaps because their day was over. On the other hand where the Porretans were involved the Lombard was far from being silent and vigorously showed his mettle. These *veritatis adversarii* deny the convertibility of the proposition 'three persons are one

[1] I, 3, I (p. 33).
[2] I, 2, 4 (pp. 23–8). Cf. *Theol.* 'Schol.', I, 13–14 (PL. 178, 998–1004).
[3] I, 13, I (p. 85); I, 13, 3 (p. 86).
[4] I, II, 1–2 (pp. 77–81). Cf. *Theol. Christiana*, IV; *Theol.* 'Schol.', II, 15 (PL. 178, 1300D–6C, 1075A–80B).
[5] I, 12, 2 (pp. 82–4). Cf. *Theol. Christiana*, IV (1304 *et seq.*); *Theol.* 'Schol.', II, 15 (1078 *et seq.*).
[6] 'Pierre Lombard', col. 1991. The Trinity occupies about forty columns in the Migne impression of the *De sacramentis* (PL. 176, 208–46) and about twenty columns of the *Summa Sent.* (PL. 176, 50–70). The *Theol.* 'Schol.' fills 135 columns (PL. 178, 979–1114) and in Migne, PL. 192, 521–652, Book I of the Sentences fills 131 columns.

God.'[1] Against them the Lombard interrupts the regular progress of his exposition[2] and shows his capacity to pursue advanced and tough reasoning.[3] He and Robert of Melun were, according to John of Salisbury, two principal adversaries of Gilbert at the council of Rheims in 1148.[4] The Porretans aroused Peter's wrath: 'haereticorum improbitas instinctu diabolicae fraudulentiae excitata'.[5]

In order to exclude mutability from the divine power and knowledge Abelard had taught that God cannot do or know more or other things than he does or knows.[6] Peter Lombard opposes Abelard with forceful and direct argument. Whereas the Victorines did not furnish much encouragement to him to combat Abelard on the nature of the Trinity, the Lombard could take his cue from them on questions concerning God's power and knowledge[7] and in doing so he broadened the discussion and made original contributions. He agreed with the Abelardians that God's knowledge could not be increased or diminished, but he did not agree that God cannot know more than he knows. He distinguished between the divine knowledge and the subjects of that knowledge. Something could be or could not be a subject of God's knowledge without altering God's knowledge; God can know more than he does but his knowledge is immutable.[8]

[1] I, 4, 2 (pp. 40–1).
[2] 'Nunc ad praemissam quaestionem revertamur . . . ', I, 4, 2 (p. 42).
[3] Cf. E. Bertola, 'Il problema di Dio in Pier Lombardo'.
[4] Hist. Pont., c. 8 (ed. Chibnall, p. 16). Cf. F. Pelster, 'Petrus Lombardus und die Verhandlungen über die Streitfrage des Gilbertus'; J. Leclercq, 'Textes sur S. Bernard et Gilbert de la Porrée' in Recueil d'Etudes, II, 341–71, here 342–3.
[5] I, 33, I (p. 209); cf. I, 34, I (pp. 212–13). Pelster, op. cit., p. 72, considers that the Lombard in his Sentences opposed Gilbert's pupils rather than Gilbert himself.
[6] On divine power see above, pp. 134–6. The thesis concerning divine knowledge is more clearly conveyed by Abelard's disciples; cf. above, pp. 161, 247, 255.   [7] Cf. above, pp. 189–91, 209.
[8] 'Et tamen conceditur posse scire quod non scit, et posse non scire quod scit; quia posset aliquid esse subiectum eius scientiae, quod non est, et posset non esse subiectum aliquid, quod est, sine permutatione ipsius scientiae', I, 39, I (p. 246); cf. I, 39, 3 (p. 247).

The forty-third distinction of Book I of the Sentences concerns divine power and is entirely directed against the Abelardians. The rubric reads: 'Invectio contra illos qui dicunt Deum nil posse, nisi quod vult et facit.'[1] The Lombard describes his opponents in the words of Hugh: 'quidam tamen de suo sensu gloriantes, Dei potentiam coarctare sub mensura conati sunt'.[2] But the richest meat in this long polemical chapter is largely provided by Peter himself. The Abelardians say that God can only do what is good and just and what justice requires, but the Lombard detects an ambiguity in this manner of argument which he proceeds to expose by distinguishing the senses of the statement.[3] If the statement 'God can only do what is good and just' means that God is unable to do many things which are neither good nor just, it is false, for there are many things which are neither good nor just because they do not and will never exist if God does not do them. However the statement 'God can only do what is good and just' is true in the sense that God can only do what, if he did it, would be good and just.[4] Peter says too that his opponents add that God can only do what he ought to do and conversely that he ought only to do what he does. Quoting the *Summa*[5] he replies that the word 'ought', when applied to God, contains poison and he again distinguishes two meanings of the Abelardian thesis.[6] In the sense that God cannot do other than he ought, that is wills, to do, it is false, but it is true that God can only do what, if it were done, would suit him well.[7]

The Lombard applies his exposure of the ambiguity of the Abelardian thesis to Abelard's so-called optimism. He argues

---

[1] I, 43, *cap. unicum* (p. 263). The *magister ignotus* of the Lombard's school rallied to his master's support on this question, A. Landgraf, 'Abaelard und die Sentenzen des *magister ignotus*', pp. 78–9.

[2] I, 43, *cap. unicum* (p. 263). Cf. above, p. 190.

[3] 'his autem respondemus, duplicem verborum intelligentiam aperientes, et ab eis involuta evolventes . . . ', *ibid.* (p. 264).

[4] *Ibid.*   [5] Cf. above, p. 209.

[6] 'Multiplicem enim et involutam tenet intelligentiam, nec Deo proprie competit, qui non est debitor nobis, nisi forte ex promisso . . . Ut autem venenum evacuetur, distingue verbi sensus . . . ', I, 43, *cap. unicum* (p. 265).

[7] *Ibid.*

('ambiguitatem locutionis determinantes') that it is not true that
divine actions, because they are prompted by the best reasons,
cannot be altered. It is true that God cannot act against his eternal
reason, but under this reason he can do other reasonable and good
things.[1] Abelard argued that divine perfection implied that God
was unable to improve upon his work, for otherwise he would
be remiss in not always acting perfectly.[2] Here Peter reproduces
almost verbally against the *scrutatores* the argument of the *Summa*
which is derived from the stand taken by Hugh in the *De sacramentis*.[3] Contrary to his usual habit Peter in these chapters employs
authority sparingly. He relies largely upon the Victorines, but
succeeds in developing their criticisms. On divine omnipresence,
however, he is more content to follow Victorine arguments;
he almost certainly envisages Abelard's school when he insists
that more is implied by omnipresence than mortals can understand. The fault of some is that they rely too much upon their
own capabilities.[4]

In a famous distinction, the sixth of the third book of the
Sentences, Peter Lombard sets out three opinions on Christ.
The distinction opens with an enunciation of the intention to
probe the meaning of certain *locutiones* such as 'Deus est homo'
or 'Deus factus est homo', but with a view, now that Christological disputes have gained in momentum, to discover whether

[1] *Ibid.* (pp. 265–6).
[2] *Theol. 'Schol.'*, III, 5 (PL. 178, 1093D *et seq.*)
[3] I, 44, I (pp. 268–70). Cf. above, pp. 209, 190.
[4] 'Quidam tamen, immensa ingenio suo metiri praesumentes, hoc ita fore
intelligendum tradiderunt, quod Deus ubique esse per essentiam dicitur, non
quod Dei essentia proprie sit in omni loco et in omni creatura, sed quia omnis
natura atque omne quod naturaliter est, in quocumque loco sit per eum habet
esse ... Ipsi iidem etiam dicunt, ideo Deum ubique dici esse per praesentiam
vel per potentiam, quia cuncta loca sunt ei praesentia, et quae in eis sunt, nec
in eis aliquid operari cessat ... Sed licet haec vera sint, quae asserunt in explanan-
dis intelligentiis praedictionum, in illis tamen verbis, quibus dicitur Deus ubique
esse per essentiam, plus contineri credendum est; quod homo vivens capere
non valet', I, 37, 3 (p. 234). Cf. L. Ott, *Untersuchungen*, pp. 208–11. Peter does
not seem to envisage Abelard in discussing Christ's descent into Hell, III, 22, 2
(pp. 651–2). In his *Sermo de ascensione* he distinguishes between incarnation
secundum deitatem which is not local and ascension *secundum humanitatem* which
is a local movement, ed. Van den Eynde, 'Deux sermons inédits', pp. 80–6,
here 81.

these *locutiones* imply that God has been made, or is, *aliquid*. Abelard had concentrated the attention of theologians upon such *locutiones*, as his disciple termed them, some twenty years before;[1] by so doing he seems to have aroused disputes which, as the decades passed by, increased in scale and in complexity. The Lombard in mid century was only too well aware of the difficulties of the problem ('nimium difficultatis atque perplexitatis') and of the disagreements among its students ('plurimum differre inveniuntur sapientes').[2]

According to the first of the three opinions set out by the Lombard, at the incarnation of the Word a certain man with a rational soul and human flesh became God and God became that man. The Lombard presents some authorities, principally Augustine, with whom the upholders of this opinion support their argument that this man became God, not in nature or by merit, but by grace, acquiring all the knowledge and power of the Word.[3] The opinion is now generally known as the *assumptus* theory and it was probably the most widely accepted theory of the incarnation in the twelfth century. Robert of Melun and Maurice of Sully preferred it. John of Cornwall, writing in 1176 in the hope that Pope Alexander III would proclaim it officially, quoted in its support from Anselm of Canterbury, Bernard of Clairvaux, Hugh and Achard of St Victor.[4] The thesis was not always presented without naivety. Abelard had criticized some improper implications, such as that to say baldly 'God became man' implies divine mutability. The author of the *Summa* had also criticized Hugh's association of omnipotence with the human soul of Christ.[5] But Abelard would probably not have rejected the theory once certain qualifications were added. He interprets such expressions as 'fieri hominem' not literally as a

---

[1] *Theol. 'Schol.'*, III, 6 (PL. 178, 1105D–9A); *Sententie* of Hermann, c. 24 (1732A–34A, here 1733C).
[2] Peter Lombard, *Sent.*, III, 6, 1 (p. 573).
[3] III, 6, 2 (pp. 574–6).
[4] *Eulogium ad Alexandrum III*, c. 4 (ed. Haring, pp. 266–8). Cf. B. Barth, 'Ein neues Dokument' (1919), pp. 423–4, and J. Châtillon, 'Achard de S. Victor', pp. 319–21.
[5] Cf. above, pp. 205–6.

divine transmutation but as a union, 'unire personam in unam'. He writes of the assumption of manhood by the Son but warns that what is assumed by God is not properly speaking God, just as the flesh assumed by a human soul is not the soul. To this the *Summa* had responded that 'Deus est homo' is more meaningful than 'anima est caro'.[1] In his next distinction, the seventh, where the Lombard himself outlined an objection that could be raised against the *assumptus* theory, he followed the lead given by Abelard in remarking that the idea of becoming or beginning to be, if associated with God, compromises the divine immutability.[2] The Lombard adds that this opinion can be opposed in many other ways which he will pass over, leaving the exercise to the reader.[3]

The second theory described by the Lombard in his sixth distinction is maintained by men who partly subscribe to the *assumptus* theory. They explain the Son as a person who before his incarnation was simple, having one substance and one nature in his divinity, but who at the incarnation became a composite person to whom had been added a second nature, humanity, and two more substances, a rational soul and a human body. Christ is therefore a composite person consisting of two natures or three substances. The person, the Word, 'ut quibusdam placet', did not become a person or a substance or a nature, but 'quoddam subsistens ex anima et carne', 'subsistens' of (*ex*) two natures or three substances.[4] In the seventh distinction the Lombard presents at some length objections to this theory, especially against its apparent tendency to introduce firm divisions into Christ which detract from the perfection of the union of two natures in his person. Hilary seems to have been clearly ('aperte') opposed to any suggestion that the Son of God was one thing and the Son of man another when he cited the Evangelist, John: 'Verbum caro factum est.'[5] Augustine, referring to St Paul's words, 'forma Dei formam servi accepit', asserted that both the form of God and

---

[1] Cf. above, p. 210, n. 3.   [2] Peter Lombard, *Sent.*, III, 7, 1–2 (pp. 582–3).
[3] A. Gaudel thought that the Lombard supported this theory, 'La théologie de l'Assumptus homo' (1937), p. 218.
[4] *Sent.*, III, 6, 3 (pp. 576–8).   [5] *De Trinitate*, IX, 40 (PL. 10, 313).

the form of a slave are God and man.[1] Augustine also resisted the fragmentation of Christ when he wrote that God and man are not parts of Christ.[2] Although the Lombard does not make explicit his attitude to this theory and although he always shows how its exponents respond to their own difficulties, from the way in which he emphasizes the criticisms formulated against it, it would seem that he betrays a measure of distaste for it.[3]

This theory, by which Christ is analysed as if he were a composition, is usually known as the subsistence theory. Its clearest advocates were the Porretans,[4] who seem to have been motivated by a concern to guard against the danger, present in the *assumptus* theory, of confusing the natures in Christ. Abelard showed a like concern about the *assumptus* theory and he has been hailed as a supporter of the subsistence theory.[5] One of his disciples in the *Commentarius Cantabrigiensis* described Christ as a composition.[6] Hermann wrote of the parts of Christ,[7] and Adam, the obscure canon in Rome, is reported by Gerhoh of Reichersberg to have asserted the existence of parts in Christ.[8] There is, however, no passage in Abelard's extant writings which teaches that Christ had parts. In the printed version of his *Theologia Christiana* Abelard guards carefully against such a 'figurative and improper' term as 'parts'.[9] Even if Abelard at some stage in his career countenanced the theory of parts in addition to popularizing its discussion, the Lombard's account of the subsistence theory did not principally envisage the Abelardians and the theory of parts occupies only a small place in his analysis.[10] When Abelard's

[1] *De Trinitate*, I, 7, n. 14 (PL. 42, 829).
[2] *Contra Maximinum*, II, 10, n. 2 (PL. 42, 765).
[3] *Sent.* III, 7, 1–2 (pp. 583–7).
[4] Cf. John of Cornwall, *Eulogium*, c. 3 (ed. Haring, p. 263); Barth, 'Ein neues Dokument' (1919), p. 424; P. Glorieux, 'L'Orthodoxie de III Sentences', p. 139; N. Haring, 'Sprachlogische und philosophische Voraussetzungen zum Verständnis der Christologie Gilberts.'
[5] Cf. John of Cornwall, *loc. cit.* (Haring, pp. 263–4); Barth, *op. cit.* (1919), p. 425. I have not been able to obtain R. F. Studeny, *John of Cornwall. An Opponent of Nihilianism* (Modling, 1939).
[6] Ed. Landgraf, I, 45.
[7] C. 24 (PL. 178, 1753BC).   [8] Cf. above, p. 24.
[9] IV (PL. 178, 1273D–4B). Cf. *Theol. 'Schol.'*, III, 6 (1107AB).
[10] *Sent.*, III 7, 2 (p. 587).

disciples showed their unwillingness to acknowledge a communication of natures or other kinds of change or development than an increase or decrease of substances, they resembled the Porretans, but they did not themselves arrive at an elaboration of the subsistence theory and it is this that the Lombard considered.

The third opinion described by the Lombard is the antithesis of the second. The third theory discards the notion that Christ was composed of natures and even the notion that the man, Christ, or a substance in Christ was composed or made of body and soul. It affirms that a body and soul were united to the person or nature of the Word, not in a three-sided composition forming a person, but as a garment ('indumentum', 'habitus') clothing the Word so that he could appear appropriately before human eyes. The Word was truly man because he truly accepted flesh and soul, but as a sort of covering. This human nature does not therefore increase the number of persons in the Trinity nor does the assumption of the 'indumentum' divide or change the Word.[1]

The *habitus* theory has also been hailed as Abelard's, both by John of Cornwall in the twelfth century[2] and by modern scholars.[3] But as with the *assumptus* and subsistence theories, it must again be emphasized that Abelard's Christological thinking did not reach the point of elaboration or definitiveness that was later achieved in mid century. No doubt Abelard's analysis of Christ's person was a spur to further discussion[4] but Abelard himself does not seem to have elaborated or appropriated a theory. The most that can be read in his own writings or in those of his closest disciples, in this matter as often in others, are miscellaneous and limited analytical observations, among which we can perceive elements of the *habitus* theory as of the subsistence and *assumptus* theories. Hermann in fact wrote in terms which suit both the *habitus* and the subsistence theories. In Peter's Sentences on the other hand, the three theories are quite separate, more developed

---

[1] III, 6, 4–6 (pp. 578–82).

[2] *Eulogium*, c. 3 (Haring, pp. 263–5).

[3] Cf. O. Baltzer, *Beiträge zur Geschichte des christologischen Dogmas*, pp. 65 et seq.; P. Glorieux, 'L'Orthodoxie de III Sentences', p. 139.

[4] A. Landgraf, *Dogmengeschichte*, II, i, 116 et seq., observed that the *habitus* theory was used by writers prior to Abelard.

and now autonomous. Abelard in his own surviving writings nowhere uses the term 'indumentum' nor the expression 'Verbum habens hominem'. His school was not vigorous in promoting the image of the Son of God clothing himself in manhood. Hermann merely wrote of 'Verbum habens hominem'.[1] Thus there is no immediate relationship between the remarks of Abelard and the *habitus* theory expounded by the Lombard. The Lombard explains that a major source of this theory is Augustine's consideration of the Pauline sentence 'habitu inventus ut homo' (Phil. 2, 7). Augustine taught that the Son of God was not transfigured into a man, but was found resembling man, having put on a man's habit.[2] The Lombard quotes Augustine's teaching at considerable length and concludes that he seemed to have clearly ('aperte') said that God became man *secundum habitum*.[3] In the seventh distinction where the Lombard presents difficulties against this opinion,[4] he is gentle, whereas he had subjected the second opinion to a rough handling. Although he does not himself state an explicit preference for any of the three theories,[5] there can be little doubt that he sympathized most with the *habitus* theory.[6]

From the *habitus* theory to nihilism is only a short step. If it is conceded that Christ 'wore' manhood like a garment, this manhood is difficult to qualify. In 1150 Roland in his Sentences concluded that as man Christ was not *aliquid*. Peter Lombard courted this opinion in his Sentences and probably did so more boldly in his oral teaching.[7] It was because he was credited with its

[1] C. 24 (1734A).
[2] *Quaest.* 73, n. 12 (PL. 40, 84 *et seq.*).
[3] *Sent.*, III, 6, 5–6 (pp. 580–1).
[4] III, 7, 1–2 (pp. 587–8).
[5] Cf. III, 7, 3 (p. 589).
[6] Cf. J. Bach, *Die Dogmengeschichte des Mittelalters*, II, 205; Sikes, *Peter Abailard*, pp. 174–5; Châtillon, 'Achard de S. Victor', p. 317; L. Ott, *Untersuchungen*, p. 644; Barth, 'Ein neues Dokument' (1919), p. 422; A. M. Ethier, *Le 'De Trinitate' de Richard de S. Victor*, p. 30.
[7] I. Brady, 'Peter Manducator and the Oral Teachings of Peter Lombard', p. 473, prints an anonymous report which probably refers to the Lombard's teaching: 'Quod queritur, utrum Christus inquantum est homo est aliquid. Magister, inquit, non semper negabat, immo quandoque concedebat extraneis. Cum tautem negabat, tutis auribus loquebatur, id est illis quos instruxerat. Dicebat enim, quia quamvis nomina neutri generis soleant accipi in designatione

adoption that his Sentences encountered such strong opposition throughout a whole half century after their appearance.[1] In the tenth distinction of the third book Peter asks whether the man in Christ or Christ as man is a person or something. If he is something, he must be either a person or a rational substance which is not always the same as a person. If he is a person, he must be a third person of the Trinity. But it is inconvenient to say that Christ as man is the third person of the Trinity or God. The Abelardians earlier had been concerned to avoid saying that a human nature had entered the Trinity, and one text, not by Abelard himself but produced by the anonymous *Excerptor*, proclaimed that Christ, as God and man, was not a third person of the Trinity *per se*.[2] The Lombard faces the same difficulty, but it is now more developed. He describes, without espousing, the view held by some that Christ 'secundum hominem' is not a person or anything.[3] He notes that the word 'secundum' is equivocal: it may express the unity of the person in which case perhaps Christ 'secundum hominem' is a person, but it may also mean that the man is a *habitus* or a property of the divine or human nature in which case the man is not *aliquid*. What was at issue was not the concrete humanity of Christ or his psychological personality as man, but the dialectical qualification of that humanity which was not itself a person and which therefore seemed to some not to be qualifiable as anything.[4]

That Christ did not possess the spirit of fear of the Lord and

---

[1] Cf. J. de Ghellinck, *Le Mouvement théologique*, pp. 251 *et seq*. On Robert of Cricklade see R. W. Hunt, 'English Learning', pp. 37–8: 'In quo, inquit, hereticus est magister Petrus? In multis inquam. Unum inquit proferatur. Separat inquam hominem a Deo, ut non sit una persona cum Deo in Trinitate, qui revera filius Dei est.' On Walter of St Victor's sermon *De superexcellenti baptismo Christi* (PL. 196, 1011–8) see J. Châtillon, 'Un sermon théologique de Gauthier de S. Victor'.

[2] Cf. above, p. 137.

[3] *Sent.*, III, 10, 1 (pp. 593–4).

[4] Cf. Glorieux, 'L'Orthodoxie de III Sentences', pp. 141–2.

---

nature, plerumque tamen accipiuntur in designatione persone. Ideo quoque concedebat: "Christus in quantum est homo est aliquid", id est, alicuius nature. Negabat tamen, quia "aliquid" ibi videtur accipi in designatione persone. Christus enim non, in quantum est homo, est aliqua persona.'

that hallowed fear or reverence ('castus timor') will cease in the future life are two of the condemned propositions which Abelard was alleged to have taught. The authorities upon which Abelard erected a question were collected in chapter 78 of the *Sic et Non*: 'Quod Christus servilem timorem habuisse videatur, et non.'[1] The Lombard discusses these texts in the third chapter of the thirty-fourth distinction of the third book of the Sentences, a model example of the method suggested by the *Sic et Non*.[2] Isaiah (11, 1–3) prophesied that Christ will be filled with the spirit of the fear of the Lord. But Bede wrote that servile fear of the Lord cannot coexist with charity in the future life, and Augustine stated that salvation drives out fear of the Lord. Bede and Augustine seem to believe that fear will not exist in the future and is not present in the souls of the saints. The Lombard distinguishes, however, the purposes and effects of fear now and in the future. Filial fear, which now is fear of offending those we love lest we be separated from them, will have a different purpose in the future when it will make us revere those from whom we do not now fear separation. This reverence is found in the angels and in the souls of the saints now and it will still be present in the future. It was also in Christ. Similarly 'castus timor' or friendly fear will not cease in the future; fear of separation will cease but reverence of God will remain.[3]

Peter Lombard does not debate Abelard's pronounced opinions on the redemption. He taught clearly and repeatedly that Christ redeemed man from the devil, from sin and from the penalties of sin.[4] He does not discuss with any thoroughness the devil's power over mankind.[5] With Hugh of St Victor he affirms that man was justly held in captivity by the devil.[6] But in spite of an unwillingness to debate Abelard's thesis, J. Rivière concluded that the initiatives of St Anselm and of Abelard in reacting against an exaggerated soteriology, are felt in the Sentences in so far as the Lombard devotes comparatively little attention to the place

[1] PL. 178, 1453–5. Cf. above, p. 128.   [2] Pp. 700–1.
[3] *Sent.*, III, 34, 5 (pp. 702–4).   [4] III, 19, 1 (p. 634); III, 18, 5 (p. 633).
[5] III, 20, 2 (p. 641).
[6] III, 20, 4 (p. 642). Cf. Hugh, *De sac.*, I, 8, 4 (PL. 176, 308A).

of the devil in the redemptive process.[1] Moreover, Peter Lombard, like Abelard, emphasizes the exemplary value of Christ's passion in the liberation from sin as distinct from the liberation from the devil which follows the liberation from sin. Paul teaches[2] that Christ's death commends God's charity to us: 'Exhibita autem tantae erga nos dilectionis arrha, et nos movemur accendimurque ad diligendum Deum, qui pro nobis tantum fecit; et per hoc iustificamur, id est soluti a peccatis, iusti efficimur. Mors igitur Christi nos iustificat, dum per eam caritas excitatur in cordibus nostris.'[3] This passage is very reminiscent of Abelard's own argument in the *Expositio in 'ad Romanos'*.[4] But the Lombard adds, as if to supplement Abelard, that the death of Christ also justifies us through faith in his death.[5] Throughout the Lombard is concerned to bring out the meaning of justification and sacrifice, the merit of Christ which opens to man the approach to the kingdom. In this perhaps he shows a better sense of proportion than Abelard.

Peter Lombard affirms through the words of Augustine that man cannot will and do good without the assistance of grace.[6] Although Abelard was condemned for teaching that free will alone suffices unto goodness, in his writings he clearly assumed that the free will was prepared by faith and he only denied that successive additional graces are granted before each good act of the will. The Lombard does not directly discuss Abelard's rejection of these enabling graces; he employs different terms and his arguments are more elaborate.[7] But J. de Ghellinck was probably right to believe that the Lombard here consciously rejected with insight and penetration Abelard's errors.[8] Each soul has a natural will for good which is tenuous and weak unless grace assists. The power of the rational soul to discern good and evil is called free will.[9] 'Gratia operans' which is 'fides cum dilectione' prepares the will

---

[1] *Le Dogme de la rédemption*, pp. 382–4.   [2] Rom. 5, 8–9.
[3] *Sent.*, III, 19, 1 (p. 634).   [4] PL. 178, 836AB.
[5] *Sent.*, III, 19, 1 (p. 635).
[6] II, 26, 1 (pp. 436–7). A survey of the Lombard's moral teaching is given by P. Delhaye, *Pierre Lombard, sa vie, ses œuvres, sa morale.*
[7] II, 24, 3 (p. 421); II, 26, 1–7 (pp. 436–43).
[8] 'Pierre Lombard', col. 1995.   [9] *Sent.*, II, 24, 3 (p. 421).

T

to do good and to will the good effectively, but it is followed by other gifts, particularly by 'gratia cooperans' which assists the already good will.[1] With Abelard perhaps in mind, he asks whether operating and cooperating graces are not one and the same grace which both operates and cooperates. Such a view, he says, would not be unreasonable, but the plural is used to indicate their different effects.[2]

In Book II, dist. 35, chapter 1 the Lombard asks what is sin. He immediately corrects Abelard's unique emphasis upon the inner disposition of the sinner. Relying especially upon the words of Augustine ('omne dictum vel factum vel concupitum')[3] he argues that sin comprises both internal and external evil acts of the will.[4] In the following chapter he presents three views of the nature of sin: 'de peccato plurimi diversa senserunt'.[5] His discussion of these views is full and frank. The first opinion presented is Abelard's; sin is an evil will and does not embrace external actions.[6] The other two opinions hold sin to be, on the one hand, will and action, and on the other, neither will nor action since evil is nothing.[7] Far from adopting a severe attitude to the condemned thesis, the Lombard proceeds as if the question were open: 'Quid igitur in hac tanta varietate tenendum, quid dicendum?'[8] Against Abelard he affirms that sin is an external as well as an internal evil action, an evil thought, word or deed, but sin consists chiefly ('praecipue') in the evil will; evil actions are the bad fruits of a bad tree.[9] Later in distinction 40, chapter 1, the Lombard returns to Abelard in discussing the role of motive in determining the morality of actions.[10] He presents two opinions on the question whether the morality of all actions is determined by the end and the intention. The first is that of Abelard: all actions are morally indifferent in themselves and become good or bad only through the goodness or badness of the intention of their agent.[11] Others maintain that some actions are good or bad in

---

[1] II, 26, 1 (pp. 436–7).   [2] Ibid.
[3] Lib. XXII Contra Faustum Manich., c. 27 (PL. 142, 418).
[4] P. 491.   [5] II, 35, 2 (p. 492).   [6] P. 492.   [7] Ibid.   [8] P. 493.
[9] Ibid.   [10] Pp. 518–22.
[11] 'Quibusdam ita esse videtur, qui dicunt, omnes actus esse indifferentes, ut nec boni nec mali per se sint, sed ex intentione bona bonus, ut ex mala malus

themselves, whatever the intention of the doer. The Lombard steers a middle course between these two opinions. He concedes to Abelard that all actions are judged according to intention and cause, but some actions are evil in themselves, whatever the motive by which they are pursued. Peter insists forcefully upon this breach of the thesis of the amorality of all actions: 'Intende, lector, propositis verbis tota mentis consideratione, quae non inutilem habent exercitationem; et dignosces, quis actus sit peccatum, qui scilicet malam habet causam; nec ille tantum, quia sunt nonnulli actus, qui etsi bonam habeant causam, tamen peccata sunt.'[1] Here the Lombard reveals that Abelard is foremost in his mind by referring to the example of the crucifiers of Christ who thought that they were serving God: 'aliqui ponunt actum Iudaeorum, qui crucifigendo Christum arbitrabantur, "se obsequium praestare Deo" '.[2] To the Lombard this is an example of an action which is sin *per se*: 'omnia igitur opera hominis secundum intentionem et causam iudicantur bona vel mala, exceptis his, quae per se mala sunt, id est quae sine praevaricatione fieri nequeunt'.[3] Others say that such actions which can never have a good motive include stealing to give to the poor and committing adultery to save one's life.

In Book II, dist. 30, chapter I the Lombard introduces the subject of original sin in a manner which appears to be a direct reply to Abelard's condemned opinion that the descendants of Adam inherit the penalty but not the fault of original sin. Peter says that 'peccatum simul ac poenam per eum transisse in posteros'.[4] His concern is not to consider Abelard's error as dead but to reveal the genuine difficulties which arise in attempting to define original sin: 'de hoc enim sancti doctores subobscure locuti sunt, atque scholastici lectores varie senserint'.[5] In chapter 6 he

---

[1] P. 521. The author of the *Enarrationes in Evangelium S. Matthaei* (PL. 162, 1311B, 1363C) also combines the principle that the morality of an act depends on the presiding intention with the supposition that *mala per se* cannot become good by virtue of a good intention. Cf. D. Van den Eynde, 'Autour des "Enarrationes",' p. 75.
[2] P. 521.   [3] P. 522.   [4] P. 460.   [5] II, 30, 6 (p. 462).

sit omnis actus. Secundum quos, quilibet actus potest esse bonus, si bona intentione geratur', p. 519.

describes Abelard's opinion ('quidam . . . putant') that original sin in us is the 'reatus poenae' or the 'debitum vel obnoxietas' for Adam's sin. However the Lombard does no more than reproduce the reply to Abelard given by the *Summa Sententiarum*.[1] If mankind contracts the debt for the penalty owing on account of Adam's sin, then mankind does not contract the penalty itself. The Lombard writes that some Abelardians ('quidam eorum') admit this when they speak of the 'obnoxietas poenae' which little children bear.[2] He proceeds to affirm through the *auctoritates* that men contract the fault of Adam's sin; original sin is the 'fomes peccati' or concupiscence with which all are born.[3]

Peter defines the power of the keys, in dependence upon the *Summa*, as *scientia discernendi* and *potentia iudicandi*.[4] He enquires particularly into the role of God and the priest in the remission of sin and also into the transmission of the power of the keys. On the first problem the Lombard conducts an open debate: 'Ecce, quam varia a doctoribus super his traduntur. Et in hac tanta varietate quid tenendum?'[5] God alone remits sin yet we must reckon with a power of binding and loosing men which was conceded to the Apostles. He quotes Hugh's opinion that sinners are bound by mental disease and blindness and also by the debt of future punishment; from these he is loosed by God and the priest respectively.[6] Others say that the debt of eternal death is dismissed by God alone when he illumines the mind and inspires contrition; the power of the keys was entrusted to the Apostles so that they could show men that they are bound in or loosed from sin.[7] When Christ cured the leper he forthwith sent him to the priests so that by their acknowledgement of the cure he would be shown to be clean. Jerome inveighed against the Pharisaical attitude of those priests who believed that they remitted sin.[8] Yet Christ committed Lazarus to his disciples for loosing after raising him from death. The Lombard distinguishes between forgiveness by God and the realization of that forgive-

---

[1] Cf. above, pp. 209–10.   [2] P. 462.   [3] II, 30, 7–9 (pp. 462–5).
[4] IV, 18, 2 (p. 858). Cf. *Summa Sent.*, VI, 11 (PL. 176, 152A).
[5] *Sent.*, IV, 18, 5 (p. 862).   [6] IV, 18, 4 (pp. 859–61). Cf. above, p. 195.
[7] IV, 18, 5–6 (pp. 861–4).   [8] *Super Matth.* III, 16, 19 (PL. 26, 118).

ness by the church. In this the Lombard reminds us of Abelard's teaching. The authorities that he presents are similar to those discussed by Abelard who also emphasized that the power of the keys was a declaratory power.[1]

On the second question the Lombard follows the *Summa*: although not all priests have discretion ('unde dolendum est atque lugendum') they do have the power of judging.[2] He makes a clear allusion to the Abelardians who, he says, argue that the power of the keys pertains only to those priests who copy the teachings and the lives of the Apostles. But the Lombard maintains that all priests have the power; they do not, however, have it rightly and worthily unless they are true imitators of the Apostles.[3] When the power is exercised without discretion, the sentence is not confirmed in heaven.[4]

'Abaelardus catholicus spiritu Hugonis repletus.' The editors of the Quaracchi edition of the Sentences perhaps exaggerated the debt of the Lombard to Abelard, although not to Hugh.[5] But John of Cornwall affirmed that he often had Abelard's *Theologia* in his hands[6] and he knew how to use the excellent documentation contained within that work. Unlike Abelard he expected nothing from philosophers and he excluded them in favour of an exclusive cultivation of theological tradition. The large extent of his dependence upon the *Summa* is, when one approaches the Sentences by way of their antecedents, somewhat disappointing. Nonetheless the attitudes adopted by Peter Lombard to Abelard's teachings are not always identical with those of the *Summa*. And

---

[1] *Sent.*, IV, 18, 4–6 (pp. 858–64). 'In remittendis vel retinendis culpis id iuris et officii habent evangelici sacerdotes, quod olim sub lege habebant legales in curandis leprosis. Hi ergo peccata dimittunt vel retinent, dum dimissa a Deo vel retenta iudicant et ostendunt', IV, 18, 6 (p. 863). The Lombard also explains that the power of binding and loosing is a power of admitting and excluding from communion and a power of imposing satisfaction. For Abelard see *Ethica*, c. 36 (PL. 178, 673 *et seq.*) and above pp. 140–1, 152. Cf. L. Hödl, *Geschichte der scholastischen Literatur*, p. 193.

[2] *Sent.*, IV, 19, 1 (pp. 866–9). Cf. *Summa Sent.*, VI, 14 (PL. 176, 152).

[3] *Sent.*, IV, 19, 1 (p. 868).

[4] IV, 18, 7 (pp. 864–5).

[5] *Prolegomena*, p. xlvi.

[6] *Eulogium*, c. 3 (Haring, p. 265).

who will say that when he makes his own incursions into the criticism of Abelard's opinions or when he lifts material from the *Theologia* and perhaps from the *Sic et non*, he does not show good sense? His interpretation of the redemption is, in comparison with his predecessors, more rounded. His handling of the morality of acts, while not distinguished, is a belated recognition of the theological importance of Abelard's conceptual analyses. His readiness to use offending terms in Trinitarian thought, while not very important in itself, reveals a measure of independence from Victorine examples. In his polemic concerning divine power and knowledge, he succeeded in advancing the debate a little. In comparison with the *Summa* and with Hugh Peter Lombard had put Abelard to greater profit and revealed less hostility than they had done.

CHAPTER XII

ROBERT OF MELUN

The connections between Britain and the scholastic centres of France in the twelfth century are important and many reputable scholars and writers either came to France from across the Channel or were eventually to be domiciled in England. They include Achard of St Victor, Adam of Balsham and of the Petit Pont, Adelard of Bath, Alexander Nequam, Andrew of St Victor, Bartholomew of Exeter, Daniel Morley, Ervisius of St Victor, Gilbert Crispin, Gilbert the Universal, Gerald of Wales, John of Cornwall, John of Salisbury, Lawrence of Westminster, Ralph of Beauvais, Richard of St Victor, Robert of Melun, Robert Pullen and Stephen Langton.

Robert of Melun was English by birth and died as bishop of Hereford in 1167. The greater part of his career was spent in French schools, notably Melun and Paris which he left finally in 1160.[1] In the 1150s and perhaps in the early 1160s he composed his Sentences but without, it seems, completing his work.[2] In about 1157 or in previous years, Robert issued 125 *Questiones de divina pagina*, most of them centred on Matthew's Gospel and arranged rather weakly.[3] At a similar period he issued his *Questiones de epistolis Pauli*.[4] Robert had played, in concert with Peter Lombard, a leading role against Gilbert of Poitiers at Paris in 1147.[5] Later with Maurice of Sully he opposed the Christology

[1] On Robert's life see R. M. Martin, *Oeuvres de Robert de Melun*, I, vi–xii, and U. Horst, *Die Trinitäts- und Gotteslehre des Robert von Melun*, pp. 3–11. On Robert's character see especially M. D. Knowles, *The Episcopal Colleagues of Archbishop Thomas Becket*, pp. 28–9, 104–6.

[2] Cf. Martin, *Oeuvres*, III, 1, vi who assigned them to the period 1152–60; Horst, *Die Trinitäts- u. Gotteslehre*, pp. 20–3 suggests 1155/6–1163/4.

[3] Martin, *Oeuvres*, I, li–lii, suggested 1143–7; D. Van den Eynde, 'Nouvelles précisions chronologiques', pp. 86–100 preferred *c.* 1157; Horst, *Die Trinitäts- u. Gotteslehre*, pp. 12–17 now advises *c.* 1147–55.

[4] 1145–55 according to Martin, *Oeuvres*, II, lvi–lviii; *c.* 1157 for Van den Eynde, 'Nouvelles précisions chronologiques', pp. 86–100; *c.* 1150–5 for Horst, *Die Trinitäts- u. Gotteslehre*, pp. 17–20.

[5] Robert's name does not appear in the list of participants in the council of

of Peter Lombard.[1] The mid-century was no period of calm following the freshness and rapid fluidity of the time of Abelard, but it was a time when reflection upon earlier and perhaps more hectic debates was possible and when most questions, particularly those raised by Abelard, had a tradition of disputation behind them. Robert had been prominent in Paris in 1137 when John of Salisbury found him engaged in teaching the *trivium*, a penetrating and diligent scholar, always ready with answers and delighted with discovery.[2] No dialectical work by Robert survives, although his theological writing is impregnated by dialectical modes of expression and exposition. The later Robert may have been somewhat altered from the logician of the thirties, for his writings, or at least his Sentences, are very prolix and thorough; here the diligence has become wearying. Nonetheless in the 1150s Robert was one of the most active students of Abelard's teaching, differing in this from Peter Lombard by the vigour of his reasoning and less interested than Peter Lombard in Abelard's collections of texts. In no sense was Robert committed to the *corpus* of Abelard's doctrines, but he disputed the questions which Abelard had raised, referred to Abelard for the framework of his often contrary arguments and kept alive the stimulus of Abelard.[3]

Robert's editor, the late R. Martin, found that in the *Questiones de divina pagina* Robert discussed Abelard's theories as found in his writings and lectures,[4] and with reference to the *Questiones de epistolis Pauli* and especially to the questions on Romans, Martin observed: 'Robert a eu constamment sous les yeux le commentaire d'Abélard sur cette même épître et en a fait des

[1] Cf. John of Cornwall, *Eulogium*, c. 5 (ed. Haring, p. 268); Robert of Cricklade, *Speculum fidei*, III, 5, cited by R. W. Hunt, 'English Learning in the Twelfth Century', pp. 37 *et seq.*
[2] *Metalogicon*, II, 10 (ed. Webb, p. 78).
[3] Horst, *Die Trinitäts- u. Gotteslehre*, p. 9, rightly regards as questionable the opinion of Martin, *Oeuvres*, I, ix, that Robert taught within the walls of St Victor.
[4] *Oeuvres*, I, xlvii.

Rheims published by Leclercq and Pelster; see above, p. 265 and n.; cf. also John of Salisbury, *Hist. Pont.*, c. 8 (ed. Chibnall, p. 16).

emprunts fréquents, des citations d'auteurs, des gloses, des doctrines.'[1] The plan[2] of his Sentences shows affinities with the *De sacramentis* of Hugh. The first of the two books concerns the sacraments of the Old Testament and discusses the Creation, God and the Trinity, angéls and man, free will and original sin. The second book on the sacraments of the New Testament concerns Christ, his nature and work. The remainder of this book, which does not survive and which may not have been written, was meant to include the sacraments instituted by Christ, the theological virtues and eschatology. But in the general preface we find indications that Robert has not forgotten Abelard's three-fold division of theology into faith, charity and sacrament and that his work may be based upon Abelard as well as upon the *De sacramentis*. Without mentioning names Robert singles out for praise 'duo precipui auctores' who have set the best standard for the composition of comprehensive treatises of theology: 'Horum autem tractatuum auctores pauci inveniuntur, sed ex illis tamen duo precipui, qui tam *de sacramentis fidei quam de ipsa fide ac caritate* ratione inquirenda ac reddenda, omnibus qui post illos sacre scripture expositores exstiterunt, omnibus omnium iuditio prepollent.'[3] Since Robert has heard these two masters *viva voce* he feels better able to present and discuss their opinions than other masters who rely on the written word alone.[4] The two are very different in their views and in the thoroughness of

---

[1] *Oeuvres*, II, xxxvii–xxxviii.

[2] Described by Martin, *Oeuvres*, III, 1, vi–x, and by Horst, *Die Trinitäts- u. Gotteslehre*, pp. 191–9.

[3] *Sententie* (1, 45 = Martin, *Oeuvres*, III, 1, p. 45). A strong case has now been made for identifying the two authors with Hugh and Abelard by U. Horst, 'Beiträge zum Einfluss Abaelards auf Robert von Melun', pp. 321–3. The same view has also been advocated by M. Grabmann, *Geschichte*, II, 295 (Grabmann, in his *Geschichte*, II, 323–58 was the first modern historian to recognize the importance of Robert), and by R. Baron, 'Note sur l'énigmatique Summa Sententiarum', pp. 35–6. The influence of Hugh's lectures (*Sent. de divinitate*) is discussed by Horst, *Die Trinitäts- u. Gotteslehre*, pp. 105–11.

[4] 'Eis ergo qui auctores predictorum tractatuum viva voce, ut dici solet, suam exponentes sententiam presentes audierunt magis credendum est in eorundem tractatuum expositione, quam illis qui ex scripturis eorum quid senserint opinantur.' 'Ab eisque eadem suscepi que ipsi ante meam cum eis conversationem vel post scriptis signaverunt', *Sententie* (1, 48 and 47).

their considerations, but sometimes beneath their apparent differences they are firmly united. Robert boasts that he who follows these models and amalgamates them and harmonizes their differences will produce 'unum sententiarum excellentissimum corpus'.[1] This then is Robert's plan, to produce a harmonious combination of the work of the two leading masters of the time, Hugh certainly and probably also Abelard. The ambition was in accordance with much contemporary feeling; as we have seen, some chroniclers selected the condemned heretic and the 'secundus Augustinus' for special praise as the 'duo luminaria', the twin beacons of French thought. Early codices frequently presented alongside of each other the writings of Victorines and of Abelardians. Abelard's own followers soon came to include in their own sentence works much material from the school of Hugh. In their opinions Abelard and Hugh kept at a distance from each other in their lifetime, but the theological movement of the twelfth century, instead of becoming polarized around the one or the other, sought its progress through their combination. This is true of the work of the Lombard and it is true of the thinking found in Robert's Sentences, if not also in their preface.

As a master of logic Robert shared Abelard's keen interest in Trinitarian problems. He adopts directly from Abelard the belief, which the Lombard had not shared, that the ancient gentile philosophers knew of the Trinity.[2] Robert argues that no one

---

[1] 'Ex istorum itaque sententiarum tractatibus unum sententiarum excellentissimum corpus posse conpingi dubitandum non est, si ea que in illis differentia videntur hic in unitate quadam convenire monstrentur, et que ibi aversitate sibi obviare creduntur, hic sola diversitate sibi consona distare ostendantur. Et si quod aput unum brevius vel prolixius quam oportuit dictum est, hic vero aput alterum prolixa abbrevientur vel abbreviata producantur; vel que ab uno vel ab utroque pretermissa sunt vel minus congrue dicta, hic et ab uno et ab utroque pretermissa suppleantur et minus congrue dicta convenientius dicantur. Cuius operis quanta sit utilitas, et effectus ipse docebit et hec que loco exemplaris sunt proponenda presignant', *Sententie* (1, 47). Cf. *ibid.*, 1, 47 *l*. 16: 'tractatus illos qui non immerito sententiarum nomine inscribuntur'. Abelard was not usually thought of as the author of Sentences, but as the author of, for example, the *Theologia*; this *caveat* constitutes a reason for not placing complete confidence in the identification with Abelard.

[2] *Sent.* (1, 294) and *Questiones de epistolis Pauli*, ed. Martin, *Oeuvres*, II, 24

should be disturbed by the revelation of this faith through divine grace to pagans, for their knowledge strengthens ours and can be used to oppose those pagans who resist Christianity.[1] Nonetheless Robert himself shows none of the zeal of Abelard to present pagan witnesses to the Trinity but he does use, as Peter Lombard did, Abelard's collection of Old Testament materials which refer to the Trinity.[2] He is content to refer to Augustine's acceptance that Plato believed in the eternal generation of the Son. Of the world-soul he is more circumspect; he reports that some believe the world-soul signifies the Spirit and that this is a sensible view, but it cannot be supported with ecclesiastical authority and therefore Robert is not inclined to espouse it.[3] Robert also shows his wariness on the question of the procession and generation of the divine persons. With the Victorines he underlines our ignorance of how the Son is engendered or how the Spirit proceeds.[4] He finds that the analogy between the love of a rational mind and the Spirit of God is not a substantial similarity. The affections of the mind are not *de substantia mentis*; they are its extensions, proceeding from the mind. The Spirit, however, which is also love, is *de substantia Patris*. Robert does not ask whether the Spirit is also *ex substantia Patris*, as Abelard would not have it, but it is clear that he is rejecting what he considers to be someone's error 'quod multum fidei catholice adversatur'.[5]

Robert is fond of similes which are used to demonstrate the truths of the Trinity. That of the cithara, in which string, hands

[1] *Sent.* (I, 293–4).
[2] *Sent.* (I, 301–6). Cf. *Theol.* 'Summi boni', I, 2–3 (ed. Ostlender, pp. 4–6), *Theol. Christiana*, I, 5 (PL. 178, 1137D–8A), *Theol.* 'Schol.', I, 13 (998–9). To the parallels noted by Martin add *Ps.* 2, 7, *Is.* 53, 8, *Mic.* 5, 2, *Prov.* 8, 12 *et seq.*
[3] *Sent.* (I, 296): 'Illud vero quod per animam mundi Spiritum sanctum eum intellixisse quidam estimant, etsi sanus eorum sit sensus, nos tamen asserere nolumus: quoniam nulla Ecclesie auctoritate hoc ostendere possumus, id est, quod anima mundi Spiritus sanctus sit aut credenda aut predicanda.'
[4] *Sent.* (2, 131–3 = Martin, *Oeuvres*, III, 2, pp. 131–3). Cf. above, pp. 208–9, 240.
[5] *Sent.* (2, 115–20). The 'unknown author of the second half of the twelfth century' cited by Horst, *Die Trinitäts- u. Gotteslehre*, p. 136 n. 15, is the anonymous *Excerptor*; cf. *Cap. Haeresum*, 2 (PL. 182, 1049BC).

(= QEP (24)). Cf. Abelard, *Theol.* 'Summi boni' I, 5 (ed. Ostlender, pp. 12–13). Cf. also Horst, *Die Trinitäts- u. Gotteslehre*, pp. 93–5.

and skill cooperate but only the string sounds, is helpful in elucidating the Incarnation. The sun helpfully illustrates the coeternity of the Word, symbolized by the splendour of the sun, with the Father. The spring usefully indicates the identity of essence, since the same water passes from the spring through the stream to the lake. But although all similes are defective in some respect or other, in his *Questiones de epistolis Pauli* Robert considered Abelard's simile of the seal the most suitable to describe the different properties of the persons and the identity of the divine essence.[1] In the Sentences on the other hand he argues against his earlier preference;[2] he still believes that similes have their uses[3] and he is most concerned with drawing parallels between the soul and God, but now he finds that the simile of the wax does not demonstrate the distinction of persons nor do the seal and the potentiality of sealing denote a difference of property.[4]

In the Sentences Robert also qualifies Abelard's enumeration of reasons why God is the Trinity.[5] He cites the three reasons given by Abelard in his *Theologia*.[6] A plurality of persons where the Father is omnipotent, the Son supremely wise and the Spirit supremely loving, reveals a *summum bonum*. Supreme power, wisdom and love reveal that God is to be feared for his power and wisdom and loved because he is supremely loving. Thirdly, the works of God, because they are effected by supreme power, wisdom and love, are appreciable as excellent. These reasons are, however, merely useful; they do not appear to Robert to be the sufficient explanations which they have seemed to some, for even if the

---

[1] QEP (26-7, here 27): 'Est eciam illa de sigillo qua expressior nulla invenitur, et ad diversas personarum proprietates, et ad identitatem essentie demonstrandum.'   [2] *Sent.* (2, 108-10).

[3] 'Quid ergo? Omnesne reprehendende sunt a sanctis doctoribus . . ? Absit. Eas enim . . . Spiritu sancto docente in suis reliquerunt scriptis', *Sent.* (2, 110).

[4] 'Illa vero similitudo que de ere, sigillo ac sigillabili a quibusdam solet proponi, illam unitatem essentie trium personarum, ut quibusdam visum est, ceteris similitudinibus evidentius exprimit, ad rem pertinere non videtur, eo quod sigillum in quo tria diversa proprietate assignare volunt, nulla est persona, nec sigillabile a sigillo est proprietate aliqua diversum', *Sent.* (2, 109). Cf. *Theol. 'Schol.'*, II, 13 (1068C-70B).   [5] *Sent.* (1, 284-6).

[6] *Theol. 'Summi boni'*, I, 2 (ed. Ostlender, pp. 3, 4); *Theol. 'Schol.'*, I, 9 (989D-990C). Cf. also *Theol. Christiana*, I, 3 (1127BC).

Trinity was not predicated, God would still appear to be the *summum bonum*.

Robert rallies to Abelard's defence in the matter of the divine attributes both in the *Questiones de epistolis Pauli* and in eleven consecutive chapters of the first book of his Sentences.[1] In the *Questiones* he gives in brief outline what is expanded in the Sentences. The Father is omnipotence, the Son wisdom and the Spirit goodness; this is the teaching of Augustine, Jerome, Maximus and others, but in espousing it we in no way explain the mystery of the Trinity.[2] In other words the attributes of the persons do not serve to demonstrate the existence of the persons or the relationships between them. The cautionary qualification may well be a discreet dissociation from Abelard's utilization of the personal attributes for these purposes.[3]

In the Sentences Robert returns to this theme with the confidence that this is the teaching of the holy doctors and that contemporary doctors have followed their opinion, that it is also the church's teaching based on Scripture.[4] Objections to such a view are therefore troublesome and emanate from those who do not understand and who are presumptuous. Indeed it was an obstinate custom with such people in matters of which they were ignorant to condemn others without discussion and without rational enquiry.[5] The offensive against the abbot of Clairvaux has commenced.[6]

[1] I have not been able to see R. M. Martin, 'Pro Petro Abaelardo, un plaidoyer de Robert de Melun contre S. Bernard' in *Revue des sciences philosophiques et théologiques*, XII (1923), pp. 308–33.

[2] 'Nec est hoc ineffabilem Trinitatem determinare, sed est noticia quedam quid debeamus credere', QEP (27–8, here 28). No quotations from Augustine and Jerome are offered. The text of Maximus, *Hom. LXXXIII de traditione symboli* (PL. 57, 433–4) was much used by Abelard to indicate the omnipotence of the Father.

[3] Cf. the criticism of Walter of Mortagne, *Tract. de trinitate*, c. 13 (PL. 209, 588–90). Also Robert, *Sent.* (1, 280, 282).

[4] *Sent.* (2, 65). Cf. Horst, *Die Trinitäts- u. Gotteslehre*, pp. 119–32.

[5] 'Hanc tamen . . . quidam reprehendere presumpsere. Quorum erat obstinata consuetudo omnia que scire non poterant sine omni discussione et absque omni rationis examinatione dampnare, ut ea sola catholica et fidei christiane consona viderentur, quorum ipsi se scientiam habere profitebantur', *Sent.* (2, 65).

[6] Robert's diatribe suggests that he did not act against Gilbert in order to

Robert intends to make plain the insufferable arrogance of his opponents and the frivolity of their objections[1] and he plays a game of cat and mouse, refusing to move straight into the kill but unleashing scorn and irony as he proceeds. Do the critics grant that Augustine supports these attributions or do they not? Perhaps they do not know of Augustine's teaching? If so they may not censure others. Perhaps they deny that Augustine gave this teaching? Then they may easily be convinced by Augustine's text. Or perhaps they consider that Augustine had erred? But Augustine made no confession of his error in the *Retractationes*.[2] The critics say that these distinctions between the persons render certain properties exclusive to certain persons, *specialiter ac proprie*. But this, the criticism of Bernard against Abelard,[3] is scarcely worthy of a reply. It receives, however, a lengthy and sarcastic reply.[4] Critics claim that the distinctions are dangerous because they are liable to lead to error or to be misinterpreted. Robert wonders who will be their misinterpreter. If the opposition itself misinterprets, they have no claims to authority. The church itself has made no condemnation.[5] What authority do the objectors accept? 'How can they say that the promoter of this opinion did not understand it well when they do not know how he understood it and when it was more likely that he would have a catholic rather than an erroneous or unorthodox meaning, given that he was a catholic doctor who gave it and a celebrated authority in the holy church, namely Aurelius

---

[1] 'Primum itaque eos esse arrogantie intolerabilis ostendamus, deinde quam frivola sit ratio quam obiciunt', *Sent.* (2, 66).

[2] *Sent.* (2, 66). Cf. *Sent.* (1, 277 and 2, 79–82).

[3] *Epist.* 190, c. 3 (PL. 182, 1059B). Cf. William of St Thierry, *Disputatio adversus Abael.*, c. 2 (PL. 180, 250B–1A).   [4] *Sent.* (2, 67–8).

[5] *Sent.* (2, 69). Horst, *Die Trinitäts- u. Gotteslehre*, p. 122 suggests that this passage indicates that Robert did not view the condemnation at Sens as an authoritative condemnation of the *predicta assignatio*. This is correct in the sense that the condemnation did not proscribe all use of the ternary of power, wisdom and love, but did exclude the inequalities within the Trinity which resulted from a particular use of the ternary. Bernard and William, however, had attacked the use of the ternary in general.

---

please Bernard; John of Salisbury (*Hist. Pont.*, c. 8, (ed. Chibnall, p. 16)) wondered whether this was one of his reasons.

Augustine.'¹ The hammering is slow and ponderous, but it
should not delude the reader into imagining that Robert himself
has demonstrated that he has Augustine's support. He does not
quote Augustine.² He takes what Abelard and the Victorines
taught for granted. The association of power, wisdom and goodness with the persons respectively, although suggested by Augustine,³ needs to be demonstrated as Abelard did demonstrate it
by the discussion of texts; it is not self evident. Robert is somewhat more effective in dealing with the objection, made by
Bernard,⁴ that power cannot be attributed *proprie ac specialiter*
to the Father if it is common to the three persons. He admits that
the special appropriation of a common name usually implies
a special excellence, as is the case when we call Paul simply
'the Apostle' in regard to his excellence as a preacher. In the
Trinity, on the other hand, there is equality between the persons.⁵
However, in Scripture many of the divine operations, which
are common to the whole Trinity, are attributed to particular
persons and the suggestion that Scripture should not name one
of the persons rather than another when referring to particular
operations of the Trinity astounds Robert. It is the custom of
Scripture to use names common to all the persons in distinguishing
between the persons; 'Deus genuit Deum' (*Ps.* 2, 7) is a reference
first to the Father and next to the Son.⁶ Moreover, Maximus
provides support for affirming that it is because the Father is
unbegotten that power is particularly attributed to him. Otherwise
we would say, falsely, that the Son or Spirit is *potens ex se*.⁷
Robert agrees with Abelard that only the Father has power and
being from himself alone, but whereas Abelard had indicated a
difference in the *modus substantiae* or the *modus subsistendi* of the
persons,⁸ Robert more carefully suggests that this difference

¹ *Sent.* (2, 69).
² Cf. Horst, *Die Trinitäts- u. Gotteslehre*, pp. 120–1, 125.
³ *De Trinitate*, xv, 17, nn. 27–31 (PL. 42, 1079–82).
⁴ Cf. above, pp. 118, 133.
⁵ *Sent.* (2, 71–4)
⁶ *Sent.* (2, 76–9).
⁷ *Sent.* (2, 82–3). Cf. Maximus, *Hom. LXXXIII de traditione symboli* (PL.
57, 433–4).   ⁸ Cf. above, pp. 132–3.

between the power of the Father on the one hand and of the Son and Spirit on the other reveals the diversity of the persons only and not that there are various *modi habendi potentiam* in God.[1] Unlike Abelard, Robert also regards divine power, wisdom and goodness to be susceptible of mutual predication; not only is the divine wisdom divine power, but also divine goodness is divine power and divine power is divine goodness.[2] For Robert, as for Abelard, the attraction of these attributions is that however God is described they are invoked. To speak of his eternity, immensity and incorruptibility is to indicate his power; his knowledge and providence are his wisdom and his meekness and mercy are his goodness. These attributes perfectly distinguish the Trinity.[3]

Why did Robert indulge in such ponderous polemic against Bernard of Clairvaux? U. Horst has suggested that the relationship of pupil to master (if, indeed, we can be sure that Robert was ever a pupil and not merely a hearer of Abelard) is partly explanatory and he has underlined that Robert was engaged in a broad attempt to establish ways in which natural reason, under grace, can know the Trinity.[4] Another possible cause for Robert's strong feeling is that Bernard's criticisms of Abelard, which could not have been wholly accepted even by the Victorines, had gone unanswered, except for Abelard's own *Apologia*, and were in some respects extreme and misconceived.

---

[1] 'Unde cum dicitur, Filius hoc modo potens est quia a solo Patre est, non modus distinguitur quo nec Pater nec Spiritus sanctus potens sit, sed Persona ostenditur que nec Pater nec Spiritus sanctus est', *Sent.* (2, 85). Later in an inedited part of the *Sent.*, cod. Bruges, Bibl. de la ville 191, ff. 79vb–81rb (cf. Horst, *Die Trinitäts- u. Gotteslehre*, pp. 246–51) Robert develops further implications of Abelard's thesis. Power, the special attribute of the Father who is *ex se potens* and the common attribute of the three persons, also *is* the Trinity. The Trinity is powerful by its power and by the Father. Each person is powerful *ex ea Trinitate*.

[2] *Sent.* (1, 277).

[3] *Sent.* (1, 277–8). S. Otto, *Die Funktion des Bildbegriffes in der Theologie*, pp. 83 *et seq.*, has underlined that Robert diverges from Abelard in returning, through the Victorines, to the triads *mens–notitia–amor* and *memoria–intelligentia–dilectio* which in Augustine's psychology were more fully developed than *potentia–sapientia–charitas* which Abelard employed in an aprioristic way.

[4] Horst, *Die Trinitäts- u. Gotteslehre*, pp. 129–30.

Robert was very much occupied with Abelard's thought concerning the operation of divine power. In the *Questiones de divina pagina* he raised four questions which he briefly considered here and again at a much greater length in the Sentences.[1] The first of his questions in the *Questiones de divina pagina* is whether God can do now all that he can do. He offers two lines of thought between which he does not choose. If God can in fact do now an infinity of things, there remains nothing left for the exercise of his power. If on the other hand he can only do some things now, he is not omnipotent[2]. In the Sentences Robert puts a similar question: can God do all that he can do? If he did, his power would be terminated; so Robert slightly qualifies this answer by saying that God can do whatever it is possible to do.[3]

In his second question concerning divine power in the *Questiones de divina pagina* Robert asks whether God can do less well what he in fact does.[4] Here Robert is turning upside down Abelard's question whether God can do what he does better than he does. Robert indicates a line of thought according to which God's capacity to do something less well involves the capacity to do it still less well again and so on *ad infinitum* where (or so Robert rather curiously believes) the point is reached at which further deterioration is impossible. At this stage God's power is terminated. In the Sentences Robert establishes two limits (*termini*) to God's power, the *summum malum* on the one hand and the *summum bonum* on the other; God cannot do what is *summum malum*.[5] The third of the series of questions in the *Questiones de divina pagina* puts the corollary to the previous question: can God do better than he does?[6] If he can, then he can do everything in-

---

[1] *Sent., lib.* I, *pars* vii, c. 1–29 are inedited and I follow U. Horst, *Die Trinitäts- u. Gotteslehre*, pp. 207–51, in his exact analysis of Robert's thought and in his plentiful illustration from cod. Bruges, Bibl. de la ville, 191, ff. 69vb–75rb. Horst does not, incidentally, relate the teaching of the Sentences to the *Questiones de divina pagina*, 52–5, ed. Martin, *Oeuvres*, I, 29–8 (= QDP, 52–5 (28–9)).

[2] QDP, 52 (28).

[3] Cod. Bruges 191, ff. 71rb, 74va; cf. Horst, *op. cit.*, pp. 221–2.

[4] QDP, 53 (28–9).

[5] Cod. Bruges 191, ff. 71rb, 74vb; cf. Horst, *op. cit.*, p. 222.

[6] QDP, 54 (29).

U

creasingly better until the *summum bonum* is reached when either his power is terminated or an equal is made; both alternatives are inconvenient. However, to say that God cannot do or make the *summum bonum* is not to dispose of the question whether he can do things better, and in the Sentences Robert gives Abelard's thesis, that God cannot do better than he does, a most thorough refutation.[1] Abelard had invoked Plato; Robert retorts that Plato is not a certain authority.[2] The Platonic thesis that the world is perfect is an affirmation that the totality of creation could not be made better; it does not entail that every particular aspect of creation cannot be made better. The perfection of the whole world is in fact evaluated by comparison with the lesser perfection of its particular contents. Moreover, the perfection of the Creator does not necessarily entail the perfection of his works. It is true that Augustine wrote that God could not engender a better Son,[3] but this is inapplicable to anything other than the Son. It is also true that Augustine considered that God would be failing if he did not do what he did as well as possible,[4] but this must be considered as a human manner of speech.

In the fourth and last of Robert's series of questions in the *Questiones de divina pagina* Robert firmly pronounces against Abelard that God can do what he does not will to do and that he can do many things which he does not do.[5] In the Sentences he gives the same question an exhaustive consideration.[6] He affirms the equality of the divine power and the divine will, but God's will is not restricted by his power. His power, moreover, is only

---

[1] Cod. Bruges 191, ff. 69vb–72ra; Horst, *op. cit.*, pp. 207–11.

[2] It would be wrong to infer from this and from Robert's lack of theological interest in the world-soul that he was anti-Platonic. In general he is enthusiastic for Plato; cf. *Sent.*, (1, 296) on the eternal generation of the Son, (1, 245, 265) on the excellence of the *Timaeus*, (1, 211–2) on creation.

[3] 'Deus, quem genuit, quoniam meliorem se generare non potuit (nihil enim Deo melius), generare debuit aequalem. Si enim voluit et non potuit, infirmus est: si potuit et non voluit, invidus est', *Lib. Quaestionum LXXXIII*, c. 50 (PL. 40, 31–2).

[4] 'Si mundum Deus facere potuisset meliorem et noluisset, invidus esset, si voluisset et non potuisset, inpotens esset', *De Genesi ad litteram*, IV, 16 (PL. 34, 307).

[5] QDP, 55 (29).

[6] Cod. Bruges 191, ff. 70ra–75r; cf. Horst, *Die Trinitäts- u. Gotteslehre*, p. 211.

restricted by his will in the sense that God can will no evil and in the sense that God acts only with reason and cause. The Victorines come to mind when Robert insists that God is bound by no *debitum* or *necessitas* which prevents him from doing what he does not do or from not doing what he does.[1] It is not true that it is always wrong not to do what it would be just to do. There are many things which can be done with equal utility; the selection of some of these and the non-selection of others is made because it is convenient for God to do so; he is not obliged to do all such things.

It is a pronounced feature of Robert's writing in the Sentences that he attempts to exhaust all the possibilities of thought and meaning before he finally accepts or rejects an argument. Although the stimulus of Abelard's reasoning or that of the Victorines is perceptible in his discussion of the attributions to the persons and of the operation of divine power, Robert broadens the framework of argument. As U. Horst has remarked,[2] although Robert refutes Abelard's thesis on the operation of divine power, it is through Abelard's acuteness that a problem was raised with so many implications; in affirming the sovereignty of God Robert throughout tackles questions which arose from Abelard's thesis.

Robert also owes a great debt to Abelard in his thought on the person and natures of Christ and on the redemption. Like the Lombard, whose opponent Robert was in Christological matters, he used Abelard's arguments and considered questions which Abelard had raised. In particular he focused his attention upon linguistic problems and the meaning of such propositions as 'man is God' and 'God is man'. For Robert such statements are valid provided we do not mean that 'this' is 'that' and absorb the subject into the predicate. The proposition 'God is man', unlike the proposition 'Socrates is a man', means that God has united to himself a man or that the Word has assumed a man. This critique is like Abelard's, but whereas the result of Abelardian analysis was to pronounce the *locutiones* under discussion to be improper, Robert, guided perhaps by Victorine stimulus, continues to accept their soundness: 'bene tamen dicitur, quod Deus

[1] Cf. above, p. 209. [2] *Die Trinitäts- u. Gotteslehre*, pp. 224–8.

est homo'.[1] John of Cornwall hailed him as a supporter of the *assumptus* theory.[2] Robert also criticized the theory which was cultivated by some members of Abelard's school that Christ had parts; this Robert considers, somewhat mysteriously, to be an error and a heresy which died with the death of its author.[3]

Like Abelard Robert stresses that the divine choice of the way of the Cross, more than any other possible way of redeeming mankind, leads man to humility and inspires him with love for God.[4] Robert argues that Christ did not pay a price to the devil for man's redemption. A recompense is that which is paid to one who is injured, but the power that the devil exercised over mankind as gaoler and torturer was held only during the judge's pleasure. Christ was a victim offered to God; his death diminished the power of the devil by granting to man the humility and love with which to resist the devil.[5] In his own argument Abelard had attempted to show that the price of satisfaction for Adam's sin was paid to God, but he neglected to describe from whom man was redeemed; Robert is clear that man was redeemed from the yoke of the devil, his authorized gaoler and tormenter.

Robert reports and criticizes Hugh's opinion, among those of others, that original sin is concupiscence of evil and ignorance of good.[6] He also reports Abelard's opinion, which he says is held

---

[1] QEP (10–11). Cf. QDP, 63 (33).

[2] 'Eorum . . . super his . . . scripta . . . non legi sed multis eorum lectionibus et disputationibus interfui, in quibus et de homine assumpto et de aliis quibusdam magistri Petri Lombardi doctrinam falsitatis arguebant ne dicam erroris' *Eulogium*, c. 5 (ed. Haring, p. 268).

[3] See the abbreviation of an inedited part of the Sentences published by F. Anders, *Die Christologie des Robert von Melun*, p. 58; also Anders' introduction, *ibid.*, p. lix.

[4] QEP (62–3, 266, 295).

[5] QEP (64–7, 92); also the abbreviation of the Sentences published by Anders, *op. cit.*, pp. 13–15 (cf. Anders' introduction, p. xxiii). For the Sentences themselves I have used cod. British Museum, Royal 2. F. 1, f. 207vb. Cf. J. Rivière, *Le Dogme de la rédemption*, pp. 184–6, 232–7.

[6] QEP (84). The teaching of the Sentences is inedited and I follow its description by R. M. Martin, 'Les idées de Robert de Melun sur le péché originel' (1913) together with Martin's illustrations from cod. Bruges 191. On Hugh's opinion cf. Bruges 191, ff. 243r–4v and Martin, *op. cit.*, pp. 703–5. Robert also rejects the view that original sin is 'inobedientia primi hominis' (Bruges 191, ff. 244v–5r) and 'languor nature' (Bruges 191, ff. 245r–v) and considers the view

by very many, that original sin in us is not concupiscence but the guilt for which eternal punishment is owing or the debt for which man is held to be guilty until he is baptized. He considers Abelard's opinion to be worse than Pelagianism and asks why, if the descendants of Adam do not inherit his sin, the debt or the penalty should be imputed to them.[1] Perhaps Robert takes insufficiently into account Abelard's distinction between the *culpa* of the first parents and the absence of that *culpa* or fault but the presence of sin nonetheless in their descendants; there can, however, be no mistaking the object of his criticism. In his turn Robert offers a definition of original sin in us as the proneness to sin which the soul contracts on union with the corrupt body. The corruption of the body is vice and of the soul, sin. He implies that the authors of the rejected opinions were confused by the variety of their own vocabulary.[2] Robert is nonetheless personally concerned with the precise meaning of the notion of sin and his own distinctions of the meanings of sin are based upon Abelard's.[3] Like Abelard, Robert in glossing *Romans* 2, 6 ('qui reddet unicuique secundum opera eius') interprets *opus* as *voluntas* and teaches that the quality of works depends on the intention or will of the doer.[4] Robert similarly asks whether, when Paul zealously persecuted the church, his zeal rendered his persecution worthy, and like Abelard he distinguishes between the will and the intention. By his zeal Paul earned merit for his will was good, but the intention was not pure because its object was wrong.[5] However, in his discussion of involuntary sin Robert departs somewhat from Abelard. He considers the case of a man who throws a stone and accidentally kills another. To Abelard such a

[1] Bruges 191, f. 245v. Cf. R. M. Martin, 'Les idées de Robert' (1913), pp. 711–16. Abelard's teaching was also criticized in the *Quaestiones super epistolas Pauli* written by a disciple of Robert, qu. 104 (PL. 175, 460).

[2] Bruges 191, f. 249r–v; cf. R. M. Martin, 'Les idées de Robert' (1913), pp. 723–5. Also QEP (84).

[3] QDP, 7 (6); QEP (54–5). Cf. Abelard, *Expos. in 'ad Romanos'*, II (PL. 178, 866BC); *Ethica*, c. 14 (654AB).

[4] QEP (41). Cf. *Expos. in 'ad Romanos'*, I (810A).

[5] QDP, 6 (5); QEP (164–5). Cf. *Ethica*, c. 11–13 (PL. 178, 652–3).

that it is 'fomes peccati' or 'membrorum lex' or 'concupiscentia' (Bruges 191, ff. 247r–8v; Martin, *op. cit.*, pp. 716–23).

killing, which is not accompanied by consent, would not be sin. But Robert argues that the man who threw the stone sinned because his action proceeded from a prior evil will of which he may even have been unaware.[1] This is a curious deviation from an otherwise sympathetic following of Abelard's analysis of sin. Elsewhere he quotes approvingly an 'authority' who declares that our works do not avail to 'much' good or evil[2] and perhaps here Robert has Abelard again in mind, although Abelard had been concerned to show that works themselves earn no merit or blame. In signalling the imperfection of ecclesiastical courts which judge an accused by external evidence alone, Robert may again have had Abelard in his mind, for Abelard made the same point.[3]

On grace Robert mentions three opinions. The first is that a root of charity exists in some men which enables them to achieve eternal life when grace is offered to them; this is dismissed as heresy. The second is that God gives grace in common to all and salvation or damnation is consequent upon grasping or not grasping it. To take hold of the proferred grace requires another grace, but this establishes an infinite series of graces, each required to enable a man to grasp the previously offered grace, and no place is therefore left for merit. The third opinion is that grace is offered to man and he must grasp it. Without grace there would be no merit, but man nonetheless must exert himself to grasp it. Robert presents the parallel of a man who is trapped in a well and who cannot be pulled out by the rope which is offered to him unless he himself takes hold of it. But Robert warns against this opinion also.[4] The analogy is equivalent to Abelard's simile of the doctor and the patient and, like Robert, Abelard did not in his commentary on Romans say that the man in need of help assists himself,[5] although one of his followers did say this.[6] But Robert, like Abelard, has also rejected the theory of enabling graces with the rejection of the second opinion and it still remained for him

---

[1] QDP, 92 (47); QEP (96). Cf. *Expos. in 'ad Romanos'*, III (894C *et seq.*).
[2] QEP (81).   [3] QEP (161). Cf. *Ethica*, c. 5 (648A–C).
[4] QEP (124): 'Unde et hec sententia cavenda est.'
[5] *Expos. in 'ad Romanos'*, II (918).   [6] Cf. above, pp. 162–3.

to show that the soul has a natural power to do good which is not independent of the assistance provided by grace. To show this Robert presents a rather lovely simile of the sun's ray which touches the human eye. If the eye is shut, the ray is repelled; if it is open, the eye sees the ray. Sight will not come unless the eye is touched by the ray and when it is touched, it sees by its own nature. Similarly the soul has the natural power of doing good, but it cannot exercise this power unless it is touched with the splendour of grace; when it is touched, it acts and earns merit. Robert also offers another simile of a young man who has a natural capacity to walk, but needs someone to guide him in doing so; likewise the ability to ride a horse cannot be exercised without a horse.[1] Robert appears by these similes to be building upon Abelard's rejection of enabling graces a new theory which closely combines natural power and the virtue of grace.

On the power of the keys Robert quotes the Abelardian opinion that there is only one key, namely the power of binding and loosing; the knowledge that should accompany the conferring of the key does not belong to every priest. To this Robert responds coolly that Christ knew what he was doing and that the person on whom he conferred the keys had small knowledge or none.[2] He also reports the opinion of some that to bind and loose is to show that someone has been bound or loosed; the lepers healed by Christ showed themselves to priests. Robert himself prefers to say that men are bound or loosed by priests when it is fitting that they should be.[3] In this way he preserves a real, as distinct from declaratory, power of binding and loosing sin, but without involving in this power the errors of priestly judgment. Robert also believes that the penitent is forgiven in contrition, but it is a condition of forgiveness that he does not neglect to be released by a priest from the debt of external satisfaction.[4] Abelard had not included this condition in his evaluation of the effectiveness of contrition in the remission of sin.

The striking feature of Robert's debt to Abelard is the independence of judgment with which he pursues his discussion of Abelard's theses. He is much less guided by the Victorine

[1] QEP (124–6). [2] QDP, 26 (16). [3] QDP (16–17). [4] QDP, 72 (37–8).

example in criticism of Abelard than is Peter Lombard and even less guided by Bernard of Clairvaux or by the council of Sens. It is no exaggeration to say that Robert's disagreements with Abelard present him with the opportunity to develop vigorously either counter-theses of his own or theses which incorporate the foundations and premises of Abelard's own discussions. In one sense Robert is, for all his divergences of views, Abelard's most authentic follower, for Abelard had wished to develop his own opinions on certain problems without the obligation to accept that these were the only possible opinions which could be formulated or that they were meant to be always right. Robert seems to regard many of Abelard's teachings as opinions which sometimes seem right and sometimes wrong, but which do not, when they are wrong, need to be denigrated in a moralistic fashion. Of his Trinitarian teaching U. Horst has concluded that Robert was second to none in detecting Abelard's weaknesses and in the subtlety of his own answers.[1] In influence, however, he ranks behind Peter Lombard.[2] Robert is a difficult thinker to read who often becomes weighed down with the effort of his own reasoning and with the fineness of his own distinctions.

[1] *Die Trinitäts- u. Gotteslehre*, p. 32. John of Cornwall said of Robert 'in theologia certissimum est nichil hereticum docuisse', *Eulogium*, c. 4 (ed. Haring, p. 268).

[2] On Robert's influence see Horst, *Die Trinitäts- u. Gotteslehre*, pp. 318–27; Martin, *Oeuvres*, II, xlvi–liv; Landgraf, *Introducción*, pp. 116–19.

CHAPTER XIII

RICHARD OF ST VICTOR

Richard of St Victor (d. 1173) seems to exert an ever increasing fascination over students of the theological literature of the twelfth century. He was most active as a writer in the fifties and sixties,[1] which were no period of calm, yet, daring and influential as he was, he, like Hugh, engaged in no known public controversy and aroused no recorded antagonism.

Recent historians have been unanimous in underlining Richard's unusual sense of proportion. Formerly B. Hauréau described Richard and other Victorines as mystics who had turned their backs upon philosophy,[2] while another writer, T. Heitz, reproached Richard for being too influenced by Abelard's excessively rationalist appeal.[3] But more recent writers have almost without exception praised in Richard the admirably balanced union of scholasticism and mysticism.[4]

In some respects Richard approaches theological speculation as a philosopher, moving through the sensible to the world above sense and proving the Trinity by an analysis of the notion of charity. He is rightly considered an important figure in his own right in the history of medieval philosophy.[5] In the *De trinitate*

---

[1] J. Ribaillier, in his introduction to his edition of Richard's *De trinitate*, pp. 11–13, finds it impossible to settle when it was written; it is a mature work finished perhaps over the course of several years.

[2] 'Ce système, c'est en deux mots, le mépris, la négation même de la philosophie', *Histoire de la philosophie scolastique*, I, 513.

[3] Reference from G. Fritz, 'Richard de S. Victor', cols. 2691–2. I have been unable to obtain T. Heitz, *Essai historique sur les rapports entre la philosophie et la foi de Bérenger de Tours à S. Thomas d'Aquin* (Paris, 1909).

[4] 'La spéculation trinitaire se lie à l'idéal d'une vie mystique', P. Vignaux, *La Pensée au moyen âge*, p. 61; 'das connubium von Scholastik und Mystik', Grabmann, *Geschichte*, II, 310; 'nicht bloss ein kontemplativer, sondern auch ein philosophischer Genius', *ibid.*, p. 315; 'Scholastiker und Mystiker zugleich', B. Geyer, *Patristische und Scholastische Philosophie*, p. 267.

[5] Cf. Geyer, *Patristische u. Scholastische Philosophie*, pp. 267–71; G. Dumeige, 'Efforts métaphysiques chez Richard de S. Victor'; Vignaux, *La Pensée au moyen âge*, chapter 2.

he is conscious of the possibilities of equivocity: 'utrobique dictio una, sed ratio nominis diversa'.[1] A master of allegory and famous as the author of the two *Benjamins*, Richard was also a technical expositor of the literal difficulties found in Scripture and the author of an *Expositio difficultatum suborientium in expositione tabernaculi foederis*, of a *Concordia temporum regnorum congregantium super Judam et super Israel* and of an *Explicatio aliquorum passuum difficilium Apostoli*. He inevitably reminds us of Abelard by his desire to formulate commonsense rules for the interpretation of the sense of the *auctoritates*.[2]

Richard also shared with Abelard a concern to affirm explicitly the value of a rational approach to theology. In the *De trinitate* he wrote: 'I have read of my God that he is one and triune . . . All this I frequently hear or read but how it is proved I do not remember reading. Authorities exist in abundance—not so arguments.'[3] Richard is not as thorough-going as Abelard in the place which he accords to natural theology and he does not, for example, succumb to the allure of pagan philosophy.[4] His standpoint is rather Anselmian, but the road from Anselm of Canterbury to Richard passed by not only Achard[5] but also Abelard. The first two books of his *De trinitate* rise from contingent being, by means of the principle of causality, to the idea of supreme substance and to the study of the divine attributes of eternity, immensity, simplicity and so on. Without the impetuosity of an Abelard, Richard continues in this work to supply what was incomplete in patristic tradition. He writes in the third book that in his remaining enquiries he must adopt greater diligence and proceed with greater earnestness according as he finds less

[1] II, 13 (ed. Ribaillier, p. 120; PL. 196, 908D). G. Dumeige confidently describes this as a trace of Abelard, *Richard de S. Victor et l'idée chrétienne de l'amour*, p. 20.

[2] 'Si ea quae de lege ab Apostolo diversis in locis dicuntur ad invicem conferantur, multa eis contrarietas inesse videtur. Videtur namque esse contrarius sibi ipsi, contrarius rationi, contrarius veritati, et quod his omnibus amplius est, sententiae ipsius Domini', *Explicatio* (PL. 196, 665AB).

[3] *De trinitate*, I, 5 (ed. Ribaillier, pp. 90–1; PL. 196, 893BC).

[4] Cf. *Benjamin major*, II, 2 (PL. 196, 81AB).

[5] Cf. Ribaillier, in the introduction to his edition of the *De trin.*, pp. 27–33.

in the writings of the Fathers to support the testimony of reason.[1] In his commentary upon the book of Ezechiel he insists that we must supply what the Fathers have omitted to discuss, although had they done this, their contribution would be worthier than that of any modern. Reverence for the Fathers does not oblige us to ignore what they ignored.[2] Perhaps Richard is declaring the end of the prolongation of the patristic era.

Richard surpassed Abelard in deep spiritual insight and purpose. As A. M. Ethier remarked, Richard is neither an artist nor a poet, neither historian nor philosopher, but a theologian of the spiritual life.[3] It is difficult to discuss his theological achievement in relation to the activities of the French schools. He is at once withdrawn from the circles of academic masters and yet full of contemporary relevance. From Anselm of Canterbury he derived the desire to understand what is believed and the search for necessary reasons.[4] His writings stand under the shadow of the influence of Hugh, whom Richard thought the leading theologian of the time.[5] He opposed Gilbert Porreta. He chastized

---

[1] 'Oportet autem in his que ad querendum restant tanto majorem diligentiam inpendere eoque ardentius insistere quanto minus in Patrum scriptis invenitur unde possimus ista . . . ex rationis attestatione convincere', III, I (ed. Ribaillier, p. 135; PL. 196, 915D).

[2] '. . . Hinc contigisse arbitror, ut litterae expositionem in obscurioribus quibusdam locis antiqui Patres tacite praeterirent, vel paulo negligentius tractarent, qui si plenius insisterent multo perfectius procul dubio, quam aliquis ex modernis id potuissent. Sed nec illud tacite praetereo, quod quidam quasi ob reverentiam Patrum nolunt ab illis omissa attentare, ne videantur aliquid ultra majores praesumere . . . Nos autem a Patribus pertractata cum omni aviditate suscipiamus, et ab ipsis omissa cum omni alacritate perquiramus, et sagaciter inventa cum omni liberalitate in commune proferamus', *Prolog.* (PL. 196, 527CD). [3] *Le De Trinitate de Richard de S. Victor*, p. 8.

[4] 'Satagamus, in quantum possumus, ut intelligamus quod credimus . . . Nitamur semper, in quantum fas est vel fieri potest, comprehendere ratione quod tenemus ex fide', *De Trin., Prolog.* (ed. Ribaillier, p. 81; PL. 196, 889). 'Erit itaque intentionis nostre in hoc opere ad ea que credimus, in quantum Dominus dederit, non modo probabiles sed etiam necessarias rationes adducere et fidei nostre documenta veritatis enodatione et explanatione condire', *De Trin.*, I, 4 (ed. Ribaillier, p. 89; PL. 196, 892C).

[5] 'Praecipuus ille nostri temporis theologus', *Benjamin major*, I, 4 (PL. 196, 67D); 'Magni illius (magistrum Hugonem loquor) nostri temporis theologi sententia', *De spiritu blasphemiae* (1189B). G. Dumeige, on the other hand (*Richard de S. Victor*, p. 12), considers this to be curiously small praise.

Peter Lombard scornfully; of one of his opinions Richard re-marked that 'it is so ludicrous that it seems we must jeer rather than refute it'.[1] Yet Richard could also make important borrow-ings from the censured Abelard.

Richard leaned towards Abelard in his use of the divine attri-butes of power, wisdom and goodness. In his *De tribus appro-priatis* he answered one Master Bernard who had asked why in Scripture power, wisdom and goodness were attributed *specialiter* to the Father, Son and Spirit. Richard prefaced his reply with a caution, no doubt mindful of earlier troubles.[2] But he reaffirms that the attributions are warranted by tradition.[3] With Richard, as with Robert of Melun[4] and Peter Lombard, Abelard's phrasing and expressions return to some favour after being subjected to disfavour at the time of the council of Sens. Richard nonetheless

---

[1] 'Tam frivola, ut ridenda videatur potius quam refellenda', *De potestate ligandi et solvendi*, c. 12 (PL. 196, 1168A). The reference is to Peter Lombard, *Sentences*, IV, 18, 6 (pp. 862–4). Richard also wrote in the *De trinitate*, VI, 22 (ed. Ribaillier, p. 259; PL. 196, 986D–7A): 'Multi temporibus nostris surrexere qui . . . contra sanctorum Patrum auctoritatem et tot attestationes paternarum traditionum audent negare . . . Nullo modo concedunt quod substantia gignat substantiam . . . Afferant, si possunt, auctoritatem, non dicam plures, sed saltem unam, que neget substantiam gignere substantiam.' Cf. Lombard, *Sent.*, I, 5, 1 (pp. 42–9), I, 4, 1 (pp. 39–40).

[2] 'Merito eiusmodi timere debuissem si nescirem apud quem in aure loquens sermonem seu sensum effunderem. Tibi utique; tibi, inquam, libenter dico quod sentio', PL. 196, 993D.

[3] 'Quoniam ergo in potentia exprimitur proprietas ingeniti, speciali quodam considerationis modo merito ascribatur illi. Sed quoniam in sapientia expri-mitur proprietas geniti, merito et illa iuxta eundem modum ascribitur ipsi. Item, quia in bonitate proprietas Spiritus sancti invenitur, merito et ei bonitas specialius assignatur', 994CD. The passage is almost exactly reproduced in the *De trin.*, VI, 15: 'Libet me hoc loco repetere quod recolo me alias scripsisse . . . ', ed. Ribaillier, p. 247; PL. 196, 979B–80B. Cf. also the *De spiritu blasphemiae*, 'in Scripturis sanctis specialiter attribuitur potentia Patri, sapientia Filio, bonitas vero Spiritui sancto', PL. 196, 1187C; also the *De statu interioris hominis*, II, 3: 'Nam quamvis una eademque sit potentia, sapientia et bonitas Patris, et Filii, et Spiritus sancti, secundum quemdam tamen modum loquendi in quibusdam Scripturae locis, potentia Patri, sapientia Filio, benignitas Spiritui sancto (quasi specialiter) videntur assignari', 1148B. Cf. L. Ott, *Untersuchungen*, pp. 569–94, and G. Salet, in his edition of the *De trinitate*, pp. 500–3.

[4] For R. M. Martin, 'Pro Petro Abaelardo', p. 333 (cited in Ott, *Untersuchun-gen*, p. 592, n. 51), Richard's view was 'simplement l'écho des leçons professées sur la question par Robert de Melun'.

takes care to avoid inventing various *modi* by which the attributes belong to particular persons; he insists that the *modus* by which the Father has power is the same as that by which the Son has wisdom.[1] Unlike Hugh or Robert, Richard does not find in the appropriations a mere convenience, correcting for example any tendency to represent the Father as infirm or the Son as inexperienced. With Abelard Richard finds that power, wisdom and goodness are related to each other by what they are and these relationships correspond with those which exist between the divine persons. Power is prior to wisdom and goodness; wisdom depends on power and goodness; the good will is nothing without wisdom with which to discern good and evil.[2]

Richard possibly owes another debt of greater magnitude to Abelard's Trinitarian thought. His demonstration in the *De trinitate*[3] why there are three divine persons includes an argument which asserts the fact of a plurality of divine persons. Richard proceeds from the idea that God is supreme charity. But charity requires a plurality of persons; love has to be extended from one person to another and supreme charity necessitates a plurality of divine persons. 'Oportet itaque ut amor in alterum tendat, ut caritas esse queat.'[4] This sentence, as has long been known,[5] is an unacknowledged quotation from a sermon by Gregory the Great.[6] Here Gregory explains that the sending forth by Christ of his disciples in pairs exemplifies both love of God and love of one's neighbour, for charity cannot exist between less than two persons.[7] Gregory therefore excludes self-love from this notion of charity. He was not, however, writing about the Trinity. Recently an English scholar, John Bligh, has noticed that Gregory's idea of charity had been applied to the Trinity

---

[1] *De tribus appropriatis*, cited above, p. 303, n. 3.   [2] *Ibid.*

[3] III, 2 (ed. Ribaillier, pp. 136–7; PL. 196, 916C–7B).

[4] *Ibid.* (ed. Ribaillier, p. 136; PL. 196, 916D).

[5] Cf. Ethier, *Le De Trinitate de Richard*, p. 91, n. 2; F. Guimet, 'Notes en marge d'un texte de Richard', p. 376.

[6] *Homilia in Evang.*, I, 17 (PL. 76, 1139A).

[7] 'Minus quam inter duos charitas haberi non potest. Nemo enim proprie ad semetipsum habere charitatem dicitur, sed dilectio in alterum tendit, ut charitas esse possit', *ibid.*

before Richard did so and by Abelard.[1] Abelard used Gregory's notion on several occasions and he may have been Richard's source, although Richard and Abelard did not share exactly the same purpose. Abelard did not demonstrate from this the plurality of divine persons as such, but he illustrated the procession of the Spirit who is love and love extends itself to another.[2] For Abelard as for Richard the mutual aspect of charity is important, and in the opening of the *Theologia 'Scholarium'* Abelard, following Cicero, defined love as good will towards another on his behalf rather than our own.[3]

The influence of Abelard upon Richard's *De trinitate* should not, however, be overstated; it is not 'ubiquitous' as has been suggested.[4] In particular Richard probably did not owe to Abelard his joke that he seems to hear Balaam's ass (Numbers 22) telling him that if God could make an ass speak for him, he could doubtless give Richard the same benefit.[5] Abelard, who was perhaps less disposed to describe himself as an ass, uses the allusion

[1] 'Richard of St Victor's De Trinitate: Augustinian or Abelardian?', pp. 135–6.

[2] 'Charitas autem, teste Gregorio.... Procedere itaque Dei est sese ad aliquam rem per affectum charitatis quodammodo extendere, ut eam videlicet diligat, ac se ei per amorem conjungat', *Theol. Christiana* (PL. 178, 1299CD). '... Spiritus ... procedere, hoc est se per charitatem ad alterum extendere, quia quodammodo per amorem unusquisque a seipso ad alterum procedit', *ibid.* (1300A). Cf. also *Theol. 'Schol.'*, II, 14 (1072B, 1072D–3A). On the extension of divine love to creation cf. also *Theol. 'Summi boni'*, III, 3 (ed. Ostlender, p. 103): 'Procedere itaque dei est se ad creaturas per affectum caritatis quodammodo extendere, ut eis gratiae suae dona largiatur.'

[3] 'Amicitia est voluntas erga aliquem rerum bonarum, ipsius illius causa quem diligit', I, 1 (982D). Cf. Cicero, *De Inventione*, II, 55. Abelard does not exclude self-love from his definition provided that its end is outside self: 'nequaquam peccamus nos amando; sed amoris ... finem in nobis collocando' (983B); 'nihil igitur amandum est ... nisi propter Deum, ut in Deo finem omnium constituamus' (983C).

[4] 'While reading the *Theologia Christiana* one has the impression of reading Richard's source book. Even his pedantic little jokes about Balaam's ass and Goliath's sword are borrowed from Abelard', Bligh, *op. cit.*, p. 136. In the edition by Ribaillier of the *De trinitate*, the list of authors actually cited by Richard does not include Abelard's name.

[5] 'Audio et ego adhuc loquentem et dicentem michi: "Qui quod loquerer potuit dare michi, poterit procul dubio dare et tibi",' III, 1 (ed. Ribaillier, p. 136; PL. 196, 916C).

to defend the thesis that God could also work through infidels.[1] Richard's source is more likely to be Gregory the Great who prefaces his *Moralia* with a similar modest disclaimer.[2]

In his discussion of the generation of the Son and specifically of the question whether substance engendered substance, Richard remarked that his opponents fly in the face of patristic testimony and turn the authorities against their correct interpreters, subduing Goliath with his own weapon: 'et in morem Golie gladium in quo jugulentur deferentes'.[3] Abelard promised Goliath's fate to his opponents and did so in different contexts from that of Richard;[4] in some of these Abelard quotes the words of Jerome[5] and it is therefore difficult to be confident that Abelard rather than Jerome was the cause of this further popularization of an already accessible allusion. In another passage, where Richard argues that divinity is incommunicable, he uses as a help to understanding the word 'Danielitas' which signifies that quality which belongs only to Daniel, unlike, for example, 'humanitas' which is common to others besides Daniel.[6] J. Bligh considers that Abelard is the source of Richard's idea and he refers to Abelard's commentary upon the Boethian exposition of Por-

---

[1] 'Bene autem et per indignos sive infideles maxima Deus operatur, qui verbis asini prophetam docuit', *Theol. 'Schol.'*, I, 15 (1007A). Cf. *Theol. Christiana*, I (1140D). The parallels discussed by Bligh with reference to the *Theol. Christiana* recurred in the *Theol. 'Schol'*.

[2] 'Fore quippe idoneum me ad ista desperavi ... Quid igitur mirum, si intellectum stulto homini praebeat, qui veritatem suam, cum voluerit, etiam per ora jumentorum narrat', *Moralium libri, Epistola missoria,* c. 2 (PL. 75, 512BC). This reference is given by G. Salet in his edition of the *De trin.*, p. 167, n. 5, though not by Ribaillier, p. 135 *in notis*.

[3] *De trin.*, VI, 22 (ed. Ribaillier, p. 259; PL. 196, 986D–7A). Cf. 1 *Kings* 17, 51.

[4] *Theol. 'Summi boni'*, II (ed. Ostlender, p. 36), *Theol. Christiana,* II, III, (1166D, 1212B, 1227C), *Theol. 'Schol.'*, II (1035C, 1040A).

[5] 'Didicerat enim a vero David, extorquere de manibus hostium gladium, et Goliae superbissimi caput proprio mucrone truncare', *Theol. 'Schol.'*, II (1035C). Cf. *Theol. Christiana,* II (1166D). Here Abelard is quoting Jerome, *Epist.* 70 (2e), (PL. 22, 665). The reference to Jerome is given by G. Salet, in his edition of the *De trin.*, p. 444, n. 2, who, however, adduces for comparison *Theol. Christiana,* III (1227C) where Abelard does not quote Jerome. Ribaillier, in his edition, p. 259 *in notis*, does not offer parallels.

[6] *De trin.*, II, 12 (ed. Ribaillier, pp. 118–20; PL. 196, 907C–8C).

phyry's *Isagoge*.[1] In fact on this particular point Abelard is merely following a discussion by Boethius in another commentary, that on Aristotle's *De interpretatione*, concerning 'Platonitas' which Boethius[2] and Abelard offer as an example of a *qualitas singularis*. Neither Boethius nor Abelard is here concerned with the Trinity.[3] As G. Dumeige justly remarked, Abelard in general exercised a distant influence upon Richard.[4]

Richard may, however, have been indebted to Abelard in some considerations of the nature of sin which he offered in the *De statu interioris hominis*, II, 2–4. Here he made a sharp distinction between vice and sin, seeing in vice that which leads us to consent to evil and therefore to commit sin.[5] Richard's expressions can be paralleled in both Abelard's *Ethica*[6] and in Hugh's *De sacramentis*.[7] Richard, however, also seems to follow the Abelardian tradition in distinguishing between venial and mortal sin and in considering the latter subjectively as a contempt of God.[8] According to both Richard and Hermann the difference between

[1] *Logica 'Ingredientibus'*, ed. Geyer, p. 64.

[2] *In Perihermenias, ed. secunda*, II, c. 7 (rec. Meiser, pp. 136–7).

[3] G. Salet in his edition of the *De trin.*, p. 128, n. 3 indicates that Marius Victorinus in *Adversus Arianos*, I, 52 (PL. 8, 1080) had applied the argument to the Trinity as had also Jerome and Cassiodore to whom he offers no references.

[4] *Richard de S. Victor*, p. 27.

[5] 'aliud est vitium atque aliud est peccatum . . . Vitium est ipse appetitus mali, qui solet praecedere vel provocare consensum, peccatum autem ipse est consensus mali', II, 2 (PL. 196, 1147AB).

[6] 'Vitium itaque est quo ad peccandum proni efficimur, hoc est inclinamur ad consentiendum ei quod non convenit, ut illud scilicet faciamus aut dimittamus. Hunc vero consensum proprie peccatum nominamus', c. 3 (PL. 178, 636A).

[7] 'Quando autem tentanti vitio consensus adhibetur actus injustitiae est quod peccatum dicitur. Itaque vitium est infirmitas spiritualis corruptionis, peccatum autem ex corruptione oriens per consensum actus iniquitatis . . . Actus vero peccati solo consensu perficitur, etiamsi foris opus non fuerit, quia quod iniquitatis est per consensum pravum in sola voluntate completur', II, 13, 1 (PL. 176, 525AB).

[8] 'In cogitatione vero peccatur mortaliter, vel voluntate peccandi, vel consentiendo delectationi cogitationis, et moram habendo in delectatione . . . Si enim duraverit ipsa delectatio ratione non consentiente, vel illam non advertente, mortalis non dicitur', *Explicatio in Cantica Canticorum*, c. 25 (PL. 196, 480A). 'Veniale quoque per contemptum fit mortale', *ibid.* (481D). For Abelard's views on consent and contempt see *Ethica*, c. 3 (PL. 178, 636).

mortal and venial sin lies in the fact that the former in itself alone suffices for damnation.[1]

Richard's debt to Abelard is, then, slight but interesting.[2] To say that Richard is 'le seul penseur (spirituel) qui ait compris et sauvé Abélard'[3] is perhaps to overstate the amount of attention which Richard accorded to Abelard's thought. No aspect of Abelard's thinking stimulated Richard in his writing to criticism or to a reformulation. He knew the need for caution in using Abelard's expression of the theory of divine appropriations. He borrowed too a few of Abelard's ethical considerations and he was very inspired by a text of Gregory which his eye had perhaps chanced upon in reading Abelard's *Theologia*. In this Richard serves to show that in mid century Abelard could be more favourably considered at St Victor. But in the elaboration of the distinctively Victorine mystical and doctrinal achievement Abelard's positive doctrinal influence was most restrained.

[1] 'Videtur mihi veniale peccatum quod in Christo renatis per se solum nunquam inducit aeternum supplicium, etiamsi defuerit poenitentiae remedium. Mortale vero peccatum etiamsi fuerit solum, si poenitentiae remedium defuerit, aeternam mortem inducit', *De differentia peccati mortalis et venialis* (PL. 196, 1193C). Cf. L. Ott, *Untersuchungen*, pp. 614-23, who considers this work to be addressed to Master Bernard. Cf. also the *Sententie* of Hermann, c. 33: 'Veniale dicitur, quod per se ad damnationem non sufficit ... Mortale vero illud peccatum, quod solum ad mortem sufficiens est', PL. 178, 1753D-4A.

[2] The *De superexcellenti baptismo Christi*, which appears among Richard's works in PL. 196, 1011-8, and which contains an attack on Christological nihilism (cf. L. Ott, *Untersuchungen*, pp. 641-51) is now considered by J. Chatillon ('Un sermon théologique de Gauthier de S. Victor') to be by Walter of St Victor.

[3] R. Javelet, 'Psychologie des auteurs spirituels', p. 223.

CHAPTER XIV

CONCLUSION

The twelfth century was notable for the activity which preceded and achieved the appearance of several books which came to be accepted as classical and standard manuals of the subjects of which they treated: the *Decretum* of Gratian, the *Summa super Priscianum* of Peter Helyas, the History of Peter Comestor, the Sentences and the Gloss of Peter Lombard. Abelard did not become such an authority even in logic or on account of his *Sic et Non*. His teaching, although wide ranging, was not everyone's guide to the sum of theological or logical knowledge. Nor could Abelard be accepted as an authoritative representative of faith. His scholarship and his mastery of source materials as well as his opinions caused his work to be remembered and consulted by the most prominent of his successors in the schools, but the condemnations had made clear that his teaching was to lack episcopal approval.

Abelard knew, perhaps better than his critics, that he was less a teacher of truth than an analyst and a reviewer of formulae and of the mass of *auctoritates*. His Confession of faith to Héloïse is a touchstone of his sincerity to uphold the teaching of Christ and the Apostles but in understanding that teaching he was most concerned to reveal and to elucidate problems, to reorganize the vocabulary of thought and to highlight what had been neglected or exaggerated among the themes contained in Scripture and the Fathers. He is 'one whose infallible instinct leads straight to dangerous questions and provoking replies'.[1] The challenge contained in such enquiries when cultivated by an intelligence of Abelard's power is an unusually demanding one in any academic society. To try to represent this teaching, as his closest disciples attempted, was to risk falsification by abbreviation. The interventions of a Bernard or a William of St Thierry, who tried to outlaw it, represent an opposite extreme of feeling and, largely, of

---

[1] E. Gilson, *Héloïse and Abelard*, p. 105.

falsification. But the condemnation of 1140, which Abelard's followers tried to prevent, does not appear to have occasioned as much participation by other masters of the schools as the trial of Gilbert in 1148. The masters were nonetheless faced with the task of determining their own attitudes towards Abelard.

The results of the condemnation of 1140 were mixed. Abelard was silenced but he continued to write. His reputation had received an adverse endorsement and only a Berengar protested violently and openly. But some Cardinals were offended by the proceedings and Bernard did not succeed as clearly with his prosecution of Gilbert. The analysis of the relations between the divine persons in the light of the divine attributes continued to appeal to certain minds, for example to Richard of St Victor; some of Bernard's criticisms were not heeded. The enthusiasm for what was thought to be Plato's teaching on God and particularly of the world-soul went out of fashion but was perhaps doomed to do so even without Abelard's condemnation. On the procession of the Spirit *ex* or *de substantia Patris* Bernard pushed Abelard to make a logical defence of his position which was correct and useless and his disciples were unable to follow him in devising a new language to express the Trinitarian relationships. Keen debates were occasioned in a rush to criticize Abelard's thesis on the operation of the divine power. Discussion of Abelard's considerations of the interior aspects of morality continued although the condemnation of the thesis that actions being morally indifferent earn neither merit nor blame, marked an acceptable boundary for such discussion. His thesis on original sin and on grace was buried, but the implications remained to provoke debate. His emphasis on the exemplarist aspects of Christ's work was slow to find its way into the general current of teaching and perhaps because of the manner in which Abelard originally propounded it.

The negative reaction to Abelard is well documented, but the condemnation left work for others to do. It seems that those closest to Hugh had not constituted a *via media* between Abelard and Bernard nor did they generally filter his teachings to collect what was useful and to discard what was unacceptable. On the contrary, Hugh and the author of the *Summa Sententiarum* raised a flag of determined opposition based upon a more thorough understanding of what Abelard taught than was achieved by Bernard. The fusion of the teachings of the two schools of Abelard and of Hugh began when Abelard's disciples bowed to the Victorine thrust and in greater or less degree incorporated Victorine criticisms as well as other material into their work, and when Victorine followers, such as the author of the *Ysagoge* or Roland, diverged markedly from Hugh to incorporate controversial teaching by Abelard. This fusion largely characterizes the work of Robert of Melun and of Peter Lombard.

The use of Abelard's thought, shorn of its more notable peculiarities, was considerable in mid century. By being frequently tentative and experimental, by advancing opinions which seemed to be logically required even when the paucity of authoritative support was manifest to him, Abelard invited not only disagreement but also debate and further thought. The constructive vigour with which he was refuted and controverted by Robert of Melun and the Victorines indicates the nature of his influence upon creative minds. Like Gilbert he provoked much of the keenest thinking which appears in scholastic writing for some twenty years after his death.

APPENDICES

AN INEDITED FRAGMENT OF THE SENTENCES OF HERMANN

There are a few texts from Abelard's school which are still inedited, notably the Sentences of Omnebene and *Sententie Parisienses II*. The justification for printing the following short passage is simply that on occasion it has been referred to, but not cited, in the foregoing pages. In any new edition of Hermann's Sentences other passages besides this would need to be revised. Chapters 10 and 11 in the Rheinwald-Migne edition are extensively altered in two manuscripts, Pavia, Aldini 49, and Carpentras, Inguimbertine 110, and wholly omitted in St Gall 69. The concern here is with the Carpentras manuscript which contains a late thirteenth-century copy of the work together with a fragmentary continuation not printed in the Rheinwald-Migne edition nor found in any of the other six extant MSS. of Hermann's Sentences. The fragment is short and it continues the discussion of the forgiveness of sin with which other exemplars of this work end.[1] The continuation appears on f. 65v of the Carpentras manuscript and is itself manifestly incomplete. It is copied by the second of the two hands which have transcribed the text (ff. 55r–63v and ff. 64r–5v) and the copyist would appear to have failed to resume his task for the text ends in the middle of the first column of f. 65v; the rest of the folio is blank.

A marginal rubric mentions the particular problem under discussion: 'Utrum sacerdos dimittat peccata.' Reason, the author affirms, seems to prove that a priest can neither save nor damn a man. But the argument from reason is not expounded. Instead authorities are produced from the Old and New Testaments and from the writings of St Jerome. The raising of Lazarus from the tomb is interpreted here to signify the calling of a man by Christ away from the habits of sin. Christ's call comes through an inner inspiration; it is Christ who grants life. Only then does the sinner show himself to the priest in confession. Christ's gift to the apostles of the power to remit sin refers to the release not from sin, but from the temporal punishment and the excommunication which are imposed as a result of sin. Consequently, the power of the keys, that is the power of binding and loosing, is simply the power

---

[1] C. 37 (PL. 178, 1757–8).

to open and to close the church to sinners, that is to excommunicate and to free from the bond of excommunication.

Abelard discusses this question of the power of priests to bind and to loose the sinner in the *Ethica*. The citations from Jerome and Gregory and the example of Lazarus which are given in the *Sentences* are also found in Abelard's *Ethica*,[1] and the interpretation of the power of the keys as purely a power to impose and to abrogate temporal punishments is suggested by Abelard.[2] The understanding of the keys by their effects is found in other works belonging to Abelard's school, in the Sentences of Roland[3] and of Omnebene,[4] and it is attributed to Abelard in a question from the school of Laon.[5] In this fragment Hermann faithfully represents the teaching of Abelard. Had the Carpentras copy of these Sentences continued further, the question whether the apostles received a special gift of the power of the keys which was not transmitted to their successors, might have appeared.

. . . inde graviter est puniendus.[6]

Utrum sacerdos dimittat peccata

Nunc si sacerdos dimittere valeat inquirendum relinquitur. Sed quod non possit dampnare nec salvare, posse ratio
5 comparare videtur. Quod autem non possit da⟨m⟩pnare, David aperte ostendit cum dicat: 'Anima mea in manibus meis semper.'[7] Si enim in manu nostra hoc situm est quod nosmet dampnemus, nec alius homo potest. Quod autem salvare non potest—quod quidem faceret si peccata dimit-
10 teret—Dominus ⟨per⟩ Prophetam ostendit: 'Ego, inquit, solus debeo iniquitates et peccata populi.'[8] Item Ambrosius: 'Ille solus peccata dimittit qui pro peccatis nostris mortuus est.'[9] Item Ieronimus super Matthaeum,[10] ubi dicit Petro:

2: Utrum . . . peccata *in marg.*   6: in) In *cod.*   10: inquit) inquid *cod.*

[1] PL. 178, 674CD, 676A–7A, 676CD.
[2] *Ethica*, cod. Oxford, Balliol College 296, f. 78v–9v.
[3] Ed. Gietl, pp. 264–9.
[4] Cited by Gietl in his edition, p. 265 *in notis.*   [5] Cited above, p. 177, n. 6.
[6] Cod. Carpentras f. 65v. Migne, PL. 178, 1758 ends thus. Omissions are noted within square brackets [] and additions within angular brackets ⟨⟩.   [7] Ps. 118 (119), 109.   [8] Isa. 43, 25.
[9] *Exposit. in Evang. Lucae, lib.* VI, 109 (PL. 15, 1698).
[10] *Commentariorum in Evang. Matthaei lib.* III, 16 (PL. 26, 118A).

'Quodcunque ligaveris super terra⟨m⟩' etc.:[1] 'Hunc locum quidam intelligentes aliquid sibi sumunt de supercilio Phariseorum, ut da⟨m⟩pnare innoxios vel solvere se putent noxios, cum apud Deum non sacerdotum sententia, sed
5 reorum vita queratur'. Sed non aliud possunt in peccatoribus quam sacerdotes levitici potuerant, neque enim eos leprosos faciebant, sed qui mundi vel immundi essent ostendebant. Unde et Dominus in Evangelio: 'Ite, ostendite vos sacerdotibus'[2] per . . . siquidem nostri sacerdotes qui digni vel
10 indigni ecclesie communione discesserunt, ut illi qui mundi vel immundi existerent. Hoc quod Dominus per Lazarum, per quem omnes in consuetudine peccati quasi iacentes in sepulcro signatum ostendit, accessit enim et vocavit eum et vocatum vivificavit et vivificato ait: 'Exi foras',[3] et de eo dixit
15 discipulis: 'Solvite et s⟨inite⟩ a⟨bire⟩.'[4] Similiter venit ad peccatorem et vocavit eum per internam inspirationem et morte peccati discedente vivficatur et eo vivificato dicit ut foras exeat, id est per confessionem se sacerdotibus ostendat. [De quo et sacerdotibus ostendat] De quo et
20 sacerdotibus dicitur: 'Solvite eum', id est, revocate eum ad ecclesiam, et 'Sinite abire', cum aliis fidelibus conversari et permanere. Quod igitur dictum est: 'Quorum peccata dimiseritis' etc.,[5] de temporalibus penis intelligendum ⟨est⟩. Quod tamen cum discretione faciendum est, ut solis scilicet
25 devote satis facientibus huius pene remissio adhibeatur. [de hoc non] Quod dictum est: 'Quodcunque ligaveris super terram' etc.,[6] de excommunicatione a presenti ecclesia accipiendum est. Si igitur intelligas: 'quoscunque in hac vita abieceris vel in ecclesiam introduxeris, sic erit ratum in
30 celis', id est in omnibus ecclesiis, quia si quis episcopus aut et presbyter aliquis de parochia sua excommunicaverit, pro

9: per . . .) per m̄ *cod.*   23: dimiseritis) remiseritis *Vulg.*

[1] Matt. 16, 19.   [2] Luc. 17, 14.
[3] Joh. 11, 43.
[4] Joh. 11, 44.
[5] Joh. 20, 23.
[6] Matt. 16, 19.

excommunicato habetur apud omnes alias ecclesias. Sive autem iuste sive iniuste hoc fiat, nichil refert quin subiectus obedire debeat. Unde Gregorius:[1] 'Sententia pastoris, sive iusta sive iniusta sit, timenda est ne ex tumida reprehensione,
5   quod prius non erat culpa, postea fiat'. De clavibus quoque dicimus, quod non sint nisi potentia ligandi vel solvendi, id est claudendi ecclesiam peccatoribus vel aperiendi, sed propter duos effectus, quia ea scilicet peccator ligatur, id est extra ecclesiam eicitur, et ea solvitur, id est in ecclesiam
10 reducitur. Per hos, inquam, duos effectus due claves dicuntur.

4: reprehensione) responsione *cod.*

[1] *XL Homiliarum in Evangelia Lib.* ii, *Homil.* xxvi, 6 (PL. 76, 1201b).

APPENDIX II

Open an edition or a study of Abelard and it is likely that you will find in it a discussion of the correct way to spell Abelard's name. Usually a few spellings are given, but medieval writers used many more. Here are thirty-seven forms which have been encountered in the course of writing this book. Now it will be possible to know how this name should be correctly written—or will it? Abaalardus, Abaalarz, Abaelardi, Abaelardus, Abaialardi, Abaielardus, Abailar, Abailardus, Abailart, Abaillardus, Abaiolardus, Abaiulardus, Abalardus, Abarlardus, Abaulardus, Abaulart, Abaylardus, Abbaalardus, Abbaelardus, Abelardi, Abelardus, Abellardus, Abulart, Abylardus, Adbaiolardi, Alardi, Baalardus, Baalaurdus, Baelardi, Bailardus, Baiolardus, Baiulardus, Balaardus, Baylardus, Bealaardus, Habaelardus, Habelardus.

BIBLIOGRAPHY

The bibliography contains details of works referred to above. The place of publication is not mentioned in the case of French and English works published in Paris and London respectively.

WORKS BY ABELARD
Collected editions

PL. 178.

Duchesne, A. *Petri Abaelardi . . . et Heloissae conjugis eius . . . Opera nunc primum edita ex MSS. Codd . . . Francisci Amboesii . . .* Paris, 1616.

Cousin, V. *Opera Petri Abaelardi.* 2 vols. Paris, 1849, 1859.

—— *Ouvrages inédits d'Abélard pour servir à l'histoire de la philosophie scolastique.* 1834.

—— *Fragments philosophiques pour servir à l'histoire de la philosophie, II. Philosophie du moyen âge.* 5th. ed., 1866.

Editions of one or more works

Dal Pra, M. *Pietro Abelardo. Scritti filosofici.* Nuova Biblioteca Filosofica, Serie II, vol. 3, Rome-Milan, 1954.

De Rijk, L. M. *Petrus Abaelardus. Dialectica.* Wijsgerige Teksten en Studies, vol. I, Assen, 1956.

Dreves, G. M. *Petri Abaelardi Peripatetici Palatini Hymnarius Paraclitensis sive Hymnarius libelli tres.* Paris, 1891.

—— *Hymnographi latini. Lateinische Hymnendichter des Mittelalters. Erste Folge.* Analecta Hymnica Medii Aevi, C. Blume and G. M. Dreves, vol. XLVIII, Leipzig, 1905, pp. 141–232.

Geyer, B. *Peter Abaelards Philosophische Schriften, I. Die Logica 'Ingredientibus'.* BGPTMA, XXI, Hefte 1–3, 1919–27; *II. Die Logica 'Nostrorum Petitioni Sociorum'.* BGPTMA, XXI, Heft 4, 1933.

Hauréau, B., a fragment of Abelard's *Expositio in Hexaemeron* in *Notices et Extraits*, vol. V, 1892, pp. 237–44.

Henke, E. L. T. and Lindenkohl, G. S. *Petri Abaelardi Sic et Non.* Marburgi Cattorum, 1851.

Klibansky, R. 'Epistula Petri Abailardi contra Bernardum abbatem'. *Medieval and Renaissance Studies*, vol. V, 1961, pp. 6–7.

Leclercq J., another ed. of the above letter in ASOC, IX, 1953, pp. 104–5.

McLaughlin T. P. 'Abelard's Rule for Religious Women'. *Medieval Studies*, vol. XVIII, 1956, pp. 241–92.

Minio-Paluello L. *Twelfth Century Logic. Texts and Studies, II. Abaelardiana Inedita*. Rome, 1959.

Monfrin, J. *Abélard, Historia Calamitatum. Texte critique avec une introduction*. Bibliothèque des textes philosophiques, 1962.

Muckle, J. T. 'Abaelard's Letter of Consolation to a Friend (Historia Calamitatum)', *Medieval Studies*, vol. XII, 1950, pp. 163–213.

—— 'The Personal Letters between Abelard and Héloïse'. *Medieval Studies*, vol. XV, 1953, pp. 47–94.

—— 'The Letter of Héloïse on the Religious Life and Abaelard's First Reply'. *Medieval Studies*, vol. XVII, 1955, pp. 240–81.

Ostlender, H. *Peter Abaelards Theologia 'Summi Boni'*. BGPTMA, XXXV, 2/3, 1939.

Ottaviano, C. 'Un brano inedito della Theologia Christiana di Abelardo'. *Giornale critico della filosofia italiana*, vol. XI, 1930, pp. 326–32.

—— 'Frammenti abelardiani'. *Rivista di cultura*, vol. XII, 1931, pp. 425–45.

Pez, B. *Thesaurus anecdotorum novissimus*. vol. III. Augustae Vindelicorum & Graecii, 1721.

Rheinwald, F. H. *Dialogus Petri Abaelardi inter Philosophum, Judaeum et Christianum*. Berlin, 1831.

Ruf, P. and Grabmann, M. 'Ein neuaufgefundenes Bruchstück der Apologia Abaelards'. *Sitzungsberichte der Bayerischen Akademie der Wissenschaften. Philos.-hist. Abteilung*, V, 1930.

Stölzle, R. *Abaelards 1121 zu Soissons verurtheilter 'Tractatus de Unitate et Trinitate Divina'*. Freiburg, 1891.

WORKS WRITTEN BEFORE 1500

Abbreviatio: Petri Abaelardi Expositionis in Epistolam S. Pauli ad Romanos Abbreviatio, ed. A. M. Landgraf in *Bohoslavia*, vol. XIII, Lemberg, 1935, pp. 1–45.

Adam Balsamiensis Parvipontani, *Ars disserendi*, ed. L. Minio-Paluello, *Twelfth Century Logic. Texts and Studies*, vol. I, Rome, 1956.

Alberic of Tre Fontane, *Chronicon*, MGH.SS. vol. XXIII, 1874, pp. 631–950.

Ambrose, St. *Opera, pars VII*, ed. O. Faller. CSEL, vol. LXXIII, 1955.

Annales Sancti Taurini Ebroicensis, ed. Bouquet, *Recueil*, vol. XII, pp. 776–7.

Anselm of Laon, *Sententie*, in *Liber Pancrisis*, ed. O. Lottin, *Psychologie et Morale*, vol. v, pp. 32–81.

Augustine, St. *Opera*, PL. 32–46 and *Opera*, ed. I. Zycha. CSEL, vol. XXVIII, Sectio III, Pars 2, 1894.

Becket, Thomas. *Materials for the History of Thomas Becket*, ed. J. C Robertson and J. B. Sheppard, 8 vols. RS, 1875–85.

Berengar of Poitiers, *Opera*. PL. 178, 1854–80.

Bernard, Abbot, *Sententie*. Clm. 4600, ff. 68r–72v.

Bernard of Clairvaux, *Opera*. PL. 182–5 and ed. J. Leclercq, etc., I– , Rome, 1957– .

—— *Select Treatises*, ed. W. W. Williams. Cambridge, 1926.

Biblia sacra vulgatae editionis . . . P. M. Hetzenauer. Ratisbonae et Romae, 1914.

Boethius, A. M. *Operum pars I. In Isagogen Porphyrii Comment.* rec. S. Brandt. CSEL, vol. XLVIII, 1906.

Bonaventure, St. *Opera omnia*. Quaracchi, 1882–1902.

Bruno the Carthusian, *Opera*, PL. 152–3.

Capitula Haeresum, PL. 182, 1049–54.

Chronicon anonymi, ed. Bouquet. *Recueil*, vol. XII, 1781, pp. 118–21.

Chronicon Britannicum, ed. Bouquet. *Recueil*, vol. XII, 1781, pp. 557–8.

Chronicon Burchardi et Cuonradi Urspergensium. MGH.SS. vol. XXIII, 1874, pp. 333–83.

Chronicon Mauriniacensis, ed. L. Mirot. *La Chronique de Morigny, 1095–1152*, 1909.

Chronicon Senonense Gaufridi de Collone, cit. V. Cousin. *Opera Petri Abaelardi*, vol. I, p. 46.

Chronicon Turonense, ed. Bouquet. *Recueil*, vol. XII, 1781, pp. 461–78.

Clarembald of Arras, Commentary on Boethius' *De trinitate*, ed. W. Jansen. *Der Kommentar des Clarenbaldus von Arras zu Boethius, De trin.* Breslauer Studien zur historischen Theologie, VIII, Breslau, 1926.

Clarius of Sens, *Chronicon*, ed. Bouquet. *Recueil*, vol. XII, 1781, pp. 279–85.

Claudianus Mamertus, *Opera*, ed. A. Engelbrecht. CSEL, vol. XI, 1885.

Commentarius Cantabrigiensis in Epistolas Pauli e Schola P. Abaelardi, ed. A. Landgraf. Notre-Dame University Publications in Medieval Studies, vol. II, 4 parts. Notre-Dame, Indiana, 1937–45.

Commentarius Porretanus in primam Epistolam ad Corinthios, ed. A. Landgraf. Studi e Testi, vol. CXVII, Vatican City, 1945.

Enarrationes in Evangelium S. Matthaei. PL. 162, 1227–1500.

Eugenius III, Pope, *Epistolae et privilegia*, PL. 180.

Eusebius of Vercelli, *De trinitate*, ed. V. Bulhart. Corpus Christianorum Series Latina, IX, Turnholti, 1957.

Everard of Ypres, *Dialogus Ratii et Everardi*, ed. N. Haring. 'A Latin Dialogue on the Doctrine of Gilbert of Poitiers'. *Medieval Studies*, vol. XV, 1953, pp. 243–89.

Excerptor, see *Capitula Haeresum*.

Filius a patre gigni, ed. O. Lottin. *Psychologie et morale*, vol. V, pp. 338–42.

Fulk of Deuil, *Epistola ad Abaelardum*. PL. 178, 371–6.

Geoffrey of Auxerre, *Opera*. PL. 185.

—— *Fragmenta de Vita et Miraculis S. Bernardi*, ed. R. Lechat. *Analecta Bollandiana*, vol. L, 1932, pp. 83–122.

Gerald of Wales, *Giraldi Cambrensis Opera*, ed. J. S. Brewer and J. F. Dimock, 8 vols. RS, 1861–91.

Gerhoh of Reichersberg, *Opera*. PL. 193–4.

—— *Libelli selecti*, ed. E. Sackur. MGH, Libelli de lite, vol. III, 1897, pp. 131–525.

—— *Opera inedita*, ed. D. Van den Eynde, etc., 3 vols. Spicilegium Pontificii Athenaei Antoniani, fasc. 8–10, Rome, 1955–6.

Gerson, John, *Opera omnia . . . opera & studio L. Ellies du Pin*, 5 vols, Antwerp, 1706.

Gilbert Crispin, *Disputatio Iudei et Christiani*, ed. B. Blumenkranz. Stromata patristica et mediaevalia, vol. III, Utrecht, 1956.

Glossa ordinaria. PL. 113–114.

Glossae super librum Porphyrii secundum vocales, ed. C. Ottaviano. Fontes Ambrosiani, vol. III, Florence, 1933, pp. 106–207; also incompletely by B. Geyer in BGPTMA, XXI, 4, 1933, pp. 583–8.

Gratian, *Decretum* in *Corpus Juris Canonici, editio Lipsiensis*, A. Friedberg, Leipzig, 1879–81.

Gregory the Great, *Opera*. PL. 75–9.

Helinand of Froidmont, *Opera*. PL. 212.

Henry of Brussels, *De scriptoribus illustribus*, ed. A. Miraeus. *Bibliotheca ecclesiastica*, Antwerp, 1639, pp. 161–76.

Hermann, *Sententie*, ed. R. H. Rheinwald. *Petri Abaelardi Epitome Theologiae Christianae*, Berlin, 1835 and PL. 178, 1695–1758.

Hermann of Kappensberg, *Opera*. PL. 170.

Hilary, *Versus et ludi*, ed. J. J. Champollion-Figeac, 1838.

—— *Elegia*, PL. 178, 1851–6.

Hilary of Poitiers, *Opera*. PL. 9–10.

Historiae Tornacenses. MGH.SS. vol. xiv, 1883, pp. 327–52.

Horatius Flaccus Q., *Carmina*, ed. F. Vollmer. Bibl. Teubneriana. Leipzig, 1907.

Hugh of Amiens, *Opera.* PL. 192.

Hugh Métel, *Epistolae*, ed. C. L. Hugo. *Sacrae antiquitatis monumenta*, vol. ii, Saint Die, 1731.

Hugh of St Victor, *Opera.* PL. 175–7.

—— *Questiones*, ed. O. Lottin, 'Questions inédites de Hugues de Saint Victor'. *RTAM*, vol. xxvi, 1959, pp. 177–213; xxvii, 1960, pp. 42–66.

—— *Didascalicon*, trans. with an introduction and notes by J. Taylor. Records of Civilization. Sources and Studies, vol. lxiv, New York, 1961.

—— *Tractatus de trinitate et de reparatione hominis*, ed. from cod. Douai 365 by R. Baron in *Mélanges de science religieuse*, vol. xviii, 1961, pp. 111–123.

Innocent II, Pope, *Opera omnia*, PL. 179.

Ivo of Chartres, *Opera.* PL. 161–2.

James of Vitry, *Exempla*, ed. J. Greven. *Die Exempla aus den Sermones feriales et communes des Jakob von Vitry*, Heidelberg, 1914.

Jerome St., *Opera.* PL. 22–30.

John of Cornwall, *Eulogium quod Christus sit aliquis homo ad Alexandrum III*, ed. N. Haring. *Medieval Studies*, vol. xiii, 1951, pp. 253–300.

John of Salisbury, *Epistolae.* PL. 199.

—— *Historia Pontificalis*, ed. M. Chibnall. Edinburgh, 1956.

—— *Metalogicon*, ed. C. C. J. Webb. Oxford, 1929.

—— *Policraticus*, ed. C. C. J. Webb. 2 vols. Oxford, 1909.

Laborans, Cardinal, *Opuscula*, ed. A. M. Landgraf. Florilegium patristicum, fasc. xxxii, Bonn, 1932.

Macrobius, Ambrosius Theodosius, *Opera*, ed. I. Willis. 2 vols. Bibl. Teubneriana, Leipzig, 1963.

Map, Walter, *De nugis curialium*, ed. M. R. James. Anecdota Oxoniensia. Medieval and Modern Series, vol. xiv, Oxford, 1914; also MGH.SS. vol. xxvii, 1885, pp. 61–74.

Maximus of Turin, *Opera.* PL. 57.

Metamorphosis Goliae episcopi, ed. R. B. C. Huygens, 'Mitteilungen aus Handschriften'. *Studi medievali, Terza serie*, iii (1962), pp. 764–72.

Moralium dogma philosophorum, ed. J. Holmberg. *Das Moral. dog. philos. des Guillaume de Conches, lateinisch, altfranzösisch und mittelniederfränkisch*, Uppsala, 1929.

Morigny, Chronicle of, see *Chronicon Mauriniacensis*.

Netter, Pseudo-Thomas Netter of Walden, *Confessio Magistri Johannis Tyssyngton. Fasciculi Zizaniorum Magistri Johannis Wyclif cum Tritico*, ed. W. Waddington Shirley. RS, 1858.

Nicholas of Amiens, *Chronicon*, ed. Bouquet. *Recueil*, vol. XIV, 1806, pp. 21–3.

Nicholas of Cusa, *De pace fidei*, ed. R. Klibansky and H. Bascour. *Medieval and Renaissance Studies*, Supplement 3, 1956.

Odo of Ourscamp, *Questiones*, ed. J. B. Pitra, *Questiones Magistri Odonis Suessionis*. Analecta novissima Specilegii Solesmensis. Continuatio altera, vol. II, 1888.

Omnebene, *Sententie*, Clm. 19,134, ff. 151r–228r; cod. Monte Cassino 386 G, pp. 57–87; cod. Naples, Bibl. nazionale VII C 43, ff. 1r–90v.

Otto of Freising, *Gesta Friderici*, ed. G. Waitz. *Ottonis et Rahewini Gesta Friderici I. Imperatoris. Ed. tertia.* Scriptores rerum germanicarum, Hanover and Leipzig, 1912.

Otto of St Blaise, *Chronicon*. MGH.SS. vol. XX, 1868, pp. 302–37.

Peter of Blois, *Opera*. PL. 207.

Peter Cantor, *Opera*. PL. 205.

Peter Damian, *Opera*. PL. 144–5.

Peter Lombard, *Opera*. PL. 191–2.

—— *Libri IV Sententiarum, ed. secunda*. Ad Claras Aquas, 1916.

Peter the Venerable, *Opera*. PL. 189.

Petrarch F., *Librorum F. Petrarchae impressorum annotatio*. Venice, 1501.

—— *De vita solitaria*, trans. J. Zeitlin. *The Life of Solitude*. Illinois, 1924.

Phillip of Harvengt, *Opera*. PL. 203.

Plato, *Timaeus a Calcidio translatus . . .*, ed. J. H. Waszink. Plato latinus 4. Corpus Platonicum Medii Aevi, London-Leiden, 1962.

Quaestiones super epistolas Pauli. PL. 175, 431–634.

Ralph of Coggeshall, *Chronicon Anglicanum*, ed. J. Stevenson. RS, 1875.

Ralph of Laon, *Sententie*, ed. O. Lottin. *Psychologie et morale*, vol. V, pp. 183–8.

Ralph Tortaire, *Carmina*, ed. M. B. Ogle and D. M. Schullian. Papers and Monographs of the American Academy in Rome, vol. 8, 1933.

—— Verses, ed. C. Cuissard. *Documents inédits sur Abélard tirés des manuscrits de Fleury*. Orleans, 1880.

Richard of Poitiers, *Chronicon*. MGH.SS. vol. XXVI, 1882, pp. 74–82.

Richard of St Victor, *Opera*. PL. 196.

—— *De trinitate. Texte critique avec introduction, notes et tables*, J. Ribaillier. Textes philosophiques du moyen âge, vol. VI, 1958.

Richard of St. Victor, *De trinitate. Texte latin, introduction, traduction et notes*, G. Salet. Sources chrétiennes, vol. 63, 1959.

Robert of Auxerre, *Chronicon*. MGH.SS. vol. XXVI, 1882, pp. 219–76.

Robert of Melun, *Quaestiones de divina pagina*, ed. R. J. Martin. *Oeuvres de Robert de Melun*, vol. I. Spicilegium Sacrum Lovaniense, fasc. 13. Louvain, 1932.

—— *Quaestiones de epistolis Pauli*, ed. R. J. Martin. *Oeuvres* . . . II. Spicil. Sac. Lovan., fasc. 18, 1938.

—— *Sententiae*, ed. R. J. Martin. *Oeuvres* . . . III, 1. Spicil. Sac. Lovan., fasc. 21, 1947; *Oeuvres* . . . *III*, 2, *auxiliante* R. M. Gallet. Spicil. Sac. Lovan., fasc. 25, 1952.

Robert of Torigny, *Chronicon*, ed. L. Delisle. *Chronique de Robert de Torigni*, 2 vols, Rouen, 1872–3.

Roland Bandinelli, *Stroma*, ed. F. Thaner. *Die Summa Magistri Rolandi nachmals Papstes Alexander III*, Innsbruck, 1874.

—— *Sententie*, ed. A. M. Gietl. *Die Sentenzen Rolands*, Freiburg, 1891.

Roscelin of Compiègne, *Epistola ad Abaelardum*, PL. 178, 357–72; also ed. J. Reiners, *Der Nominalismus in der Frühscholastik. Ein Beitrag zur Geschichte der Universalienfrage im Mittelalter. Nebst einer neuen Textausgabe des Briefes Roscelins an Abaelard.* BGPTMA, VIII. 1910, pp. 63–80.

Sententie Anselmi, ed. F. Bliemetzrieder. *Anselms von Laon systematische Sentenzen.* BGPTMA, XVIII, 2–3, 1919, pp. 47–153.

Sententie Atrebatenses, ed. O. Lottin. *Psychologie et morale*, vol. V, pp. 400–40.

Sententie divine pagine, ed. F. Bliemetzrieder. *Anselms von Laon systematische Sentenzen.* BGPTMA, XVIII, 2–3, 1919, pp. 3–46.

Sententie Florianenses, ed. H. Ostlender. Florilegium Patristicum, fasc. XIX, Bonn, 1929.

Sententie Magistri A., ed. N. Haring. 'The Sententiae Magistri A. (Vat. MS. lat. 4361) and the School of Laon'. *Medieval Studies*, vol. XVII, 1955, pp. 1–45.

Sententie Parisienses I, ed. A. Landgraf. *Ecrits théologiques de l'école d'Abélard.* Spicilegium Sacrum Lovaniense, vol. XIV, Louvain, 1934, pp. 1–60.

Sententie Parisienses II, cod. Paris, Bibl. nat. lat. 18,108, ff. 170r–177v.

Sententie Varsavienses, ed. F. Stegmüller. 'Sententiae Varsavienses', *Divus Thomas*, Piacenza, vol. XLV, 1942, pp. 316–42.

Serlo of Bayeux, ed. T. Wright. *The Satirical Poets and Epigrammatists of the Twelfth Century*, vol. II. RS, 1872, pp. 232–58.

Sigeberti Auctarium Affligemense. MGH.SS. vol. VI, 1844, pp. 398–405.

Sigeberti Continuatio Praemonstratensis. MGH.SS. vol. VI, 1844, pp. 447–56.

Stephen of Tournai, *Epistolae*, ed. J. Desilve. Valenciennes, 1893.

Summa Sententiarum. PL. 176, 41–174.

Thomas of Morigny, *Disputatio Catholicorum Patrum adversus Dogmata Petri Abaelardi.* PL. 180, 283–328; also ed. W. Meyer, 'Die Anklagesätze', p. 417 (introductory fragment).

Tractatus de intellectibus, ed. V. Cousin. *Opera Petri Abaelardi*, vol. II, 733–55, and formerly Cousin, *Fragments philosophiques*, vol. II, 461–92.

Victorinus, Marius, *Opera.* PL. 8.

Vincent of Beauvais, *Bibliotheca mundi.* 4 vols. Douai, 1624.

Vita Gosvini, ed. Bouquet. *Recueil*, vol. XIV, 1806, pp. 442–8.

Walter of Mortagne, *Epistola ad Abaelardum*, ed. H. Ostlender. Florilegium Patristicum, fasc. XIX, Bonn, 1929, pp. 34–40.

—— *Epistola ad Theodoricum Carnotensem*, ed. L. d'Achéry. *Spicilegium sive collectio veterum aliquot scriptorum qui in Galliae bibliothecis delituerant. Nova ed.*, vol. II, 1723, 462–6.

—— *Tractatus de trinitate*, PL. 209, 575–90.

Walter of St Victor, *Contra Quatuor Labyrinthos Franciae*, ed. P. Glorieux. *AHDLMA*, vol. XIX, 1952, pp. 187–335.

—— *Sermo de superexcellenti baptismo Christi.* PL. 196, 1011–8.

William of Champeaux, *Sententie*, ed. O. Lottin. *Psychologie et morale*, vol. V, pp. 189–227.

William of Conches, *Glosae super Platonem*, ed. E. Jeauneau. Textes philosophiques du moyen âge, vol. XIII, 1965.

William Godell, *Chronicon*, ed. Bouquet. *Recueil*, vol. XIII, 1786, pp. 671–7.

William of Nangis, *Chronicon*, ed. H. Géraud. *Chronique latine de Guillaume de Nangis . . . nouvelle éd.*, 2 vols. 1843.

William of St Thierry, *Opera.* PL. 180, 182, 184.

—— *Epistola ad Fratres de Monte Dei, Prologus*, ed. A. Wilmart, 'La Préface de la lettre aux Frères du Mont-Dieu'. *Revue bénédictine*, vol. XXXVI, 1924, pp. 229–47.

—— *Speculum fidei, Aenigma fidei*, ed. M. M. Davy. *Deux traités sur la foi. Le Miroir de la foi. L'Enigme de la foi.* Bibliothèques des textes philosophiques, 1959.

Ysagoge in theologiam, ed. A. Landgraf. *Ecrits théologiques de l'école d'Abélard.* Spicilegium Sacrum Lovaniense, vol. XIV, Louvain, 1934, pp. 61–289.

Zachary of Besançon, *Super Unum ex quattuor.* PL. 186, 11–620.

WORKS WRITTEN AFTER 1500

Affeldt, W. 'Verzeichniss der Römerbriefkommentare der lateinischen Kirche bis zu Nikolaus von Lyra'. *Traditio*, vol. XIII, 1957, pp. 369–406.

Alszeghy, Z. *'Nova Creatura'. La nozione della grazia nei commentari medievali di S. Paolo.* Analecta Gregoriana, vol. LXXXI. Rome, 1956.

Alverny, M. T. d'. *Alain de Lille, textes inédits avec une introduction sur sa vie et ses oeuvres.* Etudes de philosophie médiévale, vol. LII, 1965.

Amanieu, A. 'Alger de Liège'. DDC, vol. I, 1935, cols. 390–403.

Anciaux, P. *La Théologie du sacrement de pénitence au XIIe siècle.* Louvain, Gembloux, 1949.

Anders, F. *Die Christologie des Robert von Melun.* Forschungen zur christlichen Literatur- und Dogmengeschichte, Band XV, Heft V, Paderborn, 1927.

Anstey, H. ed., *Epistolae academicae oxonienses*, 2 vols. Oxford History Society Publications, vols. XXXV, XXXVI. Oxford, 1898.

Aristoteles Latinus. Codices descripsit G. Lacombe, etc. vols. I–II. Rome, 1939, Cambridge, 1955.

Bach, J. *Die Dogmengeschichte des Mittelalters vom christologischen Standpunkte*, vols. I–II. Vienna, 1873–5.

Baltzer, O. *Beiträge zur Geschichte des christologischen Dogmas im 11. und 12. Jahrhundert.* Studien zur Geschichte der Theologie und der Kirche, vol. III, Leipzig, 1898/9.

Bandinius, A. M. *Bibliotheca Leopoldina Laurentiana seu catalogus manuscriptorum qui iussu Petri Leopoldi in Laurentianam translati sunt.* 3 vols, Florence, 1791–3.

Baron, R. 'L'influence de Hugues de Saint Victor'. *RTAM*, vol. XXII, 1955, pp. 56–71.

—— 'Etude sur l'authenticité de l'oeuvre de Hugues de Saint Victor d'après les MSS. Paris Maz. 717, B.N. 14506 et Douai 360–6'. *Scriptorium*, vol. X, 1956, pp. 182–220.

—— 'Notes biographiques sur Hugues de Saint Victor'. *RHE*, vol. LI, 1956, pp. 920–34.

—— *Science et sagesse chez Hugues de Saint Victor.* 1957.

—— 'Le Sacrement de la foi selon Hugues de Saint Victor'. *RSPT*, vol. XLII, 1958, pp. 50–78.

—— 'Note sur l'énigmatique "Summa Sententiarum"'. *RTAM*, vol. XXV, 1958, pp. 26–42.

—— *Etudes sur Hugues de Saint Victor*. 1963.

Barth, B. 'Ein neues Dokument zur Geschichte der frühscholastische Christologie'. *Theologische Quartalschrift*, vol. C, 1919, pp. 409–26, vol. CI, 1920, pp. 235–62.

Bauer, O. 'Frowin von Engelberg (1147–1178), De laude liberi arbitrii libri septem'. *RTAM*, vol. XV, 1948, pp. 27–75, 269–303.

Becker, G. *Catalogi Bibliothecarum Antiqui*. Bonn, 1885.

Beonio-Brocchieri Fumagalli, M. T. *La Logica di Abelardo*. Pubblicazioni dell'Istituto di Storia della Filosofia dell'Università degli Studi di Milano, vol. VI, Florence, 1964.

Bernard, E. *Catalogi Librorum MSS. Angliae et Hiberniae*. Oxford, 1697.

Bernards, M. 'Zur Überlieferung mittelalterlicher theologischer Schriften. Neue Handschriften'. *RTAM*, vol. XIX, 1952, pp. 327–36.

Bernhard von Clairvaux. Mönch und Mystiker; internationaler Bernhardkongress, Mainz 1953, ed J. Lortz. Veröffentlichungen des Institut für europäische Geschichte, Mainz, vol. VI, Wiesbaden, 1955.

Bertola, E. 'Le "Sententiae Florianenses" della scuola di Abelardo'. *Sophia*, vol. XVIII, 1950, pp. 368–78.

—— 'Il problema di Dio in Pier Lombardo'. *RFNS*, vol. XLVIII, 1956, pp. 135–50.

—— *San Bernardo e la teologia speculativa*. Pubbl. dell'Istituto Universitario di Magistero di Catania. Serie filosofica—Monografie, N. 11, Padua, 1959.

—— 'Le critiche di Abelardo ad Anselmo di Laon ed a Guglielmo di Champeaux'. *RFNS*, vol. LII, 1960, pp. 495–522.

—— 'I precedenti storici del metodo del "Sic et Non" di Abelardo'. *RFNS*, vol. LIII, 1961, pp. 255–80.

Bibliotheca Casinenis seu codicum manu scriptorum qui in Tabulario Casinensi asservantur series, 5 vols. Ex typographia Casinensi, 1873–94.

Bischoff, B. 'Aus der Schule Hugos von St. Viktor'. *Aus der Geisteswelt des Mittelalters*. BGPTMA, Supplementband III, 1, 1935, pp. 246–50.

Bliemetzrieder, F. 'L'oeuvre d'Anselme de Laon et la littérature théologique contemporaine, 1. Honorius von Autun, 2. Hugues de

Rouen'. *RTAM*, vol. v, 1933, pp. 275–91, vol. vi, 1934, pp. 261–83, vol. vii, 1935, pp. 28–51.

Bligh, J. 'Richard of St Victor's De Trinitate: Augustinian or Abelardian?' *Heythrop Journal*, vol. i, 1960, pp. 118–39.

Blomme, R. *La Doctrine du péché dans les écoles théologiques de la première moitié du XIIe siècle.* Louvain, 1958.

Blumenkranz, B. and Chatillon, J. 'De la polémique antijuive à la catéchèse chrétienne. L'objet, le contenu et les sources d'une anonyme *Altercatio Synagogae et Ecclesiae* du XIIe siècle'. *RTAM*, vol. xxiii, 1956, pp. 40–60.

Boeckler, A. *Die Regensburg-Prüfeninger Buchmalerei des XII-XIII Jahrhunderts.* Munich, 1924.

Bonnard, Fourier, *Histoire de l'abbaye royale et de l'ordre des chanoines réguliers de S. Victor de Paris,* 2 vols. 1904.

Borst, H. 'Abälard und Bernhard'. *Historische Zeitschrift*, vol. clxxxvi, 1958, pp. 497–526.

Bradley, J. W. *A Dictionary of Miniaturists, Illuminators, Calligraphers and Copyists,* 3 vols. 1887–9.

Brady, I. 'Peter Lombard: Canon of Notre-Dame'. *RTAM*, vol. xxxii, 1965, pp. 277–95.

—— 'Peter Manducator and the Oral Teachings of Peter Lombard'. *Antonianum*, vol. xli, 1966, pp. 454–490.

Bredero, A. H. *Etudes sur la 'Vita Prima' de Saint Bernard.* ASOC, vol. xvii, 1961, pp. 3–71, 215–61; vol. xviii, 1962, pp. 3–59.

Brinkmann, H., 'Die Metamorphosis Goliae'. *Zeitschrift für deutsches Altertum. Neue Folge,* vol. l, 1925, pp. 27–36.

Brooke, O. 'The Speculative Development of the Trinitarian Theology of William of St. Thierry in the *Aenigma fidei'. RTAM*, vol. xxvii, 1960, pp. 193–211, vol. xxviii, 1961, pp. 26–58.

Brückner, A. *Scriptoria Medii Aevi Helvetica*, III. *Schreibschulen der Diözese Konstanz. St. Gallen,* ii. Geneva, 1938; IV. *Schreibschulen der Diözese Konstanz. Stadt und Landschaft Zürich.* Geneva, 1940; V. *Stift Einsiedeln.* Geneva, 1943.

Buytaert, E. M. 'St John Damascene, Peter Lombard and Gerhoh of Reichersberg'. *Franciscan Studies*, vol. x, 1950, pp. 323–43.

—— 'An Earlier Redaction of the "Theologia Christiana" of Abelard'. *Antonianum*, vol. xxxvii, 1962, pp. 481–95.

—— 'Critical Observations on the "Theologia Christiana" of Abelard'. *Antonianum*, vol. xxxviii, 1963, pp. 384–433.

—— 'Thomas of Morigny and the "Theologia 'Scholarium'"' of Abelard'. *Antonianum*, vol. XL, 1965, pp. 71–95.

—— 'The Greek Fathers in Abelard's "Sic et Non"'. *Antonianum*, vol. XLI, 1966, pp. 413–53.

Carra de Vaux Saint Cyr, M. B. 'Disputatio catholicorum patrum adversus dogmata Petri Abaelardi'. *RSPT*, vol. XLVII, 1963, pp. 205–20.

Catalogue général des manuscrits des bibliothèques publiques en France. Départements, XXXI. 1898.

Catalogue général des manuscrits latins de la Bibliothèque nationale, P. Lauer etc., vol. I- . 1939- .

Catalogue of the Harleian MSS. in the British Museum, R. Nares etc., 4 vols. 1808–12.

Catalogue of the MSS. preserved in the Library of the University o, Cambridge, 6 vols. Cambridge, 1856–67.

Catalogus Codicum MSS. Bibliothecae Regiae, 4 vols. Paris, 1739–44.

Catalogus Codicum MSS. Latinorum Bibliothecae Regiae Monacensis, vol. I, 3, Munich, 1873, vol. II, 1–4, 1874–81; *ed. altera emendatior*, vol. I, 1–2, 1892–4.

Cave, W. *Scriptorum Ecclesiasticorum Historia Literaria.* 2 vols, 1688–98.

Certain, E. de, 'Raoul Tortaire'. *Bibliothèque de l'Ecole des Chartes.* 4th Series, vol. I, 1855, pp. 489–521.

Chabanne, R. 'Omnibonus'. DDC, vol. VI, 1957, cols. 1111–12.

Chatillon, J. 'Achard de Saint Victor et les controverses christologiques au XIIe siècle'. *Mélanges F. Cavallera*, Toulouse, 1948, pp. 316–37.

—— 'De Guillaume de Champeaux à Thomas Gallus: Chronique d'histoire littéraire et doctrinale de l'école de Saint Victor'. *Revue du moyen âge latin*, vol. VIII, 1952, pp. 139–62, 247–72.

—— 'Un Sermon théologique de Gauthier de Saint Victor égaré parmi les oeuvres du prieur Richard'. *Revue du moyen âge latin*, vol. VIII, 1952, pp. 43–50.

—— 'Les Régions de la dissemblance et de la ressemblance selon Achard de Saint Victor'. *Hommage au R. P. Fulbert Cayré. Recherches Augustiniennes*, vol. II, 1962, pp. 237–50.

Chenu, M. D. 'La Psychologie de la foi au XIIIe siècle'. *Etudes d'histoire littéraire et doctrinale du XIIIe siècle, 2e série.* Publications de l'Institut d'Etudes médiévales d'Ottawa, vol. II, Ottawa-Paris, 1932, pp. 163–191.

—— 'Un essai de méthode théologique au douzième siècle'. *RSPT*, vol. XXIV, 1935, pp. 258–67.

Chenu, M. D. 'Platon à Cîteaux'. *AHDLMA*, vol. XXI, 1954, 99–106.
—— 'Involucrum. Le mythe selon les théologiens médiévaux'. *AHDLMA*, vol. XXII, 1955, pp. 75–9.
Chossat, M. *La Somme des Sentences, oeuvre de Hugues de Mortagne vers 1155*. Spicilegium Sacrum Lovaniense, vol. V, Louvain, 1932.
Claeys-Boúúaert, P. 'La Summa Sententiarum, appartient-elle à Hugues de Saint Victor?' *RHE*, vol. X, 1909, pp. 278–89, 710–19.
Classen, P. *Gerhoch von Reichersberg*. Wiesbaden, 1960.
—— 'Zur Geschichte der Frühscholastik in Österreich und Bayern'. *Mitteilungen des Instituts für Österreichische Geschichtsforschung*, vol. LXVII, 1959, pp. 249–77.
Cloes, H. 'La systématization théologique pendant la première moitié du XIIe siècle'. *Ephemerides theologicae Lovanienses*, vol. XXXIV, 1958, pp. 277–329.
Collon, M. *Catalogue général des mss. des bibliothèques publiques en France. Départements, XXXVII. Tours*, vol. I. 1900.
Cottiaux, J. 'La Conception de la théologie chez Abélard'. *RHE*, vol. XXVIII, 1932, pp. 247–95, 533–51, 788–828.
Courcelle, P. *Les Confessions de Saint Augustin dans la tradition littéraire*. 1963.
Cuissard, C. *Documents inédits sur Abélard tirés des manuscrits de Fleury*. Orleans, 1880.
—— *Catalogue général des manuscrits des bibliothèques en France. Départements, XII*. Orléans, 1889.
Czerny, A. *Die Handschriften der Stiftsbibliothek Sankt Florian*. Linz, 1871.
Davy, M. M. *Un traité de la vie solitaire. Lettre aux Frères du Mont-Dieu. Guillaume de Saint Thierry*. Etudes de philosophie médiévale, vol. XXIX, 1946.
—— *Théologie et mystique de Guillaume de Saint Thierry, I. La Connaissance de Dieu*. Etudes de théologie et d'histoire de la spiritualité, 1954.
Debil, A. 'La première distinction du "De Poenitentia" de Gratien'. *RHE*, vol. XV, 1914, pp. 251–73, 442–55.
Déchanet, J. M. 'L'amitié d'Abélard et de Guillaume de Saint Thierry'. *RHE*, vol. XXXV, 1939, pp. 761–73.
—— *Guillaume de Saint Thierry. L'Homme et son oeuvre*. (Bibliothèque médiévale. Spirituels préscolastiques, vol. I, Bruges-Paris, 1942.
Dehaisnes, C. *Catalogue général des mss. des bibliothèques publiques des départements. Ancienne série, VI. Douai*. 1878.

Delhaye, P. 'Une adaptation du "De Officiis" au XIIe siècle. Le Moralium Dogma Philosophorum'. *RTAM*, vol. XVI, 1949, pp. 227–58, vol. XVII, 1950, pp. 5–28.

—— 'Le Dossier antimatrimonial de l'Adversus Jovinianum et son influence sur quelques écrits latins du XIIe siècle'. *Medieval Studies*, vol. XIII, 1951, pp. 65–86.

—— *Pierre Lombard, sa vie, ses oeuvres, sa morale.* Publications de l'Institut d'Etudes Médiévales, Montreal, 1961.

Delisle, L. *Le Cabinet des manuscrits de la Bibliothèque impériale.* 3 vols, 1868–81.

—— *Inventaire des mss. latins de Notre-Dame et divers petits fonds conservés à la Bibliothèque nationale sous les nos. 16719–18613.* 1871; also in *Bibliothèque de l'Ecole des Chartes*, vol. XXXI, 1870.

—— *Catalogue général des mss. des bibliothèques publiques des départements. Ancienne série, IV.* 1872.

Denifle, H. 'Die Sentenzen Abaelards und die Bearbeitungen seiner Theologia vor Mitte des 12. Jahrhunderts'. *Archiv für Literatur- und Kirchengeschichte des Mittelalters*, vol. I, 1885, pp. 402–69, 584–624.

—— *Die abendländischen Schriftausleger bis Luther über Justitia Dei (Rom. I, 17) und Justificatio.* Mainz, 1905.

Denis, M. *Codices Manu Scripti Theologici Bibliothecae Vindobonensis Latini, I.* Vienna, 1794.

Desroches, Abbé, 'Notice sur les mss. de la Bibliothèque d'Avranches'. *Mémoires de la Société des Antiquaires de Normandie, 2e série*, vol. I, 1837, pp. 70–156.

Deutsch, S. M. *Peter Abaelard, ein kritischer Theologe des zwölften Jahrhunderts.* Leipzig, 1883.

Dickinson, J. C. *The Origins of the Austin Canons and their Introduction into England.* London, 1950.

Dimier, M. A. 'Les premiers Cisterciens étaient-ils ennemis des études?' *Studia Monastica*, vol. IV, 1962, pp. 69–91.

Dobschütz, E. von. *Das Decretum Gelasianum.* Leipzig, 1912.

Duhamel, M. *Catalogue général des mss. des bibliothèques publiques de France. Départements, XXXIV. Carpentras*, vol. I, 1901.

Dumeige, G. *Richard de Saint Victor et l'idée chrétienne de l'amour.* 1952.

—— 'Dissemblance'. *Dictionnaire de Spiritualité*, vol. III, M. Viller, etc., 1957, cols. 1330–46.

—— 'Efforts métaphysiques chez Richard de Saint Victor'. *Die Metaphysik im Mittelalter. Vorträge des II. Internationalen Kongresses für Mittelalterliche Philosophie*, Köln, 1961, ed. P. Wilpert. Miscellanea Mediaevalia, vol. II, Berlin 1963, pp. 207–14.

Ehrle, F. *I più antichi statuti della facoltà teologica dell'università di Bologna.* Universitatis Bononiensis Monumenta, vol. I, Bologna, 1932.

Ethier, A. M. *Le 'De Trinitate' de Richard de Saint Victor.* Publications de l'Institut d'Etudes médiévales d'Ottawa, vol. IX, Ottawa, 1939.

Fischer, H. *Katalog der Handschriften der Universitätsbibliothek Erlangen. Neubearbeitung I. Die lateinische Pergamenthandschriften*, Erlangen, 1928.

Fischer, J. 'Die hebräischen Bibelzitate des Scholastikers Odos'. *Biblica*, vol. XVI, 1934, pp. 50–93.

Folz, R. 'Otton de Freising, témoin de quelques controverses intellectuelles de son temps'. *Bulletin de la Société historique et archéologique de Langres*, vol. XIII, 1958, pp. 70–6, 77–89.

Fortia d'Urban, Marquis de. *Histoire et ouvrages de Hugues Métel.* 1839.

Fournier, P. and Le Bras, G. *Histoire des collections canoniques en Occident depuis les fausses Décrétales jusqu'au Décret de Gratien.* 2 vols, 1931–2.

Franklin, A. *Les Anciennes bibliothèques de Paris.* 3 vols, 1867–73.

Fritz, G. 'Richard de Saint Victor'. DTC, vol. XIII, 1937, cols. 2676–95.

Frugoni, A. *Arnaldo di Brescia nelle fonti del secolo XII.* Studi storici, fasc. 8–9, Rome, 1954.

Gagner, S. A. *Studien zur Ideengeschichte der Gesetzgebung.* Acta Universitatis Upsaliensis. Studia iuridica Upsaliensia, vol. I, Uppsala, 1960.

Gallia Christiana . . . Opera et studio monachorum Congregationis S. Mauri, vols 4–13. 1715–86.

Gaudel, A. 'La théologie de l'assumptus homo. Histoire et valeur doctrinale'. *Revue des sciences religieuses*, vol. XVII, 1937, pp. 64–90, 214–34, vol. XVIII, 1938, pp. 45–71, 201–17.

Geyer, B. 'Verfasser und Abfassungszeit der sogenannter Summa Sententiarum'. *Theologische Quartalschrift*, vol. CVII, 1926, pp. 89–107.

—— *Patristische und Scholastische Philosophie.* Ueberweg/Heinze, *Grundriss der Geschichte der Philosophie, II. Neubearbeitung.* Berlin, 1927.

—— *Untersuchungen.* Peter Abaelards Philosophische Schriften, II, BGPTMA, vol. XXI, 4, 1933, pp. 589–633.

—— 'Neues und Altes zu den Sententiae Divinitatis'. *Mélanges J. de Ghellinck*, vol. II, Gembloux, 1951, pp. 617–30.

Ghellinck, J. de. 'A propos de l'hypothèse des deux rédactions ou des deux éditions successives de la "Somme des Sentences".' *Recherches de science religieuse*, vol. XV, 1925, pp. 449–54.

—— 'Pierre Lombard'. DTC, vol. XII, 1934, cols. 1941–2019.

—— 'La Carrière de Pierre Lombard. Nouvelle précision chronologique'. *RHE*, vol. XXX, 1934, pp. 95–100.

—— *L'Essor de la littérature latine au XIIe siècle*. Museum Lessianum. Section historique, vols. IV–V, Brussels, 1946.

—— *Le Mouvement théologique du XIIe siècle. Nouvelle édition*. Museum Lessianum. Section historique, vol. X, Bruges, etc., 1948. See also *Mélanges J. de Ghellinck*.

Gilson, E. *The Mystical Theology of St Bernard*, trans. A. H. C. Downes. 1940.

—— *Héloïse and Abelard*, trans. L. K. Shook. Chicago, 1951.

—— *History of Christian Philosophy in the Middle Ages*. 1955.

Glorieux, P. 'Les "Deflorationes" de Werner de S. Blaise'. *Mélanges J. de Ghellinck*, vol. II, Gembloux, 1951, pp. 699–721.

—— 'Mauvaise action et mauvais travail. Le "Contra quatuor labyrinthos Franciae". ' *RTAM*, vol. XXI, 1954, pp. 179–93.

—— *Aux Origines de la Sorbonne, I. Robert de Sorbon*. Etudes de philosophie médiévale, t. 53, 1966.

Grabmann, M. *Die Geschichte der Scholastischen Methode*. 2 vols, Freiburg i.B., 1909.

—— 'Bearbeitungen und Auslegungen der aristotelischen Logik aus der Zeit von Peter Abaelard bis Petrus Hispanus. Mitteilungen aus Handschriften deutscher Bibliotheken'. *Abhandlung der Preussischen Akademie der Wissenschaften. Philos.-hist. Klasse*, 1937, no. V.

—— 'Kommentare zur aristotelischen Logik aus dem 12. und 13. Jahrhundert in MS. lat. fol. 624 der Preussischen Staatsbibliothek in Berlin'. *Sitzungsberichte der Preussischen Akademie der Wissenschaften*, 1938, pp. 185–210.

—— 'Ein Tractatus de Universalibus und andere logische Inedita aus dem 12. Jahrhundert in Cod. lat. 2486 der Nationalbibliothek in Wien'. *Medieval Studies*, vol. IX, 1947, pp. 56–70.

Greenaway, G. W. *Arnold of Brescia*. Cambridge, 1931.

Gregory, T. *Anima mundi. La filosofia di Guglielmo di Conches e la scuola di Chartres*. Pubblicazioni dell'Istituto di Filosofia dell' Università di Roma, vol. III, Rome, 1955.

—— 'Nuove note sul platonismo medievale. Dall'anima mundi all' idea di natura'. *Giornale critico della filosofia italiana*, vol. XXXVI, 1957, pp. 37–55.

Grill, L. 'Die neunzehn "Capitula" Bernhards von Clairvaux gegen Abälard'. *Historisches Jahrbuch*, vol. LXXX, 1961, pp. 230–9.

Grillmeier, A. 'Fulgentius von Ruspe, De Fide ad Petrum und die Summa Sententiarum. Eine Studie zum Werden der frühscholastischen Systematik'. *Scholastik*, vol. XXXIV, 1959, pp. 526–65.

Gross, J. 'Die Ur- und Erbsünde bei Hugo von Sankt Viktor'. *ZKG*, 4e Folge, vol. XI, 1962, pp. 42–61.

—— 'Abälards Umdeutung des Erbsündendogmas'. *Zeitschrift für Religions- und Geistesgeschichte*, vol. XV, 1963, pp. 14–33.

—— 'Die Ur- und Erbsündenlehre der Schule von Laon'. *ZKG*, vol. LXXVI, 1965, pp. 12–40.

Gsell, B. *Xenia Bernardina. Pars Secunda. Die Handschriften Verzeichnisse der Cistercienserstifte der österreich.-ungar. Ordensprovinz*. Vienna, 1891.

Guimet, F. 'Notes en marge d'un texte de Richard de S. Victor'. *AHDLMA*, vol. XIV, 1943–5, pp. 371–94.

Haring, N. 'The Commentary of Gilbert of Poitiers on Boethius' De Hebdomadibus'. *Traditio*, vol. IX, 1953, pp. 177–211.

—— 'The Commentary of Gilbert, bishop of Poitiers, on Boethius' Contra Eutychen et Nestorium'. *AHDLMA*, vol. XXI, 1954, pp. 241–357.

—— 'The Cistercian Everard of Ypres and his Appraisal of the Conflict between St Bernard and Gilbert of Poitiers'. *Medieval Studies*, vol. XVII, 1955, pp. 143–72.

—— 'The Creation and Creator of the World according to Thierry of Chartres and Clarenbaldus of Arras'. *AHDLMA*, vol. XXII, 1955, pp. 137–216.

—— 'The Sententiae Magistri A. (Vat. MS. lat. 4361) and the School of Laon'. *Medieval Studies*, vol. XVII, 1955, pp. 1–45.

—— 'A Third MS. of Peter Abelard's Theologia Summi boni (MS. Oxford, Bodleian Lyell 49, ff. 101–28v)'. *Medieval Studies*, vol. XVIII, 1956, pp. 215–24.

—— 'Sprachlogische und philosophische Voraussetzungen zum Verstandnis der Christologie Gilberts von Poitiers'. *Scholastik*, vol. XXXII, 1957, pp. 373–98.

Haskins, C. H. *Studies in the History of Mediaeval Science*. New York, 1927.

Haureau, B. *Histoire de la philosophie scolastique*, 2 parts, 1872, 1880.

—— 'Mémoire sur quelques maîtres du XIIe siècle'. *Mémoires de l'Académie des Inscriptions et Belles-Lettres*, vol. XXVIII, 2, 1876.

—— *Notices et extraits de quelques manuscrits latins de la Bibliothèque nationale*. 6 vols, 1890–3.

Hayen, A. 'Le Concile de Reims et l'erreur théologique de Gilbert de la Porrée'. *AHDLMA*, vols. X–XI, 1935–6, pp. 29–102.

Heinemann, O. von. *Die Handschriften der Herzoglichen Bibliothek zu Wolfenbüttel.* 10 vols, Wolfenbüttel, 1884–1913.

Hiss, W. *Die Anthropologie Bernhards von Clairvaux.* Quellen und Studien zur Geschichte der Philosophie, ed. P. Wilpert, Band VII, Berlin, 1964.

Histoire Littéraire de la France par les religieux bénédictins de la Congréga- tion de S. Maur. 1733– .

Hödl, L. *Die Geschichte der scholastischen Literatur und der Theologie der Schlüsselgewalt,* I. BGPTMA, vol. XXXVIII, 4, 1960.

Hofmeier, J. *Die Trinitätslehre des Hugo von St Viktor.* Münchener Theologische Studien, 11. Systematische Abteilung, 25. Band, Munich, 1963.

Hofmeister, A. 'Studien über Otto von Freising'. *Neues Archiv,* vol. XXXVII, 1911–12, pp. 99–161, 633–768.

Horst, U. 'Beiträge zum Einfluss Abaelards auf Robert von Melun'. *RTAM,* vol. XXVI, 1959, pp. 314–26.

—— *Die Trinitäts- und Gotteslehre des Robert von Melun.* Walberberger Studien der Albertus-Magnus-Akademie, vol. I, Mainz, 1964.

Hüffer, G. 'Handschriftliche Studien zum Leben des hl. Bernhard von Clairvaux, III. Ungedruckte Briefe'. *Historisches Jahrbuch,* vol. VI, 1885, pp. 232–70.

Hunt, R. W. 'English Learning in the Twelfth Century'. *Transactions of the Royal Historical Society, 4th Series,* vol. XIX, 1936, pp. 19–42.

—— 'Studies on Priscian in the Twelfth Century, I'. *Medieval and Renaissance Studies,* vol. I, 1943, pp. 194–231; II, *ibid.,* vol. II, 1950, pp. 1–56.

—— 'The Disputation of Peter of Cornwall against Symon the Jew'. *Studies in Medieval History presented to F. M. Powicke,* Oxford, 1948, pp. 143–56.

—— 'The Introductions to the "Artes" in the Twelfth Century'. *Studia Mediaevalia R. J. Martin,* Bruges, 1948, pp. 85–112.

—— 'The Lyell Bequest'. *Bodleian Library Record,* vol. III, 1950, pp. 68–82.

Inguanez, M. *Codicum Casinensium MSS. Catalogus,* vol. II. 2 parts, Monte Cassino, 1928, 1934.

Irmischer, J. C. *Handschriften Katalog der Königlichen Universitätsbiblio- thek zu Erlangen.* Frankfurt, 1852.

Jacquin, M. *Etude sur l'abbaye de Liessies, 1095–1147.* Bulletin de la

Commission royale d'histoire de Belgique, tom. 71, n. 4, Brussels, 1903.

James, M. R. *A Descriptive Catalogue of the MSS. in the Library of Corpus Christi College, Cambridge,* 7 parts. Cambridge, 1912.

—— *The Western MSS. in the Library of Trinity College, Cambridge.* 4 vols, Cambridge, 1900–4.

Javelet, R. 'Psychologie des auteurs spirituels du XIIe siècle'. *Revue des sciences religieuses,* vol. XXXIII, 1959, pp. 18–64, 97–164, 209–68.

Jeauneau, E. 'Glane chartraine dans un manuscrit de Rouen'. *Mémoires de la Société archéologique d'Eure et Loir,* vol. XXI, 1957, pp. 1 *et seq.*

—— 'L'Usage de la notion d'*integumentum* à travers les gloses de Guillaume de Conches'. *AHDLMA,* vol. XXIV, 1957, pp. 35–100.

—— 'Note sur l'école de Chartres', *Studi medievali, Serie III,* vol. V, 1964, pp. 821–65.

Jolivet, J. 'Sur quelques critiques de la théologie d'Abélard'. *AHDLMA,* vol. XXXVIII, 1963, pp. 7–51.

Kaiser, E. *Pierre Abélard critique.* Freiburg, 1901.

Keuffer, M. *Beschreibendes Verzeichniss der Handschriften der Stadtbibliothek zu Trier,* 1– . Trier 1888– .

Klibansky, R. 'The Rock of Parmenides'. *Medieval and Renaissance Studies,* vol. I, 1943, pp. 178–86.

—— 'L'Epître de Bérenger de Poitiers contre les Chartreux'. *Revue du moyen âge latin,* vol. II, 1946, pp. 314–16.

—— 'Peter Abailard and Bernard of Clairvaux'. *Medieval and Renaissance Studies,* vol. V, 1961, pp. 1–27.

Knowles, D. *The Episcopal Colleagues of Archbishop Thomas Becket,* Cambridge, 1951.

—— Review of A. Bredero, *Etudes sur la Vita prima . . .* in *English Historical Review,* vol. LXXVII, 1962, pp. 748–9.

Krarup, A. *Katalog over Universitetsbibliotekets Haandskriften.* 2 vols. Copenhagen, 1935.

Kuttner, S. 'Zur Frage der theologischen Vorlagen Gratians'. *Zeitschrift der Savigny Stiftung. Kanonistische Abteilung,* vol. LIV, 1934, pp. 243–68.

—— *Kanonistische Schuldlehre von Gratian bis auf die Dekretalen Gregors IX.* Studi e testi, vol. LXIV, Vatican City, 1935.

—— *Repertorium von Kanonistik, 1140–1234, I. Prodromus Corporis glossarum.* Studi e testi, vol. LXXI, Vatican City, 1937.

—— 'De Gratiani opere noviter edendo'. *Apollinaris,* XXI, 1948, pp. 118–28.

Landgraf, A. M. 'Zur Methode der Biblischen Textkritik im 12. Jahrhundert'. *Biblica*, vol. x, 1929, pp. 445–74.
—— 'Beiträge zur Erkenntnis der Schule Abaelards'. *Zeitschrift für Katholische Theologie*, vol. LIV, 1930, pp. 360–405.
—— 'Zur Lehre von der Gotteserkenntnis in der Frühscholastik'. *New Scholasticism*, vol. IV, 1930, pp. 261–96.
—— 'Zwei Gelehrte aus der Umgebung des Petrus Lombardus'. *Divus Thomas* (Freiburg), vol. XI, 1933, pp. 157–82.
—— 'Quelques collections de "Quaestiones" de la seconde moitié du XIIe siècle'. *RTAM*, vol. VI, 1934, pp. 368–93, vol. VII, 1935, pp. 113–28.
—— 'Abaelard und die Sentenzen des *magister ignotus*'. *Divus Thomas* (Freiburg), vol. XIX, 1941, pp. 75–80.
—— *Dogmengeschichte der Frühscholastik.* 4 parts in 8 vols, Regensburg, 1952–6.
—— *Introducción a la historia de la literatura teológica de la escolástica incipiente.* Barcelona, 1956.
Le Bras, G. 'Un second ms. de l'Abbreviatio Decreti d'Omnebene'. *Revue des sciences religieuses*, vol. VII, 1927, pp. 649–52.
—— 'Manuscrits canoniques, a.- Un troisième ms. de l'Abbreviatio Decreti d'Omnebene'. *Revue des sciences religieuses*, vol. VIII, 1928, pp. 270–1.
—— 'Les Ecritures dans le Décret de Gratien'. *Zeitschrift der Savigny-Stiftung für Rechtsgeschichte. Kanonistische Abteilung*, vol. XXVII, 1938, pp. 47–80.
—— 'Pierre Lombard, Prince du droit canon'. *Miscellanea Lombardiana*, Novara, 1957, pp. 245–52.
Le Bras, G., Lefebvre, G. and Rambaud, J. *L'Age classique 1140–1378. Sources et théorie du droit.* Histoire du Droit et des Institutions de l' Eglise en Occident, dirigé par G. Le Bras, vol. VII, 1965.
Lebreton, M. M. 'Recherches sur les manuscrits contenant les sermons de Pierre le Mangeur. *Bulletin de l'Institut de Recherches et d'Histoire des Textes*, vol. II, 1953, pp. 25–44.
Leclercq, J. 'Une liste de docteurs dans un ms de Tolède'. *Hispania Sacra*, vol. II, 1949, pp. 23–4.
—— 'Les mss. de l'abbaye de Liessies'. *Scriptorium*, vol. VI, 1952, pp. 51–62.
—— 'Pour l'histoire de l'expression "philosophie chrétienne" '. *Mélanges de science religieuse*, vol. IX, 1952, pp. 221–6.

Leclercq, J. *Etudes sur S. Bernard et le texte de ses écrits*. ASOC, vol. IX, 1–2, 1953.

—— *L'Amour des lettres et le désir de Dieu: initiation aux auteurs monastiques du moyen âge*. 1957.

—— 'Les deux rédactions du prologue de Pierre Lombard sur les épîtres de S. Paul'. *Miscellanea Lombardiana*, Novara, 1957, pp. 109–112.

—— *Recueil d'études sur S. Bernard et ses écrits, I, II*. Storia e letteratura, vols XCII, CIV, Rome, 1962, p. 196.

—— 'Les Etudes bernardines en 1963'. *Bulletin de la Société internationale pour l'étude de la philosophie médiévale*, vol. V, 1963, pp. 121–38.

—— 'Les Formes successives de la lettre-traité de saint Bernard contre Abélard'. *Revue bénédictine*, vol. LXXVIII, 1968, pp. 87–105.

Lehmann, P. 'Mitteilungen aus Handschriften, III'. *Sitzungsberichte der philos.- philol. und der hist. Klasse der Bayerischen Akademie der Wissenschaften*, 1931–2, no. 6.

—— *Die Parodie im Mittelalter, 2e Auflage*. Stuttgart, 1963.

Lehmann, P. and Glauning, O. *Mittelalterliche Handschriftenbruchstücke der Universitätsbibliothek und des Georgianum zu München*. 72. Beiheft zum Zentralblatt für Bibliothekswesen, Leipzig, 1940.

Lesne, E. *Les Ecoles de la fin du VIIIe siècle à la fin du XIIe*. Histoire de la propriété ecclésiastique en France, vol. V, Lille, 1940.

Lieftinck, G. I. 'The *Psalterium Hebraycum* from St Augustine's Canterbury rediscovered at Leyden'. *Transactions of the Cambridge Bibliographical Society*, vol. II, 1954–8, pp. 97–104.

Lindner, P. *Familia S. Quirini in Tegernsee. Die Äbte und Mönche der Benediktiner Abtei Tegernsee von den ältesten Zeiten bis zu ihrem Aussterben* (1861). *Ie Teil*, Munich, 1897; also in *Oberbayerisches Archiv für vaterländische Geschichte*, vol. L.

Loewe, R. 'Herbert of Bosham's Commentary on Jerome's Hebrew Psalter'. *Biblica*, vol. XXXIV, 1953, pp. 44–77, 159–92, 275–98.

—— 'The Medieval Christian Hebraists of England—Herbert of Bosham and earlier Scholars'. *Transactions of the Jewish Historical Society of England*, vol. XVII, 1953, pp. 225–49.

Lottin, O. 'Pierre Bérenger'. *DHGE*, vol VIII, 1935, cols. 379–80.

—— 'Aux origines de l'école théologique d'Anselme de Laon'. *RTAM*, vol. X, 1938, pp. 102–22.

—— 'Nouveaux fragments théologiques de l'école d'Anselme de Laon'. *RTAM*, vol. XI, 1939, pp. 242–59, vol. XII, 1940, pp. 49–77, vol. XIII, 1946, pp. 202–21, vol. XIV, 1947, pp. 5–31.

—— *Psychologie et morale aux XIIe et XIIIe siècles*. 6 vols, Louvain-Gembloux, 1942–60.

—— 'A propos des sources de la Summa Sententiarum'. *RTAM*, vol. xxv, 1958, pp. 42–58.

Luchaire, A. *Etudes sur quelques mss de Rome et de Paris: Recueils épistolaires de S. Victor.* Bibliothèque de la Faculté des Lettres de l'Université de Paris, vol. VII, 1899.

Luscombe, D. E. 'Towards a new edition of Peter Abelard's *Ethica* or *Scito te ipsum*: An introduction to the manuscripts'. *Vivarium*, vol. III, 1965, pp. 115–27.

—— *Peter Abelard and his School.* Fellowship Dissertation, 1961, King's College Library, Cambridge.

—— *Peter Abelard's Following.* Ph.D. Thesis, 1963, University Library, Cambridge.

—— 'The Authorship of the *Ysagoge in Theologiam*'. *AHDLMA* (forthcoming).

Manitius, M. *Geschichte der lateinischen Literatur des Mittelalters*, III. Müllers Handbuch der klassischen Altertums-Wissenschaft, vol. IX, 11, Munich, 1931.

Mansi, J. D. *Sacrorum Conciliorum nova et amplissima collectio . . . ed. novissima.* 56 vols, Florence, etc., 1759–1927.

Marchegay, P. 'Charte en vers de l'an 1121 composée par Hilaire, disciple d'Abailard et chanoine du Ronceray d'Angers'. *Bibliothèque de l'Ecole des Chartes*, vol. XXXVII, 1876, pp. 245–52.

Marchi, L. de. *Inventario dei manoscritti della R. Biblioteca Universitaria di Pavia*, vol. I. Milan, 1894.

Martin, H. *Catalogue des mss. de la Bibliothèque de l'Arsenal.* 2 vols, 1885–6.

Martin, R. M. 'Les Idées de Robert de Melun sur le péché originel'. *RSPT*, vol. VII, 1913, pp. 700–25, vol. VIII, 1914, pp. 439–66, vol. IX, 1920, pp. 103–20, vol. XI, 1922.

Martini, A. and Bassi, D. *Catalogus codicum graecorum bibliothecae Ambrosianae.* 2 vols, Milan, 1906.

Mazzuchelli, G. M. *Gli scrittori d'Italia.* 2 vols in 6, Brescia, 1753–63.

Meier, G. *Catalogus codicum mss. qui in bibliotheca monasterii Einsidlensis OSB servantur*, vol. I. Einsiedeln-Leipzig, 1899.

—— *Heinrich von Ligerz, Bibliothekar von Einsiedeln in 14. Jahrhundert.* Centralblatt für Bibliothekswesen. Beihefte. Leipzig, 1896.

Meier, L. 'Vier Jahre Skotusforschung in Deutschen Bibliotheken'. *Zentralblatt für Bibliothekswesen*, vol. LX, 1943, pp. 145–67.

Mélanges J. de Ghellinck. 2 vols, Museum Lessianum. Section historique, vols. XIII–XIV, Gembloux, 1951.

Mélanges offerts au R. P. Ferdinand Cavallera. Toulouse, 1948.

Mélanges Saint Bernard. Dijon, 1954.

Meyer, W. 'Die Anklagesätze des hl. Bernhard gegen Abälard'. *Nachrichten der k. Gesellschaft der Wissenschaften zu Göttingen. Phil.-hist. Klasse*, 1898, 4. *Abhandlung*, pp. 397–468.

Meyier, K. A. de. *Paul en Alexandre Petau en de Geschiednis van hun Handschriften*. Leiden, 1947.

Minio-Paluello, L. 'Iacobus Veneticus Grecus, Canonist and Translator of Aristotle'. *Traditio*, vol. VIII, 1952, pp. 265–304.

Miscellanea Lombardiana. Novara, 1957

Mittelalterliche Bibliothekskataloge Österreichs, I. Niederösterreich. T. Gottlieb, Vienna, 1915; *III. Steiermark*. G. Möser-Mersky, Graz, 1961.

Mohlberg, C. *Katalog der Handschriften der Zentralbibliothek Zürich, I. Mittelalterliche Handschriften*. 4 parts, Zurich, 1932–52.

Molinier, A. *Catalogue général des mss. des bibliothèques publiques de France. Départements, XXXI*. 1898.

Mols, R. 'Célestin II'. *DHGE*, vol. XII, 1953, cols. 59–62.

—— 'Célestin III'. *DHGE*, vol. XII, 1953, cols. 62–77.

Montebaur, J. *Studien zur Geschichte der Bibliothek der Abtei St. Eucharius-Matthias zu Trier*. Römische Quartalschrift, vol. XXVI, Supplementheft, 1931.

Montfaucon, B. *Bibliotheca Bibliothecarum MSS. Nova*. 2 vols, 1739.

Morin, G. in *Revue bénédictine*, vol. XIII, 1896, pp. 340 *et seq.*

Motte, A. R. 'Une fausse accusation contre Abélard et Arnaud de Brescia'. *RSPT*, vol. XXII, 1933, pp. 27–46.

Mynors, R. A. B. *Durham Cathedral MSS. to the End of the Twelfth Century*. Oxford, 1939.

—— *Catalogue of the Manuscripts of Balliol College, Oxford*. Oxford, 1963.

Nolhac, P. de. *Pétrarque et l'humanisme*. 2 vols, 1907.

Nortier, G. 'Les bibliothèques médiévales des abbayes bénédictines de Normandie'. *Revue Mabillon*, vol. XLVII, 1957, pp. 57–83, 135–71, vol. L, 1960, pp. 229–43, vol. LI, 1961, pp. 332–47, vol. LII, 1962, pp. 118–34, 182–96.

Olwer, N. d'. 'Sur la date de la Dialectica d'Abélard'. *Revue du moyen âge latin*, vol. I, 1945, pp. 375–90.

Omont, H. *Catalogue général des mss. des bibliothèques publiques de France. Départements, X. Avranches*, etc. 1889.
—— *Catalogue général des mss. des bibliothèques publiques de France. Départements, I. Rouen.* 1886.
Ostlender, H. in *Bulletin Thomiste*, vol. VIII, 1931, p. 229.
—— 'Die Theologia Scholarium des Peter Abaelard'. *Aus der Geisteswelt des Mittelalters.* BGPTMA, Supplementband III, 1, 1935, pp. 262–81.
—— 'Die Sentenzenbücher der Schule Abaelards'. *Theologische Quartalschrift*, vol. CXVII, 1936, pp. 208–52.
Ott, L. *Untersuchungen zur theologischer Briefliteratur der Frühscholastik.* BGPTMA, vol. XXXIV, 1937.
—— 'Der Trinitätstraktat Walters von Mortagne als Quelle der Summa Sententiarum'. *Scholastik*, vol. XVIII, 1943, pp. 78–90, 219–39.
—— 'Die Trinitätslehre der Summa Sententiarum als Quelle des Petrus Lombardus'. *Divus Thomas* (Freiburg), vol. XXI, 1943, pp. 159–86.
—— 'Hugo von St. Viktor und die Kirchenväter'. *Divus Thomas* (Freiburg), *3e Folge*, vol. XXVII, 1949, pp. 180–208, 293–332.
—— 'Walter von Mortagne und Petrus Lombardus in ihrem Verhältnis zueinander'. *Mélanges J. de Ghellinck*, vol. II, Gembloux, 1951, pp. 646–97.
——'Petrus Lombardus. Personlichkeit und Werk'. *Münchener theologischer Zeitschrift*, vol. V, 1954, pp. 99–113.
—— 'Pietro Lombardo: Personalità e Opera'. *Miscellanea Lombardiana*, Novara, 1957, pp. 11–20.
—— 'Die platonische Weltseele in der Theologie der Frühscholastik'. *Parusia. Studien zur Philosophie Platons und zur Problemgeschichte des Platonismus. Festgabe für Johannes Hirschberger*, ed. K. Flasch, Frankfurt am Main, 1965, pp. 307–31.
Ottaviano, C. 'Prolegomeni all' edizione critica delle "Sententiae" del Magister Omnibonus (†1185)'. *Sophia*, vol. XXXV, 1967, pp. 56–85.
Otto, S. *Die Funktion des Bildbegriffes in der Theologie des 12. Jahrhunderts.* BGPTMA, vol. XL, 1, 1963.
Pacaut, M. *Alexandre III. Etude sur sa conception du pouvoir pontifical dans sa pensée et dans son oeuvre.* L'Eglise et l'Etat au moyen âge, vol. XI, 1956.
—— 'Roland Bandinelli'. *DDC*, vol. VII, 1965, cols. 702–26.

z

Paré, G., Brunet, A. and Tremblay, P. *La Renaissance du XIIe siècle. Les Ecoles et l'enseignement.* Publications de l'Institut d'Etudes médié-vales d'Ottawa, vol. III, Paris-Ottawa, 1933.

Pelster, F. 'Petrus Lombardus und die Verhandlungen über die Streitfrage des Gilbertus Porreta in Paris (1147) und Reims (1148)'. *Miscellanea Lombardiana,* Novara, 1957, pp. 65–73.

Peter, J. *L'Abbaye de Liessies en Hainaut depuis ses origines jusqu'après la réforme de Louis de Blois, 764–1566.* Mémoires et travaux publiés par les professeurs des Facultés catholiques de Lille, fasc. IX, 1912.

Pitra, J. B. *Questiones Magistri Odonis Suessionis.* Analecta novissima Spicilegii Solesmensis. Continuation altera, vol. II, 1888.

Poole, R. L. 'The Early Lives of Robert Pullen and Nicholas Breaks-pear'. *Essays in Medieval History presented to T. F. Tout,* Manchester, 1925, pp. 61–70.

—— *Illustrations of the History of Medieval Thought and Learning.* 2nd ed., 1920.

Poorter, A. de. *Catalogue des manuscrits de la Bibliothèque de la Ville de Bruges.* Gembloux, 1934.

Portalié, E. 'Pierre Abélard'. DTC, vol. I, 1907, cols. 36–55.

—— 'Alexandre III'. DTC, vol. I, 1923, cols. 711–7.

Prantl, C. *Geschichte der Logik im Abendlände, II,* 2nd. ed., Leipzig, 1885.

Raby, F. J. E. *The Oxford Book of Medieval Latin Verse.* 2nd. ed., Oxford, 1959.

Rathbone, E. *The Influence of Bishops and of Members of Cathedral Bodies in the Intellectual Life of England, 1066–1216.* Ph.D. Thesis, London University, 1936.

Redlich, V. *Tegernsee und die deutsche Geistesgeschichte im 15. Jahrhundert.* Schriften zur bayerischen Landesgeschichte, vol. IX, Munich, 1931.

Ricci, S. de. *Census of Medieval and Renaissance MSS. in the United States and Canada.* 3 vols, New York, 1935–40.

Rivière, J. *Le Dogme de la Rédemption au début du moyen âge.* Bibliothèque Thomiste, vol. XIX, 1934.

—— 'Quelques faits nouveaux sur l'influence théologique d'Abélard'. *Bulletin de littérature ecclésiastique,* vol. XXXII, 1931, pp. 107–13.

—— 'Les "capitula" d'Abélard condamnés au Concile de Sens'. *RTAM* vol. V, 1933, pp. 5–22.

Robert, G. *Les Ecoles et l'enseignement de la théologie pendant la première moitié du XIIe siècle.* 1909.

Rose, V. *Verzeichniss der lateinischen Handschriften der königlichen*

Bibliothek zu Berlin, 1– . Die Handschriften Verzeichnisse der königlichen Bibliothek zu Berlin, Bd. XII– , Berlin, 1893– .

Rud, T. *Codicum MSS. Ecclesiae Cathedralis Dunelmensis Catalogus* ... (Durham, 1825).

Saint Bernard Théologien, Actes du Congrès de Dijon, 15–19 septembre 1953. ASOC, vol. IX, 1953.

Saltet, L. *Les Réordinations au moyen âge.* 1907.

San Bernardo. Pubblicazione commemorativa nell' VIII centenario della sua morte. Pubbl. dell'università cattolica del S. Cuore. Nouva serie, vol. XLVI, Milan 1954.

Schepss, G. 'Zum lateinischen Aristoteles und Boethius'. *Blätter für das bayer. Gymnasialschulwesen*, vol. XXIX, 1893, pp. 116 *et seq.*

Scherrer, G. *Verzeichniss der Handschriften der Stiftsbibliothek von St Gallen.* Halle, 1875.

Schreiber, H. *Die Bibliothek der ehemaligen Mainzer Kartause. Die Handschriften und ihre Geschichte.* Zentralblatt für Bibliothekswesen. Beiheft LX, Leipzig, 1927.

Schulte, J. F. von. *Dissertatio de Decreto ab Omnibono abbreviato.* Bonn, 1892.

—— *Geschichte der Quellen und Literatur des Canonischen Rechts von Gratian bis auf die Gegenwart.* 3 vols in 4, Stuttgart, 1875–80.

Sikes, J. G. *Peter Abailard.* Cambridge, 1932.

Silvain, R. 'La Tradition des Sentences d'Anselme de Laon'. *AHDLMA*, vol. XVI, 1947–8, pp. 1–52.

Smalley, B. 'Gilbertus Universalis, Bishop of London (1128–34) and the Problem of the "Glossa Ordinaria" '. *RTAM*, vol. VII, 1935, pp. 235–62, vol. VIII, 1936, pp. 24–60.

—— 'A Commentary on the *Hebraica* by Herbert of Bosham'. *RTAM*, vol. XVIII, 1951, pp. 29–65.

—— *The Study of the Bible in the Middle Ages.* 2nd ed., Oxford, 1952.

—— 'Jean de Hesdin, O. Hosp. S. Ioh.', *RTAM*, vol. XXVIII, 1961, pp. 283–330.

Staender, J. *Chirographorum in Regia Bibliotheca Paulina Monasteriensi Catalogus.* Bratislava, 1889.

Stegmüller, F. *Repertorium Biblicum Medii Aevi.* 7 vols, Madrid, 1940–61.

—— 'Sententiae Varsavienses. Ein neuaufgefundenes Sentenzenwerk unter dem Einfluss des Anselm von Laon und des Peter Abaelard', *Divus Thomas*, Piacenza, vol. XLV, 1942, pp. 301–42.

Stegmüller, F. 'Die Quellen der "Sententiae Varsavienses".' *Divus Thomas*, Piacenza, vol. XLVI, 1943, pp. 375–84.

—— *Repertorium commentariorum in Sententias P. Lombardi.* 2 vols, Herbipoli, 1947.

Stickler, A. M. *Historia Iuris Canonici Latini*, vol. I. Turin, 1950.

Studia Gratiana post octava decreti saecularia I–VIII, curantibus I. Forchielli, A. M. Stickler, Bologna, 1953–62.

Tabulae Codicum MSS. praeter Graecos et Orientales in Bibliotheca Palatina Vindobonensi asservatorum. 7 vols, Vienna, 1864–75.

Talbot, C. H. 'Notes on the Library of Pontigny'. ASOC, vol. X, 1954, pp. 106–8.

Taylor, J. *The Origin and Early Life of Hugh of St Victor.* Texts and Studies in the History of Medieval Education, Notre Dame, Indiana, 1957.

Teetaert, A. *La Confession aux laïques dans l'Englise latine depuis le VIIIe siècle jusqu'au XIVe siècle.* Wetteren, 1926.

Thaner, F. *Abälard und das canonische Recht. Die Persönlichkeit in der Eheschliessung. Zwei Festreden.* Graz, 1900.

Tosti, L. *Storia di Abaelardo e dei suoi tempi.* Naples, 1851.

Vacandard, E. 'Arnaud de Brescia'. *Revue des questions historiques*, vol. XXXV, 1884, pp. 52–114.

—— 'Les poèmes latins attribués à S. Bernard'. *Revue des questions historiques*, vol. XLIX, 1891, pp. 218–31.

—— *Vie de S. Bernard.* 2 vols, 2nd ed., 1897.

—— 'Bérenger de Poitiers'. *DTC*, vol. II, 1905, cols. 720–2.

Van den Eynde, D. 'Les "magistri" du Commentaire "Unum ex quattuor" de Zacharias Chrysopolitanus'. *Antonianum*, vol. XXIII, 1948, pp. 3–32, 181–220.

—— 'Précisions chronologiques sur quelques ouvrages théologiques du XIIe siècle'. *Antonianum*, vol. XXVI, 1951, pp. 223–46.

—— 'Du nouveau sur les deux maîtres lombards contemporains du Maître des Sentences: 1. Moïse de Bergame, 2. Lutolphe de Novare'. *Pier Lombardo*, vol. I, 1953, pp. 6–8.

—— 'Nouvelles précisions chronologiques sur quelques oeuvres théologiques du XIIe siècle'. *Franciscan Studies*, vol. XIII, 1953, pp. 71–118.

—— 'Deux sermons inédits de Pierre Lombard'. *Miscellanea Lombardiana*, Novara, 1957, pp. 75–87.

—— 'Essai chronologique sur l'oeuvre littéraire de Pierre Lombard'. *ibid.*, pp. 45–63.

—— *L'oeuvre littéraire de Géroch de Reichersberg.* Spicilegium Pontificii Athenaei Antoniani, vol. XI, Rome, 1957.

—— 'Autour des "Enarrationes" in Evangelium S. Matthaei attribuées à Geoffroi Babion'. *RTAM*, vol. XXVI, 1959, pp. 50–84.

—— *Essai sur la succession et la date des écrits de Hugues de S. Victor.* Spicilegium Pontificii Athenaei Antoniani, vol. XIII, Rome, 1960.

—— 'La "Theologia Scholarium" de Pierre Abélard'. *RTAM*, vol. XXVIII, 1961, pp. 225–41.

—— 'Les Rédactions de la "Theologia Christiana" de Pierre Abélard'. *Antonianum*, vol. XXXVI, 1961, pp. 273–99.

—— 'Chronologie des écrits d'Abélard à Héloïse'. *Antonianum*, vol. XXXVII, 1962, pp. 337–49.

—— 'Les Ecrits perdus d'Abélard'. *Antonianum*, vol. XXXVII, 1962, pp. 467–80.

—— 'Le Recueil des Sermons de Pierre Abélard'. *Antonianum*, vol. XXXVII, 1962, pp. 17–54.

—— 'Détails biographiques sur Pierre Abélard'. *Antonianum*, vol. XXXVIII, 1963, pp. 217–23.

Van Hove, A. 'Quae Gratianus contulerit methodo scientiae canonicae'. *Apollinaris*, vol. XXI, 1948, pp. 12–24.

Vaupel, H. 'Clarembaldus von Arras und Walter von Mortagne'. *ZKG*, vol. LXV, 1954, pp. 129–38.

Vernet, A. 'Une épitaphe inédite de Thierry de Chartres'. *Recueil de travaux offerts à M. Cl. Brunel*, vol. II, 1955, pp. 660–70.

Vernet, F. 'Arnaud de Brescia'. *DTC*, vol. I, 1903, cols. 1972–5.

—— 'Hugues de S. Victor'. *DTC*, vol. VII, 1922, cols. 240–308.

Vignaux, P. *La Pensée au moyen âge.* 1938.

Villemarque, M. Th. de la. *Barzas-Breis. Chants populaires de la Bretagne.* 1839.

Vita Comune (La) del Clero nei secoli XI e XII. Atti della Settimana di studio: Mendola, settembre 1959. 2 vols, Miscellanea del Centro di Studi Medioevali, vol. III, Pubblicazioni dell'Università Cattolica del S. Cuore, Serie terza. Scienze storiche, 2–3. Milan, 1962.

Warner, G. F. and Gilson, J. P. *Catalogue of Western MSS. in the Old Royal and King's Collections.* 4 vols, 1921.

Weisweiler, H. 'Eine neue Bearbeitung von Abaelards "Introductio" und der Summa Sententiarum'. *Scholastik*, vol. IX, 1934, pp. 346–71.

—— 'La Summa Sententiarum, source de Pierre Lombard'. *RTAM*, vol. VI, 1934, pp. 143–83.

Weisweiler, H. *Das Schrifttum der Schule Anselms von Laon und Wilhelms von Champeaux in deutschen Bibliotheken*. BGPTMA, vol. XXXIII, 1–2, 1936.

—— *Maître Simon et son groupe, De Sacramentis; textes inédits*. Spicilegium Sacrum Lovaniense, vol. XVII, Louvain, 1937.

—— 'Un ms. inconnu de Munich sur la querelle des investitures'. *RHE*, vol. XXXIV, 1938, pp. 245–69.

—— 'Hugos von St. Viktor Dialogus de sacramentis legis naturalis et scriptae als frühscholastisches Quellenwerk'. *Miscellanea G. Mercati*, vol. II. Studi e testi, CXXII. Vatican City, 1946, pp. 179–219.

—— 'Die Arbeitsmethode Hugos von St. Viktor'. *Scholastik*, vols. XX/XXIV, 1949, pp. 59–87, 232–67.

—— 'Zur Einflußsphäre der "Vorlesungen" Hugos von St. Viktor'. *Mélanges J. de Ghellinck*, vol. II, Gembloux, 1951, pp. 527–81.

—— in *Scholastik*, vol. XXXI, 1956, pp. 475.

Werner, J. *Beiträge zur Kunde der lateinischen Literatur des Mittelalters*. 2nd ed., Aarau, 1905.

Williams, J. R. 'The Cathedral School of Reims in the Time of Master Alberic, 1118–1136'. *Traditio*, vol. XX, 1964, pp. 93–114.

Wilmart, A. 'Les livres légués par Célestin II à Città di Castello'. *Revue bénédictine*, vol. XXXV, 1923, pp. 98–102.

—— 'La série et la date des ouvrages de Guillaume de S. Thierry'. *Revue Mabillon*, vol. XIV, 1924, pp. 157–67.

—— *Bibliothecae Apostolicae Vaticanae Codices Manu Scripti, I. Codices Reginenses Latini*. Vatican City, 1937.

Wright, T. *Biographia Britannica Literaria. Anglo-Norman Period*. 1846.

Young, K. in *Speculum*, vol. V, 1930, pp. 112–14.

—— *The Drama of the Medieval Church*. 2 vols, Oxford, 1933.

INDEXES

INDEX OF MANUSCRIPTS

GENERAL INDEX